By SIGMUND FREUD

THE STANDARD EDITION

OF THE COMPLETE PSYCHOLOGICAL WORKS OF

SIGMUND FREUD

24 VOLUMES

D0011780

THE PRISONER'S DREAM

Introductory Lectures on Psychoanalysis

SIGMUND FREUD

Translated and Edited by

JAMES STRACHEY

A Liveright Book

W · W · NORTON & COMPANY

NEW YORK · LONDON

W. W. Norton & Company, Inc., 500 Fifth Avenue,
New York, N.Y. 10110
W. W. Norton & Company Ltd. 37 Great Russell Street,
London WC1B 3NU

First published as a Liveright paperback 1977

W. W. Norton & Company, Inc. is also the publisher of the works of
Erik H. Erikson, Otto Fenichel, Karen Horney, Harry Stack Sulli-
van, and The Standard Edition of the Complete Psychological
Works of Sigmund Freud.

Library of Congress Cataloging in Publication Data
Freud, Sigmund, 1856-1939.
Introductory lectures on psychoanalysis.
Translation of Vorlesungen zur Einführung in die Psychoanalyse.
"A Liveright book."
Bibliography: p.
Includes index.
1. Psychoanalysis. I. Strachey, James. II. Title.
BF173.F7   1977   150.19′52   77-5779

ISBN 0-87140-118-5

Printed in the United States of America
9 0

CONTENTS

APPENDIXES

INTRODUCTORY LECTURES ON
PSYCHOANALYSIS

EDITOR'S INTRODUCTION

VORLESUNGEN ZUR EINFÜHRUNG IN DIE PSYCHOANALYSE

(a) GERMAN EDITIONS:

1916 Part I (separately), *Die Fehlleistungen.* Leipzig and Vienna: Heller.

1916 Part II (separately), *Der Traum.* Same publishers.

1917 Part III (separately), *Allgemeine Neurosenlehre.* Same publishers.

1917 The above, three parts in one volume. Same publishers. Pp. viii + 545.

1918 2nd ed. (With index and inserted list of 40 corrigenda.) Same publishers. Pp. viii + 553.

1920 3rd ed. (Corrected reprint of above.) Leipzig, Vienna and Zurich: Internationaler Psychoanalytischer Verlag. Pp. viii + 553.

1922 4th ed. (Corrected reprint of above.) Same publishers. Pp. viii + 554. (Also Parts II and III separately, under titles *Vorlesungen über den Traum* and *Allgemeine Neurosenlehre.*)

1922 Pocket ed. (No index.) Same publishers. Pp. iv + 495.

1922 Pocket ed. (2nd ed., corrected and with index.) Same publishers. Pp. iv + 502.

1924 *G.S.,* 7. Pp. 483.

1926 5th ed. (Reprint of *G.S.*) I.P.V. Pp. 483.

1926 Pocket ed. (3rd ed.) Same publishers.

1930 Small 8vo. ed. I.P.V. Pp. 501.

1933 (By licence.) Berlin: Kiepenheuer. Pp. 524.

1940 *G.W.,* 11, Pp. 495.

(*b*) ENGLISH TRANSLATIONS:

A General Introduction to Psychoanalysis

1920   New York: Boni & Liveright. Pp. x + 406. (Tr. un-
        specified; Foreword G. Stanley Hall.)

Introductory Lectures on Psycho-Analysis

1922   London: Allen & Unwin. Pp. 395. (Tr. Joan Riviere;
        without Freud's preface; with preface by Ernest
        Jones.)

1929   2nd ed. (revised). Same publishers. Pp. 395.

A General Introduction to Psychoanalysis

1935   New York: Liveright. Pp. 412. (The London ed. under
        the title of the old New York one. Tr. Joan Riviere;
        with prefaces by Ernest Jones and G. Stanley Hall.
        Freud's preface included.)

The present translation is a new one by James Strachey.

This book had a wider circulation than any of Freud's
works, except, perhaps, *The Psychopathology of Everyday Life*.[1] It
is also distinguished by the number of misprints in it. As is
recorded above, 40 were corrected in the second edition; but
there were many more, and a considerable number of slight
variations in the text may be observed in the various editions.
The present translation follows the text of the *Gesammelte Werke*,
which is in fact identical with that of the *Gesammelte Schriften*;
and only the more important deviations from earlier versions
have been recorded.

The actual date of publication of the three parts is not clear.
Part I was certainly out before the end of July, 1916, as is
shown by a reference to it in a letter of Freud's to Lou Andreas-
Salomé of July 27, 1916 (cf. Freud, 1960). In the same letter he

---

[1] The *Lectures* were certainly the most translated of any. In Freud's lifetime (apart from English) they appeared in Dutch (1917), French (1922),
Italian (1922), Russian (1922–3), Spanish (1923), Japanese (1928),
Norwegian (1929), Hebrew (1930), Hungarian (1932), Serbo-Croatian
(1933), Chinese (1933), Polish (1935) and Czech (1936). They had probably also appeared by then in Portuguese, Swedish, and later in Arabic.

also speaks of Part II as being on the point of appearing. Part III seems to have been published in May, 1917.

The academic year of the University of Vienna fell into two parts: a winter term (or semester) running from October to March, and a summer one from April to July. The lectures printed here were delivered by Freud in two successive winter terms during the first World War: 1915–16 and 1916–17.[1] The fullest account of the circumstances leading to their publication will be found in the second volume of Ernest Jones's biography (1955, 245 ff.).

Although, as Freud himself remarked in his preface to the *New Introductory Lectures*, his membership of the University of Vienna had only been 'a peripheral one', he had nevertheless, from the time of his appointment as Privatdozent (University Lecturer) in 1885 and as Professor Extraordinarius (Assistant Professor) in 1902, given many courses of University lectures. These remained unrecorded, though some accounts of them may be found—for instance, by Hanns Sachs (1945, 39 ff.) and Theodor Reik (1942, 19 ff.), as well as by Ernest Jones (1953, 375 ff.). Freud decided that the series beginning in the autumn of 1915 should be the last, and it was at Otto Rank's suggestion that he agreed upon their publication. In his preface to the *New Introductory Lectures* which has just been quoted Freud tells us that the first half of the present, earlier, series 'were improvised, and written out immediately afterwards' and that 'drafts of the second half were made during the intervening summer vacation, at Salzburg, and delivered word for word in the following winter'. He adds that at that time he 'still possessed a phonographic memory', for, however carefully his lectures might have been prepared, his actual delivery of them was invariably extempore[2] and usually without notes. There is general agreement upon his technique of lecturing: that he was never rhetorical and that his tone was always one of quiet and

[1] The opening lecture of the series was delivered, according to Ernest Jones, on October 23, 1915, but according to a contemporary notice (*Int. Z. Psychoan.*, **3**, 376) on October 16. It is agreed that they were given on Saturdays.

[2] A single exception to this rule is recorded in the case of his Budapest Congress paper (1919a); cf. Jones (1953, 375 n.).

even intimate conversation. But it must not be supposed from this that there was anything slovenly or disordered about his lectures. They almost always had a definite form—a head, body and tail—and might often give the hearer the impression of possessing an aesthetic unity.

It has been said (Reik, 1942, 19) that he disliked lecturing, but it is difficult to reconcile this, not only with the number of lectures he delivered in the course of his life, but with the remarkably high proportion of his actually published work which is in the form of lectures. There is, however, a possible explanation of this inconsistency. Examination shows that among his publications it is predominantly the *expository* works that appear as lectures: for instance, the early lecture on 'The Aetiology of Hysteria' (1896c), the somewhat later one 'On Psychotherapy' (1905a), as well, of course, as the *Five Lectures* delivered in America (1910a) and the present series. But beyond this, when, many years afterwards, he undertook an exposition of the later developments of his views, he, for no obvious reason, once more threw them into lecture form and published his *New Introductory Lectures* (1933a), though there was never any possibility of their being delivered as such. Thus lectures as a method of putting forward his opinions evidently appealed to Freud, but only subject to a particular condition: he must be in a lively contact with his real or supposed audience. Readers of the present volume will discover how constantly Freud retains this contact—how regularly he puts objections into his audience's mouth and how frequently there are imaginary arguments between him and his hearers. He in fact carried over this method of stating his case to some of his works which are not lectures at all: the whole of *The Question of Lay Analysis* (1926e) and the greater part of *The Future of an Illusion* (1927c) take the form of dialogues between the author and a critical listener. Contrary, perhaps, to some mistaken notions, Freud was entirely opposed to laying down his views in an authoritarian and dogmatic fashion: 'I shall not tell it you', he says to his audience at one point below (p. 431), 'but shall insist on your discovering it for yourselves.' Objections were not to be shouted down but brought into the open and examined. And this, after all, was no more than an extension of an essential feature of the technique of psycho-analysis itself.

The *Introductory Lectures* may justly be regarded as a stock-taking of Freud's views and the position of psycho-analysis at the time of the first World War. The secessions of Adler and Jung were already past history, the concept of narcissism was some years old, the epoch-making case history of the 'Wolf Man' had been written (with the exception of two passages) a year before the lectures began, though it was not published till later. So, too, the great series of 'metapsychological' papers on fundamental theory had been finished a few months earlier, though only three had been published. (Two more of them appeared soon after the lectures, but the remaining seven disappeared without leaving a trace.) These latter activities, and no doubt the production of the lectures as well, had been facilitated by the slackening in Freud's clinical work imposed by war conditions. A watershed had apparently been reached and the time seemed to have come for a halt. But in fact fresh creative ideas were in preparation which were to see the light in *Beyond the Pleasure Principle* (1920g), *Group Psychology* (1921c) and *The Ego and the Id* (1923b). Indeed, the line must not be drawn too sharply. Already, for instance, hints may be detected of the notion of the 'compulsion to repeat' (p. 274), and the beginnings of the analysis of the ego are quite apparent (pp. 422 and 428), while the difficulties over the multiple senses of the term 'unconscious' (see p. 227n. 1) are paving the way towards the new structural account of the mind.

In his preface to these lectures Freud speaks a little depreciatively of the lack of novelty in their contents. But no one, however well-read in psycho-analytic literature, need feel afraid of being bored by them or could fail to find plenty in them that is not to be found elsewhere. The discussions on anxiety (Lecture XXV) and on primal phantasies (Lecture XXIV), which Freud himself singles out in his preface as fresh material, are not the only ones he might have mentioned. The review of symbolism in Lecture X is probably his most complete. Nowhere does he give such a clear summary of the formation of dreams as in the last pages of Lecture XIV. There are no more understanding commentaries on the perversions than those in Lectures XX and XXI. Finally, there is no rival to the analysis of the process of psycho-analytic therapy given in the last lecture of all. And even where the subjects would seem to be well-worn, such as the mechanism of parapraxes and of dreams, they are approached from unexpected directions and throw fresh illumination on what might have seemed depressingly familiar ground. The *Introductory Lectures* have thoroughly deserved their popularity.[1]

[1] From their very nature these lectures touch upon a large variety of subjects, into some of which Freud (as he himself remarks in the last paragraph of the final lecture) has been unable to enter very deeply. Many readers, and especially students who find in this work their first approach to psycho-analysis, are likely to come upon some point about which they would wish to learn more. An attempt has accordingly been made in the footnotes of this edition to give particularly generous references to others of Freud's writings in which the topic in the text is dealt with at greater length.

PREFACE [1]
[1917]

WHAT I am here offering the public as an 'Introduction to Psycho-Analysis'[2] is not designed to compete in any way with such general accounts of this field of knowledge as are already in existence, e.g. those of Hitschmann (1913), Pfister (1913), Kaplan (1914), Régis and Hesnard (1914) and Meijer (1915). This volume is a faithful reproduction of the lectures which I delivered [at the University] during the two Winter Terms 1915/16 and 1916/17 before an audience of doctors and laymen of both sexes.

Any peculiarities of this book which may strike its readers are accounted for by the conditions in which it originated. It was not possible in my presentation to preserve the unruffled calm of a scientific treatise. On the contrary, the lecturer had to make it his business to prevent his audience's attention from lapsing during a session lasting for almost two hours. The necessities of the moment often made it impossible to avoid repetitions in treating some particular subject—it might emerge once, for instance, in connection with dream-interpretation and then again later on in connection with the problems of the neuroses. As a result, too, of the way in which the material was arranged, some important topics (the unconscious, for instance) could not be exhaustively treated at a single point, but had to be taken up repeatedly and then dropped again until a fresh opportunity arose for adding some further information about it.

Those who are familiar with psycho-analytic literature will find little in this 'Introduction' that could not have been known to them already from other much more detailed publications. Nevertheless, the need for rounding-off and summarizing the subject-matter has compelled the author at certain points (the

---

[1] [This Preface was omitted from the 1922 English translation and its re-issues.]

[2] [A literal translation of the German title of the book would be 'Lectures to Serve as an Introduction to Psycho-Analysis'.]

aetiology of anxiety and hysterical phantasies) to bring forward material that he has hitherto held back.

FREUD

VIENNA, *Spring* 1917

PREFACE TO THE
HEBREW TRANSLATION[1]
[1930]

THESE lectures were delivered in 1916 and 1917; they gave a fairly accurate account of the position of the young science at that period and they contained more than their title indicated. They provided not only an introduction to psycho-analysis but covered the greater part of its subject-matter. This is naturally no longer true. Advances have in the meantime taken place in its theory and important additions have been made to it, such as the division of the personality into an ego, a super-ego and an id, a radical alteration in the theory of the instincts, and discoveries concerning the origin of conscience and the sense of guilt. These lectures have thus become to a large extent incomplete; it is in fact only now that they have become truly 'introductory'. But in another sense, even to-day they have not been superseded or become obsolete. What they contain is still believed and taught, apart from a few modifications, in psychoanalytic training schools.

Readers of Hebrew and especially young people eager for knowledge are presented in this volume with psycho-analysis clothed in the ancient language which has been awakened to a new life by the will of the Jewish people. The author can well picture the problem which this has set its translator. Nor need he suppress his doubt whether Moses and the Prophets would have found these Hebrew lectures intelligible. But he begs their descendants (among whom he himself is numbered), for whom this book is designed, not to react too quickly to their first impulses of criticism and dislike by rejecting it. Psychoanalysis brings forward so much that is new, and among it so much that contradicts traditional opinions and wounds deeply-rooted feelings, that it is bound at first to provoke denial. A

---

[1] [This preface was first published in German in *G.S.*, **12** (1934), 383–4, and reprinted in *G.W.*, **16** (1950), 274–5. It is here translated into English for the first time by James Strachey. The Hebrew translation was published by the Verlag Stybel in Jerusalem in 1930.]

11

reader who suspends his judgement and allows psycho-analysis as a whole to make its impression on him will perhaps become open to a conviction that even this undesired novelty is worth knowing and is indispensable for anyone who wishes to understand the mind and human life.

VIENNA, *December* 1930

PART I
PARAPRAXES

LECTURE I

INTRODUCTION

LADIES AND GENTLEMEN,—I cannot tell how much knowledge about psycho-analysis each one of you has already acquired from what you have read or from hearsay. But the wording of my prospectus—'Elementary Introduction to Psycho-Analysis' —obliges me to treat you as though you knew nothing and stood in need of some preliminary information.

I can, however, assume this much—that you know that psycho-analysis is a procedure for the medical treatment of neurotic patients. And here I can at once give you an instance of how in this field a number of things take place in a different way—often, indeed, in an opposite way—from what they do elsewhere in medical practice. When elsewhere we introduce a patient to a medical technique which is new to him, we usually minimize its inconveniences and give him confident assurances of the success of the treatment. I think we are justified in this, since by doing so we are increasing the probability of success. But when we take a neurotic patient into psycho-analytic treatment, we act differently. We point out the difficulties of the method to him, its long duration, the efforts and sacrifices it calls for; and as regards its success, we tell him we cannot promise it with certainty, that it depends on his own conduct, his understanding, his adaptability and his perseverance. We have good reasons, of course, for such apparently wrong-headed behaviour, as you will perhaps come to appreciate later on.

Do not be annoyed, then, if I begin by treating you in the same way as these neurotic patients. I seriously advise you not to join my audience a second time. To support this advice, I will explain to you how incomplete any instruction in psycho-analysis must necessarily be and what difficulties stand in the way of your forming a judgement of your own upon it. I will show you how the whole trend of your previous education and all your habits of thought are inevitably bound to make you into opponents of psycho-analysis, and how much you would have to overcome in yourselves in order to get the better of this instinctive opposition. I cannot, of course, foretell how much understanding of psycho-analysis you will obtain from the information I give you, but I can promise you this: that by listening to it you will not have learnt how to set about a psycho-analytic investigation or how to carry a treatment through. If, however, there should actually turn out to be one of you who did not feel satisfied by a fleeting acquaintance with psycho-analysis but was inclined to enter into a permanent relationship to it, I should not merely dissuade him from doing so but actively warn him against it. As things stand at present, such a choice of profession would ruin any chance he might have of success at a University, and, if he started in life as a practising physician, he would find himself in a society which did not understand his efforts, which regarded him with distrust and hostility, and unleashed upon him all the evil spirits lurking within it. And the phenomena accompanying the war that is now raging in Europe will perhaps give you some notion of what legions of these evil spirits there may be.

Nevertheless, there are quite a number of people for whom, in spite of these inconveniences, something that promises to bring them a fresh piece of knowledge still has its attraction. If a few of you should be of this sort and in spite of my warnings appear here again for my next lecture, you will be welcome. All of you, however, have a right to learn the nature of the difficulties of psycho-analysis to which I have alluded.

I will begin with those connected with instruction, with training in psycho-analysis. In medical training you are accustomed to *see* things. You see an anatomical preparation, the precipitate of a chemical reaction, the shortening of a muscle as a result of the stimulation of its nerves. Later on, patients are demonstrated before your senses—the symptoms of their illness, the products of the pathological process and even in many cases the agent of the disease in isolation. In the surgical departments you are witnesses of the active measures taken to bring help to patients, and you may yourselves attempt to put them into effect. Even in psychiatry the demonstration of patients with their altered facial expressions, their mode of speech and their behaviour, affords you plenty of observations which leave a deep impression on you. Thus a medical teacher plays in the main the part of a leader and interpreter who accompanies you through a museum, while you gain a direct contact with the objects exhibited and feel yourselves convinced of the existence of the new facts through your own perception.

In psycho-analysis, alas, everything is different. Nothing takes place in a psycho-analytic treatment but an interchange of words between the patient and the analyst. The patient talks, tells of his past experiences and present impressions, complains, confesses to his wishes and his emotional impulses. The doctor listens, tries to direct the patient's processes of thought, exhorts, forces his attention in certain directions, gives him explanations and observes the reactions of understanding or rejection which he in this way provokes in him. The uninstructed relatives of our patients, who are only impressed by visible and tangible things—preferably by actions of the sort that are to be witnessed at the cinema—never fail to express their doubts whether 'anything can be done about the illness by mere talking'. That, of course, is both a short-sighted and an inconsistent line of thought. These are the same people who are so certain that patients are 'simply imagining' their symptoms. Words were originally magic and to this day words have retained much of their ancient magical power. By words one person can make another blissfully happy or drive him to despair, by words the teacher conveys his knowledge to his pupils, by words the orator carries his audience with him and determines their judgements and decisions. Words provoke affects and are in general the means of mutual influence among men. Thus we shall not depreciate the use of words in psychotherapy and we shall be pleased if we can listen to the words that pass between the analyst and his patient.[1]

But we cannot do that either. The talk of which psycho-analytic treatment consists brooks no listener; it cannot be demonstrated. A neurasthenic or hysterical patient can of course, like any other, be introduced to students in a psychiatric lecture. He will give an account of his complaints and symptoms, but of nothing else. The information required by analysis will be given by him only on condition of his having a special

[1] [Cf. a parallel passage near the beginning of *The Question of Lay Analysis* (1926e), (Norton, 1950).]

emotional attachment to the doctor; he would become silent as soon as he observed a single witness to whom he felt indifferent. For this information concerns what is most intimate in his mental life, everything that, as a socially independent person, he must conceal from other people, and, beyond that, everything that, as a homogeneous personality, he will not admit to himself.

Thus you cannot be present as an audience at a psychoanalytic treatment. You can only be told about it; and, in the strictest sense of the word, it is only by hearsay that you will get to know psycho-analysis. As a result of receiving your instruction at second hand, as it were, you find yourselves under quite unusual conditions for forming a judgement. That will obviously depend for the most part on how much credence you can give to your informant.

Let us assume for a moment that you were attending a lecture not on psychiatry but on history, and that the lecturer was telling you of the life and military deeds of Alexander the Great. What grounds would you have for believing in the truth of what he reported? At a first glance the position would seem to be even more unfavourable than in the case of psycho-analysis, for the Professor of History no more took part in Alexander's campaigns than you did. The psycho-analyst does at least report things in which he himself played a part. But in due course we come to the things that confirm what the historian has told you. He could refer you to the reports given by ancient writers, who were either themselves contemporary with the events under question or, at any rate, were comparatively close to them—he could refer you, that is to say, to the works of Diodorus, Plutarch, Arrian, and so on. He could put reproductions before you of coins and statues of the king which have survived and he could hand round to you a photograph of the Pompeian mosaic of the battle of Issus. Strictly speaking, however, all these documents only prove that earlier generations already believed in Alexander's existence and in the reality of his deeds, and your criticism might start afresh at that point. You would then discover that not all that has been reported about Alexander deserves credence or can be confirmed in its details; but nevertheless I cannot think that you would leave the lecture-room in doubts of the reality of Alexander the Great. Your decision would be determined essentially by two considerations: first, that the lecturer had no conceivable motive for assuring you of the reality of something he himself did not think real, and secondly, that all the available history books describe the events in approximately similar terms. If you went on to examine the older sources, you would take the same factors into account—the possible motives of the informants and the conformity of the witnesses to one another. The outcome of your examination would undoubtedly be reassuring in the case of Alexander, but would probably be different where figures such as Moses or Nimrod were concerned. Later opportunities will bring to light clearly enough what doubts you may feel about the credibility of your psycho-analytic informant.

But you will have a right to ask another question. If there is no objective verification of psycho-analysis, and no possibility of demonstrating it, how can one learn psycho-analysis at all, and convince oneself of the truth of its assertions? It is true that psycho-analysis cannot easily be learnt and there are not many people who have learnt it properly. But of course there is a practicable method none the less. One learns psycho-analysis on oneself, by studying one's own personality. This is not quite the same thing as what is called self-observation, but it can, if necessary, be subsumed under it. There are a whole number of very common and generally familiar mental phenomena which, after a little instruction in technique, can be made the subject of analysis upon oneself. In that way one acquires the desired sense of conviction of the reality of the processes described by analysis and of the correctness of its views. Nevertheless, there are definite limits to progress by this method. One advances much further if one is analysed oneself by a practised analyst and experiences the effects of analysis on one's own self, making use of the opportunity of picking up the subtler technique of the process from one's analyst. This excellent method is, of course, applicable only to a single person and never to a whole lecture-room of students together.

Psycho-analysis is not to be blamed for a second difficulty in your relation to it; I must make you yourselves responsible for it, Ladies and Gentlemen, at least in so far as you have been students of medicine. Your earlier education has given a

particular direction to your thinking, which leads far away from
psycho-analysis. You have been trained to find an anatomical
basis for the functions of the organism and their disorders, to
explain them chemically and physically and to view them biologically. But no portion of your interest has been directed to
psychical life, in which, after all, the achievement of this marvel-
lously complex organism reaches its peak. For that reason
psychological modes of thought have remained foreign to you.
You have grown accustomed to regarding them with suspicion,
to denying them the attribute of being scientific, and to handing
them over to laymen, poets, natural philosophers[1] and mystics.
This limitation is without doubt detrimental to your medical
activity, since, as is the rule in all human relationships, your
patients will begin by presenting you with their mental *façade*,
and I fear that you will be obliged as a punishment to leave a
part of the therapeutic influence you[2] are seeking to the lay
practitioners, nature curers and mystics whom you so much
despise.

I am not unaware of the excuse that we have to accept for
this defect in your education. No philosophical auxiliary science
exists which could be made of service for your medical purposes.
Neither speculative philosophy, nor descriptive psychology, nor
what is called experimental psychology (which is closely allied
to the physiology of the sense-organs), as they are taught in the
Universities, are in a position to tell you anything serviceable of
the relation between body and mind or to provide you with
the key to an understanding of possible disturbances of the
mental functions. It is true that psychiatry, as a part of medicine, sets about describing the mental disorders it observes and
collecting them into clinical entities; but at favourable moments
the psychiatrists themselves have doubts of whether their purely
descriptive hypotheses deserve the name of a science. Nothing
is known of the origin, the mechanism or the mutual relations
of the symptoms of which these clinical entities are composed;
there are either *no* observable changes in the anatomical organ

---

[1] [In the sense of followers of Schelling's pantheistic 'philosophy of
nature', which prevailed in Germany during the earlier part of the
nineteenth century.]

[2] ['*Sie* (you)' in the earlier German editions; '*sie* (they)' in *G.S.* and
G.W.]

of the mind to correspond to them, or changes which throw no light upon them. These mental disorders are only accessible to therapeutic influence when they can be recognized as subsidiary effects of what is otherwise an organic illness.

This is the gap which psycho-analysis seeks to fill. It tries to give psychiatry its missing psychological foundation. It hopes to discover the common ground on the basis of which the convergence of physical and mental disorder will become intelligible. With this aim in view, psycho-analysis must keep itself free from any hypothesis that is alien to it, whether of an anatomical, chemical or physiological kind, and must operate entirely with purely psychological auxiliary ideas; and for that very reason, I fear, it will seem strange to you to begin with.

I shall not hold you, your education or your attitude of mind responsible for the next difficulty. Two of the hypotheses of psycho-analysis are an insult to the entire world and have earned its dislike. One of them offends against an intellectual prejudice, the other against an aesthetic and moral one. We must not be too contemptuous of these prejudices; they are powerful things, precipitates of human developments that were useful and indeed essential. They are kept in existence by emotional forces and the struggle against them is hard.

The first of these unpopular assertions made by psycho-analysis declares that mental processes are in themselves unconscious and that of all mental life it is only certain individual acts and portions that are conscious.[1] You know that on the contrary we are in the habit of identifying what is psychical with what is conscious. We look upon consciousness as nothing more nor less than the *defining* characteristic of the psychical, and psychology as the study of the contents of consciousness. Indeed it seems to us so much a matter of course to equate them in this way that any contradiction of the idea strikes us as obvious non-

---

[1] ['*Unbewusst*' and '*bewusst*'. It should be realized from the first that in German these words have a passive grammatical form and, generally speaking, a passive sense. In English 'conscious' and 'unconscious' *may* be used passively but as often as not are used *actively*: 'I am conscious of a pain in my toe' or 'he was unconscious of his hatred'. The German usage would rather speak of the *pain* as conscious and the *hatred* unconscious, and this is the usage adopted regularly by Freud.]

sense. Yet psycho-analysis cannot avoid raising this contradiction; it cannot accept the identity of the conscious and the mental.[1] It defines what is mental as processes such as feeling, thinking and willing, and it is obliged to maintain that there is unconscious thinking and unapprehended willing. In saying this it has from the start frivolously forfeited the sympathy of every friend of sober scientific thought, and laid itself open to the suspicion of being a fantastic esoteric doctrine eager to make mysteries and fish in troubled waters. But you, Ladies and Gentlemen, naturally cannot understand as yet what right I have to describe as a prejudice a statement of so abstract a nature as 'what is mental is conscious'. Nor can you guess what development can have led to a denial of the unconscious—should such a thing exist—and what advantage there may have been in that denial. The question whether we are to make the psychical coincide with the conscious or make it extend further sounds like an empty dispute about words; yet I can assure you that the hypothesis of there being unconscious mental processes paves the way to a decisive new orientation in the world and in science.

You cannot have any notion, either, of what an intimate connection there is between this first piece of audacity on the part of psycho-analysis and the second one, which I must now tell you of. This second thesis, which psycho-analysis puts forward as one of its findings, is an assertion that instinctual impulses which can only be described as sexual, both in the narrower and wider sense of the word, play an extremely large and never hitherto appreciated part in the causation of nervous and mental diseases. It asserts further that these same sexual impulses also make contributions that must not be underestimated to the highest cultural, artistic and social creations of the human spirit.[2]

In my experience antipathy to this outcome of psycho-analytic research is the most important source of resistance which it has met with. Would you like to hear how we explain that fact? We believe that civilization has been created under the pressure of the exigencies of life at the cost of satisfaction of

[1] [The first section of Freud's paper on 'The Unconscious' (1915e), discusses this question at great length.]

[2] [The sexual instincts form the topic of Lecture XX.]

the instincts; and we believe that civilization is to a large extent being constantly created anew, since each individual who makes a fresh entry into human society repeats this sacrifice of instinctual satisfaction for the benefit of the whole community. Among the instinctual forces which are put to this use the sexual impulses play an important part; in this process they are sublimated—that is to say, they are diverted from their sexual aims and directed to others that are socially higher and no longer sexual. But this arrangement is unstable; the sexual instincts are imperfectly tamed, and, in the case of every individual who is supposed to join in the work of civilization, there is a risk that his sexual instincts may refuse to be put to that use. Society believes that no greater threat to its civilization could arise than if the sexual instincts were to be liberated and returned to their original aims.[1] For this reason society does not wish to be reminded of this precarious portion of its foundations. It has no interest in the recognition of the strength of the sexual instincts or in the demonstration of the importance of sexual life to the individual. On the contrary, with an educational aim in view, it has set about diverting attention from that whole field of ideas. That is why it will not tolerate this outcome of psycho-analytic research and far prefers to stamp it as something aesthetically repulsive and morally reprehensible, or as something dangerous. But objections of this sort are ineffective against what claims to be an objective outcome of a piece of scientific work; if the contradiction is to come into the open it must be restated in intellectual terms. Now it is inherent in human nature to have an inclination to consider a thing untrue if one does not like it, and after that it is easy to find arguments against it. Thus society makes what is disagreeable into what is untrue. It disputes the truths of psycho-analysis with logical and factual arguments; but these arise from emotional sources and it maintains these objections as prejudices, against every attempt to counter them.

We, however, Ladies and Gentlemen, can claim that in asserting this controversial thesis we have had no tendentious aim in view. We have merely wished to give expression to a

---

[1] [The antagonism between civilization and the instinctual forces received its fullest treatment by Freud in *Civilization and its Discontents* (1930a), (Norton, 1962).]

matter of fact which we believe we have established by our painstaking labours. We claim, too, the right to reject without qualification any interference by practical considerations in scientific work, even before we have enquired whether the fear which seeks to impose these considerations on us is justified or not.

Such, then, are a few of the difficulties that stand in the way of your interest in psycho-analysis. They are perhaps more than enough for a start. But if you are able to overcome the impression they make on you, we will proceed.

LECTURE II

PARAPRAXES

LADIES AND GENTLEMEN,—We will not start with postulates but with an investigation. Let us choose as its subject certain phenomena which are very common and very familiar but which have been very little examined, and which, since they can be observed in any healthy person, have nothing to do with illnesses. They are what are known as 'parapraxes',[1] to which everyone is liable. It may happen, for instance, that a person who intends to say something may use another word instead (a *slip of the tongue* [*Versprechen*]), or he may do the same thing in writing, and may or may not notice what he has done. Or a person may read something, whether in print or manuscript, different from what is actually before his eyes (a *misreading* [*Verlesen*]), or he may hear wrongly something that has been said to him (a *mishearing* [*Verhören*])—on the assumption, of course, that there is no organic disturbance of his powers of hearing. Another group of these phenomena has as its basis *forgetting* [*Vergessen*]—not, however, a permanent forgetting but only a temporary one. Thus a person may be unable to get hold of a *name* which he nevertheless knows and which he recognizes at once, or he may forget to carry out an *intention*, though he remembers it later and has thus only forgotten it at that particular moment. In a third group the temporary character is absent—for instance in the case of *mislaying* [*Verlegen*], when a person has put something somewhere and cannot find it again,

---

[1] ['*Fehlleistungen*', literally 'faulty acts' or 'faulty functions'. The general concept did not exist before Freud, and an English term was invented for its translation. The whole of *The Psychopathology of Everyday Life* (1901*b*), (Norton, 1965), is devoted to a discussion of them. Freud often used them in his didactic writings (as he does here) as the most suitable material for an introduction to his theories. They were, indeed, among the earliest subjects of his own psychological investigations. Some account of the history of his interest in them will be found in the Editor's Introduction to the sixth volume of the *Standard Edition*. Since there will be a large number of references to that work in the present lectures, the abbreviation '*P.E.L.*' will be used here in order to economize space. The page references in all such cases will be to the *Standard Ed.* and the Norton edition.]

or in the precisely analogous case of *losing* [*Verlieren*]. Here we have a forgetting which we treat differently from other kinds of forgetting, one at which we are surprised or annoyed instead of finding it understandable. In addition to all this there are particular sorts of *errors* [*Irrtümer*], in which the temporary character is present once more; for in their instance we believe for a time that something is the case which both before and afterwards we know is not so. And there are a number of other similar phenomena known by various names.

All these are occurrences whose internal affinity with one another is expressed in the fact that [in German] they begin with the syllable '*ver*'.[1] They are almost all of an unimportant kind, most of them are very transitory, and they are without much significance in human life. Only rarely does one of them, such as losing an object, attain some degree of practical importance. For that reason, too, they attract little attention, give rise to no more than feeble emotions, and so on.

It is to these phenomena, then, that I now propose to draw your attention. But you will protest with some annoyance: 'There are so many vast problems in the wide[2] universe, as well as within the narrower confines of our minds, so many marvels in the field of mental disorders, which require and deserve to have light thrown upon them, that it does really seem gratuitous to waste labour and interest on such trivialities. If you could make us understand why a person with sound eyes and ears can see and hear in broad daylight things that are not there, why another person suddenly thinks he is being persecuted by the people of whom he has hitherto been most fond, or puts forward the cleverest arguments in support of delusional beliefs which any child could see were nonsensical, then we should have some opinion of psycho-analysis. But if it can do no more than ask us to consider why a speaker at a banquet uses one word instead of another or why a housewife has mislaid her keys, and similar futilities, then we shall know how to put our time and interest to better uses.'

I should reply: Patience, Ladies and Gentlemen! I think your criticism has gone astray. It is true that psycho-analysis cannot

---

[1] [The English syllable 'mis' has a similar sense.]

[2] [In the editions from 1922 onwards this word is omitted.]

boast that it has never concerned itself with trivialities. On the contrary, the material for its observations is usually provided by the inconsiderable events which have been put aside by the other sciences as being too unimportant—the dregs, one might say, of the world of phenomena. But are you not making a confusion in your criticism between the vastness of the problems and the conspicuousness of what points to them? Are there not very important things which can only reveal themselves, under certain conditions and at certain times, by quite feeble indications? I should find no difficulty in giving you several examples of such situations. If you are a young man, for instance, will it not be from small pointers that you will conclude that you have won a girl's favour? Would you wait for an express declaration of love or a passionate embrace? Or would not a glance, scarcely noticed by other people, be enough? a slight movement, the lengthening by a second of the pressure of a hand? And if you were a detective engaged in tracing a murder, would you expect to find that the murderer had left his photograph behind at the place of the crime, with his address attached? or would you not necessarily have to be satisfied with comparatively slight and obscure traces of the person you were in search of? So do not let us under-estimate small indications; by their help we may succeed in getting on the track of something bigger. Furthermore, I think like you that the great problems of the universe and of science have the first claim on our interest. But it is as a rule of very little use to form an express intention of devoting oneself to research into this or that great problem. One is then often at a loss to know the first step to take. It is more promising in scientific work to attack whatever is immediately before one and offers an opportunity for research. If one does so really thoroughly and without prejudice or preconception, and if one has luck, then, since everything is related to everything, including small things to great, one may gain access even from such unpretentious work to a study of the great problems. That is what I should say in order to retain your interest, when we deal with such apparent trivialities as the parapraxes of healthy people.

Let us now call in someone who knows nothing of psychoanalysis, and ask him how he explains such occurrences. His first reply will certainly be: 'Oh! that's not worth explaining: they're just small chance events.' What does the fellow mean by this? Is he maintaining that there are occurrences, however small, which drop out of the universal concatenation of events —occurrences which might just as well not happen as happen? If anyone makes a breach of this kind in the determinism of natural events at a single point, it means that he has thrown overboard the whole *Weltanschauung* of science. Even the *Weltanschauung* of religion, we may remind him, behaves much more consistently, since it gives an explicit assurance that no sparrow falls from the roof without God's special will. I think our friend will hesitate to draw the logical conclusion from his first reply; he will change his mind and say that after all when he comes to study these things he can find explanations of them. What is in question are small failures of functioning, imperfections in mental activity, whose determinants can be assigned. A man who can usually speak correctly may make a slip of the tongue (1) if he is slightly indisposed and tired, (2) if he is excited and (3) if he is too much occupied with other things. It is easy to confirm these statements. Slips of the tongue do really occur with particular frequency when one is tired, has a headache or is threatened with migraine. In the same circumstances proper names are easily forgotten. Some people are accustomed to recognize the approach of an attack of migraine when proper names escape them in this way.[1] When we are excited, too, we often make mistakes over words—and over *things* as well, and a 'bungled action' follows. Intentions are forgotten and a quantity of other undesigned actions become noticeable if we are absent-minded—that is, properly speaking, if we are concentrated on something else. A familiar example of this absent-mindedness is the Professor in *Fliegende Blätter*[2] who leaves his umbrella behind and takes the wrong hat because he is thinking about the problems he is going to deal with in his next book. All of us can recall from our own experience instances of how we can forget intentions we have formed and promises we have made because in the meantime we have had some absorbing experience.

This sounds quite reasonable and seems safe from contradic-

---

[1] [This was a personal experience of Freud's. *P.E.L.*, 21.]

[2] [The comic weekly.]

tion, though it may not be very interesting, perhaps, and not what we expected. Let us look at these explanations of parapraxes more closely. The alleged preconditions for the occurrence of these phenomena are not all of the same kind. Being ill and disturbances of the circulation provide a physiological reason for the impairment of normal functioning; excitement, fatigue and distraction are factors of another sort, which might be described as psycho-physiological. These last admit of easy translation into theory. Both fatigue and distraction, and perhaps also general excitement, bring about a division of attention which may result in insufficient attention being directed to the function in question. If so, the function can be disturbed with especial ease, or carried out inaccurately. Slight illness or changes in the blood-supply to the central nervous organ can have the same effect, by influencing the determining factor, the division of attention, in a similar manner. In all these cases, therefore, it would be a question of the effects of a disturbance of attention, whether from organic or psychical causes.

This does not appear to promise much for our psychoanalytic interest. We might feel tempted to drop the subject. If, however, we examine the observations more closely, what we find does not tally entirely with this attention theory of parapraxes, or at least does not follow from it naturally. We discover that parapraxes of this kind and forgetting of this kind occur in people who are *not* fatigued or absent-minded or excited, but who are in all respects in their normal state—unless we choose to ascribe *ex post facto* to the people concerned, purely on account of their parapraxis, an excitement which, however, they themselves do not admit to. Nor can it be simply the case that a function is ensured by an increase in the attention directed upon it and endangered if that attention is reduced. There are a large number of procedures that one carries out purely automatically, with very little attention, but nevertheless performs with complete security. A walker, who scarcely knows where he is going, keeps to the right path for all that, and stops at his destination without having *gone astray [vergangen]*. Or at all events this is so as a rule. An expert pianist strikes the right keys without thinking. He may, of course, make an occasional mistake; but if automatic playing increased the danger of bungling, that danger would be at its greatest for a virtuoso, whose playing, as a result of prolonged practice, has become *entirely* automatic. We know, on the contrary, that many procedures are carried out with quite particular certainty if they are not the object of a specially high degree of attention,[1] and that the mishap of a parapraxis is liable to occur precisely if special importance is attached to correct functioning and there has therefore certainly been no distraction of the necessary attention. It could be argued that this is the result of 'excitement', but it is difficult to see why the excitement should not on the contrary *increase* the attention directed to what is so earnestly intended. If by a slip of the tongue someone says the opposite of what he intends in an important speech or oral communication, it can scarcely be explained by the psycho-physiological or attention theory.

There are, moreover, a number of small subsidiary phenomena in the case of parapraxes, which we do not understand and on which the explanations so far given shed no light. For instance, if we have temporarily forgotten a name, we are annoyed about it, do all we can to remember it and cannot leave the business alone. Why in such cases do we so extremely seldom succeed in directing our attention, as we are after all anxious to do, to the word which (as we say) is 'on the tip of our tongue' and which we recognize at once when we are told it? Or again: there are cases in which the parapraxes multiply, form chains, and replace one another. On a first occasion one has missed an appointment. On the next occasion, when one has firmly decided not to forget *this* time, it turns out that one has made a note of the wrong hour. Or one tries to arrive at a forgotten word by roundabout ways and thereupon a second name escapes one which might have helped one to find the first. If one searches for this second name, a third disappears, and so on. As is well known, the same thing can happen with misprints, which are to be regarded as the parapraxes of the compositor. An obstinate misprint of this kind, so it is said, once slipped into a social-democrat newspaper. Its report of some ceremonial included the words: 'Among those present was to be noticed His Highness the *Kornprinz*.' Next day an attempt was

---

[1] [Freud has often suggested elsewhere that functions may be performed more accurately in the absence of conscious attention. See *P.E.L.*, 132.]

made at a correction. The paper apologized and said: 'We should of course have said "the *Knorprinz*".' [1] People speak in such cases of a 'demon of misprints' or a 'type-setting fiend'— terms which at least go beyond any psycho-physiological theory of misprints. [2]

Perhaps you are familiar, too, with the fact that it is possible to *provoke* slips of the tongue, to produce them, as it were, by suggestion. An anecdote illustrates this. A stage neophyte had been cast for the important part in [Schiller's] *Die Jungfrau von Orleans* of the messenger who announces to the King that 'der Connétable schickt sein Schwert zurück [the Constable sends back his sword]'. A leading actor amused himself during the rehearsal by repeatedly inducing the nervous young man to say, instead of the words of the text: 'der Komfortabel schickt sein Pferd zurück [the cab-driver sends back his horse].' [3] He achieved his aim: the wretched beginner actually made his début at the performance with the corrupt version, in spite of having been warned against it, or perhaps *because* he had been warned.

No light is thrown on these small features of parapraxes by the theory of withdrawal of attention. The theory need not on that account be wrong, however; it may merely lack something, some addition, before it is entirely satisfying. But some of the parapraxes, too, can themselves be looked at from another point of view.

Let us take *slips of the tongue* as the most suitable sort of parapraxis for our purpose—though we might equally well have chosen slips of the pen or misreading. [4] We must bear in mind

[1] [What was intended was the '*Kronprinz* (Crown Prince)'. '*Korn*' means 'corn' and '*Knorr*' 'protuberance'.]

[2] [Cf. *P.E.L.*, 130–1.]

[3] [There seems to be some confusion here. Actually (in Act I, Scene 2 of the play) it is the King himself who announces the Constable's defection.]

[4] [It is most unfortunate from the point of view of the translator that Freud chose slips of the tongue as his most frequent examples of parapraxes in all three of these lectures, since they are from their very nature peculiarly resistant to translation. We have, however, followed our invariable practice in the *Standard Edition* and kept Freud's instances, with footnote and square bracket explanations, rather than replace them by extraneous English ones. Plenty of the latter will be found elsewhere, especially in papers by A. A. Brill (1912) and Ernest Jones (1911).]

that so far we have only asked when—under what conditions—people make slips of the tongue, and it is only to that question that we have had an answer. But we might direct our interest elsewhere and enquire why it is that the slip occurred in this particular way and no other; and we might take into account what it is that emerges in the slip itself. You will observe that, so long as this question is unanswered and no light thrown on the product of the slip, the phenomenon remains a chance event from the psychological point of view, even though it may have been given a physiological explanation. If I make a slip of the tongue, I might obviously do so in an infinite number of ways, the right word might be replaced by any of a thousand others, it might be distorted in countless different directions. Is there something, then, that compels me in the particular case to make the slip in one special way, or does it remain a matter of chance, of arbitrary choice, and is the question perhaps one to which no sensible answer at all can be given?

Two writers, Meringer and Mayer (a philologist and a psychiatrist), in fact made an attempt in 1895 to attack the problem of parapraxes from this angle. They collected examples and began by treating them in a purely descriptive way. This, of course, provides no explanation as yet, though it might pave the way to one. They distinguish the various kinds of distortions imposed by the slip on the intended speech as 'transpositions', 'pre-sonances [anticipations]', 'post-sonances [perseverations]', 'fusions (contaminations)' and 'replacements (substitutions)'. I will give you some examples of these main groups proposed by the authors. An instance of transposition would be to say '*the Milo of Venus*' instead of 'the Venus of Milo' (a transposition of the order of the words); an instance of a pre-sonance [anticipation] would be: 'es war mir *auf der Schwest* . . . auf der Brust so schwer';[1] and a post-sonance [perseveration] would be exemplified by the well-known toast that went wrong: 'Ich fordere Sie *auf, auf* das Wohl unseres Chefs *auf*zustossen' [instead of *an*zustossen].[2] These three forms of slip of the tongue are not

---

[1] [The phrase intended was : 'it lay on my breast so heavily.' The meaningless '*Schwest*' was a distortion of '*Brust* (breast)' owing to an anticipation of the '*schw*' of '*schwer* (heavily)'. This and the preceding example are also in *P.E.L.*, 53–4.]

[2] ['I call on you to *hiccough to*' (instead of 'drink to') 'the health of

exactly common. You will come on much more numerous examples in which the slip results from contraction or fusion. Thus, for instance, a gentleman addressed a lady in the street in the following words: 'If you will permit me, madam, I should like to *begleit-digen* you.' The composite word,[1] in addition to the '*begleiten* [to accompany]', evidently has concealed in it '*beleidigen* [to insult]'. (Incidentally, the young man was not likely to have much success with the lady.) As an example of a substitution Meringer and Mayer give the case of someone saying: 'Ich gebe die Präparate in den *Brief* kasten' instead of '*Brüt* kasten'.[2]

The attempted explanation which these authors base on their collection of instances is quite peculiarly inadequate. They believe that the sounds and syllables of a word have a particular 'valency' and that the innervation of an element of high valency may have a disturbing influence on one that is less valent. Here they are clearly basing themselves on the far from common cases of pre-sonance and post-sonance; these preferences of some sounds over others (if they in fact exist) can have no bearing at all on other effects of slips of the tongue. After all, the commonest slips of the tongue are when, instead of saying one word, we say another very much like it; and this similarity is for many people a sufficient explanation of such slips. For instance, a Professor declared in his inaugural lecture: 'I am not '*geneigt* [inclined]' (instead of '*geeignet* [qualified]') to appreciate the services of my highly esteemed predecessor.' Or another Professor remarked: 'In the case of the female genitals, in spite of many *Versuchungen* [temptations]—I beg your pardon, *Versuche* [experiments]. . . .'[3]

The most usual, and at the same time the most striking kind of slips of the tongue, however, are those in which one says the precise opposite of what one intended to say. Here, of course, we are very remote from relations between sounds and the effects of similarity; and instead we can appeal to the fact that

our Chief.' This, too, occurs in *P.E.L.*, 54, where, however, the translation is slightly different.]

[1] [A meaningless one.]

[2] ['I put the preparation into the letter-box' instead of 'incubator', literally, 'hatching-box'. These last two examples occur in *P.E.L.*, 68 and 54.]

[3] [*P.E.L.*, 69 and 78–9.]

contraries have a strong conceptual kinship with each other and stand in a particularly close psychological association with each other.[1] There are historical examples of such occurrences. A President of the Lower House of our Parliament once opened the sitting with the words: 'Gentlemen, I take notice that a full quorum of members is present and herewith declare the sitting *closed*.'[2]

Any other familiar association can act in the same insidious fashion as a contrary one, and can emerge in quite unsuitable circumstances. Thus, on the occasion of a celebration in honour of the marriage of a child of Hermann von Helmholtz to a child of Werner von Siemens, the well-known inventor and industrialist, it is said that the duty of proposing the young couple's health fell to the famous physiologist Du Bois-Reymond. No doubt he made a brilliant speech, but he ended with the words: 'So, long life to the new firm of Siemens and Halske!' That was, of course, the name of the *old* firm. The juxtaposition of the two names must have been as familiar to a Berliner as Fortnum and Mason would be to a Londoner.[3]

We must therefore include among the causes of parapraxes not only relations between sounds and verbal similarity, but the influence of word-associations as well. But that is not all. In a number of cases it seems impossible to explain a slip of the tongue unless we take into account something that had been said, or even merely thought, in an earlier sentence. Once again, then, we have here a case of perseveration, like those insisted upon by Meringer, but of more distant origin.—I must confess that I feel on the whole as though after all this we were further than ever from understanding slips of the tongue.

Nevertheless I hope I am not mistaken in saying that during this last enquiry we have all of us formed a fresh impression of

---

[1] [Cf. below, p. 178 ff.]

[2] [*P.E.L.*, 59. The example was also used by Freud in one of his very last writings, the unfinished 'Some Elementary Lessons in Psycho-Analysis' (1940*b* [1938]).]

[3] [In the original: 'as Riedel and Beutel would be to a Viennese'. This last was a well-known outfitter's shop in Vienna. Siemens and Halske were, of course, the great electrical engineers.]

these instances of slips of the tongue, and that it may be worth while to consider that impression further. We examined the conditions under which in general slips of the tongue occur, and afterwards the influences which determine the kind of distortion which the slip produces. But we have so far paid no attention whatever to the *product* of the slip considered by itself, without reference to its origin. If we decide to do so, we are bound in the end to find the courage to say that in a few examples what results from the slip of the tongue has a sense of its own. What do we mean by 'has a sense'? That the product of the slip of the tongue may perhaps itself have a right to be regarded as a completely valid psychical act, pursuing an aim of its own, as a statement with a content and significance. So far we have always spoken of 'parapraxes [faulty acts]', but it seems now as though sometimes the faulty act was itself quite a *normal* act, which merely took the place of the other act which was the one expected or intended.

The fact of the parapraxis having a sense of its own seems in certain cases evident and unmistakable. When the President of the Lower House with his first words *closed* the sitting instead of opening it, we feel inclined, in view of our knowledge of the circumstances in which the slip of the tongue occurred, to recognize that the parapraxis had a sense. The President expected nothing good of the sitting and would have been glad if he could have brought it to an immediate end. We have no difficulty in pointing to the sense of this slip of the tongue, or, in other words, in interpreting it. Or, let us suppose that one lady says to another in tones of apparent admiration: 'That smart new hat—I suppose you *aufgepatzt* [a non-existent word instead of *aufgeputzt* (trimmed)] it yourself?' Then no amount of scientific propriety will succeed in preventing our seeing behind this slip of the tongue the words: 'This hat is a *Patzerei* [botched-up affair].' Or, once more, we are told that a lady who was well-known for her energy remarked on one occasion: 'My husband asked his doctor what diet he ought to follow; but the doctor told him he had no need to diet: he could eat and drink what I want.' Here again the slip of the tongue has an unmistakable other side to it: it was giving expression to a consistently planned programme.[1]

---

[1] [These two last examples appear in *P.E.L.*, 87 and 70.]

If it turned out, Ladies and Gentlemen, that not only *a few* instances of slips of the tongue and of parapraxes in general have a sense, but a considerable number of them, the *sense* of parapraxes, of which we have so far heard nothing, would inevitably become their most interesting feature and would push every other consideration into the background. We should then be able to leave all physiological or psycho-physiological factors on one side and devote ourselves to purely psychological investigations into the sense—that is, the meaning or purpose—of parapraxes. We shall therefore make it our business to test this expectation on a considerable number of observations.

But before carrying out this intention I should like to invite you to follow me along another track. It has repeatedly happened that a creative writer has made use of a slip of the tongue or some other parapraxis as an instrument for producing an imaginative effect. This fact alone must prove to us that he regards the parapraxis—the slip of the tongue, for instance—as having a sense, since he has produced it deliberately. For what has happened is not that the author has made an accidental slip of the pen and has then allowed it to be used by one of his characters as a slip of the tongue; he intends to bring something to our notice by means of the slip of the tongue and we can enquire what that something is—whether perhaps he wants to suggest that the character in question is absent-minded and fatigued or is going to have an attack of migraine. If the author uses the slip as though it had a sense, we have no wish, of course, to exaggerate the importance of this. After all, a slip might in fact be without a sense, a chance psychical event, or it might have a sense in only quite rare cases, but the author would still retain his right to intellectualize it by *furnishing* it with a sense so as to employ it for his own purposes. Nor would it be surprising if we had more to learn about slips of the tongue from creative writers than from philologists and psychiatrists.

An example of this kind is to be found in [Schiller's] *Wallenstein* (*Piccolomini*, Act I, Scene 5). In the preceding scene Max Piccolomini has ardently espoused the Duke's [Wallenstein's] cause, and has been passionately describing the blessings of peace, of which he has become aware in the course of a journey while escorting Wallenstein's daughter to the camp. As he leaves the stage, his father [Octavio] and Questenberg, the emissary from the Court, are plunged in consternation. Scene 5 continues:

QUESTENBERG   Alas, alas! and stands it so?
              What, friend! and do we let him go away
              In this delusion—let him go away?
              Not call him back immediately, not open
              His eyes upon the spot?
OCTAVIO (*recovering himself out of a deep study*) He now has open'd mine,
              And I see more than pleases me.
QUEST.   What is it?
OCT.   Curse on this journey!
QUEST.   But why so? What is it?
OCT.   Come, come along friend! I must follow up
              The ominous track immediately. Mine eyes
              Are open'd now, and I must use them. Come!
                              (*Draws Q. on with him.*)
QUEST.   What now? *Where* go you then?
OCT.   To her . . .
QUEST.   To—
OCT. (*correcting himself*) To the Duke. Come let us go.
                                      [Coleridge's translation.]

Octavio had meant to say 'to him', to the Duke. But he makes a slip of the tongue, and, by saying 'to her' he betrays to *us* at least that he has clearly recognized the influence that has made the young warrior into an enthusiast for peace.[1]

A still more impressive example has been discovered by Otto Rank [1910*a*] in Shakespeare. It is from *The Merchant of Venice*, in the famous scene in which the fortunate lover chooses between the three caskets, and perhaps I cannot do better than read you Rank's short account of it:

'A slip of the tongue occurs in Shakespeare's *Merchant of Venice* (Act III, Scene 2), which is from the dramatic point of view extremely subtly motivated and which is put to brilliant technical use. Like the slip in *Wallenstein* to which Freud has drawn attention, it shows that dramatists have a clear understanding of the mechanism and meaning of this kind of parapraxis and assume that the same is true of their audience. Portia, who by her father's will has been bound to the choice of a husband by lot, has so far escaped all her unwelcome suitors by a fortunate chance. Having at last found in Bassanio

[1] [This example and the following one also occur in *P.E.L.*, 96–8.]

the suitor who is to her liking, she has cause to fear that he too
will choose the wrong casket. She would very much like to tell
him that even so he could rest assured of her love; but she is
prevented by her vow. In this internal conflict the poet makes
her say to the suitor she favours:

> I pray you tarry; pause a day or two
> Before you hazard: for, in choosing wrong,
> I lose your company; therefore forbear a while:
> There's something tells me (*but it is not love*)
> I would not lose you . . . .
>   . . . I could teach you
> How to choose right, but then I am forsworn;
> So will I never be; so may you miss me;
> But if you do you'll make me wish a sin,
> That I have been forsworn. Beshrew your eyes,
> They have o'erlooked me, and divided me;
> *One half of me is yours, the other half yours,*—
> *Mine own, I would say*; but if mine, then yours,
> And so all yours.

The thing of which she wanted to give him only a very subtle
hint, because she should have concealed it from him altogether,
namely, that even before he made his choice she was *wholly* his
and loved him—it is precisely this that the poet, with a wonderful psychological sensitivity, causes to break through openly in
her slip of the tongue; and by this artistic device he succeeds in
relieving both the lover's unbearable uncertainty and the suspense of the sympathetic audience over the outcome of his
choice.'

Observe, too, how skilfully Portia in the end reconciles the
two statements contained in her slip of the tongue, how she
solves the contradiction between them and yet finally shows that
it was the slip that was in the right:

> 'But if mine, then yours,
>   And so all yours.'

It has occasionally happened that a thinker whose field lies
outside medicine has, by something he says, revealed the sense
of a parapraxis and anticipated our efforts at explaining them.
You all know of the witty satirist Lichtenberg (1742–99), of
whom Goethe said: 'Where he makes a jest a problem lies concealed.' Sometimes the jest brings the *solution* of the problem to
light as well. In Lichtenberg's *Witzige und Satirische Einfälle*

[Witty and Satirical Thoughts, 1853] we find this: 'He had read so much Homer that he always read "*Agamemnon*" instead of "*angenommen* [supposed]".' Here we have the whole theory of misreading.[1]

We must see next time whether we can go along with these writers in their view of parapraxes.

---

[1] [Lichtenberg was a favourite author of Freud's and many of his epigrams are discussed in *Jokes and their Relation to the Unconscious* (1905c), (Norton, 1960). The Agamemnon remark is further considered below, p. 70. It is quoted in the book on jokes (p. 93) as well as in *P.E.L.*, 112, where Goethe's comment also appears (*P.E.L.*, 218).]

LECTURE III

PARAPRAXES (*continued*)

LADIES AND GENTLEMEN,—We arrived last time at the idea of considering parapraxes not in relation to the intended function which they disturbed but on their own account; and we formed an impression that in particular cases they seemed to be betraying a sense of their own. We then reflected that if confirmation could be obtained on a wider scale that parapraxes have a sense, their sense would soon become more interesting than the investigation of the circumstances in which they come about.

Let us once more reach an agreement upon what is to be understood by the 'sense' of a psychical process. We mean nothing other by it than the intention it serves and its position in a psychical continuity. In most of our researches we can replace 'sense' by 'intention' or 'purpose'.[1] Was it, then, merely a deceptive illusion or a poetic exaltation of parapraxes when we thought we recognized an intention in them?

We will continue to take slips of the tongue as our examples. If we now look through a considerable number of observations of that kind, we shall find whole categories of cases in which the intention, the sense, of the slip is plainly visible. Above all there are those in which what was intended is replaced by its contrary. The President of the Lower House [p. 34] said in his opening speech: 'I declare the sitting closed.' That is quite unambiguous. The sense and intention of his slip was that he wanted to close the sitting. 'Er sagt es ja selbst'[2] we are tempted to quote: we need only take him at his word. Do not interrupt

---

[1] [It has been thought best to translate the German word '*Tendenz*' by 'purpose' throughout these lectures. The meanings of the two words do not, however, coincide, and in a few passages some such rendering as 'trend' would be preferable. '*Tendenz*' is almost never equivalent to 'tendency', though the adjective '*tendenziös*' has become naturalized in the English form of 'tendentious', as applied, for instance, to a play 'with a purpose'.]

[2] ['He says so himself.' This is a line from the standard German translation of a phrase in *Figaro* which occurs repeatedly in the sextet in Act III.]

40

me at this point by objecting that that is impossible, that we know that he did not want to close the sitting but to open it, and that he himself, whom we have just recognized as the supreme court of appeal, could confirm the fact that he wanted to open it. You are forgetting that we have come to an agreement that we will begin by regarding parapraxes on their own account; their relation to the intention which they have disturbed is not to be discussed till later. Otherwise you will be guilty of a logical error by simply evading the problem that is under discussion—by what is called in English 'begging the question'.

In other cases, where the slip does not express the precise contrary, an opposite sense can nevertheless be brought out by it. 'I am not *geneigt* [inclined] to appreciate the services of my predecessor' [p. 33]. *Geneigt* is not the contrary of *geeignet* [qualified], but it expresses openly something which contrasts sharply with the situation in which the speech was to be made.

In yet other cases the slip of the tongue merely adds a second sense to the one intended. The sentence then sounds like a contraction, abbreviation or condensation of several sentences. Thus, when the energetic lady said: 'He can eat and drink what I want' [p. 35], it was just as though she had said: 'He can eat and drink what he wants; but what has *he* to do with wanting? *I* will want instead of him.' A slip of the tongue often gives the impression of being an abbreviation of this sort. For instance, a Professor of Anatomy at the end of a lecture on the nasal cavities asked whether his audience had understood what he said and, after general assent, went on: 'I can hardly believe that, since even in a city with millions of inhabitants, those who understand the nasal cavities can be counted *on one finger*. . . . I beg your pardon, on the fingers of one hand.' The abbreviated phrase has a sense too—namely, that there is only one person who understands them.[1]

In contrast to these groups of cases, in which the parapraxis itself brings its sense to light, there are others in which the parapraxis produces nothing that has any sense of its own, and which therefore sharply contradict our expectations. If someone twists a proper name about by a slip of the tongue or puts an abnormal series of sounds together, these very common events

[1] [Repeated from *P.E.L.*, 78.]

alone seem to give a negative reply to our question whether all parapraxes have some sort of sense. Closer examination of such instances, however, shows that these distortions are easily understood and that there is by no means so great a distinction between these more obscure cases and the earlier straight-forward ones.

A man who was asked about the health of his horse replied: 'Well, it *draut* [a meaningless word] . . . it *dauert* [will last] another month perhaps.' When he was asked what he had really meant to say, he explained that he had thought it was a '*traurige* [sad]' story. The combination of '*dauert*' and '*traurig*' had produced '*draut*'.[1]

Another man, speaking of some occurrences he disapproved of, went on: 'But then facts came to *Vorschwein* [a non-existent word, instead of *Vorschein* (light)]. . . .' In reply to enquiries he confirmed the fact that he had thought these occurrences '*Schweinereien*' ['disgusting', literally 'piggish']. '*Vorschein*' and '*Schweinereien*' combined to produce the strange word '*Vorschwein*'.[2]

You will recall the case of the young man who asked the unknown lady if he might '*begleitdigen*' her [p. 33]. We ventured to divide up this verbal form into '*begleiten* [accompany]' and '*beleidigen* [insult]', and we felt certain enough of this interpretation not to need any confirmation of it. You will see from these examples that even these obscurer cases of slips of the tongue can be explained by a convergence, a mutual '*interference*', between two different intended speeches; the differences between these cases of slips arise merely from the fact that on some occasions one intention takes the place of the other completely (becomes a substitute for it), as in slips of the tongue that express the contrary, whereas on other occasions the one intention has to be satisfied with distorting or modifying the other, so that composite structures are produced, which make sense, to a greater or lesser degree, on their own account.

We seem now to have grasped the secret of a large number of slips of the tongue. If we bear this discovery in mind, we shall be able to understand other groups as well which have puzzled us hitherto. In cases of distortion of names, for instance, we

[1] Meringer and Mayer. [*P.E.L.*, 58.]
[2] Meringer and Mayer. [*P.E.L.*, 57.]

cannot suppose that it is always a matter of competition between two similar but different names. It is not difficult, however, to guess the second intention. The distortion of a name occurs often enough apart from slips of the tongue; it seeks to give the name an offensive sound or to make it sound like something inferior, and it is a familiar practice (or malpractice) designed as an insult, which civilized people soon learn to abandon, but which they are *reluctant* to abandon. It is still often permitted as a 'joke', though a pretty poor one. As a blatant and ugly example of this way of distorting names, I may mention that in these days [of the first World War] the name of the President of the French Republic, Poincaré, has been changed into '*Schweinskarré*'.[1] It is therefore plausible to suppose that the same insulting intention is present in these slips of the tongue and is trying to find expression in the distortion of a name. Similar explanations suggest themselves along the same lines for certain instances of slips of the tongue with comic or absurd results. 'I call on you to hiccough [*aufzustossen*] to the health of our Chief [p. 32].' Here a ceremonial atmosphere is unexpectedly disturbed by the intrusion of a word which calls up an unsavoury idea, and, on the model of certain insulting and offensive phrases, we can scarcely avoid a suspicion that a purpose was trying to find expression which was in violent contradiction to the ostensibly respectful words. What the slip seems to have been saying was something like: 'Don't you believe it! I don't mean this seriously! I don't care a rap for the fellow!' Just the same thing applies to slips of the tongue which turn innocent words into indecent or obscene ones: thus, '*Apopos*' for '*à propos*' or '*Eischeissweibchen*' for '*Eiweissscheibchen*'.[2]

Many people, as we know, derive some pleasure from a habit like this of deliberately distorting innocent words into obscene ones; such distortions are regarded as funny, and when we hear one we must in fact first enquire from the speaker whether he

---

[1] [The Viennese term for a pork chop.]

[2] Both from Meringer and Meyer. [They are also in *P.E.L.*, 82. In the first of these untranslatable examples '*Apopos*' is a non-existent word; but '*Popo*' is a nursery word for 'bottom'. In the second example the nonsense word means literally 'egg-shit-female', while the intended word means 'small slices of white of egg.']

uttered it intentionally as a joke or whether it happened as a slip of the tongue.

Well, it looks now as though we have solved the problem of parapraxes, and with very little trouble! They are not chance events but serious mental acts; they have a sense; they arise from the concurrent action—or perhaps rather, the mutually opposing action—of two different intentions. But now I see too that you are preparing to overwhelm me with a mass of questions and doubts which will have to be answered and dealt with before we can enjoy this first outcome of our work. I certainly have no desire to force hasty decisions upon you. Let us take them all in due order, one after the other, and give them cool consideration.

What is it you want to ask me? Do I think that this explanation applies to *all* parapraxes or only to a certain number? Can this same point of view be extended to the many other kinds of parapraxis, to misreading, slips of the pen, forgetting, bungled actions, mislaying, and so on? In view of the psychical nature of parapraxes, what significance remains for the factors of fatigue, excitement, absent-mindedness and interference with the attention? Further, it is clear that of the two competing purposes in a parapraxis one is always manifest, but the other not always. What do we do, then, in order to discover the latter? And, if we think we have discovered it, how do we prove that it is not merely a probable one but the only correct one? Is there anything else you want to ask? If not, I will go on myself. You will recall that we do not set much store by parapraxes themselves, and that all we want is to learn from studying them something that may be turned to account for psycho-analysis. I therefore put this question to you. What are these intentions or purposes which are able to disturb others in this way? And what are the relations between the disturbing purposes and the disturbed ones? Thus, no sooner is the problem solved than our work begins afresh.

First, then, is this the explanation of *all* cases of slips of the tongue? I am very much inclined to think so, and my reason is that every time one investigates an instance of a slip of the tongue an explanation of this kind is forthcoming. But it is also true that there is no way of proving that a slip of the tongue cannot occur without this mechanism. It may be so; but theoretically it is a matter of indifference to us, since the conclusions we want to draw for our introduction to psychoanalysis remain, even though—which is certainly not the case—our view holds good of only a minority of cases of slips of the tongue. The next question—whether we may extend our view to other sorts of parapraxis—I will answer in advance with a 'yes'. You will be able to convince yourselves of this when we come to examining instances of slips of the pen, bungled actions, and so on. But for technical reasons I suggest that we should postpone this task till we have treated slips of the tongue themselves still more thoroughly.

A more detailed reply is called for by the question of what significance remains for the factors put forward by the authorities—disturbances of the circulation, fatigue, excitement, absent-mindedness and the theory of disturbed attention—if we accept the psychical mechanism of slips of the tongue which we have described. Observe that we are not denying these factors. It is in general not such a common thing for psycho-analysis to *deny* something asserted by other people; as a rule it merely adds something new—though no doubt it occasionally happens that this thing that has hitherto been overlooked and is now brought up as a fresh addition is in fact the essence of the matter. The influence on the production of slips of the tongue by physiological dispositions brought about by slight illness, disturbances of the circulation or states of exhaustion, must be recognized at once; daily and personal experience will convince you of it. But how little they explain! Above all, they are not necessary preconditions of parapraxes. Slips of the tongue are just as possible in perfect health and in a normal state. These somatic factors only serve therefore, to facilitate and favour the peculiar mental mechanism of slips of the tongue. I once used an analogy to describe this relation,[1] and I will repeat it here since I can think of none better to take its place. Suppose that one dark night I went to a lonely spot and was there attacked by a rough who took away my watch and purse. Since I did not see the robber's face clearly, I laid my complaint at the nearest police station with the words: 'Loneliness and darkness have just robbed me of my valuables.' The police officer might then say to me: 'In

[1] [*P.E.L.*, 21.]

what you say you seem to be unjustifiably adopting an extreme mechanistic view. It would be better to represent the facts in this way: "Under the shield of darkness and favoured by lone-liness, an unknown thief robbed you of your valuables." In your case the essential task seems to me to be that we should find the thief. Perhaps we shall then be able to recover the booty.'

Such psycho-physiological factors as excitement, absent-mindedness and disturbances of attention will clearly help us very little towards an explanation. They are only empty phrases, screens behind which we must not let ourselves be prevented from having a look. The question is rather what it is that has been brought about here by the excitement, the partic-ular distracting of attention. And again, we must recognize the importance of the influence of sounds, the similarity of words and the familiar associations aroused by words. These facilitate slips of the tongue by pointing to the paths they can take. But if I have a path open to me, does that fact automatically decide that I shall take it? I need a motive in addition before I resolve in favour of it and furthermore a force to propel me along the path. So these relations of sounds and words are also, like the somatic dispositions, only things that *favour* slips of the tongue and cannot provide the true explanation of them. Only consider: in an immense majority of cases my speech is not disturbed by the circumstance that the words I am using recall others with a similar sound, that they are intimately linked with their contraries or that familiar associations branch off from them. Perhaps we might still find a way out by following the philosopher Wundt, when he says that slips of the tongue arise if, as a result of physical exhaustion, the inclination to associate gains the upper hand over what the speaker otherwise intends to say. That would be most convincing if it were not contradicted by experience, which shows that in one set of cases the *somatic* factors favouring slips of the tongue are absent and in another set of cases the *associative* factors favouring them are equally absent.

I am particularly interested, however, in your next question: how does one discover the two mutually interfering purposes? You do not realize, probably, what a momentous question this is. One of the two, the purpose that is disturbed, is of course unmistakable: the person who makes the slip of the tongue knows it and admits to it. It is only the other, the disturbing purpose, that can give rise to doubt and hesitation. Now, we have already seen, and no doubt you have not forgotten, that in a number of cases this other purpose is equally evident. It is indicated by the *outcome* of the slip, if only we have the courage to grant that outcome a validity of its own. Take the President of the Lower House, whose slip of the tongue said the contrary of what he intended. It is clear that he wanted to open the sitting, but it is equally clear that he also wanted to close it. That is so obvious that it leaves us nothing to interpret. But in the other cases, in which the disturbing purpose only *distorts* the original one without itself achieving complete expression, how do we arrive at the disturbing purpose from the distortion?

In a first group of cases this is done quite simply and securely —in the same way, in fact, as with the *disturbed* purpose. We get the speaker to give us the information directly. After his slip of the tongue he at once produces the wording which he originally intended: 'It *draut* . . . no, it *dauert* [will last] another month perhaps.' [p. 42]. Well, in just the same way we get him to tell us the *disturbing* purpose. 'Why', we ask him, 'did you say "*draut*"?' He replies: 'I wanted to say "It's a *traurige* [sad] story".' Similarly, in the other case, where the slip of the tongue was '*Vorschwein*' [p. 42], the speaker confirms the fact that he had wanted at first to say 'It's a *Schweinerei* [disgusting]', but had controlled himself and gone off into another remark. Here then the distorting purpose is as securely established as the distorted one. My choice of these examples has not been un-intentional, for their origin and solution come neither from me nor from any of my followers. And yet in both these cases active measures of a kind were necessary in order to bring about the solution. The speaker had to be asked why he had made the slip and what he could say about it. Otherwise he might perhaps have passed over his slip without wanting to explain it. But when he was asked he gave the explanation with the first thing that occurred to him.[1] And now please observe that this small

[1] [The phrase 'thing that occurred to him' here stands for the German word '*Einfall*', for which there is no satisfactory English equivalent. The word appears constantly in the course of these lectures—two or three times in the present passage, repeatedly in Lecture VI, and at many

active step and its successful outcome are already a psycho-
analysis and are a model for every psycho-analytic investigation
which we shall embark upon later.

Am I too mistrustful, however, if I suspect that at the very
moment at which psycho-analysis makes its appearance before
you resistance to it simultaneously raises its head? Do you not
feel inclined to object that the information given by the person
of whom the question was asked—the person who made the slip
of the tongue—is not completely conclusive? He was naturally
anxious, you think, to fulfil the request to explain the slip, so
he said the first thing that came into his head which seemed
capable of providing such an explanation. But that is no proof
that the slip did in fact take place in that way. It *may* have been
so, but it may just as well have happened otherwise. And something else might have occurred to him which would have fitted
in as well or perhaps even better.

It is strange how little respect you have at bottom for a
psychical fact! Imagine that someone had undertaken the
chemical analysis of a certain substance and had arrived at a
particular weight for one component of it—so and so many
milligrammes. Certain inferences could be drawn from this
weight. Now do you suppose that it would ever occur to a
chemist to criticize those inferences on the ground that the
isolated substance might equally have had some other weight?
Everyone will bow before the fact that this was the weight and

points elsewhere—so that some comment on it will be useful. It is
customarily translated 'association'—an objectionable term, since it is
ambiguous and question-begging. If a person is thinking of something
and we say that he has an '*Einfall*', all that this implies is that something
else has occurred to his mind. But if we say that he has an 'association',
it seems to imply that the something else that has occurred to him is in
some way connected with what he was thinking of before. Much of the
discussion in these pages turns on whether the second thought is in fact
connected (or is necessarily connected) with the original one—whether
the '*Einfall*' is an 'association'. So that to translate '*Einfall*' by 'association' is bound to prejudge the issue. Nevertheless it is not always easy to
avoid this, more especially as Freud himself sometimes uses the German
'*Assoziation*' as a synonym for '*Einfall*', especially in the term '*freie
Assoziation*', which must inevitably be translated 'free association'.
Every endeavour will be made in the present discussion to avoid ambiguity, even at the cost of some unwieldy phraseology; later on, the need
to avoid the word 'association' will become less pressing.]

none other and will confidently draw his further inferences from it. But when you are faced with the psychical fact that a particular thing occurred to the mind of the person questioned, you will not allow the fact's validity: something else might have occurred to him! You nourish the illusion of there being such a thing as psychical freedom, and you will not give it up. I am sorry to say I disagree with you categorically over this.

You will break off at that, but only to take up your resistance again at another point. You proceed: 'It is the special technique of psycho-analysis, as we understand, to get people under analysis themselves to produce the solution of their problems. [Cf. p. 101 below.] Now let us take another example—the one in which a speaker proposing the toast of honour on a ceremonial occasion called on his audience to hiccough [*aufzustossen*] to the health of the Chief [p. 32]. You say [p. 43] that the disturbing intention in this case was an insulting one: that was what was opposing the speaker's expression of respect. But this is pure interpretation on your part, based upon observations apart from the slip of the tongue. If in this instance you were to question the person responsible for the slip, he would not confirm your idea that he intended an insult; on the contrary, he would energetically repudiate it. Why, in view of this clear denial, do you not abandon your unprovable interpretation?'

Yes. You have lighted on a powerful argument this time. I can imagine the unknown proposer of the toast. He is probably a subordinate to the Chief of the Department who is being honoured—perhaps he himself is already an Assistant Lecturer, a young man with excellent prospects in life. I try to force him to admit that he may nevertheless have had a feeling that there was something in him opposing his toast in honour of the Chief. But this lands me in a nice mess. He gets impatient and suddenly breaks out: 'Just you stop trying to cross-question me or I shall turn nasty. You're going to ruin my whole career with your suspicions. I simply said "*aufstossen* [hiccough to]" instead of "*anstossen* [drink to]" because I'd said "*auf*" twice before in the same sentence. That's what Meringer calls a perseveration and there's nothing more to be interpreted about it. D'you understand? *Basta!*'—H'm! That was a surprising reaction, a truly energetic denial. I see there's nothing more to be done with the young man. But I also reflect that he shows a strong personal interest in insisting on his parapraxis not having a sense. You may also feel that there was something wrong in his being quite so rude about a purely theoretical enquiry. But, you will think, when all is said and done he must know what he wanted to say and what he didn't.

But must he? Perhaps that may still be the question.

Now, however, you think you have me at your mercy. 'So that's your technique', I hear you say. 'When a person who has made a slip of the tongue says something about it that suits you, you pronounce him to be the final decisive authority on the subject. "He says so himself! [p. 40]". But when what he says doesn't suit your book, then all at once you say he's of no importance—there's no need to believe him.'[1]

That is quite true. But I can put a similar case to you in which the same monstrous event occurs. When someone charged with an offence confesses his deed to the judge, the judge believes his confession; but if he denies it, the judge does not believe him. If it were otherwise, there would be no administration of justice, and in spite of occasional errors we must allow that the system works.

'Are you a judge, then? And is a person who has made a slip of the tongue brought up before you on a charge? So making a slip of the tongue is an offence, is it?'[2]

Perhaps we need not reject the comparison. But I would ask you to observe what profound differences of opinion we have reached after a little investigation of what seemed such innocent problems concerning the parapraxes—differences which at the moment we see no possible way of smoothing over. I propose a provisional compromise on the basis of the analogy with the judge and the defendant. I suggest that you shall grant me that there can be no doubt of a parapraxis having a sense if the subject himself admits it. *I* will admit in return that we cannot arrive at a direct proof of the suspected sense if the subject refuses us information, and equally, of course, if he is not at hand to give us the information. Then, as in the case of the

---

[1] [A long discussion of this difficulty will be found in one of Freud's last papers, on 'Constructions in Analysis' (1937*d*).]

[2] [The German words are on the same pattern: '*Versprechen*' and '*Vergehen*'.]

administration of justice, we are obliged to turn to circumstantial evidence, which may make a decision more probable in some instances and less so in others. In the law courts it may be necessary for practical purposes to find a defendant guilty on circumstantial evidence. We are under no such necessity; but neither are we obliged to disregard the circumstantial evidence. It would be a mistake to suppose that a science consists entirely of strictly proved theses, and it would be unjust to require this. Only a disposition with a passion for authority will raise such a demand, someone with a craving to replace his religious catechism by another, though it is a scientific one. Science has only a few apodeictic propositions in its catechism: the rest are assertions promoted by it to some particular degree of probability. It is actually a sign of a scientific mode of thought to find satisfaction in these approximations to certainty and to be able to pursue constructive work further in spite of the absence of final confirmation.

But if the subject does not himself give us the explanation of the sense of a parapraxis, where are we to find the starting-points for our interpretation—the circumstantial evidence? In various directions. In the first place from analogies with phenomena apart from parapraxes: when, for instance, we assert that distorting a name when it occurs as a slip of the tongue has the same insulting sense as a deliberate twisting of a name. Further, from the psychical situation in which the parapraxis occurs, the character of the person who makes the parapraxis, and the impressions which he has received before the parapraxis and to which the parapraxis is perhaps a reaction. What happens as a rule is that the interpretation is carried out according to general principles: to begin with there is only a suspicion, a suggestion for an interpretation, and we then find a confirmation by examining the psychical situation. Sometimes we have to wait for subsequent events as well (which have, as it were, announced themselves by the parapraxis) before our suspicion is confirmed.

I cannot easily give you illustrations of this if I limit myself to the field of slips of the tongue, though even there some good instances are to be found. The young man who wanted to 'begleitdigen' a lady [p. 33] was certainly a timid character. The lady whose husband could eat and drink what *she* wanted [p. 35] is known to me as one of those energetic women who wear the breeches in their home. Or let us take the following example: At the General Meeting of the 'Concordia'[1] a young member made a speech of violent opposition, in the course of which he addressed the committee as '*Vorschussmitglieder* [lending members]', a word which seems to be made up of '*Vorstand* [directors]' and '*Ausschuss* [committee]'. We shall suspect that some disturbing purpose was at work in him, acting against his violent opposition, based on something connected with a loan. And in fact we learnt from our informant that the speaker was constantly in financial difficulties and just at that time had applied for a loan. The disturbing intention could therefore be replaced by the thought: 'Moderate your opposition; these are the same people who will have to sanction your loan.'

But I can give you a large selection of circumstantial evidence of this kind if I pass over to the wide field of the other parapraxes.

If anyone forgets a proper name which is familiar to him normally or if, in spite of all his efforts, he finds it difficult to keep it in mind, it is plausible to suppose that he has something against the person who bears the name so that he prefers not to think of him. Consider, for instance, what we learn in the following cases about the psychical situation in which the parapraxis occurred.

'A Herr Y. fell in love with a lady, but he met with no success, and shortly afterwards she married a Herr X. Thereafter, Herr Y., in spite of having known Herr X. for a long time and even having business dealings with him, forgot his name over and over again, so that several times he had to enquire what it was from other people when he wanted to correspond with Herr X.' Herr Y. evidently wanted to know nothing of his more fortunate rival: 'never thought of shall he be.'[2]

Or: A lady enquired from her doctor for news of a common acquaintance, but called her by her maiden name. She had

---

[1] [The Society of Journalists in Vienna. This anecdote will be found in *P.E.L.*, 88; it was originally supplied by Max Graf.]

[2] From Jung [1907, 52. This appears in *P.E.L.*, 25–6. The quotation at the end, 'Nicht gedacht soll seiner werden', forms the first line and a repeated refrain in a poem of Heine's from the *Nachlese*, 'Aus der Matratzengruft', No. IV.]

forgotten her friend's married name. She admitted afterwards
that she had been very unhappy about the marriage and disliked her friend's husband.[1]

We shall have a good deal to say about forgetting names in
other connections [p. 74 f. below]; for the moment we are
principally interested in the psychical situation in which the
forgetting occurs.

The forgetting of intentions can in general be traced to an
opposing current of thought, which is unwilling to carry out the
intention. But this view is not only held by us psycho-analysts;
it is the general opinion, accepted by everyone in their daily
lives and only denied when it comes to theory. A patron who
gives his *protégé* the excuse of having forgotten his request fails
to justify himself. The *protégé* immediately thinks: 'It means
nothing to him; it's true he promised, but he doesn't really want
to do it.'[2] For that reason forgetting is banned in certain
circumstances of ordinary life; the distinction between the
popular and the psycho-analytic view of these parapraxes seems
to have disappeared. Imagine the lady of the house receiving
her guest with the words: 'What? have you come to-day? I'd
quite forgotten I invited you for to-day.' Or imagine a young
man confessing to his *fiancée* that he had forgotten to keep their
last *rendez-vous*. He will certainly not confess it; he will prefer to
invent on the spur of the moment the most improbable obstacles
which prevented his appearing at the time and afterwards made
it impossible for him to let her know. We all know too that in
military affairs the excuse of having forgotten something is of no
help and is no protection against punishment, and we must all
feel that that is justified. Here all at once everyone is united in
thinking that a particular parapraxis has a sense and in knowing what that sense is. Why are they not consistent enough to
extend this knowledge to the other parapraxes and to admit
them fully? There is of course an answer to this question
too.

Since laymen have so little doubt about the sense of this
forgetting of intentions, you will be the less surprised to find
writers employing this sort of parapraxis in the same sense.
Any of you who have seen or read Bernard Shaw's *Caesar and*

[1] From Brill [1912, 191; also *P.E.L.*, 224].
[2] [This situation is considered further below, p. 72 f.]

Cleopatra will remember that in the last scene Caesar, as he is leaving Egypt, is haunted by the idea that there is something else he had intended to do but has forgotten. In the end it turns out what this was: he had forgotten to say good-bye to Cleopatra. The dramatist is seeking by this little contrivance to ascribe to the great Caesar a superiority which he did not in fact possess and which he never desired. For historical sources will tell you that Caesar made Cleopatra follow him to Rome, that she was living there with her little Caesarion when Caesar was murdered, and that she thereupon fled from the city.[1]

Cases of forgetting an intention are in general so clear that they are not of much use for our purpose of obtaining circumstantial evidence of the sense of a parapraxis from the psychical situation. Let us therefore turn to a particularly ambiguous and obscure kind of parapraxis—to losing and mislaying. You will no doubt find it incredible that we ourselves can play an intentional part in what is so often the painful accident of losing something. But there are plenty of observations like the following one. A young man lost a pencil of his of which he had been very fond. The day before, he had received a letter from his brother-in-law which ended with these words: 'I have neither the inclination nor the time at present to encourage you in your frivolity and laziness.' The pencil had actually been given to him by this brother-in-law. Without this coincidence we could not, of course, have asserted that a part was played in the loss by an intention to get rid of the thing.[2] Similar cases are very common. We lose an object if we have quarrelled with the person who gave it to us and do not want to be reminded of him; or if we no longer like the object itself and want to have an excuse for getting another and better one instead. The same intention directed against an object can also play a part, of course, in cases of dropping, breaking or destroying things. Can we regard it as a matter of chance when a schoolchild immediately before his birthday loses, ruins or smashes some of his personal belongings, such as his satchel or his watch?

Nor will anyone who has sufficiently often experienced the torment of not being able to find something that he himself has

[1] [This quotation from Shaw appears also in *P.E.L.*, 154*n*.]
[2] From Dattner. [*P.E.L.*, 207.]

put away feel inclined to believe that there is a purpose in mislaying things. Yet instances are far from rare in which the circumstances attendant on the mislaying point to an intention to get rid of the object temporarily or permanently.

Here is the best example, perhaps, of such an occasion. A youngish man told me the following story: 'Some years ago there were misunderstandings between me and my wife. I found her too cold, and although I willingly recognized her excellent qualities we lived together without any tender feelings. One day, returning from a walk, she gave me a book which she had bought because she thought it would interest me. I thanked her for this mark of "attention", promised to read the book and put it on one side. After that I could never find it again. Months passed by, in which I occasionally remembered the lost book and made vain attempts to find it. About six months later my dear mother, who was not living with us, fell ill. My wife left home to nurse her mother-in-law. The patient's condition became serious and gave my wife an opportunity of showing the best side of herself. One evening I returned home full of enthusiasm and gratitude for what my wife had accomplished. I walked up to my desk, and without any definite intention but with a kind of somnambulistic certainty opened one of the drawers. On the very top I found the long-lost book I had mislaid.'[1] With the extinction of the motive the mislaying of the object ceased as well.

Ladies and Gentlemen, I could multiply this collection of examples indefinitely; but I will not do so here. You will in any case find a profusion of case material for the study of parapraxes in my *Psychopathology of Everyday Life* (first published in 1901).[2] All these examples lead to the same result: they make it probable that parapraxes have a sense, and they show you how that sense is discovered or confirmed by the attendant circumstances. I will be briefer to-day, because we have adopted the limited aim of using the study of these phenomena as a help towards a preparation for psycho-analysis. There are only two

[1] [This appears in *P.E.L.*, 49.]
[2] See also similar collections by Maeder [1906–7] (in French), Brill [1912] (in English), Jones [1911] (in English) and J. Stärcke [1916] (in Dutch), etc.

groups of observations into which I need enter more fully here: accumulated and combined parapraxes and the confirmation of our interpretations by subsequent events.

Accumulated and combined parapraxes are without doubt the finest flower of their kind. If we had only been concerned to prove that parapraxes have a sense we should have confined ourselves to them from the first, for in their case the sense is unmistakable even to the dull-witted and forces itself on the most critical judgement. An accumulation of these phenomena betrays an obstinacy that is scarcely ever a characteristic of chance events but fits in well with something intentional. Finally, the mutual interchangeability between different species of parapraxes demonstrates what it is in parapraxes that is important and characteristic: not their form or the method which they employ but the purpose which they serve and which can be achieved in the most various ways. For this reason I will give you an instance of repeated forgetting. Ernest Jones [1911, 483] tells us that once, for reasons unknown to him, he left a letter lying on his desk for several days. At last he decided to send it off, but he had it returned to him by the Dead Letter Office[1] since he had forgotten to address it. After he had addressed it he took it to the post, but this time it had no stamp. And then at last he was obliged to admit his reluctance to sending the letter off at all.

In another case a bungled action is combined with an instance of mislaying. A lady travelled to Rome with her brother-in-law, who was a famous artist. The visitor was received with great honour by the German community in Rome, and among other presents he was given an antique gold medal. The lady was vexed that her brother-in-law did not appreciate the lovely object sufficiently. When she returned home (her place in Rome having been taken by her sister) she discovered while unpacking that she had brought the medal with her—how, she did not know. She at once sent a letter with the news to her brother-in-law, and announced that she would send the article she had walked off with back to Rome next day. But next day the medal had been so cleverly mislaid that it could not be found and sent off; and it was at this point, that the meaning

[1] [In English in the original. This example and the next two appear *P.E.L.*, 230–1.]

of her 'absent-mindedness' dawned on the lady: she wanted to keep the object for herself.[1]

I have already given you an example of a combination of a forgetting with an error, the case of someone forgetting an appointment and on a second occasion, having firmly decided not to forget *this* time, turning up at the wrong hour [p. 30]. An exactly similar case was reported to me from his own experience by a friend with literary as well as scientific interests. 'Some years ago', he told me, 'I allowed myself to be elected to the committee of a certain literary society, as I thought that the organization might one day be able to help me to have my play produced; and I took a regular part, though without being much interested, in the meetings which were held every Friday. Then, a few months ago, I was given the promise of a production at the theatre at F.; and since then I have regularly *forgotten* the meetings of the society. When I read your book on the subject I felt ashamed of my forgetfulness. I reproached myself with the thought that it was shabby behaviour on my part to stay away now that I no longer needed these people, and resolved on no account to forget the next Friday. I kept on reminding myself of this resolution until I carried it into effect and stood at the door of the room where the meetings were held. To my astonishment it was locked; the meeting was over. I had in fact made a mistake over the day; it was now Saturday!'

It would be agreeable to add further, similar examples. But I must proceed, and give you a glimpse of the cases in which our interpretation has to wait for the future for confirmation. The governing condition of these cases, it will be realized, is that the present psychical situation is unknown to us or inaccessible to our enquiries. Our interpretation is consequently no more than a suspicion to which we ourselves do not attach too much importance. Later, however, something happens which shows us how well-justified our interpretation had been. I was once the guest of a young married couple and heard the young woman laughingly describe her latest experience. The day after her return from the honeymoon she had called for her unmarried sister to go shopping with her as she used to do, while her husband went to his business. Suddenly she noticed

[1] Reported by R. Reitler.

a gentleman on the other side of the street, and nudging her sister had cried: 'Look, there goes Herr L.' She had forgotten that this gentleman had been her husband for some weeks. I shuddered as I heard the story, but I did not dare to draw the inference. The little incident only occurred to my mind some years later when the marriage had come to a most unhappy end.[1]

Maeder tells of a lady who, on the eve of her wedding had forgotten to try on her wedding-dress and, to her dressmaker's despair, only remembered it late in the evening. He connects this forgetfulness with the fact that she was soon divorced from her husband. I know a lady now divorced from her husband, who in managing her money affairs frequently signed documents in her maiden name, many years before she in fact resumed it.—I know of other women who have lost their wedding-rings during the honeymoon, and I know too that the history of their marriages has given a sense to the accident.— And now here is one more glaring example, but with a happier ending. The story is told of a famous German chemist that his marriage did not take place, because he forgot the hour of his wedding and went to the laboratory instead of to the church. He was wise enough to be satisfied with a single attempt and died at a great age unmarried.

The idea may possibly have occurred to you that in these examples parapraxes have taken the place of the omens or auguries of the ancients. And indeed some omens were nothing else than parapraxes, as, for instance, when someone stumbled or fell down. Others of them, it is true, had the character of objective happenings and not of subjective acts. But you would hardly believe how difficult it sometimes is to decide whether a particular event belongs to the one group or to the other. An act so often understands how to disguise itself as a passive experience.

All those of us who can look back on a comparatively long experience of life will probably admit that we should have spared ourselves many disappointments and painful surprises if we had found the courage and determination to interpret small parapraxes experienced in our human contacts as auguries and to make use of them as indications of intentions that were still

[1] [This example and the two next will be found *P.E.L.*, 203–4.]

concealed. As a rule we dare not do so; it would make us feel as though, after a détour through science, we were becoming superstitious again. Nor do all auguries come true, and you will understand from our theories that they do not all need to come true.

LECTURE IV

PARAPRAXES (*concluded*)

LADIES AND GENTLEMEN,—We may take it as the outcome of our efforts so far and the basis of our further investigations that parapraxes have a sense. Let me insist once again that I am not asserting—and for our purposes there is no need to do so—that every single parapraxis that occurs has a sense, even though I regard that as probably the case. It is enough for us if we can point to such a sense relatively often in the different forms of parapraxis. Moreover, in this respect these different forms behave differently. Cases of slips of the tongue and of the pen, etc., may occur on a purely physiological basis. I cannot believe that this is so in the types depending on *forgetting* (forgetting names or intentions, mislaying, etc.). It is very probable that there are cases of *losing* which can be regarded as unintended. It is in general true that only a certain proportion of the *errors* that occur in ordinary life can be looked at from our point of view. You should bear these limitations in mind when henceforward we start from the assumption that parapraxes are psychical acts and arise from mutual interference between two intentions.

This is the first product of psycho-analysis. Psychology has hitherto known nothing of the occurrence of such mutual interferences or of the possibility that they might result in such phenomena. We have made a quite considerable extension to the world of psychical phenomena and have won for psychology phenomena which were not reckoned earlier as belonging to it.

Let us pause a moment longer over the assertion that parapraxes are 'psychical acts'. Does this imply more than what we have said already—that they have a sense? I think not. I think, rather, that the former assertion [that they are psychical acts] is more indefinite and more easily misunderstood. Anything that is observable in mental life may occasionally be described as a mental phenomenon. The question will then be whether the particular mental phenomenon has arisen immediately from somatic, organic and material influences—in which case its investigation will not be part of psychology—or whether it is derived in the first instance from other mental processes, somewhere behind which the series of organic influences begins. It is this latter situation that we have in view when we describe a phenomenon as a mental process, and for that reason it is more expedient to clothe our assertion in the form: 'the phenomenon has a sense.' By 'sense' we understand 'meaning', 'intention,' 'purpose' and 'position in a continuous psychical context'. [Cf. p. 40.]

There are a number of other phenomena which are closely akin to parapraxes but to which that name is no longer appropriate. We call them chance and symptomatic actions. Like the others, they have the character of being without a motive, insignificant and unimportant; but they have in addition, more clearly, that of being unnecessary. They are distinguished from parapraxes by their lack of another intention with which they are in collision and which is disturbed by them. On the other hand, they merge insensibly into the gestures and movements which we regard as expressions of the emotions. These chance actions include all sorts of manipulations with our clothing, or parts of our body or objects within our reach, performed as though in play and apparently with no purpose, or, again, the omission of these manipulations; or, further, tunes that we hum to ourselves. I suggest that all these phenomena have a sense and can be interpreted in the same way as parapraxes, that they are small indications of more important mental processes and are fully valid psychical acts. But I do not propose to linger over this fresh extension of the field of mental phenomena; I shall return to the parapraxes, in connection with which problems important for psycho-analysis can be worked out with far greater clarity.[1]

The most interesting questions which we have raised about parapraxes and not yet answered are perhaps these. We have said that parapraxes are the product of mutual interference between two different intentions, of which one may be called the disturbed intention and the other the disturbing one. The

[1] [Symptomatic and chance actions form the subject of Chapter IX of *P.E.L.*]

disturbed intentions give no occasion for further questions, but concerning the latter we should like to know, first, what sort of intentions emerge as a disturbance to others, and secondly what is the relation of the disturbing intentions to the disturbed ones?

If you will allow me, I will once more take slips of the tongue as representatives of the whole class and I will reply to the second question before the first.

In a slip of the tongue the disturbing intention may be related in its content to the disturbed one, in which case it will contradict it or correct it or supplement it. Or—the more obscure and more interesting case—the content of the disturbing intention may have nothing to do with that of the disturbed one.

We shall have no difficulty in finding evidence of the former relation in instances we already know and in similar ones. In almost every case in which a slip of the tongue reverses the sense, the disturbing intention expresses the contrary to the disturbed one and the parapraxis represents a conflict between two incompatible inclinations. 'I declare the sitting opened, but I should prefer it to be already closed' is the sense of the President's slip of the tongue [p. 34]. A political periodical which had been accused of corruption defended itself in an article the climax of which should have been: 'Our readers will bear witness to the fact that we have always acted in the most *unself-seeking* manner for the good of the community.' But the editor entrusted with the preparation of the article wrote 'in the most *self-seeking* manner'. That is to say, he was thinking: 'This is what I am obliged to write; but I have different ideas.' A [German] member of parliament who was insisting that the truth should be told to the Emperor '*rückhaltlos* [unreservedly]' evidently heard an inner voice that was shocked at his boldness and, by a slip of the tongue, changed the word into '*rückgratlos* [spinelessly]'.[1]

In the instances already familiar to you which give an impression of being contractions or abbreviations, what we have before us are corrections, additions or continuations, by means of which a second purpose makes itself felt alongside of the

[1] This was in the German Reichstag in November 1908. [A fuller account of this appears *P.E.L.*, 95–6. The preceding slip will be found *P.E.L.*, 120–1.]

first. 'Facts came to *Vorschein* [light]—better to say it straight out—they were *Schweinereien* [disgusting]; well then, facts came to *Vorschwein* [p. 42].' 'Those who understand this can be counted *on the fingers of one hand*—no, there's really only *one* person who understands it, so: can be counted *on one finger* [p. 41].' Or: 'My husband can eat and drink what he wants. But, as you know, *I* don't put up with his wanting anything at all, so: he can eat and drink what *I* want [p. 35].' In all these cases, then, the slip of the tongue arises from the content of the disturbed intention itself or is connected with it.

The other sort of relation between the two mutually interfering intentions seems puzzling. If the disturbing intention has nothing to do with the disturbed one, where can it have come from and why is it that it makes itself noticeable as a disturbance at this particular point? The observation which can alone give us the answer to this shows that the disturbance arises from a train of thought which has occupied the person concerned a short time before and, whether it has already been expressed in speech or not, produces this subsequent effect. It must in fact, therefore, be described as a perseveration, though not necessarily as the perseveration of spoken words. In this case too an associative link between the disturbing and the disturbed intentions is present; but it does not lie in their content but is artificially constructed, often along extremely forced associative paths.

Here is a simple example of this, derived from my own observation. I once met two Viennese ladies in the lovely Dolomites, who were dressed in walking clothes. I accompanied them part of the way, and we discussed the pleasures and also the trials of spending a holiday in that way. One of the ladies admitted that spending the day like that entailed a good deal of discomfort. 'It is certainly not at all pleasant', she said, 'if one has been tramping all day in the sun and has perspired right through one's blouse and chemise.' In this sentence she had to overcome a slight hesitation at one point. Then she continued: 'But then when one gets "nach *Hose*" and can change. . . .' This slip of the tongue was not analysed but I expect you can understand it easily. The lady's intention had obviously been to give a more complete list of her clothes: blouse, chemise and *Hose* [drawers]. Reasons of propriety led her to omit any mention of the '*Hose*'. But in the next sentence, with its quite independent

content, the unspoken word emerged as a distortion of the
similar-sounding 'nach *Hause* [home]'.[1]

We can now turn, however, to the main question, which we
have long postponed, of what sort of intentions these are, which
find expression in this unusual fashion as disturbers of other
intentions. Well, they are obviously of very different sorts,
among which we must look for the common factor. If we
examine a number of examples with this in view, they will soon
fall into three groups. The first group contains those cases in
which the disturbing purpose is known to the speaker and moreover had been noticed by him before he made the slip of the
tongue. Thus, in the '*Vorschwein*' slip [p. 42] the speaker
admitted not only that he had formed the judgement '*Schweinereien*' about the events in question, but also that he had had
the intention, from which he afterwards drew back, of expressing his judgement in words. A second group is made up of other
cases in which the disturbing purpose is equally recognized as
his by the speaker, but in which he was unaware that it was
active in him just before he made the slip. Thus, he accepts our
interpretation of his slip, but nevertheless remains to some extent
surprised at it. Instances of this kind of attitude can perhaps be
found in other sorts of parapraxes more easily than in slips of
the tongue. In a third group the interpretation of the disturbing
intention is vigorously rejected by the speaker; he not only
denies that it was active in him before he made the slip, but
seeks to maintain that it is entirely foreign to him. You will
recall the example of the 'hiccough' [p. 49] and the positively
rude denial which I brought on myself from the speaker by
uncovering his disturbing intention. As you know, we have not
yet come to any agreement in our views on these cases. *I* should
pay no attention to the denial put forward by the proposer of
the toast and should persist in my interpretation unruffled,
while *you*, I suppose, are still affected by his protest and raise
the question of whether we ought not to give up interpreting
parapraxes of this kind and regard them as purely physiological
acts in the pre-analytic sense. I can well imagine what it is that
deters you. My interpretation carries with it the hypothesis that

[1] [Freud later included this anecdote in the 1917 edition of *P.E.L.*,
64–5.]

intentions can find expression in a speaker of which he himself knows nothing but which I am able to infer from circumstantial evidence. You are brought up short in the face of such a novel and momentous hypothesis. I can understand that, and I see your point so far as that goes. But one thing is certain. If you want to apply consistently the view of parapraxes which has been confirmed by so many examples, you will have to make up your mind to accept the strange hypothesis I have mentioned. If you cannot do that, you will have once more to abandon the understanding of parapraxes which you have only just achieved.

Let us consider for a moment what it is that unites the three groups, what it is that the three mechanisms of slips of the tongue have in common. It is fortunately unmistakable. In the first two groups the disturbing purpose is recognized by the speaker; furthermore, in the first group that purpose announces itself immediately before the slip. But in both cases *it is forced back. The speaker decides not to put it into words, and after that the slip of the tongue occurs: after that, that is to say, the purpose which has been forced back is put into words against the speaker's will, either by altering the expression of the intention which he has permitted, or by mingling with it, or by actually taking its place.* This, then, is the mechanism of a slip of the tongue.

On my view, I can bring what happens in the *third* group into complete harmony with the mechanism I have described. I have only to assume that what distinguishes these three groups from one another is the differing extent to which the intention is forced back. In the first group the intention is there and makes itself noticed before the speaker's remark; only then is it rejected; and it takes its revenge in the slip of the tongue. In the second group the rejection goes further: the intention has already ceased to be noticeable before the remark is made. Strangely enough, this does not in the least prevent it from playing its part in causing the slip. But this behaviour makes it easier for us to explain what happens in the third group. I shall venture to assume that a purpose can also find expression in a parapraxis when it has been forced back and not noticed for a considerable time, for a very long time perhaps, and can for that reason be denied straight out by the speaker. But even if you leave the problem of the third group on one side, you are bound to conclude from the observations we have made in the other cases that *the suppression of the speaker's intention to say something is the indispensable condition for the occurrence of a slip of the tongue.*

We may now claim to have made further advances in our understanding of parapraxes. We know not only that they are mental acts, in which we can detect sense and intention, not only that they come about through mutual interference between two different intentions, but beyond this we know that one of these intentions must have been in some way forced back from being put into effect before it can manifest itself as a disturbance of the other intention. It must itself have been disturbed before it can become a disturber. This does not mean, of course, that we have yet achieved a complete explanation of the phenomena which we call parapraxes. We see further questions immediately cropping up, and we suspect in general that the further our understanding goes the more occasions there will be for raising fresh questions. We may ask, for instance, why things should not be much simpler. If the intention is to force back a particular purpose instead of carrying it into effect, the forcing back should be successful, so that the purpose does not manifest itself at all; or on the other hand the forcing back might fail, so that the purpose that was to have been forced back would manifest itself completely. But parapraxes are the outcome of a compromise: they constitute a half-success and a half-failure for each of the two intentions; the intention which is being challenged is neither completely suppressed nor, apart from special cases, carried through quite unscathed. We may conclude that special conditions must prevail in order that an interference or compromise of this kind shall come about, but we can form no conception of what they can be. Nor do I think that we could discover these unknown factors by going deeper into the study of parapraxes. It will be necessary, rather, to examine first yet other obscure regions of mental life: it is only from analogies which we shall meet with there that we shall find the courage to set up the hypotheses necessary for throwing a more penetrating light upon parapraxes. And one thing more. Working from small indications, as we are constantly in the habit of doing in the present field, brings its own dangers. There is a mental disease, 'combinatory paranoia', in which the exploitation of small indications like these is carried to unlimited lengths; and I will not of course claim that conclusions built on such foundations are invariably correct. We can only be guarded against these risks by the broad basis of our observations, the repetition of similar impressions from the most varied spheres of mental life.

At this point, therefore, we will leave the analysis of parapraxes. But there is one point more to which I would draw your attention. I would ask you to bear in mind as a model the manner in which we have treated these phenomena. From this example you can learn the aims of our psychology. We seek not merely to describe and to classify phenomena, but to understand them as signs of an interplay of forces in the mind, as a manifestation of purposeful intentions working concurrently or in mutual opposition. We are concerned with a *dynamic view* of mental phenomena. On our view the phenomena that are perceived must yield in importance to trends which are only hypothetical.

We shall therefore not enter more deeply into parapraxes, but we may still undertake a cursory survey of the extent of this field, in the course of which we shall come once more upon things we already know but shall also discover some novelties. In this survey I shall keep to the division into three groups which I proposed to begin with:[1] slips of the tongue together with their cognate forms (slips of the pen, misreading and mishearing); forgetting, subdivided according to the objects forgotten (proper names, foreign words, intentions or impressions); and bungled actions, mislaying and losing. Errors, in so far as they concern us, fall under the headings partly of forgetting and partly of bungled actions.

We have already treated *slips of the tongue* in great detail, but there are a few more points to be added. Slips of the tongue are accompanied by certain minor emotional phenomena which are not quite without interest. No one likes making slips of the

---

[1] [At the beginning of Lecture II (p. 25). These 'three groups' are not to be confused with the 'three groups' discussed on pp. 64–5, which relate to the quite other matter of the attitude towards slips of the tongue adopted by those who make them.]

tongue, and we often fail to hear our own slips, though never
other people's. Slips of the tongue are also in a certain sense con-
tagious; it is not at all easy to talk about slips of the tongue without making slips of the tongue oneself. The most trivial forms of
such slips, precisely those which have no special light to throw on
hidden mental processes, have reasons which are nevertheless not
hard to penetrate. For instance, if someone has pronounced a long
vowel short on account of a disturbance affecting the word for
some reason or other, he will soon afterwards pronounce a
subsequent short vowel long, thus making a fresh slip of the
tongue to compensate for the earlier one. In the same way, if he
pronounces a diphthong incorrectly and carelessly (for instance
pronouncing an '*eu*' or '*oi*' as '*ei*') he will try to make up for it by
changing a subsequent '*ei*' into an '*eu*' or '*oi*'. The decisive
factor here seems to be consideration of the impression made on
the audience, who are not to suppose that it is a matter of
indifference to the speaker how he treats his mother-tongue.
The second, compensating distortion actually has the purpose
of directing the hearer's attention to the first one and of assuring
him that the speaker has noticed it too. The commonest,
simplest and most trivial slips of the tongue are contractions
and anticipations [cf. p. 32] which occur in insignificant parts
of speech. For instance, in a longish sentence one may make a
slip of the tongue which anticipates the last word of what one
intends to say. This gives an impression of impatience to be
finished with the sentence, and is evidence in general of a
certain antipathy against communicating the sentence or
against the whole of one's remarks. We thus arrive at marginal
cases in which the distinctions between the psycho-analytic
view of slips of the tongue and the ordinary physiological one
melt into one another. It is to be assumed that a purpose of
disturbing the intention of the speech is present in these cases
but that it can only announce its presence and not what it itself
has in view. The disturbance it produces then proceeds in
accordance with certain phonetic influences or associative
attractions and can be regarded as a distraction of the attention
from the intention of the speech. But neither this disturbance of
the attention nor the inclinations to associate which have
become operative touch on the essence of the process. This
remains, in spite of everything, the indication of the existence

of an intention which is disturbing to the intention of the speech, though the *nature* of this disturbing intention cannot be guessed from its consequences, as is possible in all the better defined cases of slips of the tongue.

Slips of the pen, to which I now pass, are so closely akin to slips of the tongue that we have nothing new to expect from them. Perhaps we may glean one little further point. The extremely common small slips of the pen, contractions and anticipations of later words (especially of final words) point, once again, to a general dislike of writing and impatience to be done with it. More marked products of miswriting enable one to recognize the nature and aim of the disturbing purpose. If one finds a slip of the pen in a letter, one knows in general that there was something the matter with its author, but one cannot always discover what was going on in him. A slip of the pen is just as often overlooked by the person responsible as is a slip of the tongue. The following is a noteworthy observation. There are, as we know, people who are in the habit of reading through every letter they write before sending it off. Others do not do this as a rule; but if, as an exception, they do so they always come across some conspicuous slip of the pen, which they can then correct. How is this to be explained? It looks as though these people knew that they had made a mistake in writing the letter. Are we really to believe this?

An interesting problem attaches to the *practical* importance of slips of the pen. You may perhaps remember the case of a murderer, H., who found the means of obtaining cultures of highly dangerous pathogenic organisms from scientific institutes by representing himself as a bacteriologist. He then used these cultures for the purpose of getting rid of his near connections by this most modern of methods. Now on one occasion this man complained to the Directors of one of these institutes that the cultures that had been sent to him were ineffective; but he made a slip of the pen, and instead of writing 'in my experiments on mice or guinea-pigs' he wrote quite clearly 'in my experiments on men'.[1] The doctors at the institute were struck by the slip, but, so far as I know, drew no conclusions from it. Well, what do you think? Should not the doctors, on the contrary, have taken the slip of the pen as a confession and started

[1] ['*Menschen*' instead of '*Mäusen oder Meerschweinchen*'.]

an investigation which would have put an early stop to the murderer's activities? Was not ignorance of our view of parapraxes responsible in this case for an omission of practical significance? Well, I think a slip of the pen like this would certainly have seemed to me most suspicious; but something of great importance stands in the way of using it as a confession. The matter is not as simple as all that. The slip was certainly a piece of circumstantial evidence; but it was not enough in itself to start an investigation. It is true that the slip of the pen said that he was concerned with thoughts of infecting men, but it did not make it possible to decide whether these thoughts were to be taken as a clear intention to injure or as a phantasy of no practical importance. It is even possible that a man who had made a slip like this would have every subjective justification for denying the phantasy and would repudiate it as something entirely foreign to him. You will understand these possibilities still better when later on we come to consider the distinction between psychical and material reality.[1] But this is another instance of a parapraxis acquiring importance from subsequent events. [Cf. p. 57 f. above.]

With *misreading* we come to a psychical situation which differs sensibly from that in slips of the tongue or pen. Here one of the two mutually competing purposes is replaced by a sensory stimulation and is perhaps on that account less resistant. What one is going to read is not a derivative of one's own mental life like something one proposes to write. In a great majority of cases, therefore, a misreading consists in a complete substitution. One replaces the word that is to be read by another, without there necessarily being any connection of content between the text and the product of the misreading, which depends as a rule on verbal similarity. The best member of this group is Lichtenberg's '*Agamemnon*' for '*angenommen*' [p. 39 above]. If we want to discover the disturbing purpose which produced the misreading we must leave the text that has been misread entirely aside and we may begin the analytic investigation with the two questions: what is the first association to the product of the misreading? and in what situation did the misreading occur? Occasionally a knowledge of the latter is alone enough to explain the misreading. For instance, a man under the

[1] [See the discussion in Lecture XXIII, p. 368 below.]

pressure of an imperious need was wandering about in a strange town when he saw the word '*Closet-House*' on a large notice-board on the first storey of a building. He had just enough time to feel surprised at the notice-board being placed so high up before discovering that, strictly speaking, what he should have read was '*Corset-House*'.[1] In other cases a misreading precisely of the kind which is quite independent of the content of the text may call for a detailed analysis which cannot be carried through without practice in the technique of psycho-analysis and without reliance on it. As a rule, however, it is not so hard to find the explanation of a misreading: the word substituted immediately betrays, as in the Agamemnon example, the circle of ideas from which the disturbance has arisen. In this time of war, for instance, it is a very usual thing for the names of towns and generals and the military terms that are constantly buzzing around us to be read wherever a similar word meets our eyes. Whatever interests and concerns us puts itself in the place of what is strange and still uninteresting. After-images of [earlier] thoughts trouble new perceptions.

With misreading, too, there is no lack of cases of another sort, in which the text of what is read itself arouses the disturbing purpose, which thereupon, as a rule, turns it into its opposite. What we ought to read is something unwished-for, and analysis will convince us that an intense wish to reject what we have read must be held responsible for its alteration.

In the more frequent cases of misreading which we mentioned first, we miss two factors to which we have assigned an important role in the mechanism of parapraxes: a conflict between two purposes and a forcing-back of one of them which takes its revenge by producing a parapraxis. Not that anything contrary to this occurs in misreading. But the prominence of the thought that leads to the misreading is far more noticeable than the forcing-back which it may have experienced previously.

It is these two factors which we meet with most markedly in the different situations in which parapraxes of forgetting occur. *The forgetting of intentions* is quite unambiguous; as we have already seen [p. 53], its interpretation is not disputed even by laymen. The purpose which disturbs the intention is in every

---

[1] [Later included in the 1917 edition of *P.E.L.*, 113–14.]

instance a counter-intention, an unwillingness; and all that remains for us to learn about it is why it has not expressed itself in some other and less disguised manner. But the presence of this counter-will[1] is unquestionable. Sometimes, too, we succeed in guessing something of the motives which compel this counter-will to conceal itself; acting surreptitiously by means of the parapraxis it always achieves its aim, whereas it would be sure of repudiation if it emerged as an open contradiction. If some important change in the psychical situation takes place between the forming of the intention and its carrying-out, as a result of which there is no longer any question of the intention being carried out, then the forgetting of the intention drops out of the category of parapraxes. It no longer seems strange to have forgotten it, and we realize that it would have been unnecessary to remember it: thereafter it becomes permanently or temporarily extinct. The forgetting of an intention can only be called a parapraxis if we cannot believe that the intention has been interrupted in this latter way.

The instances of forgetting an intention are in general so uniform and so perspicuous that for that very reason they are of no interest for our investigation. Nevertheless there are two points at which we can learn something new from a study of these parapraxes. Forgetting—that is, failure to carry out—an intention points, as we have said, to a counter-will that is hostile to it. This is no doubt true; but our enquiries show that the counter-will can be of two kinds—direct or indirect. What I mean by the latter will best appear from one or two examples. If a patron forgets to put in a word with a third person on behalf of his *protégé*, this may happen because he is not really very much interested in the *protégé* and therefore has no great desire to speak on his behalf. In any case, that is how the *protégé* will understand the patron's forgetting [cf. p. 53]. But things may be more complicated. The counter-will in the patron against carrying out the intention may come from another direction and may be aimed at quite a different point. It may have nothing to do with the *protégé* but may perhaps be directed

---

[1] [The concept of a 'counter-will' played a prominent part in some of Freud's very first papers on psychopathology, e.g., in 'A Case of Successful Treatment by Hypnotism' (1892–3). It reappears at several points in *P.E.L.*]

against the third person to whom the recommendation was to have been made. So you see from this once more [cf. p. 70] the doubts that stand in the way of a practical application of our interpretations. In spite of the correct interpretation of the forgetting, the *protégé* is in danger of being too distrustful and of doing his patron a grave injustice. Or, supposing someone forgets an appointment which he has promised someone else to keep, the most frequent reason for it will be, no doubt, a direct disinclination to meeting this person. But in such a case analysis might show that the disturbing purpose did not relate to him but was directed against the place at which the meeting was planned to happen and was avoided on account of a distressing memory attaching to it. Or, again, if someone forgets to post a letter, the counter-purpose may be based on the contents of the letter; but it is by no means out of the question that the letter may be harmless in itself and may only be subject to the counter-purpose because something about it recalls another letter which had been written on some earlier occasion and which offered the counter-will a direct point of attack. It can be said, therefore, that here the counter-will was transferred from the earlier letter, which justified it, to the present one, which it had in fact no grounds for concern about. You see, then, that we must practise restraint and foresight in applying our interpretations, justified as they are: things that are psychologically equivalent may in practice have a great variety of meanings.

Phenomena such as these last may seem to you most unusual, and you will perhaps be inclined to suppose that an 'indirect' counter-will already indicates that the process is a pathological one. But I can assure you that it occurs as well within the limits of what is normal and healthy. Moreover you should not misunderstand me. I am far from admitting that our analytic interpretations are untrustworthy. The ambiguities in the forgetting of intentions which I have been mentioning exist only so long as we have not made an analysis of the case and are only making our interpretations on the basis of our general assumptions. If we carry out an analysis upon the person in question, we invariably learn with sufficient certainty whether the counter-will is a direct one or what other origin it may have.

The second point I have in mind [cf. p. 72] is this. If in a large majority of instances we find confirmation of the fact that the forgetting of an intention goes back to a counter-will, we grow bold enough to extend the solution to another set of instances in which the person under analysis does not confirm but denies the counter-will we have inferred. Take as examples of this such extremely common events as forgetting to return books one has been lent or to pay bills or debts. We shall venture to insist to the person concerned that an intention exists in him to keep the books and not to pay the debts, while he will deny this intention but will not be able to produce any other explanation of his behaviour. Thereupon we shall go on to say that he has this intention but knows nothing about it, but that it is enough for us that it reveals its presence by producing the forgetting in him. He may repeat to us that he has in fact forgotten. You will now recognize the situation as one in which we found ourselves once before [p. 64]. If we want to pursue our interpretations of parapraxes, which have so frequently proved justified, to a consistent conclusion, we are forced to the inescapable hypothesis that there are purposes in people which can become operative without their knowing about them. But this brings us into opposition to all the views that dominate both ordinary life and psychology.

The forgetting of proper names and foreign names, as well as of foreign words, can similarly be traced back to a counter-intention, which is aimed either directly or indirectly against the name concerned. I have already given you several instances of direct dislike [p. 52]. But indirect causation is particularly frequent in these cases and can usually only be established by careful analyses. For instance, during the present war, which has obliged us to give up so many of our former enjoyments, our power of remembering proper names has suffered greatly as the result of the strangest associations. A short time ago I found that I was unable to reproduce the name of the innocent Moravian town of *Bisenz*; and analysis showed that what was responsible for this was not any direct hostility to it but its resemblance in sound to the name of the Palazzo *Bisenzi* in Orvieto which I had repeatedly enjoyed visiting in the past.[1] Here for the first time, in this reason for objecting to remembering a name, we come across a principle which will later on reveal its enormous importance for the causation of neurotic

[1] [This example was added in 1917 to *P.E.L.*, 34.]

symptoms: the memory's disinclination to remembering anything which is connected with feelings of unpleasure and the
reproduction of which would renew the unpleasure. This intention to avoid unpleasure arising from a recollection or from
other psychical acts, this psychical flight from unpleasure, may
be recognized as the ultimate operative motive not only for the
forgetting of names but for many other parapraxes, such as
omissions, errors, and so on.

The forgetting of names, however, seems particularly facilitated psycho-physiologically, and for that reason cases occur
in which interference by the unpleasure motive cannot be
confirmed. If someone has a tendency to forget names, analytic
investigation will show that names escape him not only because
he does not like them themselves or because they remind him of
something disagreeable, but also because in his case the same
name belongs to another circle of associations with which he
is more intimately related. The name is, as it were, anchored
there and is kept from contact with the other associations which
have been momentarily activated. If you recall the tricks of
mnemotechnics,[1] you will realize with some surprise that the
same chains of association which are deliberately laid down in
order to *prevent* names from being forgotten can also *lead* to our
forgetting them. The most striking example of this is afforded
by the proper names of persons, which naturally possess quite
different psychical importance for different people. Let us, for
instance, take a first name such as Theodore. To one of you
it will have no special meaning, to another it will be the name
of his father or brother or of a friend, or his own name. Analytic
experience will then show you that the first of these people is in
no danger of forgetting that a particular stranger bears this
name, whereas the others will be constantly inclined to withhold
from strangers a name which seems to them reserved for
intimate connections. If you now bear in mind that this associative inhibition may coincide with the operation of the
unpleasure principle[2] and, besides that, with an indirect

[1] [Artificial methods of improving the memory—e.g. 'Pelman-
ism'.]
[2] [Since the time of *The Interpretation of Dreams* (1900a) where
the principle is so named, Freud had almost invariably spoken of
the 'pleasure principle'. It is discussed under this latter name in
Lecture XXII, p. 356 f. below.]

mechanism, you will be in a position to form an adequate idea of the complications in the causation of the temporary forgetting of a name. An appropriate analysis will however unravel every one of these tangles for you.

The forgetting of impressions and experiences demonstrates much more clearly and exclusively than the forgetting of names the operation of the purpose of keeping disagreeable things out of memory. The whole field of this kind of forgetting does not, of course, fall within the class of parapraxes, but only such cases as, measured by the standard of our usual experience, seem to us striking and unjustified: for instance, when the forgetting affects impressions that are too fresh or important, or when the missing memory tears a gap in what is otherwise a well-remembered chain of events. Why and in what way we are able to forget in general, and among other things experiences which have certainly left the deepest impression upon us, such as the events of our earliest childhood years,—that is quite another problem, in which fending off unpleasurable impulses plays a certain part but is far from being the whole explanation.[1] It is an undoubted fact that disagreeable impressions are easily forgotten. Various psychologists have noticed it and the great Darwin was so much impressed by it that he made it 'a golden rule' to note down with especial care any observations which seemed unfavourable to his theory, since he had convinced himself that precisely they would not remain in his memory.[2]

A person who hears for the first time of this principle of the fending off of unpleasurable memories by forgetting rarely fails to object that on the contrary it has been his experience that distressing things are particularly hard to forget but keep on returning to torment him against his will—memories, for instance, of insults and humiliations. This is also a true fact, but the objection is not to the point. It is important to begin in good time to reckon with the fact that mental life is the arena and battle-ground for mutually opposing purposes or, to put

[1] [Infantile amnesia is discussed in Lecture XIII, p. 199 f. below. For a discussion of forgetting in general, see a long footnote added to *P.E.L.*, 274, in 1907.]

[2] [The whole passage from Darwin's autobiography (1958, 123) is quoted *P.E.L.*, 148.]

it non-dynamically, that it consists of contradictions and pairs of contraries. Proof of the existence of a particular purpose is no argument against the existence of an opposite one; there is room for both. It is only a question of the attitude of these contraries to each other, and of what effects are produced by the one and by the other.

Losing and mislaying are of particular interest to us owing to the many meanings they may have—owing, that is, to the multiplicity of the purposes which can be served by these parapraxes. All cases have in common the fact that there was a wish to lose something; they differ in the basis and aim of that wish. We lose a thing when it is worn out, when we intend to replace it by a better one, when we no longer like it, when it originates from someone with whom we are no longer on good terms or when we acquired it in circumstances we no longer want to recall. [Cf. p. 54.] Dropping, damaging or breaking the object can serve the same purpose. In the sphere of social life experience is said to have shown that unwanted and illegitimate children are far more frail than those legitimately conceived. The crude technique of baby-farmers[1] is not necessary for bringing about this result; a certain amount of neglect in looking after the children should be quite sufficient. The preserving of *things* may be subject to the same influences as that of children.

Things may, however, be condemned to be lost without their value having suffered any diminution—when, that is, there is an intention to sacrifice something to Fate in order to ward off some other dreaded loss. Analysis tells us that it is still quite a common thing among us to exorcize Fate in this way; and thus our losing is often a voluntary sacrifice. In the same way, losing may also serve the purpose of defiance or self-punishment. In short, the more remote reasons for the intention to get rid of a thing by losing it are beyond number.

Bungled actions, like other errors, are often used to fulfil wishes which one ought to deny oneself. Here the intention disguises itself as a lucky accident. For instance, as happened to one of my friends, a man may be due, obviously against his will,

[1] [In the original literally: 'what are known as angel-makers'.]

to go by train to visit someone near the town where he lives, and then, at a junction where he has to change, may by mistake get into a train that takes him back to where he came from. Or someone on a journey may be anxious to make a stop at an intermediate station but may be forbidden from doing so by other obligations, and he may then overlook or miss some connection so that he is after all obliged to break his journey in the way he wished. Or what happened to one of my patients: I had forbidden him to telephone to the girl he was in love with, and then, when he meant to telephone to me, he asked for the wrong number 'by mistake' or 'while he was thinking of something else' and suddenly found himself connected to the girl's number.[1] A good example of an outright blunder, and one of practical importance, is provided by an observation made by an engineer in his account of what preceded a case of material damage:

'Some time ago I worked with several students in the laboratory of the technical college on a series of complicated experiments in elasticity, a piece of work which we had undertaken voluntarily but which was beginning to take up more time than we had expected. One day as I returned to the laboratory with my friend F., he remarked how annoying it was to him to lose so much time on that particular day as he had so much else to do at home. I could not help agreeing with him and added half jokingly, referring to an incident the week before: "Let us hope that the machine will go wrong again so that we can stop work and go home early."

'In arranging the work it happened that F. was given the regulation of the valve of the press; that is to say, he was, by cautiously opening the valve, to let the fluid under pressure flow slowly out of the accumulator into the cylinder of the hydraulic press. The man conducting the experiment stood by the manometer and when the right pressure was reached called out a loud "Stop!" At the word of command F. seized the valve and turned it with all his might—to the left! (All valves without exception are closed by being turned to the right.) This caused the full pressure of the accumulator to come suddenly on to the press, a strain for which the connecting-pipes are not designed, so that one of them immediately burst—quite

[1] [These last three examples are described much more fully *P.E.L.*, 222 and 226–8.]

a harmless accident to the machine, but enough to oblige us to suspend work for the day and go home.

'It is characteristic, by the way, that when we were discussing the affair some time later my friend F. had no recollection whatever of my remark, which I recalled with certainty.'[1]

This may lead you to suspect that it is not always just an innocent chance that turns the hands of your domestic servants into dangerous enemies of your household belongings. And you may also raise the question whether it is always a matter of chance when people injure themselves and risk their own safety. These are notions whose value you may care to test, if occasion arises, by analysing observations of your own.

This, Ladies and Gentlemen, is far from being all that might be said about parapraxes. Much remains that might be examined and discussed. But I am satisfied if our discussion of the subject so far has to some extent shaken your previous views and has made you a little prepared to accept new ones. I am content, for the rest, to leave you faced with an unclarified situation. We cannot establish all our doctrines from a study of parapraxes and we are not obliged to draw our evidence from that material alone. The great value of parapraxes for our purposes lies in their being very common phenomena which, moreover, can easily be observed in oneself, and which can occur without the slightest implication of illness. There is only one of your unanswered questions which I should like to put into words before I end. If, as we have found from many instances, people come so close to an understanding of parapraxes and so often behave as though they grasped their sense, how is it possible that they none the less set down these same phenomena as being in general chance events without sense or meaning, and that they can oppose the psycho-analytic elucidation of them with so much vigour?

You are right. This is a remarkable fact and it calls for an explanation. But I will not give you one. Instead, I will introduce you by degrees to fields of knowledge from which the explanation will force itself upon you without any contribution of mine.

[1] [Reproduced from *P.E.L.*, 174.]

PART II
DREAMS

LECTURE V

DIFFICULTIES AND FIRST
APPROACHES

LADIES AND GENTLEMEN,—It was discovered one day that the pathological symptoms of certain neurotic patients have a sense.[1] On this discovery the psycho-analytic method of treatment was founded. It happened in the course of this treatment that patients, instead of bringing forward their symptoms, brought forward dreams. A suspicion thus arose that the dreams too had a sense.[2]

We will not, however, follow this historical path, but will proceed in the opposite direction. We will demonstrate the sense of dreams by way of preparing for the study of the neuroses. This reversal is justified, since the study of dreams is not only the best preparation for the study of the neuroses, but dreams are themselves a neurotic symptom, which, moreover, offers us the priceless advantage of occurring in all healthy people.[3] Indeed, supposing all human beings were healthy, so long as they dreamt we could arrive from their dreams at almost all the discoveries which the investigation of the neuroses has led to.

Dreams, then, have become a subject of psycho-analytic

---

[1] By Josef Breuer in the years 1880–2. Cf. the lectures delivered by me in America in 1909 (*Five Lectures on Psycho-Analysis* [1910a]) and 'On the History of the Psycho-Analytic Movement' (1914d), (Norton, 1966).]

[2] [Freud's major work on the subject of dreams was, of course, *The Interpretation of Dreams* (1900a). There is, however, scarcely one of his writings in which the topic did not emerge, but a list of the principal discussions of it is given in an Appendix to that work. A considerable number of references to it will be found in editorial footnotes to the present set of lectures; and, to save space, the abbreviation '*I. of D.*' will be used, with application in every case to Volumes IV and V of the *Standard Edition*. It may be noted that the pagination of the text of the latest separate editions of the work (London: Allen and Unwin, 1955, and New York: Basic Books, 1955) is identical with that of the *Standard Edition* volumes.]

[3] [Freud discussed this further towards the end of the last lecture of the series (p. 456 f., below).]

research: once again ordinary phenomena, with little value set
on them, and apparently of no practical use—like parapraxes,
with which indeed they have in common the fact of occurring
in healthy people. But apart from this the conditions for our
work are a good deal less favourable here. Parapraxes had
merely been neglected by science, little attention had been paid
to them; but at least there was no harm in concerning oneself
with them. 'No doubt', people would say, 'there are more
important things. But something may possibly come of it.' But
to concern oneself with dreams is not merely unpractical and
uncalled-for, it is positively disgraceful. It brings with it the
odium of being unscientific and rouses the suspicion of a personal inclination to mysticism. Imagine a medical man going
in for dreams when there are so many more serious things even
in neuropathology and psychiatry—tumours as big as apples
compressing the organ of the mind, haemorrhages, chronic
inflammation, in all of which the changes in the tissues can be
demonstrated under the microscope! No, dreams are much too
trivial, and unworthy to be an object of research.

And there is something else which from its very nature frus-
trates the requirements of exact research. In investigating
dreams one is not even certain about the object of one's research. A delusion, for instance, meets one squarely and with
definite outlines. 'I am the Emperor of China', says the patient
straight out. But dreams? As a rule no account at all can be
given of them. If anyone gives an account of a dream, has he
any guarantee that his account has been correct, or that he may
not, on the contrary, have altered his account in the course of
giving it and have been obliged to invent some addition to it
to make up for the indistinctness of his recollection? Most
dreams cannot be remembered at all and are forgotten except
for small fragments. And is the interpretation of material of
this kind to serve as the basis of a scientific psychology or as a
method for treating patients?

An excess of criticism may make us suspicious. These objections to dreams as an object of research are obviously carried
too far. We have already dealt with the question of unimpor-
tance in connection with parapraxes [p. 26 f.]. We have told
ourselves that big things can show themselves by small indications. As regards their indistinctness—that is one of the charac-

teristics of dreams, like any other: we cannot lay down for things what their characteristics are to be. And incidentally there are clear and distinct dreams as well. There are, moreover, other objects of psychiatric research which suffer from the same characteristic of indistinctness—in many instances, for example, obsessions, and these have been dealt with, after all, by respected and esteemed psychiatrists.[1] I recall the last such case that I came across in my medical practice. This was a woman patient who introduced herself with these words: 'I have a sort of feeling as though I had injured or had wanted to injure some living creature—a child?—no, more like a dog—as though I may have thrown it off a bridge, or something else.' We can help to overcome the defect of the uncertainty in remembering dreams if we decide that whatever the dreamer tells us must count as his dream, without regard to what he may have forgotten or have altered in recalling it. And finally it cannot even be maintained so sweepingly that dreams are unimportant things. We know from our own experience that the mood in which one wakes up from a dream may last for the whole day; doctors have observed cases in which a mental disease has started with a dream and in which a delusion originating in the dream has persisted; historical figures are reported to have embarked on momentous enterprises in response to dreams. We may therefore ask what may be the true source of the contempt in which dreams are held in scientific circles.

It is, I believe, a reaction against the overvaluation of dreams in earlier days. The reconstruction of the past is, as we know, no easy matter, but we may assume with certainty, if I may put it as a joke, that our ancestors three thousand or more years ago already had dreams like ours. So far as we know, all the peoples of antiquity attached great significance to dreams and thought they could be used for practical purposes. They deduced signs for the future from them and searched in them for auguries. For the Greeks and other oriental nations, there may have been times when a campaign without dream-interpreters seemed as

[1] [The tendency of obsessional neurotics to uncertainty and vagueness had been discussed by Freud in Section B of Part II of his 'Notes upon a Case of Obsessional Neurosis' (1909d). See also the account of that form of illness in Lecture XVII, p. 258 ff. below.]

impossible as one without air-reconnaissance seems to-day. When Alexander the Great started on his conquests, his train included the most famous dream-interpreters. The city of Tyre, which at that time still stood on an island, offered the king such a stiff resistance that he considered the possibility of raising the siege. Then one night he had a dream of a satyr who seemed to be dancing in triumph, and when he reported it to his dream-interpreters they informed him that it foretold his conquest of the city. He ordered an assault and captured Tyre.[1] Among the Etruscans and Romans other methods of foretelling the future were in use; but throughout the whole of the Hellenistic-Roman period the interpretation of dreams was practised and highly esteemed. Of the literature dealing with the subject the principal work at least has survived: the book by Artemidorus of Daldis, who probably lived during the reign of the Emperor Hadrian.[2] How it came about after this that the art of interpreting dreams declined and that dreams fell into discredit I cannot tell you. The spread of enlightenment cannot have had much to do with it, for many things more absurd than the dream-interpretation of antiquity were faithfully preserved in the obscurity of the Middle Ages. The fact remains that interest in dreams gradually sank to the level of superstition and could survive only among the uneducated classes. The final abuse of dream-interpretation was reached in our days with attempts to discover from dreams the numbers fated to be drawn in the game of lotto.[3] On the other hand the exact science of to-day has repeatedly concerned itself with dreams but always with the sole aim of applying its physiological theories to them. Medical men, of course, looked on dreams as non-psychical acts, as the expression in mental life of somatic stimuli. Binz (1878,[35]) pronounced that dreams are 'somatic processes, which are in every case useless and in many cases positively pathological, to which the soul of the universe and immortality are as sublimely superior as the blue sky above some weed-grown, low-lying stretch of sand.' Maury [1878, 50] compares dreams to the disordered twitchings of St. Vitus's

[1] [The explanation of this dream is given in Lecture XV, p. 236 below.]
[2] [Some account of this work appears in Chapter II of *I. of D.*]
[3] [Something very similar to what is now known as 'Bingo'.]

dance as contrasted with the co-ordinated movements of a healthy man. According to an old analogy, the contents of a dream are like the sounds produced when 'the ten fingers of a man who knows nothing of music wander over the keys of a piano' [Strümpell, 1877, 84].

Interpreting means finding a hidden sense in something; there can of course be no question of doing that if we adopt this last estimate of the function of dreams. Look at the description of dreams given by Wundt [1874], Jodl [1896], and other more recent philosophers. They content themselves with enumerating the respects in which dream-life differs from waking thought, always in a sense depreciatory to dreams—emphasizing the fact that associations are broken apart, that the critical faculty ceases to work, that all knowledge is eliminated, as well as other signs of diminished functioning. The only valuable contribution to the knowledge of dreams for which we have to thank exact science relates to the effect produced on the content of dreams by the impact of somatic stimuli during sleep. A recently deceased Norwegian author, J. Mourly Vold, published two stout volumes of experimental researches into dreams (German translation, 1910 and 1912), which are devoted almost exclusively to the consequences of alterations in the posture of the limbs. They have been recommended to us as models of exact research into dreams. Can you imagine what exact science would say if it learnt that we want to make an attempt to discover the *sense* of dreams? Perhaps it has already said it. But we will not let ourselves be frightened off. If it was possible for parapraxes to have a sense, dreams can have one too; and in a great many cases parapraxes *have* a sense, which has escaped exact science. So let us embrace the prejudice of the ancients and of the people and let us follow in the footsteps of the dream-interpreters of antiquity.

We must begin by finding our bearings in the task before us and taking a general survey of the field of dreams. What, then, is a dream? It is hard to answer in a single sentence. But we will not attempt a definition when it is enough to point to something familiar to everyone.[1] We should, however, bring the essential feature of dreams into prominence. Where is that

[1] [Cf., however, some remarks on this in Lecture XIV, p. 223 below.]

to be found, though? There are such immense differences within the frame that comprises our subject—differences in every direction. The essential feature will presumably be something that we can point to as common to all dreams.

The first thing common to all dreams would seem to be, of course, that we are asleep during them. Dreaming is evidently mental life during sleep—something which has certain resemblances to waking mental life but which, on the other hand, is distinguished from it by large differences. This was, long ago, Aristotle's definition.[1] It may be that there are still closer connections between dreams and sleep. We can be woken by a dream; we very often have a dream when we wake up spontaneously or if we are forcibly aroused from sleep. Thus dreams seem to be an intermediate state between sleeping and waking. So our attention is turned to sleep. Well, then, what is sleep?

That is a physiological or biological problem about which much is still in dispute. On that we can come to no conclusion; but we ought, I think, to try to describe the psychological characteristics of sleep. Sleep is a state in which I want to know nothing of the external world, in which I have taken my interest away from it. I put myself to sleep by withdrawing from the external world and keeping its stimuli away from me. I also go to sleep when I am fatigued by it. So when I go to sleep I say to the external world: 'Leave me in peace: I want to go to sleep.' On the contrary, children say: 'I'm not going to sleep yet; I'm not tired, and I want to have some more experiences.' The biological purpose of sleep seems therefore to be rehabilitation, and its psychological characteristic suspense of interest in the world. Our relation to the world, into which we have come so unwillingly, seems to involve our not being able to tolerate it uninterruptedly. Thus from time to time we withdraw into the premundane state, into existence in the womb. At any rate, we arrange conditions for ourselves very like what they were then: warm, dark and free from stimuli. Some of us roll ourselves up into a tight package and, so as to sleep, take up a posture much as it was in the womb. The world, it seems, does not possess even those of us who are adults completely, but only up to two thirds; one third of us is still quite unborn. Every time we wake in the morning it is like a new

[1] [Cf. Chapter I of *I. of D.*]

birth. Indeed, in speaking of our state after sleep, we say that we feel as though we were newly born. (In saying this, incidentally, we are making what is probably a very false assumption about the general sensations of a new-born child, who seems likely, on the contrary, to be feeling very uncomfortable.) We speak, too, of being born as 'first seeing the light of day'.[1]

If this is what sleep is, dreams cannot possibly form part of its programme, but seem on the contrary to be an unwelcome addition to it. In our opinion too, a dreamless sleep is the best, the only proper one. There ought to be no mental activity in sleep; if it begins to stir, we have not succeeded in establishing the foetal state of rest: we have not been able entirely to avoid residues of mental activity. Dreaming would consist in these residues. But if so, it would really seem that there is no need for dreams to have any sense. It was different with parapraxes; they, after all, were activities during waking life. But if I am asleep and have stopped mental activity completely and have merely failed to suppress some residues of it, then there is no need whatever for these residues to have any sense. I cannot even make use of any such sense, since the rest of my mental life is asleep. So it really can only be a matter of reactions, in the nature of 'twitchings', of mental phenomena such as result directly from a somatic stimulus. Dreams would accordingly be residues of waking mental activity which were disturbing sleep, and we might well decide to drop the subject at once, as not being suited to psycho-analysis.

Even if dreams are superfluous, however, they do exist, and we can try to account for their existence. Why does mental life fail to go to sleep? Probably because there is something that will not allow the mind any peace. Stimuli impinge upon it and it must react to them. A dream, then, is the manner in which the mind reacts to stimuli that impinge upon it in the state of sleep. And here we see a way of access to an understanding of dreams. We can take various dreams and try to discover what the stimulus was which was seeking to disturb sleep and to which the reaction was a dream. Our examination of the first thing common to all dreams seems to have taken us so far.

Is there anything else common to them? Yes, something
___
[1] [In German, literally, 'seeing the light of the world'.]

unmistakable but much harder to grasp and to describe. Mental processes in sleep have a quite different character from those of waking life. We experience every sort of thing in dreams and believe in it, whereas nevertheless we experience nothing, except, perhaps, the single disturbing stimulus. We experience it predominantly in visual images; feelings may be present too, and thoughts interwoven in it as well; the other senses may also experience something, but nonetheless it is predominantly a question of images. Part of the difficulty of giving an account of dreams is due to our having to translate these images into words. 'I could draw it', a dreamer often says to us, 'but I don't know how to say it.' This is not, however, a *reduced* mental activity, like that of a feeble-minded person as compared to that of a genius: it is *qualitatively* different, though it is hard to say where the difference lies. G. T. Fechner once voiced a suspicion that the scene of action of dreams (in the mind) is different from that of waking ideational life.[1] Though we do not understand this and do not know what we are to make of it, it does in fact reproduce the impression of strangeness which most dreams make on us. The comparison between dream-activity and the effects of an unmusical hand on the piano [p. 87] does not help us here. The piano will after all respond with the same sounds, though not with tunes, to any chance pressure on its keys. Let us carefully bear this second thing common to all dreams in mind, even though we may not have understood it.

Are there any other things common to them? I cannot discover any; I can see nothing anywhere but differences, and differences in all kinds of ways: in their apparent duration, as well as in their clarity, in the amount of affect accompanying them, in the possibility of retaining them, and so on. This variety is not in fact what we might expect to find in a mere defensive reaction to a stimulus, something mechanically imposed, an empty thing, like the twitchings of St. Vitus's dance. As regards the dimensions of dreams, some are very short and comprise only a single image or a few, a single thought, or even a single word; others are uncommonly rich in their

----

[1] [The psycho-physiologist Fechner (1801–87) had a great influence on Freud's theories (see Chapter V of his *Autobiographical Study* (1925d), (Norton, 1963). The present remark is discussed in the section on Regression in Chapter VII of *I. of D.*]

content, present whole novels and seem to last a long time. There are dreams which are as clear as [waking] experience, so clear that quite a time after waking we do not realize that they were dreams; and there are others which are indescribably dim, shadowy and blurred. Indeed in one and the same dream excessively definite portions may alternate with others of scarcely discernible vagueness. Dreams may be entirely sensible or at least coherent, witty even, or fantastically beautiful; others, again, are confused, feeble-minded as it were, absurd, often positively crazy. There are dreams that leave us quite cold and others in which affects of all kinds are manifest—pain to the point of tears, anxiety to the point of waking us up, astonishment, delight, and so on. Dreams are usually quickly forgotten after waking, or they may last through the day, remembered more and more dimly and incompletely till evening; others, again—for instance, childhood dreams—are so well preserved that after thirty years they remain in the memory like some fresh experience. Dreams may appear, like individuals, on a single occasion only and never again, or they may recur in the same person unchanged or with small divergences. In short, this fragment of mental activity during the night has an immense repertory at its disposal; it is capable, in fact, of all that the mind creates in daytime—yet it is never the same thing.

We might try to account for these many variations in dreams by supposing that they correspond to different intermediate stages between sleeping and waking, different degrees of incomplete sleep. Yes, but if this were so, the value, content and clarity of a dream's product—and the awareness, too, of its being a dream—would have to increase in dreams in which the mind was coming near to waking; and it would not be possible for a clear and rational fragment of dream to be immediately followed by one that was senseless and obscure and for this in turn to be followed by another good piece. The mind could certainly not alter the depth of its sleep so quickly as that. So this explanation is of no help: there can be no short cut out of the difficulty.

We will for the moment leave on one side the 'sense' of dreams, and try to make our way to a better understanding of them from what we have found is common to them. We inferred from the relation of dreams to the state of sleep that dreams are the reaction to a stimulus which disturbs sleep. We have learnt that this too is the single point on which exact experimental psychology is able to come to our assistance: it brings us evidence that stimuli which impinge during sleep make their appearance in dreams. Many investigations of this kind have been made, most recently those by Mourly Vold which I have already mentioned [p. 87]; and each of us, no doubt, has been in a position to confirm this finding from personal observation. I will select a few of the earlier experiments. Maury [1878] had some experiments performed on himself. He was given some eau-de-cologne to smell in his sleep. He dreamt he was in Cairo, in Johann Maria Farina's shop, and some further absurd adventures followed. Or, he was pinched lightly on the neck; he dreamt of a mustard plaster being applied to him and of a doctor who had treated him as a child. Or again, a drop of water was dropped on his forehead; he was in Italy, was sweating violently and was drinking white Orvieto wine.[1]

The striking thing about these experimentally produced dreams will perhaps be even more plainly visible in another series of stimulus-dreams. They are three dreams reported by an intelligent observer, Hildebrandt [1875], all of them reactions to the ringing of an alarm-clock:

'I dreamt, then, that one spring morning I was going for a walk and was strolling through the green fields till I came to a neighbouring village, where I saw the villagers in their best clothes, with hymn-books under their arms, flocking to the church. Of course! It was Sunday, and early morning service would soon be beginning. I decided I would attend it; but first, as I was rather hot from walking, I went into the church-yard which surrounded the church, to cool down. While I was reading some of the tombstones, I heard the bell-ringer climbing up the church tower and at the top of it I now saw the little village bell which would presently give the signal for the beginning of devotions. For quite a while it hung there motionless, then it began to swing, and suddenly its peal began to ring out clear and piercing—so clear and piercing that it put an end to my sleep. But what was ringing was the alarm-clock.

[1] [For these and several other of Maury's experiments see the section on the Stimuli and Sources of Dreams in Chapter I of *I. of D.*]

'Here is another instance. It was a bright winter's day and the streets were covered with deep snow. I had agreed to join a party for a sleigh-ride; but I had to wait a long time before news came that the sleigh was at the door. Now followed the preparations for getting in—the fur rug spread out, the foot-muff put ready—and at last I was sitting in my seat. But even then the moment of departure was delayed till a pull at the reins gave the waiting horses the signal. Then off they started, and, with a violent shake, the sleigh bells broke into their familiar jingle—with such violence, in fact, that in a moment the cobweb of my dream was torn through. And once again it was only the shrill sound of the alarm-clock.

'And now yet a third example. I saw a kitchenmaid, carrying several dozen plates piled on one another, walking along the passage to the dining-room. The column of china in her arms seemed to me in danger of losing its balance. "Take care," I exclaimed, "or you'll drop the whole load." The inevitable rejoinder duly followed: she was quite accustomed to that kind of job, and so on. And meanwhile my anxious looks followed the advancing figure. Then—just as I expected—she stumbled at the threshold and the fragile crockery slipped and rattled and clattered in a hundred pieces on the floor. But the noise continued without ceasing, and soon it seemed no longer to be a clattering; it was turning into a ringing—and the ringing, as my waking self now became aware, was only the alarm-clock doing its duty.'[1]

These are very nice dreams, entirely sensible and by no means as incoherent as dreams are usually apt to be. I am not objecting to them on that account. What they have in common is that in each case the situation ends in a noise, which, when the dreamer wakes up, is recognized as being made by the alarm-clock. So we see here how a dream is produced; but we learn something more than this. The dream does not recognize the alarm-clock—nor does it appear in the dream—but it replaces the noise of the alarm-clock by another; it interprets the stimulus which is bringing sleep to an end, but it interprets it differently each time. Why does it do that? There is no answer to this; it seems a matter of caprice. Understanding the dream would mean being able to say why this particular noise and

[1] [Also quoted in the last mentioned section of *I. of D.*]

none other was chosen for the interpretation of the stimulus from the alarm-clock. We may make an analogous objection to Maury's experiments: we can see quite clearly that the imping-ing stimulus appears in the dream; but why it should take this particular form we are not told, and it does not seem by any means to follow from the nature of the stimulus that disturbed sleep. In Maury's experiments, too, a quantity of other dream-material usually appears in addition to the direct effect of the stimulus—for instance, the 'absurd adventures' in the eau-de-cologne dream—, which cannot be accounted for.

And now consider that *arousal* dreams offer the best chance of establishing the influence of external sleep-disturbing stimuli. In most other cases it will become more difficult. We do not wake out of every dream, and if we remember a dream of the past night in the morning, how are we to discover a disturbing stimulus which may perhaps have made its impact on us during the night? I once succeeded in identifying a sound-stimulus of that kind retrospectively, but only, of course, owing to special circumstances. I woke up one morning in a mountain resort in the Tyrol, knowing I had had a dream that the Pope was dead. I could not explain the dream to myself; but later on my wife asked me if I had heard the fearful noise made by the pealing of bells towards morning which had broken out from all the churches and chapels. No, I had heard nothing, my sleep is more resistant than hers; but thanks to her information I understood my dream.[1] How often may stimuli of this kind instigate dreams in a sleeper without his getting news of them afterwards? Perhaps very often, but perhaps not. If the stimulus can no longer be pointed to, we cannot be convinced of its existence. And in any case we have changed our view of the importance of external stimuli that disturb sleep since we learnt that they can explain only a small portion of the dream and not the whole dream-reaction.

There is no need to give up this theory entirely on that account. Moreover it is capable of extension. It is obviously a matter of indifference what it is that disturbs sleep or instigates the mind to dream. If it cannot invariably be a sensory stimulus coming from outside, there may instead be what is called a somatic stimulus, arising from the internal organs. This is a

[1] [Told at greater length in the discussion of The Somatic Sources of Dreams in Chapter V of *I. of D.*]

very plausible notion and agrees with the most popular view of the origin of dreams: 'dreams come from indigestion', people often say. Here too unluckily we must often suspect that there are cases when a somatic stimulus which has impinged on a sleeper during the night is no longer manifest after waking and can therefore not be proved to have occurred. But we shall not overlook the number of clear experiences which support the origin of dreams from somatic stimuli. In general, there can be no doubt that the condition of the internal organs can influence dreams. The relation of the content of some dreams to an over-full bladder or to a state of excitation of the genital organs is too plain to be mistaken. These clear cases lead to others in which the content of the dreams give rise to a justifiable suspicion that there has been an impact from somatic stimuli because there is something in the content which can be regarded as a working-over, a representation or an interpretation of such stimuli. Scherner (1861), who made researches into dreams, argued particularly strongly in favour of this derivation of dreams and brought forward some good examples of it. For instance, in one dream he saw 'two rows of pretty boys with fair hair and delicate complexions facing one another in pugnacious array, making an onset and attacking one another, and then drawing back and taking up their old position again, and then starting the whole business once more.' His interpretation of these two rows of boys as teeth is plausible in itself and seems fully confirmed when we learn that after this scene the dreamer 'pulled a long tooth out of his jaw.'[1] Similarly, the interpretation of 'long, narrow, winding passages' as derived from an intestinal stimulus seems valid, and confirms the assertion by Scherner that dreams seek above all to represent the organ that sends out the stimulus by objects resembling it.

Thus we must be prepared to admit that internal stimuli can play the same part in dreams as external ones. Any estimate of their importance is unfortunately open to the same objections. In a large number of cases an interpretation pointing to a somatic stimulus is uncertain or unprovable. Not all dreams, but only a certain number of them give rise to a suspicion that internal organic stimuli had a share in their origin. And lastly, internal somatic stimuli are as little able as external sensory

[1] [*I. of D.*]

stimuli to explain more of a dream than what corresponds in it to a direct reaction to the stimulus. Where the rest of the dream comes from remains obscure.

Let us notice, however, one peculiarity of dream-life which comes to light in this study of the effects of stimuli. Dreams do not simply reproduce the stimulus; they work it over, they make allusions to it, they include it in some context, they replace it by something else. This is a side of the dream-work[1] which is bound to interest us since it may perhaps bring us nearer to the essence of dreams. When a person constructs something as a result of a stimulus, the stimulus need not on that account exhaust the whole of the work. Shakespeare's *Macbeth*, for instance, was a *pièce d'occasion* composed to celebrate the accession of the king who first united the crowns of the three kingdoms. But does this immediate historical occasion cover the content of the tragedy? Does it explain its greatnesses and its enigmas? It may be that the external and internal stimuli, too, impinging on the sleeper, are only the *instigators* of the dream and will accordingly betray nothing to us of its essence.

The second thing that is common to dreams, their psychical peculiarity [p. 89 f.], is on the one hand hard to grasp and on the other offers us no starting-point for further enquiry. We experience things in dreams as a rule in visual forms. Can the stimuli throw any light on this? Is what we experience in fact the stimulus? But, if so, why is the experience visual, while it is only in the rarest cases that optical stimulation has instigated the dream? Or if we dream spoken words, can it be shown that during sleep a conversation, or some noise resembling one, made its way into our ears? I venture to dismiss that possibility decisively.

If we can get no further with what is common to dreams, let us see whether their differences can help us. Dreams are, of course, often senseless, confused and absurd; but there are also sensible, matter-of-fact, and reasonable ones. Let us enquire whether the latter, the sensible ones, can throw any light on the senseless ones. Here is the latest reasonable dream that I

---

[1] [The process which transforms the latent thoughts behind the dream into its manifest form. This is the subject of Lecture XI below.]

have had reported to me. It was dreamt by a young man: 'I went for a walk along the Kärntnerstrasse[1] and met Herr X. there and joined him for a time. Then I went into a restaurant. Two ladies and a gentleman came and sat at my table. I was annoyed at this to begin with and wouldn't look at them. Then I did look and found that they were quite nice.' The dreamer commented on this that on the evening before the dream he had in fact walked along the Kärntnerstrasse, which is the way he usually goes, and had met Herr X. there. The other part of the dream was not a direct recollection, and only had some similarity to an experience a considerable time earlier. Or here is another matter-of-fact dream, this time a lady's: 'Her husband asked her: "Don't you think we ought to have the piano tuned?" And she replied: "It's not worth while; the hammers need reconditioning in any case." '[2] This dream repeated, without much alteration, a conversation which had taken place between her and her husband the day before the dream. What do we learn from these two reasonable dreams? Nothing except that they contain repetitions from daily life or things connected with it. That would already be something, if it could be said of dreams generally. But there is no question of that; it applies only to a minority, and in most dreams there is no sign of a connection with the day before,[3] and no light is thrown by this on the senseless and absurd dreams. It only shows that we have come upon a new task. We not only want to know what a dream says, but, if it speaks clearly, as it does in these examples of ours, we also want to know why and for what purpose this familiar material, only recently experienced, has been repeated in the dream.

I think that, like me, you must be tired of pursuing enquiries like those we have so far been making. All one's interest in a problem is evidently insufficient unless one knows as well of a path of approach that will lead to its solution. We have not yet found such a path. Experimental psychology has brought us nothing but some very valuable information on the significance of stimuli as instigators to dreaming. We have nothing to expect

[1] [The principal shopping street in Vienna.]
[2] [See Chapter V of *I. of D.*]
[3] [A qualification of this statement is to follow shortly (p. 106).]

from philosophy except that it will once again haughtily point out to us the intellectual inferiority of the object of our study. Nor have we any wish to borrow anything from the occult sciences. History and popular opinion tell us that dreams have a sense and a meaning: that they look into the future—which is hard to accept and certainly incapable of proof. So our first effort leaves us completely at a loss.

Unexpectedly, a hint reaches us from a direction in which we have not so far looked. Linguistic usage, which is no chance thing, but the precipitate of old discoveries, though, to be sure, it must not be employed incautiously—our language, then, is acquainted with things that bear the strange name of 'day-dreams'. Day-dreams are phantasies (products of the imagination); they are very general phenomena, observable, once more, in healthy as well as in sick people, and are easily accessible to study in our own mind. The most remarkable thing about these imaginative structures is that they have been given the name of 'day-dreams', for there is no trace in them of the two things that are common to dreams [p. 88 ff.]. Their relation to sleep is already contradicted by their name; and, as regards the second thing common to dreams, we do not experience or hallucinate anything in them but imagine something, we know that we are having a phantasy, we do not see but think. These day-dreams appear in the prepubertal period, often in the later part .of childhood even; they persist until maturity is reached and are then either given up or maintained till the end of life. The content of these phantasies is dominated by a very transparent motive. They are scenes and events in which the subject's egoistic needs of ambition and power or his erotic wishes find satisfaction. In young men the ambitious phantasies are the most prominent, in women, whose ambition is directed to success in love, the erotic ones. But in men, too, erotic needs are often enough present in the background: all their heroic deeds and successes seem only to aim at courting the admiration and favour of women. In other respects these day-dreams are of many different kinds and pass through changing vicissitudes. They are either, each one of them, dropped after a short time and replaced by a fresh one, or they are retained, spun out into long stories and adapted to the changes in the circumstances of the subject's life. They go along with the times, so to speak, and receive a 'date stamp' which bears witness to the influence of the new situation. They are the raw material of poetic production, for the creative writer uses his day-dreams, with certain remodellings, disguises and omissions, to construct the situations which he introduces into his short stories, his novels or his plays. The hero of the day-dreams is always the subject himself, either directly or by an obvious identification with someone else.[1]

It may be that day-dreams bear their name on account of having the same relation to reality—in order to indicate that their content is to be looked on as no less unreal than that of dreams. But perhaps they share this name because of some psychical characteristic of dreams which is still unknown to us, one which we are in search of. It is also possible that we are being quite wrong in trying to make use of this similarity of name as something significant. Only later will it be possible to clear this up.

[1] [Freud's chief discussion of phantasies and of their relation to artistic creation will be found in two of his earlier papers: 'Creative Writers and Day-Dreaming' (1908e) and 'Hysterical Phantasies and their Relation to Bisexuality' (1908a). He returns to the subject below, in the later part of Lecture XXIII.]

LECTURE VI

THE PREMISSES AND TECHNIQUE
OF INTERPRETATION

LADIES AND GENTLEMEN,—What we need, then, is a new path, a method which will enable us to make a start in the investigation of dreams. I will put a suggestion to you which presents itself. Let us take it as a premiss from this point onwards that *dreams are not somatic but psychical phenomena*. You know what that means, but what justifies our making the assumption? Nothing: but there is nothing either to prevent our making it. Here is the position: if dreams are somatic phenomena they are no concern of ours, they can only interest us on the assumption that they are mental phenomena. We will therefore work on the assumption that they really are, to see what comes of it. The outcome of our work will decide whether we are to hold to this assumption and whether we may then go on to treat it in turn as a proved finding. But what is it actually that we want to arrive at? What is our work aiming at? We want something that is sought for in all scientific work—to understand the phenomena, to establish a correlation between them and, in the latter end, if it is possible, to enlarge our power over them.

We proceed with our work, accordingly, on the supposition that dreams are psychical phenomena. In that case they are products and utterances of the dreamer's, but utterances which tell us nothing, which we do not understand. Well, what do you do if I make an unintelligible utterance to you? You question me, is that not so? Why should we not do the same thing to the dreamer—*question him as to what his dream means*?

As you will remember, we found ourselves in this situation once before. It was while we were investigating certain parapraxes—a case of a slip of the tongue. Someone had said [p. 42]: 'Then facts came to *Vorschwein*' and we thereupon asked him—no, it was luckily not we but some other people who had no connection at all with psycho-analysis—these other people, then, asked him what he meant by this unintelligible remark. And he replied at once that he had intended to say 'these facts were *Schweinereien* [disgusting]', but had forced this intention back in favour of the milder version 'then facts came to *Vorschein* [light]'. I pointed out to you at the time [p. 48] that this piece of information was the model for every psycho-analytic investigation, and you will understand now that psycho-analysis follows the technique of getting the people under examination so far as possible themselves to produce the solution of their riddles [p. 49]. Thus, too, it is the dreamer himself who should tell us what his dream means.

But, as we know, things are not so simple with dreams. With parapraxes it worked all right in a number of cases; but then others came along in which the person who was questioned would say nothing, and even indignantly rejected the answer we proposed to him. With dreams cases of the first sort are entirely lacking; the dreamer always says he knows nothing. He cannot reject our interpretation as we have none to offer him. Are we to give up our attempt then? Since he knows nothing and we know nothing and a third person could know even less, there seems to be no prospect of finding out. If you feel inclined, then, give up the attempt! But if you feel otherwise, you can accompany me further. For I can assure you that it is quite possible, and highly probable indeed, that the dreamer *does* know what his dream means: *only he does not know that he knows it and for that reason thinks he does not know it.*

You will point out to me that I am once more introducing an assumption, the second already in this short argument, and that in doing so I am enormously reducing my procedure's claim to credibility: 'Subject to the premiss that dreams are psychical phenomena, and subject to the further premiss that there are mental things in a man which he knows without knowing that he knows them . . .' and so on. If so, one has only to consider the internal improbability of each of these two premisses, and one can quietly divert one's interest from any conclusions that may be based on them.

I have not brought you here, Ladies and Gentlemen, to delude you or to conceal things from you. In my prospectus, it is true, I announced a course of 'Elementary Lectures to Serve as

an Introduction to Psycho-Analysis',[1] but what I had in mind
was nothing in the nature of a presentation *in usum Delphini*,[2]
which would give you a smooth account with all the difficulties
carefully concealed, with the gaps filled in and the doubts
glossed over, so that you might believe with an easy mind that
you had learnt something new. No, for the very reason of your
being beginners, I wanted to show you our science as it is, with
its unevennesses and roughnesses, its demands and hesitations.
For I know that it is the same in all sciences and cannot possibly
be otherwise, especially in their beginnings. I know also that
ordinarily instruction is at pains to start out by concealing such
difficulties and incompletenesses from the learner. But that will
not do for psycho-analysis. So I have in fact laid down two premisses, one within the other; and if anyone finds the whole
thing too laborious and too insecure, or if anyone is accustomed
to higher certainties and more elegant deductions, he need go
no further with us. I think, however, that he should leave
psychological problems entirely alone, for it is to be feared that
in this quarter he will find impassable the precise and secure
paths which he is prepared to follow. And, for a science which
has something to offer, there is no necessity to sue for a hearing
and for followers. Its findings are bound to canvass on its behalf
and it can wait until these have compelled attention to it.

But for those who would like to persist in the subject, I can
point out that my two assumptions are not on a par. The first,
that dreams are psychical phenomena, is the premiss which we
seek to prove by the outcome of our work; the second one has
already been proved in another field, and I am merely ven-
turing to bring it over from there to our own problems.

Where, then, in what field, can it be that proof has been
found that there is knowledge of which the person concerned
nevertheless knows nothing, as we are proposing to assume of
dreamers? After all, this would be a strange, surprising fact and
one which would alter our view of mental life and which would
have no need to hide itself: a fact, incidentally, which cancels
itself in its very naming and which nevertheless claims to be

---

[1] [The 'elementary' was dropped from the title of the lectures in their
published form. See footnote 2, p. 9.]
[2] ['For the use of the Dauphin'—an edition of the Classics prepared for
his son by order of Louis XIV: 'bowdlerized'.]

something real—a contradiction in terms. Well, it does not hide itself. It is not its fault if people know nothing about it or do not pay enough attention to it. Any more than we are to blame because judgement is passed on all these psychological problems by people who have kept at a distance from all the observations and experiences which are decisive on the matter.

The proof was found in the field of hypnotic phenomena. When, in 1889, I took part in the extraordinarily impressive demonstrations by Liébeault and Bernheim at Nancy,[1] I witnessed the following experiment among others. If a man was put into a state of somnambulism, was made to experience all kinds of things in a hallucinatory manner, and was then woken up, he appeared at first to know nothing of what had happened during his hypnotic sleep. Bernheim then asked him straight out to report what had happened to him under hypnosis. The man maintained that he could remember nothing. But Bernheim held out against this, brought urgent pressure to bear on him, insisted that he knew it and must remember it. And, lo and behold! the man grew uncertain, began to reflect, and recalled in a shadowy way one of the experiences that had been suggested to him, and then another piece, and the memory became clearer and clearer and more and more complete, and finally came to light without a break. Since, however, he knew afterwards what had happened and had learnt nothing about it from anyone else in the interval, we are justified in concluding that he had known it earlier as well. It was merely inaccessible to him; he did not know that he knew it and thought he did not know it. That is to say, the position was exactly the same as what we suspected in our dreamer.

I hope you will be surprised that this fact has been established and will ask me: 'Why did you omit to bring this proof forward earlier, in connection with the parapraxes, when we came to the point of attributing to a man who had made a slip of the tongue an intention to say things of which he knew nothing and which he denied? If a person thinks he knows nothing of experiences the memory of which he nevertheless has within him, it is no longer so improbable that he knows nothing of other mental processes within him. This argument would certainly have impressed us, and helped us to understand parapraxes.' Of course

[1] [Freud returns to this on p. 277.]

I could have brought it forward then, but I reserved it for another place, where it was more needed. The parapraxes explained themselves in part, and in part left us with a suggestion that, in order to preserve the continuity of the phenomena concerned, it would be wise to assume the existence of mental processes of which the subject knows nothing. In the case of dreams we are compelled to bring in explanations from elsewhere and moreover I expect that in their case you will find it easier to accept my carrying over of the explanations from hypnosis. The state in which a parapraxis occurs is bound to strike you as being the normal one; it has no similarity with the hypnotic state. On the other hand there is an obvious kinship between the hypnotic state and the state of sleep, which is a necessary condition of dreaming. Hypnosis, indeed, is described as an artificial sleep. We tell the person we are hypnotizing to sleep, and the suggestions we make are comparable to the dreams of natural sleep. The psychical situations in the two cases are really analogous. In natural sleep we withdraw our interest from the whole external world; and in hypnotic sleep we also withdraw it from the whole world, but with the single exception of the person who has hypnotized us and with whom we remain in rapport. Incidentally, the sleep of a nursing mother, who remains in rapport with her child and can be woken only by him, is a normal counterpart of hypnotic sleep. So it scarcely seems a very bold venture to transpose a situation from hypnosis to natural sleep. The assumption that in a dreamer too a knowledge about his dreams is present, though it is inaccessible to him so that he himself does not believe it, is not something entirely out of the blue. It should be noticed, moreover, that a third line of approach to the study of dreams is opened at this point: from the stimuli which disturb sleep, from day-dreams, and now in addition from the suggested dreams of the hypnotic state.

We may now go back to our task with increased confidence perhaps. It is very probable, then, that the dreamer knows about his dream; the only question is how to make it possible for him to discover his knowledge and communicate it to us. We do not require him to tell us straight away the sense of his dream, but he will be able to find its origin, the circle of thoughts and interests from which it sprang. You will recall that in the case of the parapraxis the man was asked how he had arrived at the wrong word '*Vorschwein*' and the first thing that occurred to him[1] gave us the explanation. Our technique with dreams, then, is a very simple one, copied from this example. We shall once more ask the dreamer how he arrived at the dream, and once more his first remark is to be looked on as an explanation. Thus we disregard the distinction between his thinking or not thinking that he knows something, and we treat both cases as one and the same.

This technique is certainly very simple, but I fear it will rouse your liveliest opposition. You will say: 'A fresh assumption! the third! And the most unlikely of all! If I ask the dreamer what occurs to him in connection with the dream, is precisely the first thing that occurs to him going to bring the explanation we are hoping for? But nothing at all may occur to him, or heaven knows what may occur to him. I cannot see what an expectation of that kind is based on. That is really showing too much trust in Providence at a point where rather more exercise of the critical faculty would be appropriate. Besides, a dream is not a single wrong word; it consists of a number of elements. So which association are we to take up?'

You are correct on all your minor points. A dream differs from a slip of the tongue, among other things, in the multiplicity of its elements. Our technique must take this into account. I therefore suggest to you that we should divide the dream into its elements and start a separate enquiry into each element; if we do this, the analogy with a slip of the tongue is re-established. You are also right in thinking that when the dreamer is questioned about the separate elements of the dream he may reply that nothing occurs to him. There are some instances in which we let this reply pass, and you will later hear which these are [cf. p. 149]; strangely enough, they are instances in which definite ideas may occur to us ourselves. But in general if the dreamer asserts that nothing occurs to him we contradict him; we bring urgent pressure to bear on him, we insist that something must occur to him—and we turn out to be right. He will produce an idea—some idea, it is a matter of indifference to us which. He will give us certain pieces of information,

[1] [See footnote, p. 47 f.]

which may be described as 'historical', with particular ease. He may say: 'That's something that happened yesterday' (as was the case in our two 'matter-of-fact' dreams [p. 97]), or: 'That reminds me of something that happened a short time ago'—and we shall discover in this way that dreams are connected with impressions of the last day or two much more often than we thought to begin with [loc. cit.]. And finally he will also recall, starting from the dream, events from further back and even perhaps from the far distant past.

But on your main point you are wrong. If you think it is arbitrary to assume that the first thing that occurs to the dreamer is bound to bring what we are looking for or to lead us to it, if you think that what occurs to him might be anything in the world and might have no connection with what we are looking for, and that it is only exhibiting my trust in Providence if I expect something different—then you are making a great mistake. Once before [p. 49] I ventured to tell you that you nourish a deeply rooted faith in undetermined psychical events and in free will, but that this is quite unscientific and must yield to the demand of a determinism whose rule extends over mental life. I beg you to respect it as a fact that *that* is what occurred to the man when he was questioned and nothing else. But I am not opposing one faith with another. It can be proved that the idea produced by the man was not arbitrary nor indeterminable nor unconnected with what we were looking for. Indeed, not long ago I learnt—without, I may say, attaching too much importance to the fact—that experimental psychology too had brought up evidence to that effect.[1]

In view of the importance of the matter, I will ask for your special attention. If I ask someone to tell me what occurs to him in response to a particular element of a dream, I am asking him to surrender himself to free association *while keeping an idea in mind as a starting-point*. This calls for a special attitude of the attention which is quite different from reflection and which excludes reflection. Some people achieve this attitude with ease; others show an incredibly high degree of clumsiness when they attempt it. There is, however, a higher degree of freedom of

[1] [A footnote dealing with this was added by Freud in 1919 to his discussion of Recent and Indifferent Material in Dreams in *I. of D.*]

association: that is to say, I may drop the insistence on keeping an initial idea in mind and only lay down the sort or kind of association I want—I may, for instance, require the experimenter to allow a proper name or a number to occur to him freely. What then occurs to him would presumably be even more arbitrary and more indeterminable than with our own technique. It can be shown, however, that it is always strictly determined by important internal attitudes of mind which are not known to us at the moment at which they operate—which are as little known to us as the disturbing purposes of parapraxes and the provoking ones of chance actions [p. 61].

I and many others after me have repeatedly made such experiments with names and numbers thought of at random, and a few of these have been published.[1] Here the procedure is to produce a series of associations to the name which has emerged; these latter associations are accordingly no longer completely free but have a link, like the associations to the elements of dreams. One continues doing this until one finds the impulse exhausted. But by then light will have been thrown both on the motive and the meaning of the random choice of the name. These experiments always lead to the same result; reports on them often cover a wealth of material and call for extensive expositions. The associations to *numbers* chosen at random are perhaps the most convincing; they run off so quickly and proceed with such incredible certainty to a hidden goal that the effect is really staggering. I will give you only one example of an analysis like this of a name, since dealing with it calls for a conveniently small amount of material.

In the course of treating a young man I had occasion to discuss this topic, and mentioned the thesis that, in spite of an apparently arbitrary choice, it is impossible to think of a name at random which does not turn out to be closely determined by the immediate circumstances, the characteristics of the subject of the experiment and his situation at the moment. Since he was sceptical, I suggested that he should make an experiment of the kind himself on the spot. I knew that he carried on particularly numerous relationships of every kind with married women and

---

[1] [Several examples are given in Section A of Chapter XII of *The Psychopathology of Everyday Life* (1901*b*), (Norton, 1965), where the whole topic is discussed at length.]

girls, so I thought he would have a specially large choice open to him if it were to be a woman's name that he was asked to choose. He agreed to this. To my astonishment, or rather, perhaps, to his, no avalanche of women's names broke over me; he remained silent for a moment and then admitted that only a single name had come into his head and none other besides: 'Albine'.—How curious! But what does that name mean to you? How many 'Albines' do you know?—Strange to say, he knew no one called 'Albine' and nothing further occurred to him in response to the name. So it might be thought that the analysis had failed. But not at all: it was already complete, and no further associations were needed. The man had an unusually fair complexion and in conversation during the treatment I had often jokingly called him an albino. We were engaged at the time in determining the feminine part of his constitution. So it was he himself who was this 'Albine', the woman who was the most interesting to him at the moment.

In the same way tunes that come into one's head without warning turn out to be determined by and to belong to a train of thought which has a right to occupy one's mind though without one's being aware of its activity. It is easy to show then that the relation to the tune is based on its text or its origin. But I must be careful not to extend this assertion to really musical people, of whom, as it happens, I have had no experience. It may be that for such people the musical content of the tune is what decides its emergence. The earlier case is certainly the commoner one. I know of a young man, for instance, who was positively persecuted for a time by the tune (incidentally a charming one) of Paris's song in [Offenbach's] *La belle Hélène*, till his analysis drew his attention to a contemporary competition in his interest between an 'Ida' and a 'Helen'.[1]

If then things that occur to one quite freely are determined in this way and form parts of a connected whole, we shall no doubt be justified in concluding that things that occur to one with a single link—namely their link with the idea which serves as their starting-point—cannot be any less determined. Investigation shows, in fact, that, apart from the link we have given

[1] [Paris, who eloped with Helen, was at one time a shepherd on Mount Ida, where he delivered his judgement between three competing goddesses.]

them with the initial idea, they are found to be dependent as well on groups of strongly emotional thoughts and interests, 'complexes', whose participation is not known at the moment —that is to say, is unconscious.

The occurrence of ideas with links of this kind has been the subject of very instructive experimental researches, which have played a notable part in the history of psycho-analysis. The school of Wundt had introduced what are known as association-experiments, in which a *stimulus word* is called out to the subject and he has the task of replying to it as quickly as possible with any *reaction* that occurs to him. It is then possible to study the interval that passes between the stimulus and the reaction, the nature of the answer given as a reaction, possible errors when the same experiment is repeated later, and so on. The Zurich school, led by Bleuler and Jung, found the explanation of the reactions that followed in the association-experiment by getting the subjects to throw light on their reactions by means of subsequent associations, if those reactions had shown striking features. It then turned out that these striking reactions were determined in the most definite fashion by the subject's complexes. In this manner Bleuler and Jung built the first bridge from experimental psychology to psycho-analysis.

Having learnt thus much, you will be able to say: 'We acknowledge now that thoughts that occur to one freely are determined and not arbitrary as we supposed. We admit that this is also true of thoughts occurring in response to the elements of dreams. But that is not what we are concerned with. You assert that what occurs to the dreamer in response to the dream-element will be determined by the psychical background (unknown to us) of that particular element. This does not seem to us to be proved. We quite expect that what occurs to the dreamer in response to the dream-element will turn out to be determined by one of the dreamer's complexes, but what good does that do us? This does not lead us to an understanding of dreams but, like the association-experiment, to a knowledge of these so-called complexes. But what have they got to do with dreams?'

You are right, but you are overlooking one factor. Moreover it is precisely the factor on account of which I did not choose the association-experiment as the starting-point of this exposition. In that experiment the single determinant of the reaction—that is, the stimulus-word—is arbitrarily chosen by us. The reaction is in that case an intermediary between the stimulus-word and the complex which has been aroused in the subject. In dreams the stimulus-word is replaced by something that is itself derived from the dreamer's mental life, from sources unknown to him, and may therefore very easily itself be a 'derivative of a complex'. It is therefore not precisely fantastic to suppose that the further associations linked to the dream-elements will be determined by the same complex as that of the element itself and will lead to its discovery.

Let me show you from another instance that the facts are as we expect. The forgetting of proper names is actually an excellent model of what happens in dream-analysis; the difference is only that events that are shared between two people in dream-analysis are combined in a single person in the parapraxis. If I forget a name temporarily, I nevertheless feel in myself a certainty that I know it—a certainty which in the case of the dreamer we only arrived at by the round-about path of the Bernheim experiment [p. 103]. The name which I have forgotten but which I know is, however, not accessible to me. Experience soon teaches me that thinking about it, with however much effort, is of no help. But in place of the forgotten name I can always call up one or several substitute names. It is only after a substitute name of this kind has occurred to me spontaneously that the conformity of this situation with that of dream-interpretation becomes obvious. Like this substitute name, the dream-element is not the right thing, but only takes the place of something else—of the genuine thing which I do not know and which I am to discover by means of the dream-analysis. The difference is once more only that in the case of forgetting the name, I recognize the substitute unhesitatingly as something ungenuine, whereas we had to acquire this view laboriously in the case of the dream-element. Now in the case of forgetting a name there is also a method by which we can start from the substitute and arrive at the unconscious genuine thing, the forgotten name. If I direct my attention to the substitute names and allow further ideas in response to them to occur to me, I arrive by shorter or longer détours at the forgotten name, and I find when this happens that both the spontaneous substitute name and the ones that I have called up are connected with the forgotten one and were determined by it.

I will describe an analysis of this kind to you. I noticed one day that I could not recall the name of the small country on the Riviera, of which Monte Carlo is the chief town. It was very tiresome, but so it was. I summoned up all that I knew about that country. I thought of Prince Albert of the House of Lusignan, of his marriages, of his devotion to deep-sea researches, and everything else I could bring together, but it was of no avail. So I gave up reflection and allowed substitute names to occur to me instead of the lost one. They came rapidly: Monte Carlo itself, then Piedmont, Albania, Montevideo, Colico. Of this series I was struck first by Albania, which was at once replaced by Montenegro, no doubt because of the contrast between white and black.[1] I then saw that four of these substitute names contained the same syllable 'mon', then suddenly I had the forgotten word and exclaimed aloud: 'Monaco!' So the substitute names had in fact arisen from the forgotten one: the first four came from its first syllable while the last reproduced its syllabic structure and its whole last syllable. Moreover I was able to discover quite easily what it was that had temporarily deprived me of the name. Monaco is also the Italian name for Munich; and it was that town which exerted the inhibitory influence.[2]

No doubt this example is a good one, but it is too simple. In other cases it would have been necessary to call up a longer string of ideas in response to the first substitute name. I have had experiences of that sort too. On one occasion a stranger had invited me to drink some Italian wine with him, but when we were in the inn it turned out that he had forgotten the name of the wine which he intended to order because of his very agreeable recollections of it. From a quantity of substitute ideas of different kinds which came into his head in place of the forgotten name, I was able to infer that thoughts about someone called Hedwig had made him forget the name. And he not only confirmed the fact that he had first tasted this wine when he

[1] ['*Albus*' the Latin for 'white', and '*negro*' the Italian for 'black'.]

[2] [This episode is decribed more briefly in *The Psychopathology of Everyday Life*, p. 55.]

was with someone of that name, but with the help of this discovery he recalled the name of the wine. He was happily married at the present time and this Hedwig belonged to earlier days which he had no wish to remember.

But if it is possible in the case of forgetting a name, it must also be possible in interpreting dreams to proceed from the substitute along the chain of associations attached to it and so to obtain access to the genuine thing which is being held back. From the example of the forgotten name we may conclude that the associations to the dream-element will be determined both by the dream-element and also by the unconscious genuine thing behind it. In this way, then, we seem to have produced some justification of our technique.

LECTURE VII

THE MANIFEST CONTENT OF DREAMS AND THE LATENT DREAM-THOUGHTS

LADIES AND GENTLEMEN,—As you see, our study of parapraxes has not been unprofitable. Thanks to our labours over them we have, subject to the premises I have explained to you,[1] achieved two things: a conception of the nature of dream-elements and a technique for interpreting dreams. The conception of dream-elements tells us that they are ungenuine things [p. 110], substitutes for something else that is unknown to the dreamer (like the purpose of a parapraxis), substitutes for something the knowledge of which is present in the dreamer but which is inaccessible to him. We are in hopes that it will be possible to carry over the same conception to whole dreams, which are made up of such elements. Our technique lies in employing free association to these elements in order to bring about the emergence of other substitutive structures, which will enable us to arrive at what is concealed from view.

I now propose that we should introduce a change into our nomenclature which will give us more freedom of movement. Instead of speaking of 'concealed', 'inaccessible', or 'ungenuine',[2] let us adopt the correct description and say 'inaccessible to the dreamer's consciousness' or *'unconscious'*.[3] I mean nothing else by this than what may be suggested to you when you think of a word that has escaped you or the disturbing purpose in a parapraxis—that is to say, I mean nothing else than *'unconscious at the moment'*. In contrast to this, we can of course speak of the dream-elements themselves, and the substitutive ideas that have been newly arrived at from them by association, as *'conscious'*. This nomenclature so far involves no

---

[1] [See pp. 100 and 101.]

[2] ['*Uneigentlich*' in all the German editions. The sense would seem to require '*eigentlich* (genuine)'.]

[3] [Cf. Lecture I, p. 21; the discussion is continued below in Lecture XIII, p. 212.]

theoretical construction. No objection can be made to using the word 'unconscious' as an apt and easily understandable description.

If we carry over our conception of the separate elements to the whole dream, it follows that the dream as a whole is a distorted substitute for something else, something unconscious, and that the task of interpreting a dream is to discover this unconscious material. From this, however, there at once follow three important rules, which we must obey during the work of interpreting dreams.

(1) We must not concern ourselves with what the dream *appears* to tell us, whether it is intelligible or absurd, clear or confused, since it cannot possibly be the unconscious material we are in search of. (An obvious limitation to this rule will force itself on our notice later [p. 126].) (2) We must restrict our work to calling up the substitutive ideas for each element, we must not reflect about them, or consider whether they contain anything relevant, and we must not trouble ourselves with how far they diverge from the dream-element. (3) We must wait till the concealed unconscious material we are in search of emerges of its own accord, exactly as the forgotten word 'Monaco' did in the experiment I have described [p. 111].

Now, too, we can understand to what extent it is a matter of indifference how much or how little the dream is remembered and, above all, how accurately or how uncertainly. For the remembered dream is not the genuine material but a distorted substitute for it, which should assist us, by calling up other substitutive images, to come nearer to the genuine material, to make what is unconscious in the dream conscious. If our memory has been inaccurate, therefore, it has merely made a further distortion of this substitute—a distortion, moreover, which cannot have been without a reason.

The work of interpreting can be performed on one's own dreams just as on other people's. In fact one learns more from one's own: the process carries more conviction. If, then, we make the attempt, we notice that something is opposing our work. It is true that ideas occur to us, but we do not allow all of them to count; testing and selecting influences make themselves felt. In the case of one idea we may say to ourselves: 'No, this is not relevant, it does not belong here'; in the case of another: 'this is too senseless' and of a third: 'this is totally un-important'. And we can further observe how with objections of this sort we may smother ideas and finally expel them alto-gether, even before they have become quite clear. Thus on the one hand we keep too close to the idea which was our starting-point, the dream-element itself; and on the other hand we inter-fere with the outcome of the free associations by making a selection. If we are not by ourselves while interpreting the dream, if we get someone else to interpret it, we become very clearly aware of yet another motive which we employ in making this illicit selection, for sometimes we say to our-selves: 'No, this idea is too disagreeable; I will not or cannot report it.'

These objections are obviously a threat to the success of our work. We must guard against them, and in our own case we do so by firmly resolving not to give way to them. If we are analysing someone else's dream, we do so by laying it down as an inviolable rule that he must not hold back any idea from us, even if it gives rise to one of the four objections—of being too unimportant or too senseless or of being irrelevant or too dis-tressing to be reported.[1] The dreamer promises to obey the rule, and we may be annoyed afterwards to find how badly he keeps his promise when the occasion arises. We may explain this to ourselves to begin with by supposing that, in spite of our authoritative assurance, he has not yet realized the justification for free association, and we may perhaps have the notion of first convincing him theoretically by giving him books to read or by sending him to lectures which may convert him into a supporter of our views on free association. But we shall be held back from blunders like this when we consider that in the case of our-selves, as to the strength of whose convictions we can, after all, hardly be in doubt, the same objections arise to certain ideas and are only set aside subsequently—by a court of appeal, as it were.

Instead of being annoyed by the dreamer's disobedience, we may take advantage of these experiences by learning something new from them—something which is all the more important the

[1] [Freud returns to this 'fundamental technical rule of analysis' in Lecture XIX, p. 287 below, where an Editor's footnote gives further references.]

less we are expecting it. We perceive that the work of interpreting dreams is carried out in the face of a *resistance*, which
opposes it and of which the critical objections are manifestations.[1] This resistance is independent of the dreamer's theoretical conviction. We learn still more, indeed. We discover that a
critical objection of this kind never turns out to be justified. On
the contrary, the ideas which people try to suppress in this way
turn out *invariably* to be the most important ones and those
which are decisive in our search for the unconscious material.
It amounts, in fact, to a special distinguishing mark, if an idea
is accompanied by an objection like this.

This resistance is something entirely new: a phenomenon
which we have come upon in connection with our premises
[p. 101 f.], but one which was not included among them. The
appearance of this new factor in our reckoning comes to us as a
not altogether pleasant surprise. We suspect at once that it is
not going to make our work any easier. It might mislead us into
abandoning our whole concern with dreams: something so unimportant as a dream and, on top of that, all these difficulties
instead of a simple straightforward technique! But, on the other
hand, the difficulties might act precisely as a stimulus and make
us suspect that the work will be worth the trouble. We regularly
come up against resistance when we try to make our way forward from the substitute which is the dream-element to the unconscious material hidden behind it. So we may conclude that
there must be something of importance concealed behind the
substitute. Otherwise, what is the point of the difficulties that
are trying to keep the concealment going? If a child refuses to
open his clenched fist to show what he has in it, we may feel
sure that it is something wrong—something he ought not to
have.

The moment we introduce the dynamic idea of a resistance
into the facts of the case, we must simultaneously reflect that
this factor is something variable in quantity. There may be
greater and smaller resistances, and we are prepared to find
these differences showing themselves during our work as well.
We may perhaps be able to link with this another experience
we also meet with during the work of interpreting dreams:
sometimes it requires only a single response, or no more than a

---

[1] [The subject of 'resistance' is fully dealt with in Lecture XIX.]

few, to lead us from a dream-element to the unconscious material behind it, while on other occasions long chains of associations and the overcoming of many critical objections are required for bringing this about. We shall conclude that these differences relate to the changing magnitude of the resistance, and we shall probably turn out to be right.[1] If the resistance is small, the substitute cannot be far distant from the unconscious material; but a greater resistance means that the unconscious material will be greatly distorted and that the path will be a long one from the substitute back to the unconscious material.

And now perhaps it is time to take a dream and try our technique upon it and see whether our expectations are confirmed. Yes, but what dream are we to choose for the purpose? You cannot imagine how hard I find it to decide; nor can I yet make the nature of my difficulties plain to you. There must obviously be dreams which have on the whole been subjected to only a little distortion, and the best plan would be to begin with them. But what dreams have been least distorted? The ones that are intelligible and not confused, two examples of which I have already put before you [p. 97]? That would be leading us quite astray. Investigation shows that such dreams have been subjected to an extraordinarily high degree of distortion. If, however, I were to disregard particular requirements and were to select a dream at haphazard, you would probably be greatly disappointed. We might have to notice or record such a profusion of ideas in response to the separate dream-elements that we should be unable to make head or tail of the work. If we write down a dream and then make a note of all the ideas that emerge in response to it, these may prove to be many times longer than the text of the dream. The best plan would therefore seem to be to choose out a number of short dreams for analysis, each of which will at least tell us something or confirm some point. So we will make up our minds to take that course, unless experience may perhaps show us where we can really find dreams that have been only slightly distorted.[2]

---

[1] [Freud discussed the effects on dream-interpretation of a high or low pressure of resistance in Section II of his 'Remarks on the Theory and Practice of Dream-Interpretation' (1923c).]

[2] [See the following lecture.]

I can however think of something else that will make things easier for us—something, moreover, which lies along our path. Instead of starting on the interpretation of *whole* dreams, we will restrict ourselves to a few dream-elements, and we will trace out in a number of examples how these can be explained by applying our technique to them.

(*a*) A lady reported that she very often dreamt when she was a child that *God wore a paper cocked-hat on his head.* What can you make of that without the dreamer's help? It sounds completely nonsensical. But it ceases to be nonsense when we hear from the lady that she used to have a hat of that sort put on her head at meals when she was a child, because she could never resist taking furtive glances at her brothers' and sisters' plates to see whether they had been given larger helpings than she had. So the hat was intended to act like a pair of blinkers. This, incidentally, was a piece of historical information [p. 105 f.] and was given without any difficulty. The interpretation of this element and at the same time of the whole short dream was easily made with the help of a further idea that occurred to the dreamer: 'As I had heard that God was omniscient and saw everything', she said, 'the dream can only mean that I knew everything and saw everything, even though they tried to prevent me.' [1] Perhaps this example is too simple.

(*b*) A sceptical woman patient had a longish dream in the course of which some people told her about my book on jokes [1905*c*] and praised it highly. Something came in then about *a 'channel', perhaps it was another book that mentioned a channel, or something else about a channel . . . she didn't know . . . it was all so indistinct.*

No doubt you will be inclined to expect that the element 'channel', since it was so indistinct, would be inaccessible to interpretation. You are right in suspecting a difficulty; but the difficulty did not arise from the indistinctness: both the difficulty and the indistinctness arose from another cause. Nothing occurred to the dreamer in connection with 'channel', and *I* could of course throw no light on it. A little later—it was the next day, in point of fact—she told me that she had thought of

[1] [This dream is reported in Section F of Chapter VI of *I. of D.*]

something that *might* have something to do with it. It was a joke, too,—a joke she had heard. On the steamer between Dover and Calais a well-known author fell into conversation with an Englishman. The latter had occasion to quote the phrase: 'Du sublime au ridicule il n'y a qu'un pas. [It is only a step from the sublime to the ridiculous.]' 'Yes,' replied the author, *'le Pas de Calais'*—meaning that he thought France sublime and England ridiculous. But the *Pas de Calais* is a channel—the English Channel. You will ask whether I think this had anything to do with the dream. Certainly I think so; and it provides the solution of the puzzling element of the dream. Can you doubt that this joke was already present before the dream occurred, as the unconscious thought behind the element 'channel'? Can you suppose that it was introduced as a subsequent invention? The association betrayed the scepticism which lay concealed behind the patient's ostensible admiration; and her resistance against revealing this was no doubt the common cause both of her delay in producing the association and of the indistinctness of the dream-element concerned. Consider the relation of the dream-element to its unconscious background: it was, as it were, a fragment of the background, an allusion to it, but it was made quite incomprehensible by being isolated.[1]

(c) As part of a longish dream a patient dreamt that *several members of his family were sitting round a table of a peculiar shape,* etc. It occurred to him in connection with the table that he had seen a piece of furniture of the kind when he was on a visit to a particular family. His thoughts then went on to say that there was a peculiar relationship between the father and son in this family; and he soon added that the same thing was true of the relationship between himself and his own father. So the table had been taken into the dream in order to point out this parallel.

This dreamer had been long familiar with the requirement of dream-interpretation. Another person might perhaps have taken objection to such a trivial detail as the shape of a table being made the subject of investigation. But in fact we regard nothing in a dream as accidental or indifferent, and we expect

[1] [The whole of this example (*b*) was inserted by Freud into *I. of D.* as a footnote in 1919. See Section A of Chapter VII.]

to obtain information precisely from the explanation of such trivial and pointless details. You may perhaps also feel surprised that the thought that 'the same thing was true of us and of them' should have been expressed by, in particular, the choice of a table [*Tisch*]. But this too becomes clear when you learn that the name of the family in question was *Tischler* [literally, 'carpenter']. By making his relations sit at this *Tisch*, he was saying that they too were *Tischlers*. Incidentally, you will notice how inevitably one is led into being indiscreet when one reports these dream-interpretations. And you will guess that this is one of the difficulties I have hinted at over the choice of examples. I could easily have taken another example in place of this one, but I should probably merely have avoided *this* indiscretion at the price of committing another.

The moment seems to me to have arrived for introducing two terms, which we could have made use of long ago. We will describe what the dream actually tells us as the *manifest dream-content*, and the concealed material, which we hope to reach by pursuing the ideas that occur to the dreamer, as the *latent dream-thoughts*. Thus we are here considering the relations between the manifest content of the dream and the latent dream-thoughts as shown in these examples. These relations may be of very many different kinds. In examples (*a*) and (*b*) the manifest element is also a constituent of the latent thoughts, though only a small fragment of them. A small piece of the large and complicated psychical structure of unconscious dream-thoughts has made its way into the manifest dream as well—a fragment of them, or, in other cases, an allusion to them, a caption, as it were, or an abbreviation in telegraphic style. It is the business of the work of interpretation to complete these fragments or this allusion into a whole—which was achieved particularly nicely in the case of example (*b*). Thus one form of the distortion which constitutes the dream-work is replacement by a fragment or an allusion. In example (*c*) another kind of relation is to be observed in addition; and we shall find this expressed in a purer and clearer form in the examples which follow.

(*d*) The dreamer *was pulling a lady* (a particular one, of his acquaintance) *out from behind a bed*. He himself found the meaning of this dream-element from the first idea that occurred to him. It meant that he was giving this lady preference.[1]

(*e*) Another man dreamt that *his brother was in a box* [*Kasten*]. In his first response '*Kasten*' was replaced by '*Schrank* [cupboard]', and the second gave the interpretation: his brother was restricting himself ['*schränkt sich ein*'].[2]

(*f*) The dreamer *climbed to the top of a mountain, which commanded an unusually extensive view*. This sounds quite rational and you might suppose that there is nothing to interpret in it and that all we have to do is to enquire what memory gave rise to the dream and the reason for its being stirred up. But you would be wrong. It turned out that this dream stood in need of interpreting just as much as any other, more confused one. For none of his own mountain climbs occurred to the dreamer, but he thought of the fact that an acquaintance of his was the editor of a 'Survey', dealing with our relations with the most remote parts of the earth. Thus the latent dream-thought was an identification of the dreamer with the 'surveyor'.

Here we have a new type of relation between the manifest and latent dream-elements. The former is not so much a distortion of the latter as a representation of it, a plastic, concrete, portrayal of it, taking its start from the wording. But precisely on that account it is once more a distortion, for we have long since forgotten from what concrete image the word originated and consequently fail to recognize it when it is replaced by the image. When you consider that the manifest dream is made up predominantly of visual images and more rarely of thoughts and words, you can imagine what importance attaches to this kind of relation in the construction of dreams. You will see, too, that in this way it becomes possible in regard to a large number of abstract thoughts to create pictures to act as substitutes for them in the manifest dream while at the same time serving the purpose of concealment. This is the technique of the familiar

[1] [This example, like the next, depends on a purely verbal point: the resemblance between the German words for 'pulling out' (*hervorziehen*) and 'preferring' (*vorziehen*). See Section F of Chapter VI of *I. of D.*]

[2] [This and the next example are also from Section F of Chapter VI of *I. of D.*]

picture-puzzles. Why it is that these representations have an appearance of being jokes is a special problem into which we need not enter here.[1]

There is a fourth kind of relation between the manifest and latent elements, which I must continue to hold back from you until we come upon its key-word in considering technique.[2] Even so I shall not have given you a full list; but it will serve our purpose.

Do you feel bold enough now to venture upon the interpretation of a *whole* dream? Let us make the experiment, to see whether we are well enough equipped for the task. I shall of course not select one of the most obscure ones; nevertheless, it will be one that gives a well-marked picture of the attributes of a dream.[3]

Very well then. A lady who, though she was still young, had been married for many years had the following dream: *She was at the theatre with her husband. One side of the stalls was completely empty. Her husband told her that Elise L. and her fiancé had wanted to go too, but had only been able to get bad seats—three for 1 florin 50 kreuzers[4]—and of course they could not take those. She thought it would not really have done any harm if they had.*

The first thing the dreamer reported to us was that the precipitating cause of the dream was touched on in its manifest content. Her husband had in fact told her that Elise L., who was approximately her contemporary, had just become engaged. The dream was a reaction to this information. We know already [p. 106] that it is easy in the case of many dreams to point to a precipitating cause like this from the previous day, and that the dreamer is often able to trace this for us without any difficulty. The dreamer in the present case put similar in-

---

[1] [See the discussion of the point in Chapter VI of Freud's book on jokes (1905c), (Norton, 1960), p. 173; cf. also p. 235 f. below.]

[2] [See below, p. 151.]

[3] [The dream which follows had been analysed, but very much less elaborately, in *I. of D.*, Chap. VI (F). It is also discussed in Chapters VII and VIII of the short work *On Dreams* (1901a), (Norton, 1952). Freud returns to it in these lectures at several points: pp. 139–40, 178, 219–21 and 224–5 below.]

[4] [This had at the time been worth approximately 2s. 6d. or 62½ cents.]

formation at our disposal for other elements of the manifest dream as well.—Where did the detail come from about one side of the stalls being empty? It was an allusion to a real event of the previous week. She had planned to go to a particular play and had therefore bought her tickets *early*—so early that she had had to pay a booking fee. When they got to the theatre it turned out that her anxiety was quite uncalled-for, since *one side of the stalls was almost empty*. It would have been early enough if she had bought the tickets on the actual day of the performance. Her husband had kept on teasing her for having been in too much of a hurry.—What was the origin of the 1 florin 50 kreuzers? It arose in quite another connection, which had nothing to do with the former one but also alluded to some information from the previous day. Her sister-in-law had been given a present of 150 florins by her husband and had been in a great hurry—the silly goose—to rush off to the jewellers' and exchange the money for a piece of jewellery.—Where did the 'three' come from? She could think of nothing in connection with that, unless we counted the idea that her newly-engaged friend, Elise L., was only three months her junior, though she herself had been a married woman for nearly ten years.—And the absurd notion of taking three tickets for only two people? She had nothing to say to that, and refused to report any further ideas or information.

But all the same, she had given us so much material in these few associations that it was possible to guess the latent dream-thoughts from them. We cannot help being struck by the fact that periods of time occur at several points in the information she gave us about the dream, and these provide a common factor between the different parts of the material. She took the theatre tickets *too early*, bought them *over-hurriedly* so that she had to pay more than was necessary; so too her sister-in-law had been *in a hurry* to take her money to the jewellers and buy some jewellery with it, as though otherwise she would *miss it*. If, in addition to the 'too early' and 'in a hurry' which we have stressed, we take into account the precipitating cause of the dream—the news that her friend, though only three months *her junior*, had nevertheless got an excellent husband—and the criticism of her sister-in-law expressed in the idea that it was *absurd* of her to be in such a hurry, then we find ourselves presented almost spontaneously with the following construction of the latent dream-thoughts, for which the manifest dream is a severely distorted substitute:

'Really it was *absurd* of me to be in such a hurry to get married! I can see from Elise's example that *I* could have got a husband later too.' (Being in too great a hurry was represented by her own behaviour in buying the tickets and by her sister-in-law's in buying the jewellery. Going to the play appeared as a substitute for getting married.) This would seem to be the main thought. We may perhaps proceed further, though with less certainty, since the analysis ought not to have been without the dreamer's comments at these points: 'And I could have got one a hundred times better with the money!' (150 florins is a hundred times more than 1 florin 50.) If we were to put her dowry in place of the money, it would mean that her husband was bought with her dowry: the jewellery, and the bad tickets as well, would be substitutes for her husband. It would be still more satisfactory if the actual element 'three tickets' had something to do with a husband. [Cf. below, p. 220.] But we have not got so far as that in our understanding of the dream. We have only discovered that the dream expresses the *low value* assigned by her to her own husband and her regret at having *married so early*.

We shall, I fancy, be more surprised and confused than satisfied by the outcome of this first dream-interpretation. We have been given too much in one dose—more than we are yet able to cope with. We can already see that we shall not exhaust the lessons of this interpretation of a dream. Let us hasten to single out what we can recognize as established new discoveries.

In the first place, it is a remarkable thing that the main emphasis in the latent thoughts lies on the element of being in too great a hurry; nothing of the sort is to be found in the manifest dream. Without the analysis, we should have had no suspicion that that factor plays any part. It seems, therefore, to be possible for what is in fact the main thing, the centre of the unconscious thoughts, to be absent in the manifest dream. This means that the impression made by the whole dream must be fundamentally altered. In the second place, there is an absurd combination in the dream: three for 1 florin 50. We detected in the dream-thoughts the assertion that 'it was absurd (to marry so early)'. Can it be doubted that this thought, 'it was absurd', is represented by the inclusion of an absurd element in the manifest dream? And in the third place, a glance of comparison shows us that the relation between the manifest and latent elements is no simple one; it is far from being the case that one manifest element always takes the place of one latent one. It is rather that there is a group-relation between the two layers, within which one manifest element can replace several latent ones or one latent element can be replaced by several manifest ones. [Cf. below, p. 173.]

As regards the meaning of the dream and the dreamer's attitude to it, we might point out much that is similarly surprising. She agreed to the interpretation indeed, but she was astonished at it. She was not aware that she assigned such a low value to her husband; nor did she know *why* she should set such a low value on him. So there is still much that is unintelligible about it. It really seems to me that we are not yet equipped for interpreting a dream and that we need first to be given some further instruction and preparation.

LECTURE VIII

CHILDREN'S DREAMS

LADIES AND GENTLEMEN,—I am under the impression that we have advanced too quickly. Let us go back a little. Before we made our last attempt at overcoming the difficulty of distortion in dreams by the help of our technique, we were saying [p. 117] that our best plan would be to get round the difficulty by keeping to dreams in which there was no distortion or only a very little—if such dreams exist. This will once more mean a divergence from the historical development of our discoveries [cf. p. 83]; for actually it was only after the technique of interpretation had been consistently applied and distorted dreams had been completely analysed that the existence of dreams that are free from distortion came to our notice.

The dreams we are in search of occur in children.[1] They are short, clear, coherent, easy to understand and unambiguous; but they are nevertheless undoubtedly dreams. You must not suppose, however, that all children's dreams are of this kind. Dream-distortion sets in very early in childhood, and dreams dreamt by children of between five and eight have been reported which bear all the characteristics of later ones. But if you limit yourselves to ages between the beginning of observable mental activity and the fourth or fifth year, you will come upon a number of dreams which possess the characteristics that can be described as 'infantile' and you will find a few of the same kind in later years of childhood. Indeed, under certain conditions even adults have dreams which are quite similar to the typically infantile ones.

From these children's dreams we can draw conclusions with great ease and certainty on the essential nature of dreams in general, and we can hope that those conclusions will prove decisive and universally valid.

(1) No analysis, no application of any technique is necessary

[1] [There is no separate chapter on children's dreams in *I. of D.*, but they are dealt with in Chapter III, where the examples in the present lecture will be found again.]

126

in order to understand these dreams. There is no need to question a child who tells us his dream. One has, however, to add a piece of information to it from the events of the child's life. There is invariably some experience of the previous day which explains the dream to us. The dream is the reaction of the child's mental life in his sleep to this experience of the previous day.

We will take a few examples on which to base our further conclusions.

(*a*) A boy of 22 months was told to hand over a basket of cherries to someone as a birthday present. He was obviously very unwilling to do it, although he was promised that he should have a few of them for himself. Next morning he reported having dreamt: '*Hermann eaten all the chewwies!*'

(*b*) A girl of 3¼ years was taken across the lake for the first time. At the landing-stage she did not want to leave the boat and wept bitterly. The crossing had been too short for her. Next morning she announced: '*Last night I went on the lake.*' We may safely add that this crossing had lasted longer.

(*c*) A boy of 5¼ years was taken on an excursion up the Echerntal near Hallstatt.[1] He had been told that Hallstatt was at the foot of the Dachstein. He had shown great interest in this mountain. There was a fine view of it from where he was staying at Aussee, and the Simony Hut on it could be made out through a telescope. The child had often tried to see it through the telescope—with what success was not known. The excursion began in an atmosphere of cheerful expectation. Whenever a fresh mountain came into view the boy asked: 'Is that the Dachstein?' and he became more and more depressed the more often he was told it was not. Finally he fell completely silent and refused to go with the rest of the party up the short ascent to the waterfall, and it was thought that he must be overtired. But next morning he said with a radiant face: 'Last night I dreamt *we were at the Simony Hut.*' So that had been what he expected to do on the excursion. He gave no further details except something he had heard before: 'You have to climb up steps for six hours.'

These three dreams will give us all the information we require.

(2) As we can see, these children's dreams are not senseless. They are intelligible, completely valid mental acts. You will

---

[1] [In the Salzkammergut district of Upper Austria.]

recall what I told you of the medical view of dreams and of the analogy with unmusical fingers wandering over the keys of a piano [p. 87]. You cannot fail to observe how sharply these children's dreams contradict this view. It would really be too strange if *children* could perform complete mental functions in their sleep while *adults* were content under the same conditions with reactions which were no more than 'twitchings'. Moreover, we have every reason to think that children's sleep is sounder and deeper.

(3) These dreams are without any dream-distortion, and therefore call for no interpretative activity. Here the manifest and the latent dream coincide. *Thus dream-distortion is not part of the essential nature of dreams.* I expect this will be a weight off your minds. But when we examine these dreams more closely, we shall recognize a small piece of dream-distortion even in them, a certain distinction between the manifest content of the dream and the latent dream-thoughts.

(4) A child's dream is a reaction to an experience of the previous day, which has left behind it a regret, a longing, a wish that has not been dealt with. *The dream produces a direct, undisguised fulfilment of that wish.* Let us recall now our discussions on the part played by somatic stimuli from outside and from within as disturbers of sleep and instigators of dreams [p. 91 ff.]. In that connection we came to know some quite undoubted facts, but by their means we were only able to explain a small number of dreams. In these children's dreams, however, there is nothing that points to the operation of somatic stimuli of that kind; we could not be mistaken in this, for the dreams are completely intelligible and easy to grasp. But this does not mean that we need abandon the stimulus aetiology of dreams. We can only ask how it has happened that from the first we have forgotten that besides somatic stimuli there are *mental* stimuli that disturb sleep. We know, after all, that it is excitations of this kind that are chiefly responsible for disturbing the sleep of an adult by preventing him from establishing the mood required for falling asleep—the withdrawing of interest from the world. He does not want to interrupt his life but would rather continue his work on the things he is concerned with, and for that reason he does not fall asleep. In the case of children, therefore, the stimulus that disturbs sleep is a mental one—the wish that has

not been dealt with—and it is to this that they react with the dream.

(5) This gives us the most direct approach to understanding the function of dreams. In so far as a dream is a reaction to a psychical stimulus, it must be equivalent to dealing with the stimulus in such a way that it is got rid of and that sleep can continue. We do not yet know how this dealing with the stimulus by the dream is made possible dynamically, but we see already that *dreams are not disturbers of sleep*, as they are abusively called, but *guardians of sleep which get rid of disturbances of sleep*. We think we should have slept more soundly if there had been no dream, but we are wrong; in fact, without the help of the dream we should not have slept at all. It is due to it that we have slept as soundly as we have. It could not avoid disturbing us a little, just as the night-watchman often cannot help making a little noise while he chases away the disturbers of the peace who seek to waken us with their noise.

(6) What instigates a dream is a wish, and the fulfilment of that wish is the content of the dream—this is one of the chief characteristics of dreams. The other, equally constant one, is that a dream does not simply give expression to a thought, but represents the wish fulfilled as a hallucinatory experience.[1] '*I should like to go on the lake*' is the wish that instigates the dream. The content of the dream itself is: '*I am going on the lake.*' Thus even in these simple children's dreams a difference remains between the latent and the manifest dream, there is a distortion of the latent dream-thought: *the transformation of a thought into an experience*. In the process of interpreting a dream this alteration must first be undone. If this turns out to be the most universal characteristic of dreams, the fragment of dream which I reported to you earlier [p. 121] 'I saw my brother in a box [*Kasten*]' is not to be translated 'my brother is restricting himself [*schränkt sich ein*]' but 'I should like my brother to restrict himself: *my brother must restrict himself.*' Of the two general characteristics of dreams which I have here brought forward, the second clearly has more prospect of being accepted without

---

[1] [It will be noted that the two 'chief characteristics' or 'general characteristics of dreams' considered in what follows are not the same as the two 'things common to all dreams' discussed in Lecture V, p. 88 ff. above.]

contradiction than the first. It is only by means of far-reaching investigations that we shall be able to establish the fact that what instigates dreams must always be a wish and cannot be a worry or an intention or a reproach; but this will not affect the other characteristic—that the dream does not simply reproduce this stimulus, but removes it, gets rid of it, deals with it, by means of a kind of experience.

(7) On the basis of these characteristics of dreams, we can return once more to a comparison between a dream and a parapraxis. In the latter we distinguished between a disturbing purpose and a disturbed one [p. 61 ff.], and the parapraxis was a compromise between them. A dream can be fitted into the same pattern. The disturbed purpose can only be that of sleeping. We may replace the disturbing one by the psychical stimulus, or let us say by the wish which presses to be dealt with, since we have not learnt so far of any other psychical stimulus that disturbs sleep. Here the dream, too, is the result of a compromise. One sleeps, but one nevertheless experiences the removing of a wish; one satisfies a wish, but at the same time one continues to sleep. Both purposes are partly achieved and partly abandoned.

(8) You will recall that at one point [p. 98] we hoped to approach an understanding of the problems of dreams from the fact that certain imaginative structures which are very transparent to us are known as 'day-dreams'. Now these day-dreams are in fact wish-fulfilments, fulfilments of ambitions and erotic wishes which are well known to us; but they are *thought*, even though vividly imagined, and never experienced as hallucinations. Of the two chief characteristics of dreams, then, the less well assured is preserved here, while the other, since it depends on the state of sleep and cannot be realized in waking life, is entirely absent. Linguistic usage, therefore, has a suspicion of the fact that wish-fulfilment is a chief characteristic of dreams. Incidentally, if our experience in dreams is only a modified kind of imagining made possible by the conditions of the state of sleep—that is, a 'nocturnal day-dreaming'—we can already understand how the process of constructing a dream can dispose of the nocturnal stimulus and bring satisfaction, since day-dreaming too is an activity bound up with satisfaction and is only practised, indeed, on that account.

But other usages of language express the same sense. There are familiar proverbs such as 'Pigs dream of acorns and geese dream of maize' or 'What do hens dream of?—Of millet.'[1] So proverbs go even lower than we do—below children to animals —and assert that the content of dreams is the satisfaction of a need. Numbers of figures of speech seem to point in the same direction: 'lovely as a dream', 'I shouldn't have dreamt of such a thing', 'I haven't imagined it in my wildest dreams'. In this, linguistic usage is evidently taking sides. For there are anxiety-dreams as well, and dreams with a distressing or indifferent content; but linguistic usage has been unmoved by them. It is true that it knows of 'bad dreams', but a dream pure and simple is only the sweet fulfilment of a wish. Nor is there any proverb which might tell us that pigs or geese dream of being slaughtered.

It is inconceivable, of course, that the wish-fulfilling characteristic of dreams should not have been noticed by writers on the subject. On the contrary, it has often been noticed; but it has not occurred to any of them to recognize this characteristic as a universal one and to make it into a corner-stone for the explanation of dreams. We can well imagine what it is that has held them back from it and we shall go into the matter later on.

But consider what a large amount of light has been thrown on things by our examination of children's dreams, and with scarcely any effort: the functions of dreams as the guardians of sleep; their origin from two concurrent purposes, one of which, the desire for sleep, remains constant, while the other strives to satisfy a psychical stimulus; proof that dreams are psychical acts with a sense; their two chief characteristics—wish-fulfilment and hallucinatory experience. And in discovering all this we were almost able to forget that we were engaged on psycho-analysis. Apart from its connection with parapraxes, our work has carried no specific mark. Any psychologist, knowing nothing of the postulates of psycho-analysis, might have been able to give this explanation of children's dreams. Why have they not done so?

If dreams of the infantile kind were the only ones, the problem would be solved and our task finished, and that without

[1] [A Hungarian and a Jewish proverb respectively. Cf. the end of Chapter III of *I. of D.*]

our questioning the dreamer or bringing in the unconscious or
resorting to free association. This is evidently where a continuation of our task lies ahead. We have already found repeatedly
that characteristics which were claimed as being of general
validity have turned out to apply only to a particular sort
and number of dreams. The question for us is therefore whether
the general characteristics we inferred from children's dreams
have a firmer footing, whether they also hold good of dreams
which are not transparently clear and whose manifest content
gives no sign of being connected with a wish left over from the
previous day. It is our view that these other dreams have under-
gone a far-reaching distortion and for that reason cannot be
judged at a first glance. We suspect too that to explain this
distortion we shall need the psycho-analytic technique which
we have been able to do without in the understanding we have
just gained of children's dreams.

In any case, there is yet another class of dreams which are
undistorted and, like children's dreams, can easily be recognized as wish-fulfilments. These are the dreams which all
through life are called up by imperative bodily needs—hunger,
thirst, sexual need—that is, they are wish-fufilments as reactions to internal somatic stimuli. Thus I have a note of a
dream dreamt by a little girl of nineteen months, which consisted of a *menu*, to which her own name was attached: '*Anna F.,
stwawbewwies, wild stwawbewwies, omblet, pudden!*' This was a
reaction to a day without food, owing to a digestive upset, which
had actually been traced back to the fruit which appeared twice
in the dream. The little girl's grandmother—their combined
ages came to seventy years—was simultaneously obliged to go
without food for a whole day on account of a disturbance due to
a floating kidney. She dreamt the same night that she had been
'asked out' and had been served with the most appetizing
delicacies.

Observations on prisoners who have been compelled to
starve, and on people who have been subjected to privations on
travels and explorations, teach us that under these conditions
the satisfaction of their needs is regularly dreamt of. Thus Otto
Nordenskjöld (1904, 1, 336 f.) writes as follows of the members
of his expedition while they were wintering in the Antarctic:
'The direction taken by our innermost thoughts was very clearly

shown by our dreams, which were never more vivid or numerous than at this time. Even those of us who otherwise dreamt but rarely had long stories to tell in the morning when we exchanged our latest experiences in this world of the imagination. They were all concerned with the outside world which was now so remote from us, though they were often adapted to our actual circumstances. . . . Eating and drinking, however, were the pivot round which our dreams most often revolved. One of us, who had a special gift for attending large luncheon parties during the night, was proud if he was able to report in the morning that he had "got through a three-course dinner". Another of us dreamt of tobacco, of whole mountains of tobacco; while a third dreamt of a ship in full sail coming in across open water. Yet another dream is worth repeating. The postman brought round the mail and gave a long explanation of why we had had to wait so long for it: he had delivered it at the wrong address and had only succeeded in recovering it with great difficulty. We dreamt, of course, of still more impossible things. But there was a most striking lack of imaginativeness shown by almost all the dreams I dreamt myself or heard described. It would certainly be of great psychological interest if all these dreams could be recorded. And it will easily be understood how much we longed for sleep, since it could offer each one of us everything that he most eagerly desired.' So too, according to Du Prel [1885, 231], 'Mungo Park, when he was almost dying of thirst on one of his African journeys, dreamt unceasingly of the well-watered valleys and meadows of his home. Similarly, Baron Trenck, suffering torments of hunger while he was a prisoner in the fortress at Magdeburg, dreamt of being surrounded by sumptuous meals; and George Back, who took part in Franklin's first expedition, when he was almost dying of starvation as a result of his fearful privations, dreamt constantly and regularly of copious meals.' [1]

Anyone who has eaten some highly-spiced dish at dinner and develops a thirst during the night is very likely to dream that he is drinking.[2] It is of course impossible to get rid of a fairly strong need for food or drink by means of a dream. One

[1] [These two quotations appear in a footnote in Chapter III of *I. of D.*]

[2] [A detailed analysis of a dream of this kind is given at the beginning of Chapter III of *I. of D.*]

wakes up from a dream of this sort still feeling thirsty, and has to have a drink of real water. The effect produced by the dream is in this instance trivial from the practical point of view; but it is none the less clear that it was produced with the aim of protecting one's sleep against a stimulus that was urging one to wake up and take action. When the need is of less intensity dreams of satisfaction often help one to get over it.

In the same way, dreams create satisfactions under the influence of sexual stimuli, but these show peculiarities which deserve mention. Since it is characteristic of the sexual instinct to be a degree less dependent on its object than hunger and thirst, the satisfaction in dreams of emission can be a real one; and in consequence of certain difficulties (which I shall have to mention later) in its relation to its object, it happens with special frequency that the real satisfaction is nevertheless attached to a dream content which is obscure or distorted. This characteristic of dreams of emission (as Otto Rank [1912a] has pointed out) makes them particularly favourable subjects for the study of dream-distortion.[1] Furthermore, all adult dreams arising from bodily needs usually contain, in addition to the satisfaction, other material which is derived from purely psychical sources of stimulation and requires interpretation before it can be understood.

Moreover I do not mean to assert that the wish-fulfilment dreams of adults which are constructed on infantile lines only appear as reactions to the imperative needs that I have mentioned. We are acquainted as well with short, clear dreams of this sort which, under the influence of some dominant situation, arise out of what are unquestionably psychical sources of stimulation. There are, for instance, dreams of impatience: if someone has made preparations for a journey, for a theatrical performance that is important to him, for going to a lecture or paying a visit, he may dream of a premature fulfilment of his expectation; he may, during the night before the event, see himself arrived at his destination, present at the theatre, in conversation with the person he is going to visit. Or there are what are justly known as dreams of convenience, in which a person who would like to sleep longer dreams that he is already up and is washing, or is already at school, whereas he is really

[1] [This is discussed more fully in Section E of Chapter VI in *I. of D.*]

still sleeping and would rather get up in a dream than in reality.[1] The wish to sleep, which we have recognized as regularly playing a part in the construction of dreams, comes into the open in these dreams and reveals itself in them as the essential dream-constructor. There is good reason for ranking the need to sleep alongside of the other great bodily needs.

Here is a reproduction of a picture by Schwind in the Schack Gallery in Munich [see Frontispiece], which shows how correctly the artist grasped the way in which dreams arise from the dominant situation. Its title is 'The Prisoner's Dream', a dream whose content is bound to be his escape. It is a happy point that he is to escape through the window, for it is the stimulus of the light pouring in by the window that is putting an end to the prisoner's sleep. The gnomes who are clambering up on one another no doubt represent the successive positions which he himself would have had to take as he climbed up to the level of the window; and, if I am not mistaken and am not attributing too much deliberation to the artist, the topmost of the gnomes, who is sawing through the bars—that is, who is doing what the prisoner would like to do—has the same features as himself.

In all dreams other than children's dreams and those of an infantile type our path is, as I have said, obstructed by dream-distortion. We cannot tell, to begin with, whether these other dreams too are wish-fulfilments as we suspect, we cannot guess from their manifest content to what psychical stimulus they owe their origin, and we cannot prove that they too are endeavouring to get rid of that stimulus or in some way deal with it. They must be interpreted—that is, translated—,their distortion must be undone, and their manifest content replaced by their latent one, before we can form a judgement as to whether what we have found in infantile dreams can claim to be valid for all dreams.

[1] [A dream of this type is reported at the beginning of Chapter III in *I. of D.*]

LECTURE IX

THE CENSORSHIP OF DREAMS

LADIES AND GENTLEMEN,—The study of the dreams of children has taught us the origin, the essential nature and the function of dreams. *Dreams are things which get rid of (psychical) stimuli disturbing to sleep, by the method of hallucinatory satisfaction.* We have, however, only been able to explain one group of the dreams of adults—those which we have described as dreams of an infantile type. What the facts are about the others we cannot yet say, but we do not understand them. We have arrived at a provisional finding, however, whose importance we must not under-estimate. Whenever a dream has been completely intelligible to us, it has turned out to be the hallucinated fulfilment of a wish. This coincidence cannot be a chance one nor a matter of indifference.

We have assumed of dreams of another sort [p. 113 f.], on the basis of various considerations and on the analogy of our views on parapraxes, that they are a distorted substitute for an unknown content, and that the first thing is to trace them back to it. Our immediate task, then, is an enquiry which will lead to an understanding of this *distortion in dreams*.

Dream-distortion is what makes a dream seem strange and unintelligible to us. We want to know a number of things about it: firstly, where it comes from—its dynamics—, secondly, what it does and, lastly, how it does it. We can also say that dream-distortion is carried out by the dream-work; and we want to describe the dream-work and trace it back to the forces operating in it.[1]

And now listen to this dream. It was recorded by a lady belonging to our group,[2] and, as she tells us, was derived from a highly-esteemed and cultivated elderly lady. No analysis was made of the dream; our informant remarks that for a psycho-analyst it needs no interpreting. Nor did the dreamer herself interpret it, but she judged it and condemned it as though she

[1] [The dream-work is discussed in Lecture XI.]
[2] Frau Dr. von Hug-Hellmuth [1915].

understood how to interpret it; for she said of it: 'And disgusting, stupid stuff like this was dreamt by a woman of fifty, who has no other thoughts day and night but worry about her child!' [1]

Here, then, is the dream—which deals with 'love services' in war-time.[2] *'She went to Garrison Hospital No. 1 and informed the sentry at the gate that she must speak to the Chief Medical Officer (mentioning a name that was unknown to her) as she wanted to volunteer for service at the hospital. She pronounced the word "service" in such a way that the N.C.O. at once understood that she meant "love service". Since she was an elderly lady, after some hesitation he allowed her to pass. Instead of finding the Chief Medical Officer, however, she reached a large and gloomy apartment in which a number of officers and army doctors were standing and sitting round a long table. She approached a staff surgeon with her request, and he understood her meaning after she had said only a few words. The actual wording of her speech in the dream was: "I and many other women and girls in Vienna are ready to . . ." at this point in the dream her words turned into a mumble ". . . for the troops—officers and other ranks without distinction." She could tell from the expressions on the officers' faces, partly embarrassed and partly sly, that everyone had understood her meaning correctly. The lady went on: "I'm aware that our decision must sound surprising, but we mean it in bitter earnest. No one asks a soldier in the field whether he wishes to die or not." There followed an awkward silence of some minutes. The staff surgeon then put his arm round her waist and said: "Suppose, madam, it actually came to . . . (mumble)." She drew away from him, thinking to herself: "He's like all the rest of them", and replied: "Good gracious, I'm an old woman and I might never come to that. Besides, there's one condition that must be observed: age must be respected. It must never happen that an elderly woman . . . (mumble) . . . a mere boy. That would be terrible." "I understand perfectly," replied the staff surgeon. Some of the officers, and among them one who had been a suitor of hers in her youth, laughed out loud. The lady then asked to be taken to the Chief Medical Officer, with whom she was*

---

[1] [This was during the 1914–18 War, in which one of her sons was engaged on active service.]

[2] ['*Liebesdienste*' means in the first instance 'services performed for love', i.e. 'unremunerated services'; but it could bear another, less respectable, meaning.]

*acquainted, so that the whole matter could be thrashed out; but she found,
to her consternation, that she could not recall his name. Nevertheless, the
staff surgeon, most politely and respectfully, showed her the way up to
the second floor by a very narrow, iron, spiral staircase, which led
directly from the room to the upper storeys of the building. As she went
up she heard an officer say: "That's a tremendous decision to make—no
matter whether a woman's young or old! Splendid of her!" Feeling
simply that she was doing her duty, she walked up an interminable
staircase.*

'The dream was repeated twice in the course of a few weeks,
with, as the lady remarked, some quite unimportant and meaningless modifications.'[1]

From its continuous nature, the dream resembles a daytime
phantasy: there are few breaks in it, and some of the details of
its content could have been explained if they had been
enquired into, but that, as you know, was not done. But what
is remarkable and interesting from our point of view is that the
dream shows several gaps—gaps not in the dreamer's memory
of the dream but in the content of the dream itself. At three
points the content was, as it were, extinguished; the speeches in
which these gaps occurred were interrupted by a mumble. As
no analysis was carried out, we have, strictly speaking, no right
to say anything about the sense of the dream. Nevertheless there
are hints on which conclusions can be based (for instance, in the
phrase 'love services'); but above all, the portions of the
speeches immediately preceding the mumbles call for the gaps
to be filled in, and in an unambiguous manner. If we make the
insertions, the content of the phantasy turns out to be that the
dreamer is prepared, by way of fulfilling a patriotic duty, to
put herself at the disposal of the troops, both officers and other
ranks, for the satisfaction of their erotic needs. This is, of course,
highly objectionable, the model of a shameless libidinal phantasy—but it does not appear in the dream at all. Precisely at the
points at which the context would call for this admission, the
manifest dream contains an indistinct mumble: something has
been lost or suppressed.

You will, I hope, think it plausible to suppose that it was

[1] [This dream was later (in 1919) added as a footnote to *I. of D.*
Cf. the beginning of Chapter IV.]

precisely the objectionable nature of these passages that was the motive for their suppression. Where shall we find a parallel to such an event? You need not look far in these days. Take up any political newspaper and you will find that here and there the text is absent and in its place nothing except the white paper is to be seen. This, as you know, is the work of the press censorship. In these empty places there was something that displeased the higher censorship authorities and for that reason it was removed—a pity, you feel, since no doubt it was the most interesting thing in the paper—the 'best bit'.

On other occasions the censorship has not gone to work on a passage *after* it has already been completed. The author has seen in advance which passages might expect to give rise to objections from the censorship and has on that account toned them down in advance, modified them slightly, or has contented himself with approximations and allusions to what would genuinely have come from his pen. In that case there are no blank places in the paper, but circumlocutions and obscurities of expression appearing at certain points will enable you to guess where regard has been paid to the censorship in advance.

Well, we can keep close to this parallel. It is our view that the omitted pieces of the speeches in the dream which were concealed by a mumble have likewise been sacrificed to a censorship. We speak in so many words of a '*dream-censorship*', to which some share in dream-distortion is to be attributed. Wherever there are gaps in the manifest dream the dream-censorship is responsible for them. We should go further, and regard it as a manifestation of the censorship wherever a dream-element is remembered especially faintly, indefinitely and doubtfully among other elements that are more clearly constructed. But it is only rarely that this censorship manifests itself so un-disguisedly—so naïvely, one might say—as in this example of the dream of 'love services'. The censorship takes effect much more frequently according to the second method, by producing softenings, approximations and allusions instead of the genuine thing.

I know of no parallel in the operations of the press-censorship to a third manner of working by the dream-censorship; but I am able to demonstrate it from precisely the one example of a dream which we have analysed so far. You will recall the dream of the 'three bad theatre-tickets for 1 florin 50' [p. 122]. In the latent thoughts of that dream the element 'over-hurriedly, too early' stood in the foreground. Thus: it was absurd to marry so *early*—it was also absurd to take the theatre-tickets so *early*—it was ridiculous of the sister-in-law to part with her money in such a *hurry* to buy jewellery with it. Nothing of this central element of the dream-thoughts passed over into the manifest dream; in it the central position is taken by the 'going to the theatre' and 'taking the tickets'. As a result of this displacement of accent, this fresh grouping of the elements of the content, the manifest dream has become so unlike the latent dream-thoughts that no-one would suspect the presence of the latter behind the former. This displacement of accent is one of the chief instruments of dream-distortion and it is what gives the dream the strangeness on account of which the dreamer himself is not inclined to recognize it as his own production.

Omission, modification, fresh grouping of the material—these, then, are the activities of the dream-censorship and the instruments of dream-distortion. The dream-censorship itself is the originator, or one of the originators, of the dream-distortion which we are now engaged in examining. We are in the habit of combining the concepts of modification and re-arrangement under the term 'displacement'.

After these remarks on the activities of the dream-censorship, we will now turn to its dynamics. I hope you do not take the term too anthropomorphically, and do not picture the 'censor of dreams' as a severe little manikin or a spirit living in a closet in the brain and there discharging his office; but I hope too that you do not take the term in too 'localizing' a sense, and do not think of a 'brain-centre', from which a censoring influence of this kind issues, an influence which would be brought to an end if the 'centre' were damaged or removed. For the time being it is nothing more than a serviceable term for describing a dynamic relation. The word does not prevent our asking by what purposes[1] this influence is exercised and against what purposes it is directed. And we shall not be surprised to learn that we have come up against the dream-censorship once already, though perhaps without recognizing it.

[1] [Or, here and in what follows, 'trends'. Cf. footnote 1, p. 40 above.]

For that is in fact the case. You will recall that when we began to make use of our technique of free association we made a surprising discovery. We became aware that our efforts at proceeding from the dream-element to the unconscious element for which it is a substitute were being met by a *resistance* [p. 116]. This resistance, we said, could be of different magnitudes, sometimes enormous and sometimes quite insignificant. In the latter case we need to pass through only a small number of intermediate links in our work of interpretation; but when the resistance is large we have to traverse long chains of associations from the dream-element, we are led far away from it and on our path we have to overcome all the difficulties which represent themselves as critical objections to the ideas that occur. What we met with as resistance in our work of interpretation must now be introduced into the dream-work in the form of the dream-censorship. The resistance to interpretation is only a putting into effect[1] of the dream-censorship. It also proves to us that the force of the censorship is not exhausted in bringing about the distortion of dreams and thereafter extinguished, but that the censorship persists as a permanent institution which has as its aim the maintenance of the distortion. Moreover, just as the strength of the resistance varies in the interpretation of each element in a dream, so too the magnitude of the distortion introduced by the censorship varies for each element in the same dream. If we compare the manifest and the latent dream, we shall find that some particular latent elements have been completely eliminated, others modified to a greater or less extent, while yet others have been carried over into the manifest content of the dream unaltered or even perhaps strengthened.

But we wanted to enquire what are the purposes which exercise the censorship and against what purposes it is directed. Now this question, which is fundamental for the understanding of dreams and perhaps, indeed, of human life, is easy to answer

---

[1] ['*Objektivierung.*' Literally, 'making objective'. The term is used several times in an early paper of Freud's on hypnotic treatment (1892–93) and again in *Studies on Hysteria* (1895d). Freud himself seems to use the term '*Realisierung*' (realization), as a synonym.]

if we look through the series of dreams which have been inter-preted. The purposes which exercise the censorship are those which are acknowledged by the dreamer's waking judgement, those with which he feels himself at one. You may be sure that if you reject an interpretation of one of your own dreams which has been correctly carried out, you are doing so for the same motives for which the dream-censorship has been exercised, the dream-distortion brought about and the interpretation made necessary. Take the dream of our fifty-year-old lady [p. 137]. She thought her dream disgusting without having analysed it, and she would have been still more indignant if Dr. von Hug-Hellmuth had told her anything of its inevitable interpretation; it was precisely because of this condemnation by the dreamer that the objectionable passages in her dream were replaced by a mumble.

The purposes *against* which the dream-censorship is directed must be described in the first instance from the point of view of that agency itself. If so, one can only say that they are invari-ably of a reprehensible nature, repulsive from the ethical, aesthetic and social point of view—matters of which one does not venture to think at all or thinks only with disgust. These wishes, which are censored and given a distorted expression in dreams, are first and foremost manifestations of an unbridled and ruthless egoism. And, to be sure, the dreamer's own ego appears in every dream and plays the chief part in it, even if it knows quite well how to hide itself so far as the manifest content goes. This 'sacro egoismo' of dreams is certainly not un-related to the attitude we adopt when we sleep, which con-sists in our withdrawing our interest from the whole external world.[1]

The ego, freed from all ethical bonds, also finds itself at one with all the demands of sexual desire, even those which have long been condemned by our aesthetic upbringing and those which contradict all the requirements of moral restraint. The desire for pleasure—the 'libido', as we call it—chooses its objects without inhibition, and by preference, indeed, the forbidden ones: not only other men's wives, but above all incestuous objects, objects sanctified by the common agreement of man-

[1] [In a footnote added in 1925 to Section D of Chapter V of *I. of D.* Freud made some qualification of his statement that dreams are entirely egoistic.]

kind, a man's mother and sister, a woman's father and brother. (The dream of our fifty-year-old lady, too, was incestuous; her libido was unmistakably directed to her son. [Cf. footnote 1, p. 137.]) Lusts which we think of as remote from human nature show themselves strong enough to provoke dreams. Hatred, too, rages without restraint. Wishes for revenge and death directed against those who are nearest and dearest in waking life, against the dreamer's parents, brothers and sisters, husband or wife, and his own children are nothing unusual. These censored wishes appear to rise up out of a positive Hell; after they have been interpreted when we are awake, no censorship of them seems to us too severe.

But you must not blame the dream itself on account of its evil content. Do not forget that it performs the innocent and indeed useful function of preserving sleep from disturbance. This wickedness is not part of the essential nature of dreams. Indeed you know too that there are dreams which can be recognized as the satisfaction of justified wishes and of pressing bodily needs. These, it is true, have no dream-distortion; but they have no need of it, for they can fulfil their function without insulting the ethical and aesthetic purposes[1] of the ego. Bear in mind, too, that dream-distortion is proportionate to two factors. On the one hand it becomes greater the worse the wish that has to be censored; but on the other hand it also becomes greater the more severe the demands of the censorship at the moment. Thus a strictly brought-up and prudish young girl, with a relentless censorship, will distort dream-impulses which we doctors, for instance, would have to regard as permissible, harmless, libidinal wishes, and on which in ten years' time the dreamer herself will make the same judgement.

Furthermore, we have not got nearly far enough yet to be able to feel indignant at this result of our work of interpretation. We do not yet, I think, understand it properly; but our first duty is to defend it against certain aspersions. There is no difficulty in finding a weak point in it. Our dream-interpretations are made on the basis of the premisses which we have already accepted [p. 100 f.]—that dreams in general have a sense, that it is legitimate to carry across from hypnotic to normal sleep the fact of the existence of mental processes which

[1] [See footnote, p. 140 above.]

are at the time unconscious, and that everything that occurs to the mind is determined. If on the basis of these premises we had arrived at plausible findings from dream-interpretation, we should have been justified in concluding that the premises were valid. But how about it if these findings seem to be as I have pictured them? We should then be tempted to say: 'These are impossible, senseless or at the least most improbable findings; so there was something wrong about the premises. Either dreams are not psychical phenomena, or there is nothing unconscious in the normal state, or our technique has a flaw in it. Is it not simpler and more satisfactory to suppose this rather than accept all the abominations which we are supposed to have discovered on the basis of our premises?'

Yes, indeed! Both simpler and more satisfactory—but not necessarily on that account more correct. Let us give ourselves time: the matter is not yet ripe for judgement. And first, we can further strengthen the criticism of our dream-interpretations. The fact that the findings from them are so disagreeable and repellent need not, perhaps, carry very great weight. A stronger argument is that the dreamers to whom we are led to attribute such wishful purposes by the interpretation of their dreams reject them most emphatically and for good reasons. 'What?' says one of them, 'you want to convince me from this dream that I regret the money I have spent on my sister's dowry and my brother's education? But that cannot be so. I work entirely for my brothers and sisters; I have no other interest in life but to fulfil my duties to them, which, as the eldest of the family, I promised our departed mother I would do.' Or a woman dreamer would say: 'You think I wish my husband was dead? That is a shocking piece of nonsense! It is not only that we are most happily married—you would probably not believe me if I said that—but his death would rob me of everything I possess in the world.' Or another man would answer us: 'You say that I have sensual desires for my sister? That is ridiculous! She means nothing at all to me. We are on bad terms with each other and I have not exchanged a word with her for years.' We might still take it lightly, perhaps, if these dreamers neither confirmed nor denied the purposes we attribute to them; we might say that these were just things they did not know about themselves. But when they feel in themselves the precise contrary of the wish we have interpreted to them and when they are able to prove to us by the lives they lead that they are dominated by this contrary wish, it must surely take us aback. Has not the time come to throw aside the whole work we have done on dream-interpretation as something which its findings have reduced *ad absurdum*?

No, not even now. Even this stronger argument collapses if we examine it critically. Granted that there are unconscious purposes in mental life, nothing is proved by showing that purposes opposed to these are dominant in conscious life. Perhaps there is room in the mind for contrary purposes, for contradictions, to exist side by side. Possibly, indeed, the dominance of one impulse is precisely a necessary condition of its contrary being unconscious. We are after all left, then, with the first objections that were raised: the findings of dream-interpretation are not simple and they are very disagreeable. We may reply to the first that all your passion for what is simple will not be able to solve a single one of the problems of dreams. You must get accustomed here to assuming a complicated state of affairs. And we may reply to the second that you are plainly wrong to use a liking or disliking that you may feel as the ground for a scientific judgement. What difference does it make if the findings of dream-interpretation seem disagreeable to you or, indeed, embarrassing and repulsive? '*Ça n'empêche pas d'exister*', as I heard my teacher Charcot say in a similar case when I was a young doctor.[1] One must be humble and hold back one's sympathies and antipathies if one wants to discover what is real in this world. If a physicist were able to prove to you that in a short period organic life on this earth would be brought to an end by freezing, would you venture to make the same reply to him: 'That cannot be so, the prospect is too disagreeable'? You would, I think, be silent, until another physicist came and pointed out to the first one an error in his premisses or calculations. When you reject something that is disagreeable to you, what you are doing is *repeating* the

[1] [Charcot's remark in full was: '*La théorie, c'est bon, mais ça n'empêche pas d'exister.*' ('Theory is good; but it doesn't prevent thing from existing' A favourite quotation of Freud's. See his obituary of Charcot (1893*f*), where the circumstances are described.]

mechanism of constructing dreams rather than understanding it and surmounting it.

You will promise now, perhaps, to disregard the repellent character of the censored dream-wishes and will withdraw upon the argument that after all it is unlikely that such a large space should be given to the evil in the constitution of human beings. But do your own experiences justify your saying this? I will not discuss how you may appear to yourselves; but have you found so much benevolence among your superiors and competitors, so much chivalry among your enemies and so little envy in your social surroundings that you feel it your duty to protest against egoistic evil having a share in human nature? Are you not aware of how uncontrolled and untrustworthy the average person is in everything to do with sexual life? Or do you not know that all the transgressions and excesses of which we dream at night are daily committed in real life by waking men? What does psycho-analysis do here but confirm Plato's old saying that the good are those who are content to dream of what the others, the bad, really do?[1]

And now turn your eyes away from individuals and consider the Great War which is still laying Europe waste. Think of the vast amount of brutality, cruelty and lies which are able to spread over the civilized world. Do you really believe that a handful of ambitious and deluding men without conscience could have succeeded in unleashing all these evil spirits if their millions of followers did not share their guilt? Do you venture, in such circumstances, to break a lance on behalf of the exclusion of evil from the mental constitution of mankind?[2]

You will represent to me that I am giving a one-sided judgement on the War: that it has also brought to light what is finest and noblest in men, their heroism, their self-sacrifice, their social sense. No doubt; but are you not now showing yourselves as accessories to the injustice that has so often been done to psychoanalysis in reproaching it with denying one thing because it has asserted another? It is not our intention to dispute the noble endeavours of human nature, nor have we ever done anything

---

[1] [Quoted in 'The Moral Sense in Dreams' in *I. of D.*, Chap. I.]
[2] [Freud's strongest impeachment of the destructive side of human nature was made in Chapters V and VI of *Civilization and its Discontents* (1930a), (Norton, 1962).]

to detract from their value. On the contrary; I am exhibiting to you not only the evil dream-wishes which are censored but also the censorship, which suppresses them and makes them unrecognizable. We lay a stronger emphasis on what is evil in men only because other people disavow it and thereby make the human mind, not better, but incomprehensible. If now we give up this one-sided ethical valuation, we shall undoubtedly find a more correct formula for the relation between good and evil in human nature.

There it is, then. We need not give up the findings of our work on the interpretation of dreams even though we cannot but regard them as strange. Perhaps we shall be able to approach an understanding of them later from another direction. For the time being let us hold fast to this: dream-distortion is a result of the censorship which is exercised by recognized purposes of the ego against wishful impulses in any way objectionable that stir within us at night-time during our sleep. Why this should happen particularly at night-time and where these reprehensible wishes come from—these are matters on which, no doubt, much still remains for questioning and research.

But it would be unfair if we neglected at this point to emphasize sufficiently another outcome of our investigations. The dream-wishes which seek to disturb us in our sleep are unknown to us and indeed we only learnt of them through dream-interpretation. They are thus to be described, in the sense we have discussed, as unconscious for the time being. But we must reflect that they are unconscious too for more than the time being. The dreamer also disavows them, as we have seen in so many instances, after he has come to know them through the interpretation of his dream. We are then faced once again with the position we first came across in the 'hiccoughing' slip of the tongue [p. 49], where the proposer of the toast protested indignantly that neither then nor at any earlier time had he become conscious of any disrespectful impulse towards his Chief. Already at the time we felt some doubts about the weight of an assurance of this kind, and suggested instead the hypothesis that the speaker was permanently unaware of the presence of this impulse in him. This situation is repeated now with every interpretation of a strongly distorted dream and consequently gains an increased importance in its bearing on the view we have taken. We are now prepared to assume that there are in the mind processes and purposes of which one knows nothing at all, has known nothing for a long time, and has even perhaps never known anything. With this the unconscious acquires a new sense for us; the characteristic of 'for the time being' or 'temporary' disappears from its essential nature. It can mean *permanently* unconscious and not merely 'latent at the time'. We shall of course have to hear more about this on some other occasion.

LECTURE X

SYMBOLISM IN DREAMS[1]

LADIES AND GENTLEMEN,—We have found that the distortion in dreams, which interferes with our understanding of them, is the result of a censoring activity which is directed against unacceptable, unconscious wishful impulses. We have not, of course, maintained that the censorship is the sole factor responsible for the distortion in dreams, and in fact when we study them further we can discover that other factors play a part in producing this result. This amounts to our saying that even if the dream-censorship was out of action we should still not be in a position to understand dreams, the manifest dream would still not be identical with the latent dream-thoughts.

We come upon this other factor which prevents dreams from being lucid, this new contribution to dream-distortion, by noticing a gap in our technique. I have already admitted to you [p. 105] that it does sometimes really happen that nothing occurs to a person under analysis in response to particular elements of his dreams. It is true that this does not happen as often as he asserts; in a great many cases, with perseverance, an idea is extracted from him. But nevertheless there remain cases in which an association fails to emerge or, if it *is* extracted, does not give us what we expected from it. If this happens during a psycho-analytic treatment, it has a peculiar significance with which we are not here concerned.[2] But it also

---

[1] [As Freud tells us in *The Interpretation of Dreams,* it was relatively late before he realized the full importance of dream-symbolism, largely under the influence of Wilhelm Stekel (1911). It was not until the fourth (1914) edition of *The Interpretation of Dreams* that a special section was devoted to the subject. That section (Chapter VI, Section E) represents, apart from the present lecture, Freud's main discussion of symbolism. The topic appears, of course, in many other places both in *The Interpretation of Dreams* and in other works throughout Freud's life, and references to these will be found at a few points below. It may be added, however, that the present lecture has claims to being regarded as the most important of all Freud's writings on symbolism.]

[2] [The reference here is to the blocking of free associations by unconscious stirring-up of the transference. Cf. 'The Dynamics of Transference' (1912*b*). See also Lecture XXVII below].

149

happens in the interpretation of normal people's dreams or in that of our own. If we convince ourselves that in such cases no amount of pressure is of any use, we eventually discover that this unwished-for event regularly occurs in connection with particular dream-elements, and we begin to recognize that a fresh general principle is at work where we had begun by thinking we were only faced by an exceptional failure of technique.

In this way we are tempted to interpret these 'mute' dream-elements ourselves, to set about translating them with our own resources. We are then forced to recognize that whenever we venture on making a replacement of this sort we arrive at a satisfactory sense for the dream, whereas it remains senseless and the chain of thought is interrupted so long as we refrain from intervening in this way. An accumulation of many similar cases eventually gives the necessary certainty to what began as a timid experiment.

I am putting all this in a rather schematic way; but that is permissable, after all, for didactic purposes, nor has it been falsified, but merely simplified.

In this way we obtain constant translations for a number of dream-elements—just as popular 'dream-books' provide them for *everything* that appears in dreams. You will not have forgotten, of course, that when we use our *associative* technique constant replacements of dream-elements never come to light.

You will object at once that this method of interpretation strikes you as far more insecure and open to attack than the earlier one by means of free association. There is, however, something further. For when, with experience, we have collected enough of these constant renderings, the time comes when we realize that we should in fact have been able to deal with these portions of dream-interpretation from our own knowledge, and that they could really be understood without the dreamer's associations. How it is that we must necessarily have known their meaning will become clear in the second half of our present discussion.

A constant relation of this kind between a dream-element and its translation is described by us as a 'symbolic' one, and the dream-element itself as a 'symbol' of the unconscious dream-thought. You will recall that earlier, when we were investigating the relations between dream-elements and the 'genuine' thing behind them, I distinguished three such relations—those of a part to a whole, of allusion and of plastic portrayal. I warned you at the time that there was a fourth, but I did not name it [p. 122]. This fourth relation is the symbolic one which I am now introducing. It gives occasion for some most interesting discussions, and I will turn to them before laying before you the detailed results of our observations of symbolism.

Symbolism is perhaps the most remarkable chapter of the theory of dreams. In the first place, since symbols are stable translations, they realize to some extent the ideal of the ancient as well as of the popular interpretation of dreams, from which, with our technique, we had departed widely. They allow us in certain circumstances to interpret a dream without questioning the dreamer, who indeed would in any case have nothing to tell us about the symbol. If we are acquainted with the ordinary dream-symbols, and in addition with the dreamer's personality, the circumstances in which he lives and the impressions which preceded the occurrence of the dream, we are often in a position to interpret a dream straightaway—to translate it at sight, as it were. A piece of virtuosity of this kind flatters the dream-interpreter and impresses the dreamer; it forms an agreeable contrast to the laborious work of questioning the dreamer. But do not allow yourselves to be led astray by this. It is not our business to perform acts of virtuosity. Interpretation based on a knowledge of symbols is not a technique which can replace or compete with the associative one. It forms a supplement to the latter and yields results which are only of use when introduced into it. And as regards acquaintance with the dreamer's psychical situation, you must bear in mind that the dreams of people you know well are not the only ones you have to analyse, that you are not as a rule familiar with the events of the previous day, which were the instigators of the dream, but that the associations of the person you are analysing will provide you precisely with a knowledge of what we call the psychical situation.

Moreover it is quite specially remarkable—having regard, too, to some considerations which we shall mention later [cf. p. 169]—that the most violent resistances have been expressed once again to the existence of a symbolic relation between dreams and the unconscious. Even people of judgement and reputation, who, apart from this, have gone a long way in agreeing with psycho-analysis, have at this point withheld their support. This behaviour is all the stranger in view, first, of the fact that symbolism is not peculiar to dreams alone and is not characteristic of them, and, secondly, that symbolism in dreams is by no means a discovery of psycho-analysis, however many other surprising discoveries it has made. The philosopher K. A. Scherner (1861) must be described as the discoverer of dream-symbolism, if its beginning is to be placed in modern times at all. Psycho-analysis has confirmed Scherner's findings, though it has made material modifications in them.

You will now want to hear something of the nature of dream-symbolism and to be given some examples of it. I will gladly tell you what I know, though I must confess that our understanding of it does not go as far as we should like.

The essence of this symbolic relation is that it is a comparison, though not a comparison of *any* sort. Special limitations seem to be attached to the comparison, but it is hard to say what these are. Not everything with which we can compare an object or a process appears in dreams as a symbol for it. And on the other hand a dream does not symbolize every possible element of the latent dream-thoughts but only certain definite ones. So there are restrictions here in both directions. We must admit, too, that the concept of a symbol cannot at present be sharply delimited: it shades off into such notions as those of a replacement or representation, and even approaches that of an allusion. With a number of symbols the comparison which underlies them is obvious. But again there are other symbols in regard to which we must ask ourselves where we are to look for the common element, the *tertium comparationis*, of the supposed comparison. On further reflection we may afterwards discover it or it may definitely remain concealed. It is strange, moreover, that if a symbol is a comparison it should not be brought to light by an association, and that the dreamer should not be acquainted with it but should make use of it without knowing about it: more than that, indeed, that the dreamer feels no inclination to acknowledge the comparison even after it has been pointed out to him. You see, then, that a symbolic relation is a comparison of a quite special kind, of which we do not as yet clearly grasp the basis, though perhaps we may later arrive at some indication of it.

The range of things which are given symbolic representation in dreams is not wide: the human body as a whole, parents, children, brothers and sisters, birth, death, nakedness—and something else besides. The one typical—that is regular—representation of the human figure as a whole is a *house*, as was recognized by Scherner, who even wanted to give this symbol a transcendant importance which it does not possess. It may happen in a dream that one finds oneself climbing down the façade of a house, enjoying it at one moment, frightened at another. The houses with smooth walls are men, the ones with projections and balconies that one can hold on to are women [cf. p. 159 below]. One's parents appear in dreams as the *Emperor* and *Empress*, the *King* and *Queen* [loc. cit.] or other honoured personages; so here dreams are displaying much filial piety. They treat children and brothers and sisters less tenderly: these are symbolized as *small animals* or *vermin*. Birth is almost invariably represented by something which has a connection with *water*: one either falls into the water or climbs out of it, one rescues someone from the water or is rescued by someone—that is to say, the relation is one of mother to child [cf. p. 160]. Dying is replaced in dreams by *departure*, by a *train journey* [cf. p. 161], being dead by various obscure and, as it were, timid hints, nakedness by *clothes* and *uniforms*. You see how indistinct the boundaries are here between symbolic and allusive representation.

It is a striking fact that, compared with this scanty enumeration, there is another field in which the objects and topics are represented with an extraordinarily rich symbolism. This field is that of sexual life—the genitals, sexual processes, sexual intercourse. The very great majority of symbols in dreams are sexual symbols. And here a strange disproportion is revealed. The topics I have mentioned are few, but the symbols for them are extremely numerous, so that each of these things can be expressed by numbers of almost equivalent symbols. The outcome, when they are interpreted, gives rise to general objection.

For, in contrast to the multiplicity of the representations in the dream, the interpretations of the symbols are very monotonous, and this displeases everyone who hears of it; but what is there that we can do about it?

Since this is the first time I have spoken of the subject-matter of sexual life in one of these lectures, I owe you some account of the way in which I propose to treat the topic. Psycho-analysis finds no occasion for concealments and hints, it does not think it necessary to be ashamed of dealing with this important material, it believes it is right and proper to call everything by its correct name, and it hopes that this will be the best way of keeping irrelevant thoughts of a disturbing kind at a distance. The fact that these lectures are being given before a mixed audience of both sexes can make no difference to this. Just as there can be no science *in usum Delphini*,[1] there can be none for schoolgirls; and the ladies among you have made it clear by their presence in this lecture-room that they wish to be treated on an equality with men.

The male genitals, then, are represented in dreams in a number of ways that must be called symbolic, where the common element in the comparison is mostly very obvious. To begin with, for the male genitals as a whole the sacred number 3 is of symbolic significance [cf. p. 163 f.]. The more striking and for both sexes the more interesting component of the genitals, the male organ, finds symbolic substitutes in the first instance in things that resemble it in shape—things, accordingly, that are long and up-standing, such as *sticks, umbrellas, posts, trees* and so on; further, in objects which share with the thing they represent the characteristic of penetrating into the body and injuring—thus, sharp *weapons* of every kind, *knives, daggers, spears, sabres,* but also fire-arms, *rifles, pistols* and *revolvers* (particularly suitable owing to their shape). In the anxiety dreams of girls, being followed by a man with a knife or a fire-arm plays a large part. This is perhaps the commonest instance of dream-symbolism and you will now be able to translate it easily. Nor is there any difficulty in understanding how it is that the male organ can be replaced by objects from which water flows—

[1] [Cf. footnote 2, p. 102.]

water-taps, watering-cans, or *fountains*—or again by other objects which are capable of being lengthened, such as *hanging-lamps, extensible pencils,* etc. A no less obvious aspect of the organ explains the fact that *pencils, pen-holders, nail-files, hammers,* and other *instruments* are undoubted male sexual symbols.

The remarkable characteristic of the male organ which enables it to rise up in defiance of the laws of gravity, one of the phenomena of erection, leads to its being represented symbolically by *balloons, flying-machines* and most recently by *Zeppelin airships.* But dreams can symbolize erection in yet another, far more expressive manner. They can treat the sexual organ as the essence of the dreamer's whole person and make him himself *fly.* Do not take it to heart if dreams of flying, so familiar and often so delightful, have to be interpreted as dreams of general sexual excitement, as erection-dreams. Among students of psycho-analysis, Paul Federn [1914] has placed this interpretation beyond any doubt; but the same conclusion was reached from his investigations by Mourly Vold [1910–12, 2, 791], who has been so much praised for his sobriety, who carried out the dream-experiments I have referred to [p. 87] with artificially arranged positions of the arms and legs and who was far removed from psycho-analysis and may have known nothing about it. And do not make an objection out of the fact that women can have the same flying dreams as men. Remember, rather, that our dreams aim at being the fulfilments of wishes and that the wish to be a man is found so frequently, consciously or unconsciously, in women. Nor will anyone with a knowledge of anatomy be bewildered by the fact that it is possible for women to realize this wish through the same sensations as men. Women possess as part of their genitals a small organ similar to the male one; and this small organ, the clitoris, actually plays the same part in childhood and during the years before sexual intercourse as the large organ in men.[1]

Among the less easily understandable male sexual symbols are certain *reptiles* and *fishes,* and above all the famous symbol of the *snake.* It is certainly not easy to guess why *hats* and *overcoats* or *cloaks* are employed in the same way, but their symbolic significance is quite unquestionable [cf. p. 157]. And finally we can ask ourselves whether the replacement of the

[1] [This is further discussed on p. 318 below.]

male limb by another limb, the foot or the hand, should be described as symbolic. We are, I think, compelled to do so by the context and by counterparts in the case of women.

The female genitals are symbolically represented by all such objects as share their characteristic of enclosing a hollow space which can take something into itself: by *pits, cavities* and *hollows*, for instance, by *vessels* and *bottles*, by *receptacles, boxes, trunks, cases, chests, pockets*, and so on. *Ships*, too, fall into this category. Some symbols have more connection with the uterus than with the female genitals: thus, *cupboards, stoves* and, more especially, *rooms*. Here room-symbolism touches on house-symbolism. *Doors* and *gates*, again, are symbols of the genital orifice. Materials, too, are symbols for women [cf. p. 160]: *wood, paper* and objects made of them, like *tables* and *books*. Among animals, *snails* and *mussels* at least are undeniably female symbols; among parts of the body, the *mouth* (as a substitute for the genital orifice); among buildings, *churches* and *chapels*. Not every symbol, as you will observe, is equally intelligible.

The breasts must be reckoned with the genitals, and these, like the larger hemispheres of the female body, are represented by *apples, peaches*, and *fruit* in general. The pubic hair of both sexes is depicted in dreams as *woods* and *bushes*. The complicated topography of the female genital parts makes one understand how it is that they are often represented as *landscapes*, with rocks, woods and water,[1] while the imposing mechanism of the male sexual apparatus explains why all kinds of complicated machinery which is hard to describe serve as symbols for it.

Another symbol of the female genitals which deserves mention is a *jewel-case*.[2] *Jewel* and *treasure* are used in dreams as well as in waking life to describe someone who is loved. *Sweets* frequently represent sexual enjoyment. Satisfaction obtained from a person's own genitals is indicated by all kinds of *playing*, including *piano-playing*. Symbolic representations *par excellence* of masturbation are *gliding* or *sliding* and *pulling off a branch* [cf. p. 164]. The *falling out of a tooth* or the *pulling out of a tooth* is a particularly notable dream-symbol. Its first meaning is

[1] [A dream with a quantity of landscape symbolism is reported below, p. 193.]

[2] [This played a prominent part in the analysis of the first dream in the case history of 'Dora' (1905e).]

undoubtedly castration as a punishment for masturbating [loc. cit.]. We come across special representations of sexual intercourse less often than might be expected from what has been said so far. Rhythmical activities such as *dancing, riding* and *climbing* must be mentioned here, as well as violent experiences such as *being run over;* so, too, certain *manual crafts,* and, of course, *threatening with weapons.*

You must not picture the use or the translation of these symbols as something quite simple. In the course of them all kinds of things happen which are contrary to our expectations. It seems almost incredible, for instance, that in these symbolic representations the differences between the sexes are often not clearly observed. Some symbols signify genitals in general, irrespective of whether they are male or female: for instance, a *small* child, a *small* son or a *small* daughter.[1] Or again, a predominantly male symbol may be used for the female genitals or vice versa. We cannot understand this till we have obtained some insight into the development of sexual ideas in human beings. In some instances the ambiguity of the symbols may only be an apparent one; and the most marked symbols, such as *weapons, pockets* and *chests* are excluded from this bisexual use.

I will now go on to make a survey, starting not from the thing represented but from the symbol, of the fields from which sexual symbols are mostly derived, and I will make a few additional remarks, with special reference to the symbols where the common element in the comparison is not understood. The *hat* is an obscure symbol of this kind—perhaps, too, head-coverings in general—with a male significance as a rule, but also capable of a female one.[2] In the same way an *overcoat* or *cloak* means a man, perhaps not always with a genital reference; it is open to you to ask why.[3] Neckties, which hang down and are not worn

[1] [That is, any one of these three may be used in a dream as a symbol for either the male or the female genitals.]

[2] [Hat-symbolism was discussed by Freud in his short paper 'A Connection between a Symbol and a Symptom' (1916c).]

[3] In *I. of D.,* VI(E), Freud suggests that the explanation may be a verbal assonance between '*Mann*' and '*Mantel*' (the German for 'overcoat' or 'cloak'). A further discussion of this symbol occurs in Lecture XXIX of the *New Introductory Lectures* (1933a), p. 488 below.]

by women, are a definitely male symbol. *Underclothing* and *linen* in general are female. *Clothes* and *uniforms*, as we have already seen, are a substitute for nakedness or bodily shapes. *Shoes* and *slippers* are female genitals. *Tables* and *wood* have already been mentioned as puzzling but certainly female symbols. *Ladders*, *steps* and *staircases*, or, more precisely, walking on them, are clear symbols of sexual intercourse. On reflection, it will occur to us that the common element here is the rhythm of walking up them—perhaps, too, the increasing excitement and breathlessness the higher one climbs [cf. p. 164].

We have earlier referred to *landscapes* as representing the female genitals. *Hills* and *rocks* are symbols of the male organ. *Gardens* are common symbols of the female genitals. *Fruit* stands, not for children, but for the breasts. *Wild animals* mean people in an excited sensual state, and further, evil instincts or passions. *Blossoms* and *flowers* indicate women's genitals, or, in particular, virginity. Do not forget that blossoms are actually the genitals of plants.[1]

We are acquainted already with *rooms* as a symbol. The representation can be carried further, for windows, and doors in and out of rooms, take over the meaning of orifices in the body. And the question of the room being *open* or *locked* fits in with this symbolism, and the *key* that opens it is a decidedly male symbol.

Here, then, is material used for symbolism in dreams. It is not complete and could be carried deeper as well as further. But I fancy it will seem to you more than enough and may even have exasperated you. 'Do I really live in the thick of sexual symbols?' you may ask. 'Are all the objects around me, all the clothes I put on, all the things I pick up, all of them sexual symbols and nothing else?' There is really ground enough for raising astonished questions, and, as a first one, we may enquire how we in fact come to know the meaning of these dream-symbols, upon which the dreamer himself gives us insufficient information or none at all.

My reply is that we learn it from very different sources—from fairy tales and myths, from buffoonery and jokes, from

[1] [A dream with a large amount of flower symbolism is reported in Section C of Chapter VI of *I. of D.* See also Section D of that chapter.]

folklore (that is, from knowledge about popular manners and customs, sayings and songs) and from poetic and colloquial linguistic usage. In all these directions we come upon the same symbolism, and in some of them we can understand it without further instruction. If we go into these sources in detail, we shall find so many parallels to dream-symbolism that we cannot fail to be convinced of our interpretations.

According to Scherner, as we have said [p. 153], the human body is often represented in dreams by the symbol of a house. Carrying this representation further, we found that windows, doors and gates stood for openings in the body and that façades of houses were either smooth or provided with balconies and projections to hold on to. But the same symbolism is found in our linguistic usage—when we greet an acquaintance familiarly as an '*altes Haus*' ['old house'], when we speak of giving someone '*eins aufs Dachl*' [a knock on the head, literally, 'one on the roof'], or when we say of someone else that 'he's not quite right in the upper storey'. In anatomy the orifices of the body are in so many words termed '*Leibespforten*' [literally, 'portals of the body'].

It seems surprising at first to find one's parents in dreams as an imperial or royal couple. But it has its parallel in fairy tales. It begins to dawn on us that the many fairy tales which begin 'Once upon a time there were a King and Queen' only mean to say that there were once a father and mother. In a family the children are jokingly called 'princes' and the eldest 'crown prince'. The King himself calls himself the father of his country. We speak of small children jokingly as '*Würmer*' ['worms'] and speak sympathetically of a child as '*der arme Wurm*' ['the poor worm'].

Let us go back to house-symbolism. When in a dream we make use of the projections on houses for catching hold of, we may be reminded of a common vulgar expression for well-developed breasts: 'She's got something to catch hold of.' There is another popular expression in such cases: 'She's got plenty of wood in front of the house', which seems to confirm our interpretation of wood as a female, maternal symbol.

And, speaking of wood, it is hard to understand how that material came to represent what is maternal and female. But here comparative philology may come to our help. Our German word '*Holz*' seems to come from the same root as the Greek '*ύλη* [hulē]', meaning 'stuff' 'raw material'. This seems to be an instance of the not uncommon event of the general name of a material eventually coming to be reserved for some particular material. Now there is an island in the Atlantic named 'Madeira'. This name was given to it by the Portuguese when they discovered it, because at that time it was covered all over with woods. For in the Portuguese language '*madeira*' means 'wood'. You will notice, however, that '*madeira*' is only a slightly modified form of the Latin word '*materia*', which once more means 'material' in general. But '*materia*' is derived from '*mater*', 'mother': the material out of which anything is made is, as it were, a mother to it. This ancient view of the thing survives, therefore, in the symbolic use of wood for 'woman' or 'mother'.

Birth is regularly expressed in dreams by some connection with water: one falls into the water or one comes out of the water—one gives birth or one is born. We must not forget that this symbol is able to appeal in two ways to evolutionary truth. Not only are all terrestrial mammals, including man's ancestors. descended from aquatic creatures (this is the more remote of the two facts), but every individual mammal, every human being, spent the first phase of its existence in water—namely as an embryo in the amniotic fluid in its mother's uterus, and came out of that water when it was born. I do not say that the dreamer knows this; on the other hand, I maintain that he need not know it. There is something else that the dreamer probably knows from having been told it in his childhood; and I even maintain of that too that his knowledge of it contributed nothing to the construction of the symbol. He was told in his nursery that the stork brings the babies. But where does it fetch them from? From the pond, or from the stream—once again, then, from the water. One of my patients after he had been given this information—he was a little Count at the time —disappeared for a whole afternoon. He was found at last lying by the edge of the castle pool, with his little face bending over the surface of the water eagerly peering down to try and see the babies at the bottom. [Cf. p. 318 below.]

In myths about the birth of heroes—to which Otto Rank [1909] has devoted a comparative study, the oldest being that of King Sargon of Agade (about 2800 B.C.)—a predominant part is played by exposure in the water and rescue from the water. Rank has perceived that these are representations of birth, analogous to those that are usual in dreams. If one rescues someone from the water in a dream, one is making oneself into his mother, or simply into *a* mother. In myths a person who rescues a baby from the water is admitting that she is the baby's true mother. There is a well-known comic anecdote according to which an intelligent Jewish boy was asked who the mother of Moses was. He replied without hesitation: 'The Princess.' 'No', he was told, 'she only took him out of the water.' 'That's what *she* says', he replied, and so proved that he had found the correct interpretation of the myth.[1]

Departure in dreams means dying. So, too, if a child asks where someone is who has died and whom he misses, it is common nursery usage to reply that he has gone on a journey. Once more I should like to contradict the belief that the dream-symbol is derived from this evasion. The dramatist is using the same symbolic connection when he speaks of the after-life as 'the undiscovered country from whose bourn no *traveller* returns'. Even in ordinary life it is common to speak of 'the last journey'. Every one acquainted with ancient rituals is aware of how seriously (in the religion of Ancient Egypt, for instance) the idea is taken of a journey to the land of the dead. Many copies have survived of *The Book of the Dead*, which was supplied to the mummy like a Baedeker to take with him on the journey. Ever since burial-places have been separated from dwelling-places the dead person's last journey has indeed become a reality.

It is just as little the case that genital symbolism is something that is found only in dreams. Every one of you has probably at one time or another spoken impolitely of a woman as an '*alte Schachtel*' ['old box'], perhaps without knowing that you were using a genital symbol. In the New Testament we find woman referred to as 'the weaker vessel'. The Hebrew scriptures, written in a style that comes close to poetry, are full of sexually symbolic expressions, which have not always been correctly understood and whose exegesis (for instance, in the case of the

---

[1] [Freud used this 'correct interpretation of the myth' as the basis of his last work, *Moses and Monotheism* (1939a).]

Song of Solomon[1]) has led to some misunderstandings. In later Hebrew literature it is very common to find a woman represented by a house, whose door stands for the sexual orifice. A man complains, for instance, in a case of lost virginity, that he has 'found the door open'. So, too, the symbol of a table for a woman in these writings. Thus, a woman says of her husband: 'I laid the table for him, but he turned it round.' Lame children are said to come about through the man's 'turning the table round'. I take these examples from a paper by Dr. L. Levy of Brünn [1914].

The fact that ships, too, in dreams stand for women is made credible by the etymologists, who tell us that '*Schiff* [ship]' was originally the name of an earthenware vessel and is the same word as '*Schaff*' [a dialect word meaning 'tub']. That ovens represent women and the uterus is confirmed by the Greek legend of Periander of Corinth and his wife Melissa. The tyrant, according to Herodotus, conjured up the shade of his wife, whom he had loved passionately but had murdered out of jealousy, to obtain some information from her. The dead woman proved her identity by saying that he (Periander) had '*pushed his bread into a cold oven*', as a disguise for an event which no one else could know of. In the periodical *Anthropophyteia*, edited by F. S. Krauss, an invaluable source of knowledge of sexual anthropology,[2] we learn that in a particular part of Germany they say of a woman who has given birth to a child that '*her oven has come to pieces*'. Kindling fire, and everything to do with it, is intimately interwoven with sexual symbolism. Flame is always a male genital, and the hearth is its female counterpart.

If you may have felt surprised at the frequency with which landscapes are used in dreams to represent the female genitals, you can learn from mythology the part played by *Mother Earth* in the concepts and cults of the peoples of antiquity and how their view of agriculture was determined by *this* symbolism. You will perhaps be inclined to trace the fact that in dreams a room represents a woman to the common usage in our language by which '*Frau*' is replaced by '*Frauenzimmer*'[3]—the

[1] [Some examples are given in Section D of Chapter VI of *I. of D.*]

[2] [Cf. Freud's appreciative letter to Krauss (1910*f*).]

[3] [Literally 'woman's apartment'. The word is very often used in German as a slightly derogatory synonym for 'woman'.]

human being is replaced by the apartment allotted to her.
Similarly we speak of the 'Sublime Porte'[1], meaning the Sultan
and his government. So too the title of the Ancient Egyptian
ruler, 'Pharaoh', means simply 'Great Courtyard'. (In the
Ancient East the courts between the double gateways of a city
were public meeting-places like the market-places of the classical world.) This derivation, however, appears to be too superficial. It seems to me more likely that a room became the symbol
of a woman as being the space which encloses human beings.
We have already found 'house' used in a similar sense; and
mythology and poetical language enable us to add 'city',
'citadel', 'castle' and 'fortress' as further symbols for 'woman'.
The question could be easily settled from the dreams of people
who do not speak or understand German. During the last few
years I have mainly treated foreign-speaking patients, and I
seem to remember that in their dreams too '*Zimmer*' ['room']
meant '*Frauenzimmer*', though they had no similar usage in their
languages. There are other indications that the symbolic relation can go beyond the limits of language—which, incidentally
was asserted long ago by an old investigator of dreams, Schubert
[1814]. However, none of my dreamers were completely
ignorant of German, so the decision must be left to psycho-
analysts who can collect data from unilingual people in other
countries.

There is scarcely one of the symbolic representations of the
male genitals which does not recur in joking, vulgar or poetic
usage, especially in the ancient classical dramatists. But here we
meet not only the symbols which appear in dreams, but others
besides—for instance tools employed in various operations, and
particularly the plough. Moreover, the symbolic representation
of masculinity leads us to a very extensive and much disputed
region, which, on grounds of economy, we shall avoid. I should
like, however, to devote a few words to one symbol, which, as it
were, falls outside this class—the number 3.[2] Whether this
number owes its sacred character to this symbolic connection
remains undecided. But what seems certain is that a number of
tripartite things that occur in nature—the clover leaf, for

---

[1] [Literally, 'Gateway', the old diplomatic term for the Otto-
man Court at Constantinople before 1923, derived *via* the French
from the Turkish title.]   [2] [Cf. p. 220 below.]

instance—owe their use for coats of arms and emblems to this symbolic meaning. Similarly, the tripartite lily—the so-called *fleur-de-lis*—and the remarkable heraldic device of two islands so far apart as Sicily and the Isle of Man—the *triskeles* (three bent legs radiating from a centre)—seem to be stylized versions of the male genitals. Likenesses of the male organ were regarded in antiquity as the most powerful *apotropaic* (means of defence) against evil influences, and, in conformity with this, the lucky charms of our own day can all be easily recognized as genital or sexual symbols. Let us consider a collection of such things—as they are worn, for instance, in the form of small silver hanging trinkets: a four-leaved clover, a pig, a mushroom, a horse-shoe, a ladder, a chimney-sweep. The four-leaved clover has taken the place of the three-leaved one which is really suited to be a symbol. The pig is an ancient fertility symbol. The mushroom is an undoubted penis-symbol: there are mushrooms [fungi] which owe their systematic name (*Phallus impudicus*) to their unmistakable resemblance to the male organ. The horseshoe copies the outline of the female genital orifice, while the chimney-sweep, who carries the ladder, appears in this company on account of his activities, with which sexual intercourse is vulgarly compared. (Cf. *Anthropophyteia.*) We have made the acquaintance of his ladder in dreams as a sexual symbol; here German linguistic usage comes to our help and shows us how the word *'steigen'* ['to climb,' or 'to mount'] is used in what is *par excellence* a sexual sense. We say *'den Frauen nachsteigen'* ['to run' (literally 'climb') 'after women'], and *'ein alter Steiger'* ['an old rake' (literally 'climber')]. In French, in which the word for steps on a staircase is *'marches'*, we find a precisely analogous term *'un vieux marcheur'*. The fact that in many large animals climbing or 'mounting' on the female is a necessary preliminary to sexual intercourse probably fits into this context.[1]

'Pulling off a branch' as a symbolic representation of masturbation is not merely in harmony with vulgar descriptions of the act[2] but has far-reaching mythological parallels. But that masturbation, or rather the punishment for it—castration—, should be represented by the falling out or pulling out of teeth

---

[1] [This is largely repeated from Freud's Nuremberg Congress paper (1910*d*).]

[2] [Cf. the English 'tossing off'.]

is especially remarkable, since there is a counterpart to it in anthropology which can be known to only a very small number of dreamers. There seems to me no doubt that the circumcision practised by so many peoples is an equivalent and substitute for castration. And we now learn that certain primitive tribes in Australia carry out circumcision as a puberty rite (at the festival to celebrate a boy's attaining sexual maturity), while other tribes, their near neighbours, have replaced this act by the knocking out of a tooth.

Here I bring my account of these specimens to an end. They are only specimens. We know more on the subject; but you may imagine how much richer and more interesting a collection like this would be if it were brought together, not by amateurs like us, but by real professionals in mythology, anthropology, philology and folklore.

A few consequences force themselves on our notice; they cannot be exhaustive, but they offer us food for reflection.

In the first place we are faced by the fact that the dreamer has a symbolic mode of expression at his disposal which he does not know in waking life and does not recognize. This is as extraordinary as if you were to discover that your housemaid understood Sanskrit, though you know that she was born in a Bohemian village and never learnt it. It is not easy to account for this fact by the help of our psychological views. We can only say that the knowledge of symbolism is unconscious[1] to the dreamer, that it belongs to his unconscious mental life. But even with this assumption we do not meet the point. Hitherto it has only been necessary for us to assume the existence of unconscious endeavours—endeavours, that is, of which, temporarily or permanently, we know nothing. Now, however, it is a question of more than this, of unconscious pieces of knowledge, of connections of thought, of comparisons between different objects which result in its being possible for one of them to be regularly put in place of the other. These comparisons are not freshly made on each occasion; they lie ready to hand and are complete, once and for all. This is implied by the fact of their agreeing in the case of different individuals—possibly, indeed, agreeing in spite of differences of language. What can

[1] [Cf. footnote, p. 21.]

be the origin of these symbolic relations? Linguistic usage covers only a small part of them. The multiplicity of parallels in other spheres of knowledge are mostly unknown to the dreamer; we ourselves have been obliged to collect them laboriously.

Secondly, these symbolic relations are not something peculiar to dreamers or to the dream-work through which they come to expression. This same symbolism, as we have seen, is employed by myths and fairy tales, by the people in their sayings and songs, by colloquial linguistic usage and by the poetic imagination. The field of symbolism is immensely wide, and dream-symbolism is only a small part of it: indeed, it serves no useful purpose to attack the whole problem from the direction of dreams. Many symbols which are commonly used elsewhere appear in dreams very seldom or not at all. Some dream-symbols are not to be found in all other fields but only, as you have seen, here and there. One gets an impression that what we are faced with here is an ancient but extinct mode of expression, of which different pieces have survived in different fields, one piece only here, another only there, a third, perhaps, in slightly modified forms in several fields. And here I recall the phantasy of an interesting psychotic patient, who imagined a 'basic language' of which all these symbolic relations would be residues.[1]

Thirdly, it must strike you that the symbolism in the other fields I have mentioned is by no means solely sexual symbolism, whereas in dreams symbols are used almost exclusively for the expression of sexual objects and relations. This is not easily explained either. Are we to suppose that symbols which originally had a sexual significance later acquired another application and that, furthermore, the toning-down of representation by symbols into other kinds of representation may be connected with this? These questions can evidently not be answered so long as we have considered dream-symbolism alone. We can only hold firmly to the suspicion that there is a specially intimate relation between true symbols and sexuality.

In this connection we have been given an important hint

---

[1] [This was Senatspräsident Schreber, whose case history was analysed by Freud (1911c).]

during the last few years. A philologist, Hans Sperber [1912], of Uppsala, who works independently of psycho-analysis, has put forward the argument that sexual needs have played the biggest part in the origin and development of speech. According to him, the original sounds of speech served for communication, and summoned the speaker's sexual partner; the further development of linguistic roots accompanied the working activities of primal man. These activities, he goes on, were performed in common and were accompanied by rhythmically repeated utterances. In this way a sexual interest became attached to work. Primal man made work acceptable, as it were, by treating it as an equivalent and substitute for sexual activity. The words enunciated during work in common thus had two meanings; they denoted sexual acts as well as the working activity equated with them. As time went on, the words became detached from the sexual meaning and fixed to the work. In later generations the same thing happened with new words, which had a sexual meaning and were applied to new forms of work. In this way a number of verbal roots would have been formed, all of which were of sexual origin and had subsequently lost their sexual meaning. If the hypothesis I have here sketched out is correct, it would give us a possibility of understanding dream-symbolism. We should understand why dreams, which preserve something of the earliest conditions, have such an extraordinarily large number of sexual symbols, and why, in general, weapons and tools always stand for what is male, while materials and things that are worked upon stand for what is female. The symbolic relation would be the residue of an ancient verbal identity; things which were once called by the same name as the genitals could now serve as symbols for them in dreams.

The parallels we have found to dream-symbolism also allow us to form an estimate of the characteristic of psycho-analysis which enables it to attract general interest in a way in which neither psychology nor psychiatry has succeeded in doing. In the work of psycho-analysis links are formed with numbers of other mental sciences, the investigation of which promises results of the greatest value: links with mythology and philology, with folklore, with social psychology and the theory of religion. You will not be surprised to hear that a periodical has grown up on psycho-analytic soil whose sole aim is to foster these links. This periodical is known as *Imago*, founded in 1912 and edited by Hanns Sachs and Otto Rank.[1] In all these links the share of psycho-analysis is in the first instance that of giver and only to a less extent that of receiver. It is true that this brings it an advantage in the fact that its strange findings become more familiar when they are met with again in other fields; but on the whole it is psycho-analysis which provides the technical methods and the points of view whose application in these other fields should prove fruitful. The mental life of human individuals, when subjected to psycho-analytic investigation, offers us the explanations with the help of which we are able to solve a number of riddles in the life of human communities or at least to set them in a true light.

Incidentally, I have said nothing at all to you yet as to the circumstances in which we can obtain our deepest insight into the hypothetical 'primal language' and as to the field in which most of it has survived. Until you know this you cannot form an opinion of its whole significance. For this field is that of the neuroses and its material is the symptoms and other manifestations of neurotic patients, for the explanation and treatment of which psycho-analysis was, indeed, created.

The fourth of my reflections takes us back to the beginning and directs us along our prescribed path. I have said [p. 149] that even if there were no dream-censorship dreams would still not be easily intelligible to us, for we should still be faced with the task of translating the symbolic language of dreams into that of our waking thought. Thus symbolism is a second and independent factor in the distortion of dreams, alongside of the dream-censorship. It is plausible to suppose, however, that the dream-censorship finds it convenient to make use of symbolism, since it leads towards the same end—the strangeness and incomprehensibility of dreams.

It will shortly become clear whether a further study of dreams may not bring us up against yet another factor that contributes to the distortion of dreams. But I should not like to leave the subject of dream-symbolism without once more [p. 152] touch-

[1] [It ceased publication in 1941. A journal with a similar aim, *The American Imago*, was founded by Hanns Sachs in Boston in 1939.]

ing on the problem of how it can meet with such violent resistance in educated people when the wide diffusion of symbolism in myths, religion, art and language is so unquestionable. May it not be that what is responsible is once again its connection with sexuality?

LECTURE XI

THE DREAM-WORK[1]

LADIES AND GENTLEMEN,—When you have thoroughly grasped the dream-censorship and representation by symbols, you will not yet, it is true, have completely mastered the distortion in dreams, but you will nevertheless be in a position to understand most dreams. In doing so you will make use of both of the two complementary techniques: calling up ideas that occur to the dreamer till you have penetrated from the substitute to the genuine thing and, on the ground of your own knowledge, replacing the symbols by what they mean. Later on we shall discuss some uncertainties that arise in this connection.

We can now take up once more a task that we tried to carry out previously with inadequate means, when we were studying the relations between the elements of dreams and the genuine things they stood for. We laid down four main relations of the kind [p. 120 ff.]: the relation of a part to a whole, approximation or allusion, the symbolic relation and the plastic representation of words. We now propose to undertake the same thing on a larger scale, by comparing the manifest content of a dream *as a whole* with the latent dream as it is revealed by interpretation.

I hope you will never again confuse these two things with each other. If you reach that point, you will probably have gone further in understanding dreams than most readers of my *Interpretation of Dreams*. And let me remind you once again that the work which transforms the latent dream into the manifest one is called the *dream-work*. The work which proceeds in the contrary direction, which endeavours to arrive at the latent dream from the manifest one, is our *work of interpretation*. This work of interpretation seeks to undo the dream-work. The dreams of infantile type which we recognize as obvious fulfilments of wishes have nevertheless experienced some amount of dream-work—they have been transformed from a wish into an actual experience and also, as a rule, from thoughts into visual images.

[1] [The whole of Chapter VI of *I. of D.* (over a third of the entire book) is devoted to the dream-work.]

In their case there is no need for interpretation but only for un-doing these two transformations. The additional dream-work that occurs in other dreams is called 'dream-distortion', and this has to be undone by our work of interpretation.

Having compared the interpretations of numerous dreams, I am in a position to give you a summary description of what the dream-work does with the material of the latent dream-thoughts. I beg you, however, not to try to understand too much of what I tell you. It will be a piece of description which should be listened to with quiet attention.

The first achievement of the dream-work is *condensation*.[1] By that we understand the fact that the manifest dream has a smaller content than the latent one, and is thus an abbreviated translation of it. Condensation can on occasion be absent; as a rule it is present, and very often it is enormous. It is never changed into the reverse; that is to say, we never find that the manifest dream is greater in extent or content than the latent one. Condensation is brought about by (1) the total omission of certain latent elements, (2) by only a fragment of some complexes in the latent dream passing over into the manifest one and (3) by latent elements which have something in common being combined and fused into a single unity in the manifest dream.

If you prefer it, we can reserve the term 'condensation' for the last only of these processes. Its results are particularly easy to demonstrate. You will have no difficulty in recalling instances from your own dreams of different people being con-densed into a single one. A composite figure of this kind may look like A perhaps, but may be dressed like B, may do some-thing that we remember C doing, and at the same time we may know that he is D. This composite structure is of course empha-sizing something that the four people have in common. It is possible, naturally, to make a composite structure out of things or places in the same way as out of people, provided that the various things and places have in common something which is emphasized by the latent dream. The process is like construct-ing a new and transitory concept which has this common

[1] [Condensation is discussed, with numerous examples, in Sec-tion A of Chapter VI of *I. of D.*]

element as its nucleus. The outcome of this superimposing of
the separate elements that have been condensed together is as a
rule a blurred and vague image, like what happens if you take
several photographs on the same plate.[1]

The production of composite structures like these must be of
great importance to the dream-work, since we can show that,
where in the first instance the common elements necessary for
them were missing, they are deliberately introduced—for instance, through the choice of the words by which a thought is
expressed. We have already come across condensations and
composite structures of this sort. They played a part in the production of some slips of the tongue. You will recall the young
man who offered to '*begleitdigen*' ['*begleiten* (accompany)' + '*beleidigen* (insult)', p. 33] a lady. Moreover, there are jokes of
which the technique is based on a condensation like this.[2] But
apart from these cases, it may be said that the process is something quite unusual and strange. It is true that counterparts to
the construction of these composite figures are to be found in
some creations of our imagination, which is ready to combine
into a unity components of things that do not belong together
in our experience—in the centaurs, for instance, and the fabu-
lous beasts which appear in ancient mythology or in Böcklin's
pictures. The 'creative' imagination, indeed, is quite incapable
of *inventing* anything; it can only combine components that are
strange to one another. But the remarkable thing about the
procedure of the dream-work lies in what follows. The material
offered to the dream-work consists of thoughts—a few of which
may be objectionable and unacceptable, but which are correctly constructed and expressed. The dream-work puts these
thoughts into another form, and it is a strange and incomprehensible fact that in making this translation (this rendering, as
it were, into another script or language) these methods of
merging or combining are brought into use. After all, a translation normally endeavours to preserve the distinctions made
in the text and particularly to keep things that are similar
separate. The dream-work, quite the contrary, tries to condense

[1] [Freud more than once compared the result of condensation
with Francis Galton's 'composite photographs', e.g. Chapter IV of
I of D.]

[2] [This technique is discussed, with many examples, in the first
section of Chapter II of Freud's book on jokes (1905c), (Norton,
1960).]

two different thoughts by seeking out (like a joke) an ambiguous word in which the two thoughts may come together. We need not try to understand this feature all at once, but it may become important for our appreciation of the dream-work.

But although condensation makes dreams obscure, it does not give one the impression of being an effect of the dream-censorship. It seems traceable rather to some mechanical or economic factor, but in any case the censorship profits by it.

The achievements of condensation can be quite extraordinary. It is sometimes possible by its help to combine two quite different latent trains of thought into one manifest dream, so that one can arrive at what appears to be a sufficient interpretation of a dream and yet in doing so can fail to notice a possible 'over-interpretation'.[1]

In regard to the connection between the latent and the manifest dream, condensation results also in no simple relation being left between the elements in the one and the other. A manifest element may correspond simultaneously to several latent ones, and, contrariwise, a latent element may play a part in several manifest ones—there is, as it were, a criss-cross relationship [cf. p. 125]. In interpreting a dream, moreover, we find that the associations to a single manifest element need not emerge in succession: we must often wait till the whole dream has been interpreted.

Thus the dream-work carries out a very unusual kind of transcription of the dream-thoughts: it is not a word-for-word or a sign-for-sign translation; nor is it a selection made according to fixed rules—as though one were to reproduce only the consonants in a word and to leave out the vowels; nor is it what might be described as a representative selection—one element being invariably chosen to take the place of several; it is something different and far more complicated.

The second achievement of the dream-work is *displacement*.[2] Fortunately we have made some preliminary examination of

---

[1] [This is commented on at several points in *I. of D.*, e.g., near the end of Chapter VII, Section A. An example of such a second interpretation will be found in Chapter IV in *I. of D.*]

[2] [Displacement is the subject of Section B of Chapter VI of *I. of D.*, but it comes up for discussion at a great many other places in the book.]

this: for we know that it is entirely the work of the dream-censorship. It manifests itself in two ways: in the first, a latent element is replaced not by a component part of itself but by something more remote—that is, by an allusion; and in the second, the psychical accent is shifted from an important element on to another which is unimportant, so that the dream appears differently centred and strange.

Replacing something by an allusion to it is a process familiar in our waking thought as well, but there is a difference. In waking thought the allusion must be easily intelligible, and the substitute must be related in its subject-matter to the genuine thing it stands for. Jokes, too, often make use of allusion. They drop the precondition of there being an association in subject-matter, and replace it by unusual external[1] associations such as similarity of sound, verbal ambiguity, and so on. But they retain the precondition of intelligibility: a joke would lose all its efficiency if the path back from the allusion to the genuine thing could not be followed easily.[2] The allusions employed for displacement in dreams have set themselves free from both of these restrictions. They are connected with the element they replace by the most external and remote relations and are therefore unintelligible; and when they are undone, their interpretation gives the impression of being a bad joke[3] or of an arbitrary and forced explanation dragged in by the hair of its head. For the dream-censorship only gains its end if it succeeds in making it impossible to find the path back from the allusion to the genuine thing.

Displacement of accent is unheard-of as a method of expressing thoughts. We sometimes make use of it in waking thought in order to produce a comic effect. I can perhaps call up the impression it produces of going astray if I recall an anecdote. There was a blacksmith in a village, who had committed a capital offence. The Court decided that the crime must be

[1] [An 'external' association is one that is based not on the *meaning* of the two associated words, but on superficial connections (such as similarity of sound) or purely accidental ones.]

[2] [An account of the 'allusion' technique of jokes with a number of examples appears in Section II of Chapter II of the book on jokes (1905c), (Norton, 1960). The necessity for their being easily intelligible is discussed ibid., 150.]

[3] [This is further discussed on p. 235 f. below.]

punished; but as the blacksmith was the only one in the village and was indispensable, and as on the other hand there were three tailors living there, one of *them* was hanged instead.[1]

The third achievement of the dream-work is psychologically the most interesting. It consists in transforming thoughts into visual images.[2] Let us keep it clear that this transformation does not affect *everything* in the dream-thoughts; some of them retain their form and appear as thoughts or knowledge in the manifest dream as well; nor are visual images the only form into which thoughts are transformed. Nevertheless they comprise the essence of the formation of dreams; this part of the dream-work is, as we already know, the second most regular one [p. 129], and we have already made the acquaintance of the 'plastic' representation of words in the case of individual dream-elements [p. 121].

It is clear that this achievement is not an easy one. To form some idea of its difficulties, let us suppose that you have undertaken the task of replacing a political leading article in a newspaper by a series of illustrations. You will thus have been thrown back from alphabetic writing to picture writing. In so far as the article mentioned people and concrete objects you will replace them easily and perhaps even advantageously by pictures; but your difficulties will begin when you come to the representation of abstract words and of all those parts of speech which indicate relations between thoughts—such as particles, conjunctions and so on. In the case of abstract words you will be able to help yourselves out by means of a variety of devices. For instance, you will endeavour to give the text of the article a different wording, which may perhaps sound less usual but which will contain more components that are concrete and capable of being represented. You will then recall that most abstract words are 'watered-down' concrete ones, and you will for that reason hark back as often as possible to the original concrete meaning of such words. Thus you will be pleased to find

---

[1] [This was a favourite anecdote of Freud's. He told it ten years earlier than this in his book on jokes (1905c), p. 206, and again eight years later in *The Ego and the Id* (1923b),   (Norton, 1960), p. 45.]

[2] [The main discussion of this is in Section C of Chapter VI of *I. of D.*]

that you can represent the 'possession' of an object by a real, physical sitting down on it.[1] And the dream-work does just the same thing. In such circumstances you will scarcely be able to expect very great accuracy from your representation: similarly, you will forgive the dream-work for replacing an element so hard to put into pictures as, for example, 'adultery' ['*Ehebruch*', literally, 'breach of marriage'], by another breach—a broken leg ['*Beinbruch*'].[2] And in this way you will succeed to

---

[1] [The German word '*besitzen*' ('to possess') is more obviously connected with sitting than its English equivalent ('*sitzen*' = 'to sit'). An example of 'sitting down on' in a dream with the meaning of 'possession' occurred in one of the dreams of 'Little Hans'. See Section II of his case history (1909*b*), *Standard Ed.*, **10**, 37 and 39.]

[2] While I am correcting the proofs of these pages chance has put into my hands a newspaper cutting which offers an unexpected confirmation of what I have written above:—

'DIVINE PUNISHMENT

'*A Broken Arm for a Broken Marriage.*

'Frau Anna M., wife of a militiaman, sued Frau Klementine K. for adultery. According to the statement of claim, Frau K. had carried on an illicit relationship with Karl M., while her own husband was at the front and was actually making her an allowance of 70 Kronen [about £3.10 or $17] a month. Frau K. had already received a considerable amount of money from the plaintiff's husband, while she and her child had to live in hunger and poverty. Fellow-soldiers of her husband had informed her that Frau K. had visited taverns with M. and had sat there drinking till far into the night. On one occasion the defendant had asked the plaintiff's husband in the presence of several other soldiers whether he would not get a divorce soon from "his old woman" and set up with her. Frau K.'s caretaker also reported that she had repeatedly seen the plaintiff's husband in the house most incompletely dressed.

'Before a court in the Leopoldstadt [district of Vienna] Frau K. yesterday denied knowing M., so that there could be no question of her having intimate relations with him.

'A witness, Albertine M., stated, however, that she had surprised Frau K. kissing the plaintiff's husband.

'At a previous hearing, M., under examination as a witness, had denied having intimate relations with the defendant. Yesterday the Judge received a letter in which the witness withdrew the statements he had made on the earlier occasion and admitted that he had had a love-affair with Frau K. up till the previous June. He had only denied his relations with the defendant at the former hearing because she had come to him before the hearing and begged him on her knees to save her and say nothing. "Today", the witness wrote, "I feel compelled

some extent in compensating for the clumsiness of the picture writing that is supposed to take the place of the alphabetic script.

For representing the parts of speech which indicate relations between thoughts—'because', 'therefore', 'however', etc.—you will have no similar aids at your disposal; those constituents of the text will be lost so far as translation into pictures goes. In the same way, the dream-work reduces the content of the dream-thoughts to its raw material of objects and activities. You will feel pleased if there is a possibility of in some way hinting, through the subtler details of the pictures, at certain relations not in themselves capable of being represented. And just so does the dream-work succeed in expressing some of the content of the latent dream-thoughts by peculiarities in the *form* of the manifest dream—by its clarity or obscurity, by its division into several pieces, and so on. The number of part-dreams into which a dream is divided usually corresponds to the number of main topics or groups of thoughts in the latent dream. A short introductory dream will often stand in the relation of a prelude to a following, more detailed, main dream or may give the motive for it[1]; a subordinate clause in the dream-thoughts will be replaced by the interpolation of a change of scene into the manifest dream, and so on. Thus the form of dreams is far from being without significance and itself calls for interpretation. When several dreams occur during the same night, they often have the same meaning and indicate that an attempt is being made to deal more and more efficiently with a stimulus of increasing insistence. In individual dreams a particularly difficult element may be represented by several symbols —by 'doublets'.[2]

If we make a series of comparisons between the dream-thoughts and the manifest dreams which replace them, we

to make a full confession to the Court, for I have broken my left arm and this seems to me to be a divine punishment for my wrong-doing."

'The Judge stated that the penal offence had lapsed under the statute of limitations. The plaintiff then withdrew her claim and the defendant was discharged.'

[1] [This is discussed, with an example, in Section C of Chapter VI of *I. of D.*]

[2] [In philology the term is used of two different words with the same etymology: e.g. 'fashion' and 'faction', both from the Latin *'factio'*.]

shall come upon all kinds of things for which we are unprepared: for instance, that nonsense and absurdity in dreams have their meaning. At this point, indeed, the contrast between the medical and the psycho-analytic view of dreams reaches a pitch of acuteness not met with elsewhere. According to the former, dreams are senseless because mental activity in dreams has abandoned all its powers of criticism; according to our view, on the contrary, dreams become senseless when a piece of criticism included in the dream-thoughts—a judgement that 'this is absurd'—has to be represented. The dream you are familiar with of the visit to the theatre ('three tickets for 1 florin 50') [p. 122] is a good example of this. The judgement it expressed was: 'it was absurd to marry so early.' [1]

Similarly, in the course of our work of interpretation we learn what it is that corresponds to the doubts and uncertainties which the dreamer so often expresses as to whether a particular element occurred in a dream, whether it was this or whether, on the contrary, it was something else. There is as a rule nothing in the latent dream-thoughts corresponding to these doubts and uncertainties; they are entirely due to the activity of the dream-censorship and are to be equated with an attempt at elimination which has not quite succeeded. [2]

Among the most surprising findings is the way in which the dream-work treats contraries that occur in the latent dream. We know already [p. 171] that conformities in the latent material are replaced by condensations in the manifest dream. Well, contraries are treated in the same way as conformities, and there is a special preference for expressing them by the same manifest element. Thus an element in the manifest dream which is capable of having a contrary may equally well be expressing either itself or its contrary or both together: only the sense can decide which translation is to be chosen. This connects with the further fact that a representation of 'no'—or at any rate an unambiguous one—is not to be found in dreams.

A welcome analogy to this strange behaviour of the dream-

[1] [Absurdity in dreams is discussed in Section G of Chapter VI of *I. of D.*]
[2] [Cf. Section A of Chapter VII in *I. of D.* Doubt as a symptom of obsessional neurosis is discussed in Lecture XVII (p. 259 f. below).]

work is provided for us in the development of language. Some philologists have maintained that in the most ancient languages contraries such as 'strong—weak', 'light—dark', 'big—small' are expressed by the same verbal roots. (What we term 'the antithetical meaning of primal words.') Thus in Ancient Egyptian *'ken'* originally meant 'strong' and 'weak'. In speaking, misunderstanding from the use of such ambivalent words was avoided by differences of intonation and by the accompanying gesture, and in writing, by the addition of what is termed a 'determinative'—a picture which is not itself intended to be spoken. For instance, *'ken'* meaning 'strong' was written with a picture of a little upright man after the alphabetic signs; when *'ken'* stood for 'weak', what followed was the picture of a man squatting down limply. It was only later, by means of slight modifications of the original homologous word, that two distinct representations were arrived at of the contraries included in it. Thus from *'ken'* 'strong—weak' were derived *'ken'* 'strong' and *'kan'* 'weak'. The remains of this ancient antithetical meaning seem to have been preserved not only in the latest developments of the oldest languages but also in far younger ones and even in some that are still living. Here is some evidence of this, derived from K. Abel (1884).[1]

In Latin, words that remained ambivalent in this way are *'altus'* ('high' and 'deep') and *'sacer'* ('sacred' and 'accursed').

As instances of modifications of the same root I may mention *'clamare'* ('to cry'), *'clam'* ('softly', 'quietly', 'secretly'); *'siccus'* ('dry'), *'succus'* ('juice'). And in German: *'Stimme'* ['voice'], *'stumm'* ['dumb'].

If we compare related languages, there are numerous examples. In English, 'to lock'; in German, *'Loch'* ['hole'] and *'Lücke'* ['gap']. In English, 'to cleave'; in German, *'kleben'* ['to stick'].

The English word 'without' (which is really 'with—without') is used to-day for 'without' alone. 'With', in addition to its combining sense, originally had a removing one; this is still to be seen in the compounds 'withdraw' and 'withhold'. Similarly with the German *'wieder'* ['together with' and *'wider'* 'against'].

[1] [Freud wrote a long review of Abel's monograph (1910*e*), from which much of what he says here is quoted in a condensed form. He returns to the subject in Lecture XV, p. 229 f. below.]

Another characteristic of the dream-work also has its counterpart in the development of language. In Ancient Egyptian, as well as in other, later languages, the order of the sounds in a word can be reversed, while keeping the same meaning. Examples of this in English and German are: '*Topf*' ['pot']—'pot'; 'boat'—'tub'; 'hurry'—'*Ruhe*' ['rest']; '*Balken*' ['beam']—'*Kloben*' ['log'] and 'club'; 'wait'—'*täuwen*' ['tarry']. Similarly in Latin and German: '*capere*'—'*packen*' ['to seize']; '*ren*'—'*Niere*' ['kidney'].

Reversals like this, which occur here with individual words, take place in various ways in the dream-work. We already know reversal of meaning, replacement of something by its opposite [p. 178]. Besides this we find in dreams reversals of situation, of the relation between two people—a 'topsy-turvy' world. Quite often in dreams it is the hare that shoots the sportsman. Or again we find a reversal in the order of events, so that what precedes an event causally comes after it in the dream —like a theatrical production by a third-rate touring company, in which the hero falls down dead and the shot that killed him is not fired in the wings till afterwards. Or there are dreams where the whole order of the elements is reversed, so that to make sense in interpreting it we must take the last one first and the first one last. You will remember too from our study of dream-symbolism that going or falling into the water means the same as coming out of it—that is, giving birth or being born [p. 153], and that climbing up a staircase or a ladder is the same thing as coming down it [p. 158]. It is not hard to see the advantage that dream-distortion can derive from this freedom of representation.

These features of the dream-work may be described as *archaic*. They are equally characteristic of ancient systems of expression by speech and writing and they involve the same difficulties, which we shall have to discuss again later in a critical sense.[1]

And now a few more considerations. In the case of the dream-work it is clearly a matter of transforming the latent thoughts which are expressed in words into sensory images, mostly of a visual sort. Now our thoughts originally arose from sensory images of that kind: their first material and their preliminary

[1] [See Lecture XIII below.]

stages were sense impressions, or, more properly, mnemic images of such impressions. Only later were words attached to them and the words in turn linked up into thoughts. The dream-work thus submits thoughts to a *regressive* treatment[1] and un-does their development; and in the course of the regression everything has to be dropped that had been added as a new acquisition in the course of the development of the mnemic images into thoughts.

Such then, it seems, is the dream-work. As compared with the processes we have come to know in it, interest in the manifest dream must pale into insignificance. But I will devote a few more remarks to the latter, since it is of it alone that we have immediate knowledge.

It is natural that we should lose some of our interest in the manifest dream. It is bound to be a matter of indifference to us whether it is well put together, or is broken up into a series of disconnected separate pictures. Even if it has an apparently sensible exterior, we know that this has only come about through dream-distortion and can have as little organic relation to the internal content of the dream as the façade of an Italian church has to its structure and plan. There are other occasions when this façade of the dream *has* its meaning, and reproduces an important component of the latent dream-thoughts with little or no distortion. But we cannot know this before we have submitted the dream to interpretation and have been able to form a judgement from it as to the amount of distortion that has taken place. A similar doubt arises when two elements in a dream appear to have been brought into a close relation to each other. This may give us a valuable hint that we may bring to-gether what corresponds to these elements in the latent dream as well; but on other occasions we can convince ourselves that what belongs together in the dream-thoughts has been torn apart in the dream.

In general one must avoid seeking to explain one part of the manifest dream by another, as though the dream had been coherently conceived and was a logically arranged narrative. On the contrary, it is as a rule like a piece of breccia, com-posed of various fragments of rock held together by a binding

[1] [The subject of 'regression' is discussed at length in Lecture XXII.]

medium, so that the designs that appear on it do not belong to the original rocks imbedded in it. And there is in fact one part of the dream-work, known as 'secondary revision',[1] whose business it is to make something whole and more or less coherent out of the first products of the dream-work. In the course of this, the material is arranged in what is often a completely misleading sense and, where it seems necessary, interpolations are made in it.

On the other hand, we must not over-estimate the dream-work and attribute too much to it. The achievements I have enumerated exhaust its activity; it can do no more than condense, displace, represent in plastic form and subject the whole to a secondary revision.[2] What appear in the dream as expressions of judgement, of criticism, of astonishment or of inference—none of these are achievements of the dream-work and they are very rarely expressions of afterthoughts about the dream; they are for the most part portions of the latent dream-thoughts which have passed over into the manifest dream with a greater or less amount of modification and adaptation to the context. Nor can the dream-work compose speeches. With a few assignable exceptions, speeches in dreams are copies and combinations of speeches which one has heard or spoken oneself on the day before the dream and which have been included in the latent thoughts either as material or as the instigator of the dream.[3] The dream-work is equally unable to carry out calculations. Such of them as appear in the manifest dream are mostly combinations of numbers, sham calculations which are quite senseless *quâ* calculations and are once again only copies of calculations in the latent dream-thoughts.[4] In these circumstances it is not to be wondered at that the interest which had turned to the dream-work soon tends to move away from it to the latent dream-thoughts, which are revealed, distorted to a greater or less degree, by the manifest dream. But there is no justification for carrying this shift of interest so far that, in looking at the matter theoretically, one replaces the dream entirely

---

[1] [This is the subject of Section I of Chapter VI of *I. of D.*]

[2] [Elsewhere Freud excluded secondary revision from the dream-work, cf. 'An Evidential Dream' (1913*a*).]

[3] [Cf. *I. of D.*, Last part of Section F of Chapter VI.]

[4] [Cf. *I. of D.*, the discussion of calculations in dreams in Chapter VI(F).]

by the latent dream-thoughts and makes some assertion about the former which only applies to the latter. It is strange that the findings of psycho-analysis could be misused to bring about this confusion. One cannot give the name of 'dream' to anything other than the product of the dream-work—that is to say, the *form* into which the latent thoughts have been transmuted by the dream-work. [Cf. p. 222 ff.]

The dream-work is a process of quite a singular kind, of which the like has not yet become known in mental life. Condensations, displacements, regressive transformations of thoughts into images—such things are novelties whose discovery has already richly rewarded the labours of psycho-analysis. And you can see once more, from the parallels to the dream-work, the connections which have been revealed between psycho-analytic studies and other fields—especially those concerned in the development of speech and thought.[1] You will only be able to form an idea of the further significance of these discoveries when you learn that the mechanism of dream-construction is the model of the manner in which neurotic symptoms arise.

I am also aware that we are not yet able to make a survey of the whole of the new acquisitions which these studies have brought to psychology. I will only point out the fresh proofs they have provided of the existence of unconscious mental acts —for this is what the latent dream-thoughts are—and what an unimaginably broad access to a knowledge of unconscious mental life we are promised by the interpretation of dreams.

But now the time has no doubt come for me to demonstrate to you from a variety of small examples of dreams what I have been preparing you for in the course of these remarks.

[1] [See also some remarks on the construction of jokes on p. 235 f. below.]

LECTURE XII

SOME ANALYSES OF
SAMPLE DREAMS

LADIES AND GENTLEMEN,—You must not be disappointed if I once again put before you fragments of dream-interpretations instead of inviting you to take part in the interpretation of a nice big dream. You will argue that after so many preparations you have a right to it, and you will express your conviction that after so many thousands of dreams have been successfully interpreted, it should have been possible long since to have brought together a collection of excellent sample dreams on which all our assertions about the dream-work and the dream-thoughts could be demonstrated. Just so. But the difficulties that stand in the way of the fulfilment of your wish are too many.

In the first place I must admit that no one carries on the interpretation of dreams as his main occupation. How does it come about, then, that people do interpret them? Occasionally, with no particular end in view, one may interest oneself in the dreams of an acquaintance, or one may work through one's own dreams for a time in order to train oneself in psycho-analytic work; but for the most part what one has to deal with are the dreams of neurotic patients who are under psycho-analytic treatment. These latter dreams are excellent material and are in no way inferior to those of healthy people; but the technique of the treatment necessitates our subordinating dream-interpretation to therapeutic aims, and we have to allow a whole number of dreams to drop after we have extracted something from them that is of service to the treatment.[1] Some dreams that occur during treatment entirely escape any full analysis: since they have arisen out of the great mass of psychical material which is still unknown to us, it is impossible to understand them before the treatment is finished. If I were to report dreams of this kind, it would oblige me to uncover all the

[1] [An account of the reasons for this is given in 'The Handling of Dream-Interpretation in Psycho-Analysis' (1911e).]

secrets of a neurosis as well; and that will not do for us, since it is precisely to prepare us for the study of the neuroses that we have attacked the problem of dreams.

You, however, would be glad to dispense with this material and would prefer to be given an explanation of the dreams of healthy people or of your own dreams. But this cannot be done, on account of their content. It is impossible to submit either oneself or anyone else whose confidence one enjoys to the ruthless exposure that would be involved in a detailed analysis of his dreams, which, as you already know, are concerned with the most intimate part of one's personality. But there is another difficulty in the way apart from that of providing the material. You are aware that dreams present an alien appearance to the dreamer himself, and much more so to anyone who is unacquainted with him personally. Our literature is not poor in good and detailed dream-analyses. I myself have published a few within the framework of case histories.[1] Perhaps the best example of the interpretation of a dream is the one reported by Otto Rank [1910b] consisting of two interrelated dreams dreamt by a young girl, which occupy about two pages of print: but their analysis extends to seventy-six pages. So I should need something like a whole term to conduct you through a piece of work of the sort. If one takes up any comparatively long and much distorted dream, one has to give so many explanations of it, to bring up so much material in the way of associations and memories, to follow up so many by-paths, that a lecture about it would be quite confusing and unsatisfactory. I must therefore ask you to be content with what can be had more easily—an account of small pieces of the dreams of neurotic patients, in which it is possible to recognize this or that point in isolation. What is easiest to demonstrate are dream-symbols and, after them, some characteristics of the regressive representation in dreams. In the case of each of the dreams that follow, I will indicate why it is that I think it worth reporting.[2]

[1] [The main instances of these are the two dreams in the analysis of 'Dora' (1905e) and the childhood dream of the 'Wolf Man' (1918b). The latter case history was not actually published until after the delivery of this lecture, though it had already been written.]

[2] [Only two of the dreams quoted here (Nos. 6 and 7) are to be found elsewhere. Very large numbers of other examples, mainly of Freud's own dreams, are reported and analysed in I. of D.]

(1) This dream consisted only of two short pictures: *His uncle was smoking a cigarette although it was a Saturday.—A woman was caressing and fondling him* [the dreamer] *as though he were her child.*

In regard to the first picture the dreamer (a Jew) remarked that his uncle was a pious man who never had done and never could do anything sinful like that. In regard to the woman in the second picture nothing occurred to him except his mother. These two pictures or thoughts must obviously be seen in connection with each other. But how? Since he expressly disputed the reality of his uncle's action, it is plausible to insert an 'if': 'If my uncle, that pious man, were to smoke a cigarette on a Saturday, then I might let myself, too, be cuddled by my mother.' This clearly means that cuddling with his mother was something impermissible, like smoking on a Saturday to a pious Jew. You will recall that I told you [p. 177] that in the course of the dream-work all the relations between the dream-thoughts drop out; these are resolved into their raw material and it is the task of the interpretation to re-insert the omitted relations.

(2) As a result of my publications on dreams I have in a sense become a public consultant on matters relating to them, and for many years I have been receiving communications from the most various sources in which dreams are reported to me or submitted to my judgement. I am of course grateful to anyone who adds enough material to the dream to make an interpretation possible or who gives an interpretation himself. The following dream, dreamt by a medical student in Munich and dating from the year 1910, falls into this category. I am bringing it up in order to show you how impossible it is in general to understand a dream till the dreamer has given us his information about it. For I suspect that at bottom you consider that the ideal method of dream-interpretation is by filling in the meaning of the symbols and that you would like to discard the technique of obtaining associations to the dream; and I am anxious to disabuse you of this damaging mistake.

'July 13, 1910. Towards morning I had this dream: *I was bicycling down the street in Tübingen when a brown dachshund rushed up behind me and seized me by the heel. After a little I got off, sat down on a step, and began to hit at the beast, which had bitten firm hold of me.* (I had no disagreeable feelings either from the bite or from the scene as a whole.) *Some elderly ladies were sitting opposite me and grinning at me. Then I woke up and, as has often happened before, at the moment of transition to waking, the whole dream was clear to me.'*

Symbols are of little help here. But the dreamer reported: 'I have recently fallen in love with a girl, but only from seeing her in the street, and I have had no means of getting in contact with her. The dachshund might have been the pleasantest way of doing so, especially as I am a great animal-lover and I liked this same characteristic in the girl.' He added that he had repeatedly intervened in furious dog-fights with great skill and often to the astonishment of the onlookers. We learn then that the girl he was attracted by was always to be seen in the company of this particular dog. As far as the manifest dream was concerned, however, the girl was omitted and only the dog associated with her was left. The elderly ladies who grinned at him may perhaps have taken the girl's place. His further remarks threw no adequate light on this point. The fact that he was bicycling in the dream is a direct repetition of the remembered situation. He never met the girl with the dog except when he was on his bicycle.

(3) When anyone has lost someone near and dear to him, he produces dreams of a special sort for some time afterwards, in which knowledge of the death arrives at the strangest compromises with the need to bring the dead person to life again. In some of these dreams the person who has died is dead and at the same time still alive, because he does not know he is dead; only if he did know would he die completely. In others, he is half dead and half alive, and each of these states is indicated in a particular way. We must not describe these dreams as simply nonsensical; for being brought to life again is no more inconceivable in dreams than it is, for instance, in fairy tales, in which it occurs as a very usual event. So far as I have been able to analyse such dreams, it has turned out that they are capable of a reasonable solution, but that the pious wish to bring the dead person back to life has been able to operate by the strangest means. I will now put before you a dream of this kind which sounds sufficiently queer and senseless and the analysis of which will show you much for which our theoretical

discussions will have prepared you. It is the dream of a man who had lost his father several years before:

His father was dead but had been exhumed and looked bad. He had been living since then and the dreamer was doing all he could to prevent him noticing it. (The dream then went on to other and apparently very remote matters.)

His father was dead; we know that. His having been exhumed did not correspond to reality; and there was no question of reality in anything that followed. But the dreamer reported that after he had come away from his father's funeral, one of his teeth began to ache. He wanted to treat the tooth according to the precept of Jewish doctrine: 'If thy tooth offend thee, pluck it out!' And he went off to the dentist. But the dentist said: 'One doesn't pluck out a tooth. One must have patience with it. I'll put something into it to kill it; come back in three days and I'll take it out.'

'That "take out",' said the dreamer suddenly, 'that's the exhuming!'

Was the dreamer right about this? It only fits more or less, not completely; for the *tooth* was not taken out, but only something in it that had died. But inaccuracies of this kind can, on the evidence of other experiences, well be attributed to the dream-work. If so, the dreamer had condensed his dead father and the tooth that had been killed but retained; he had fused them into a unity. No wonder, then, that something senseless emerged in the manifest dream, for, after all, not everything that was said about the tooth could fit his father. Where could there possibly be a *tertium comparationis* [p. 152 above] between the tooth and his father, to make the condensation possible?

But no doubt he must have been right, for he went on to say that he knew that if one dreams of a tooth falling out it means that one is going to lose a member of one's family.

This popular interpretation, as we know,[1] is incorrect or at least is correct only in a scurrilous sense. We shall be all the more surprised to find the topic thus touched upon re-appearing behind other portions of the dream's content.

The dreamer now began, without any further encouragement, to talk about his father's illness and death as well as

[1] [See pp. 156 f. and 164 f. above.]

about his own relations with him. His father was ill for a long time, and the nursing and treatment had cost him (the son) a lot of money. Yet it was never too much, he was never impatient, he never wished that after all it might soon come to an end. He was proud of his truly Jewish filial piety towards his father, of his strict obedience to Jewish Law. And here we are struck by a contradiction in the thoughts belonging to the dream. He had identified the tooth and his father. He wanted to proceed with the tooth in accordance with Jewish Law, which commanded him to pluck it out if it caused him pain or offence. He also wanted to proceed with his father, too, in accordance with the precepts of the Law, but in this case it commanded him to spare no expense or trouble, to take every burden on himself and to allow no hostile intention to emerge against the object that was causing him pain. Would not the two attitudes have agreed much more convincingly if he had really developed feelings towards his sick father similar to those towards his sick tooth—that is, if he had wished that an early death would put an end to his unnecessary, painful and costly existence?

I do not doubt that this was really his attitude towards his father during the tedious illness and that his boastful assurances of his filial piety were meant to distract him from these memories. Under such conditions the death-wish against a father is apt to become active and to hide itself under the mask of such sympathetic reflections as that 'it would be a happy release for him'. But please observe that here we have passed a barrier in the latent dream-thoughts themselves. No doubt the first portion of them was unconscious only temporarily—that is, during the construction of the dream; but his hostile impulses against his father must have been permanently unconscious.[1] They may have originated from scenes in his childhood and have occasionally slipped into consciousness, timidly and disguised, during his father's illness. We can assert this with greater certainty of other latent thoughts which have made unmistakable contributions to the content of the dream. Nothing, indeed, is to be discovered in the dream of his hostile impulses towards his father. But if we look for the roots of such hostility to a father in childhood, we shall recall that fear of a father is

[1] [This is carried further at the end of Lecture XIII, p. 212 below.]

set up because, in the very earliest years, he opposes a boy's sexual activities, just as he is bound to do once more from social motives after the age of puberty. This relation to his father applies to our dreamer as well: his love for him included a fair admixture of awe and anxiety, which had their source in his having been early deterred by threats from sexual activity.

The remaining phrases in the manifest dream can be explained now in relation to the masturbation complex. '*He looked bad*' is indeed an allusion to another remark of the dentist's to the effect that it looks bad if one has lost a tooth in that part of the month; but it relates at the same time to the 'looking bad' by which a young man at puberty betrays, or is afraid he betrays, his excessive sexual activity. It was not without relief to his own feelings that in the manifest content the dreamer displaced the 'looking bad' from himself on to his father—one of the kinds of reversal by the dream-work which is familiar to you [p. 180]. '*He had been living since then*' coincides with the wish to bring back to life as well as with the dentist's promise that the tooth would survive. The sentence 'the dreamer was doing all he could *to prevent him (his father) noticing it*' is very subtly devised to mislead us into thinking that it should be completed by the words 'that he was dead'. The only completion, however, that makes sense comes once more from the masturbation complex; in that connection it is self-evident that the young man did all he could to conceal his sexual life from his father. And finally, remember that we must always interpret what are called 'dreams with a dental stimulus' as relating to masturbation and the dreaded punishment for it. [Cf. footnote, p. 188.]

You can see now how this incomprehensible dream came about. It was done by producing a strange and misleading condensation, by disregarding all the thoughts that were in the centre of the latent thought-process and by creating ambiguous substitutes for the deepest and chronologically most remote of those thoughts.[1]

(4) We have already tried repeatedly to come to understand

---

[1] [A fragment of a dream very similar to, if not identical with, this one is discussed in *I. of D.* See an example in (II) of Section G in Chapter VI. It is also discussed in 'Formulations on the Two Principles of Mental Functioning' (1911*b*).]

the matter-of-fact and commonplace dreams which have nothing senseless or strange about them but which raise the question of why one should dream about such indifferent stuff. [Cf. pp. 96–7 and 117.] I will therefore offer you another example of this kind—three interconnected dreams dreamt by a young lady in one night.

(a) *She was walking across the hall of her house and struck her head against a low-hanging chandelier and drew blood.*

No reminiscence, nothing that had really happened. The information she produced in response to it led in quite other directions. 'You know how badly my hair's falling out. "My child," my mother said to me yesterday, "if this goes any further you'll have a head as smooth as a bottom."' So here the head stands for the other end of the body. We can understand the chandelier, without any help, as a symbol: all objects capable of being lengthened are symbols of the male organ [p. 155]. It was therefore a matter of bleeding at the lower end of the body, which had arisen from contact with a penis. This might still be ambiguous. Her further associations showed that what was in question concerned a belief that menstrual bleeding arises from sexual intercourse with a man—a piece of sexual theory which counts many faithful believers among immature girls.

(b) *She saw a deep pit in the vineyard, which she knew had been caused by a tree being torn out.* She added a remark that the tree *was missing.* She meant that she had not seen the tree in her dream; but the same wording served to express another thought which made the symbolic interpretation quite certain. The dream referred to another piece of infantile sexual theory—to the belief that girls originally had the same genitals as boys and that their later shape was the result of castration (the tearing out of a tree).

(c) *She was standing in front of the drawer of her writing-table which she was so familiar with that she could tell at once if anyone had been into it.* Like all drawers, chests and cases, the writing-table drawer stood for the female genitals [p. 156]. She knew that indications of sexual intercourse (and, as she thought, of touching) could be observed on the genitals and had long feared such a discovery. In all these three dreams, I think, the accent is to be placed on *knowledge.* She was recalling the period of her sexual researches when she was a child, of whose outcome she had been quite proud at the time.[1]

(5) Here is a little more symbolism. But this time I must start with a short preamble on the psychical situation. A gentleman who had passed a night in intercourse with a lady described her as one of those motherly characters in whom the wish for a child breaks irresistibly through in intercourse with a man. The circumstances of this meeting, however, called for a precaution which prevented the fertilizing semen from reaching the woman's uterus. On waking up after this night the woman reported the following dream:

An officer in a red cap was running after her in the street. She fled from him, and ran up the stairs with him still after her. Breathless, she reached her flat, slammed the door behind her and locked it. He stayed outside, and when she looked through the peep-hole, he was sitting on a bench outside and weeping.

You will no doubt recognize the pursuit by the officer in the red cap and the breathless climbing upstairs as representing the sexual act [p. 158]. The fact that it was the dreamer who locked herself up against her pursuer will serve as an example of the reversals that are used so commonly in dreams [p. 180], for it was the man who had avoided the consummation of the sexual act. In the same way, her grief was displaced on to the man, for it was he who wept in the dream—and this was simultaneously a representation of the emission of semen.

I feel sure that you have heard some time or other that it is asserted by psycho-analysis that every dream has a sexual meaning. Well, you yourselves are in a position to form a judgement of the incorrectness of this reproach. You have become acquainted with wishful dreams dealing with the satisfaction of the most obvious needs—hunger and thirst and the longing for freedom—with dreams of convenience and of impatience, and also with purely covetous and egoistic dreams. But at the same time you should bear in mind, as one of the results of psychoanalytic research, that greatly distorted dreams give expression mainly (though, again, not exclusively) to sexual wishes.

[1] [The sexual researches and sexual theories of children are discussed in Lecture XX (p. 317 below).]

(6) I have a particular reason for piling up instances of the use of symbols in dreams. At our first meeting [p. 16 ff.] I lamented the difficulty of providing demonstrations and so of carrying conviction in giving instruction in psycho-analysis. And I have no doubt that you have since come to agree with me. But the different theses of psycho-analysis are so intimately connected that conviction can easily be carried over from a single point to a larger part of the whole. It might be said of psycho-analysis that if anyone holds out a little finger to it it quickly grasps his whole hand. No one, even, who has accepted the explanation of parapraxes can logically withhold his belief in all the rest. A second, equally accessible position is offered by dream-symbolism. Here is the dream of an uneducated woman whose husband was a policeman and who had certainly never heard anything about dream-symbolism or psycho-analysis. Then judge for yourselves whether its explanation by the help of sexual symbols can be called arbitrary and forced:

'. . . *Then someone broke into the house and she was frightened and called out for a policeman. But he had gone into a church, to which a number of steps led up, accompanied amicably by two tramps. Behind the church there was a hill and above it a thick wood. The policeman was dressed in a helmet, gorget and cloak. He had a brown beard. The two tramps, who went along peaceably with the policeman, had sack-like aprons tied round their middles. In front of the church a path led up to the hill; on both sides of it there grew grass and brushwood, which became thicker and thicker and, at the top of the hill, turned into a regular wood.*' [1]

You will have no trouble in recognizing the symbols used. The male genitals are represented by a triad of figures, and the female ones by a landscape with a chapel, hill and wood. Once again you find steps as a symbol for the sexual act. What is called a hill in the dream is also called one in anatomy—the Mons Veneris [the hill of Venus].

(7) And here is yet another dream that must be solved by the insertion of symbols. It is notable and convincing from the fact that the dreamer himself translated all the symbols, though he had no sort of previous theoretical knowledge of

[1] [This dream, originally reported by B. Dattner, appears in *I. of D.* in a very slightly different version. See Example IV in Section E of Chapter VI.]

dream-interpretation. Such an attitude is quite unusual and its determinants are not precisely understood:[1]

'He was going for a walk with his father in a place which must certainly have been the Prater,[2] since he saw the Rotunda, with a small annex in front of it to which a captive balloon was attached, though it looked rather limp. His father asked him what all this was for; he was surprised at his asking, but explained it to him. Then they came into a courtyard which had a large sheet of tin laid out in it. His father wanted to pull off a large piece of it, but first looked around to see if anyone was watching. He told him that he need only tell the foreman and he could take some without any bother. A staircase led down from this yard into a shaft, whose walls were cushioned in some soft material, rather like a leather armchair. At the end of the shaft was a longish platform and then another shaft started. . . .'

The dreamer himself interpreted: 'The Rotunda was my genitals and the captive balloon in front of it was my penis, whose limpness I have reason to complain of.' Going into greater detail, then, we may translate the Rotunda as the bottom (habitually regarded by children as part of the genitals) and the small annex in front of it as the scrotum. His father asked him in the dream what all this was—that is, what was the purpose and function of the genitals. It seemed plausible to reverse this situation and turn the dreamer into the questioner. Since he had in fact never questioned his father in this way, we had to look upon the dream-thought as a wish, or take it as a conditional clause, such as: 'If I had asked my father for sexual enlightenment. . . .' We shall presently find the continuation of this thought in another part of the dream.

The courtyard in which the sheet of tin was spread out is not to be taken symbolically in the first instance. It was derived from the business premises of the dreamer's father. For reasons of discretion I have substituted 'tin' for another material in which his father actually dealt: but I have made no other change in the wording of the dream. The dreamer had entered his father's business and had taken violent objection to the somewhat dubious practices on which the firm's earnings in part depended. Consequently the dream-thought I have just interpreted may have continued in this way: '(If I had asked

---

[1] [Cf. some remarks on this at the beginning of Section E of Chapter VI of *I. of D.*]

[2] [The 'Bois de Boulogne' of Vienna. It includes an amusement park.]

him), he would have deceived me just as he deceives his cus-
tomers.' As regards the 'pulling off' which served to represent
his father's dishonesty in business, the dreamer himself produced
a second explanation—namely that it stood for masturbating.
Not only have we long been familiar with this interpretation
[p. 164], but there was something to confirm it in the fact that
the secret nature of masturbation was represented by its reverse: it might be done openly. Just as we should expect, the
masturbatory activity was once again displaced on to the
dreamer's father, like the questioning in the first scene of the
dream. He promptly interpreted the shaft as a vagina, having
regard to the soft cushioning of its walls. I added on my own
authority [p. 158] that climbing down, like climbing up in
other cases, described sexual intercourse in the vagina.

The dreamer himself gave a biographical explanation of the
further details—that the first shaft was followed by a longish
platform and then by another shaft. He had practised intercourse for a time but had then given it up on account of inhibitions, and he now hoped to be able to resume it by the
help of the treatment.[1]

(8) The two following dreams were dreamt by a foreigner of
a highly polygamous disposition. I repeat them to you as
evidence for my assertion [p. 142] that the dreamer's own ego
appears in every dream even if it is concealed in the manifest
content. The trunks in the dreams were symbols of women:

(a) *He was starting on a journey; his luggage was taken to the
station on a carriage, a number of trunks piled up on it, and among them
two big black ones, like boxes of samples. He said to someone con-
solingly: 'Well, they're only going with me as far as the station.'*

He did in fact travel with a great deal of luggage; but he also
brought a great many stories about women into the treatment.
The two black trunks corresponded to two dark[2] women who
were at the time playing the main part in his life. One of them
had wanted to follow him to Vienna; and on my advice he had
telegraphed to put her off.

(b) A scene at the customs-house: *Another traveller opened his*

[1] [This dream and its analysis are reprinted almost exactly from
I. of D. See Example III of Section E in Chapter VI.]
[2] [In German '*schwarz*' ('black').]

box and, coolly smoking a cigarette, said: 'There's nothing in it.' The customs officer seemed to believe him, but felt about once more inside it, and found something quite particularly prohibited. The traveller said in a resigned voice: 'There's nothing to be done about it.'

He himself was the traveller: I was the customs officer. As a rule he was very straightforward in making admissions; but he had intended to keep silent to me about a new connection he had formed with a lady, because he rightly supposed that she was not unknown to me. He displaced the distressing situation of being detected on to a stranger, so that he himself did not seem to appear in the dream.

(9) Here is an example of a symbol which I have not yet mentioned:

He met his sister in the company of two women friends who were themselves sisters. He shook hands with both of them but not with his sister.

No connection with any real occurrence. But his thoughts took him back, rather, to a period in which his observations led him to reflect on how late girls' breasts developed. So the two sisters were breasts; he would have liked to take hold of them with his hand—if only it were not his sister.

(10) Here is an example of death-symbolism in a dream:

He was walking, with two people whose names he knew but had forgotten when he woke up, across a very high, steep iron bridge. Suddenly they had both gone, and he saw a ghost-like man in a cap and linen clothes. He asked him if he was the telegraph-boy. No. Was he the driver? No. Then he walked on further. . . . While he was still dreaming he felt acute anxiety, and after he had woken up he continued the dream with a phantasy that the iron bridge suddenly broke and he fell into the abyss.

People of whom one insists that they are unknown or that one has forgotten their names are mostly people very near to one. The dreamer had a brother and sister; and if he had wished that these two were dead, it would be only fair that in return *he* should be victimized by a fear of death. Of the telegraph-boy he remarked that such people always bring bad news. By his uniform he might equally have been the lamp-lighter; but he puts out the lamps as well, just as the Spirit of Death puts out the torch. The driver made him think of Uhland's poem about King Charles's Voyage, and reminded him of a dangerous sea-voyage with two companions during which he had played the part of the King in the poem.[1] The iron bridge made him think of a recent accident and of the foolish saying: 'Life is a suspension bridge.'[2]

(11) The following dream may count as another representation of death:

An unknown gentleman left a black-edged visiting-card on him.

(12) You will be interested in the following dream in a number of ways, though a neurotic state in the dreamer was one of its preconditions:

He was travelling in a railway-train. The train came to a stop in open country. He thought there was going to be an accident and that he must think of getting away. He went through all the coaches in the train and killed everyone he met—the guard, the engine-driver, and so on.

In connection with this he thought of a story told him by a friend. A lunatic was being conveyed in a compartment on an Italian line, but through carelessness a traveller was allowed in with him. The madman killed the other traveller. Thus he was identifying himself with the madman, and based his right to do so on an obsession by which he was tormented from time to time that he must 'get rid of all accessory witnesses'. But then he himself found a better reason, and this led to the precipitating cause of the dream. At the theatre the night before he had once more seen the girl whom he had wanted to marry but had withdrawn from because she had given him ground for being jealous. In view of the intensity reached by his jealousy he would, he thought, really be mad to want to marry her. This meant that he regarded her as so untrustworthy that, in his jealousy, he would have to kill everyone who came his way. We have already come across walking through a series of rooms

[1] [In Uhland's poem, '*König Karls Meerfahrt*', King Charles and his twelve knights are overtaken by a storm on a voyage to the Holy Land. The twelve knights express their uneasiness in turn—but the King sits silently at the helm and steers the ship to safety.]

[2] [This is quoted as an example of a bad joke in a footnote added in 1912 to Freud's book on jokes (1905*c*), (Norton, 1960), p. 139.]

(here, railway coaches) as a symbol of marriage (a reversal of 'monogamy').[1]

In connection with the train coming to a stop in open country and his being afraid of an accident, he said that once when he was on a railway journey there had been a sudden stop of this kind when they were not in a station. A young lady who was travelling with him had said that there might be going to be a collision and that the safest thing to do was to lift one's legs up high. But this 'lifting the legs high' had also played a part in the many walks and excursions in the country which he had taken with the other girl in the happy early days of their love. This was a fresh argument for thinking he would be mad to marry her now. But my knowledge of the situation made me feel certain that he nevertheless wished he were mad enough to do it.

[1] [This symbol had not been mentioned earlier in these lectures. But in Section E of Chapter VI in *I. of D.*, it is stated that a suite of rooms can stand for a brothel or a harem, or alternatively (by reversal) for a monogamous marriage.]

LECTURE XIII

THE ARCHAIC FEATURES AND INFANTILISM OF DREAMS

LADIES AND GENTLEMEN,—Let us start out once more from the conclusion we arrived at that the dream-work, under the influence of the dream-censorship, transposes the latent dream-thoughts into a different mode of expression. The latent thoughts do not differ from our familiar conscious thoughts of waking life. The new mode of expression is incomprehensible to us owing to many of its features. We have said that it harks back to states of our intellectual development which have long since been superseded—to picture-language, to symbolic connections, to conditions, perhaps, which existed before our thought-language had developed. We have on that account described the mode of expression of the dream-work as *archaic* or *regressive* [p. 180 f.].

You may conclude from this that if we study the dream-work further we must succeed in gaining valuable light on the little-known beginnings of our intellectual development. I hope it will be so; but this work has not so far been started upon. The prehistory into which the dream-work leads us back is of two kinds—on the one hand, into the individual's prehistory, his childhood, and on the other, in so far as each individual somehow recapitulates in an abbreviated form the entire development of the human race, into phylogenetic prehistory too. Shall we succeed in distinguishing which portion of the latent mental processes is derived from the individual prehistoric period and which portion from the phylogenetic one? It is not, I believe, impossible that we shall. It seems to me, for instance, that symbolic connections, which the individual has never acquired by learning, may justly claim to be regarded as a phylogenetic heritage.

This, however, is not the only archaic characteristic of dreams. You are all familiar, of course, from your own experience, with the remarkable amnesia of childhood. I mean the fact that the earliest years of life, up to the age of five, six or eight, have not left behind them traces in our memory like later experiences. Here and there, it is true, we come upon people who can boast of a continuous memory from the first beginnings to the present day; but the other alternative, of gaps in the memory, is by far the more frequent. There has not, in my opinion, been enough astonishment over this fact. By the time a child is two he can speak well, and soon shows that he is at home in complicated mental situations; and he makes remarks which, if they are reported to him many years later, he himself will have forgotten. Moreover, the memory is more efficient at an early age, since it is less overburdened than it is later. Nor is there any reason for regarding the function of memory as a particularly high or difficult mental activity; on the contrary, we can find a good memory in people of very low intellectual standing.[1]

A second remarkable fact to which 1 must draw your attention, and which comes on top of the first one, is that out of the void of memories that covers the earliest years of childhood there stand out a few well-preserved recollections, mostly perceived in plastic form, which cannot justify their survival. Our memory deals with the material of the impressions which impinge on us in later life by making a selection among them. It retains what is of any importance and drops what is unimportant. But this is not true of the childhood memories that have been retained. They do not necessarily correspond to the important experiences of childhood years, nor even to those which must have seemed important from the child's point of view. They are often so commonplace and insignificant that we can only ask ourselves in astonishment why this particular detail has escaped oblivion. I attempted long ago, with the help of analysis, to attack the enigma of childhood amnesia and of the residual memories which interrupt it, and I arrived at the conclusion that even in the case of children it is true in spite of everything that only what is important remains in the memory. But through the processes, already familiar to you, of condensation and more especially of displacement, what is important is replaced in memory by something else which appears unimportant. For this reason I have called these childhood memories

[1] [A longer discussion of infantile amnesia will be found in the second of the *Three Essays* (1905*d*).]

'screen memories', and with a thorough analysis everything that has been forgotten can be extracted from them.[1]

In psycho-analytic treatments we are invariably faced by the task of filling up these gaps in the memory of childhood; and in so far as the treatment is to any extent successful—that is to say, extremely frequently—we also succeed in bringing to light the content of these forgotten years of childhood. Those impressions had never been really forgotten, they were only inaccessible, latent, and had formed part of the unconscious. But it can come about that they emerge from the unconscious spontaneously, and this happens in connection with dreams. It appears that dream-life knows how to find access to these latent, infantile experiences. Excellent examples of this have been reported in the literature and I myself have been able to provide a contribution of the kind. I once dreamt in a certain connection of a person who must have done me a service and whom I saw clearly before me. He was a one-eyed man of small stature, stout, and with his head sunk deep in his shoulders. I concluded from the context that he was a doctor. Luckily I was able to enquire from my mother, who was still alive, what the doctor at my birth-place (which I had left when I was three) had looked like; and I learnt from her that he was one-eyed, short, stout and with his head sunk deep in his shoulders; and I also learnt what the accident was for which he had come to my help and which I myself had forgotten.[2] This fact of dreams having at their disposal the forgotten material of the first years of childhood is thus a further archaic feature.[3]

This same piece of information can be further applied to another of the riddles we have come up against. You recall the amazement which was caused by our discovery that what instigates dreams are actively evil and extravagantly sexual wishes, which have made the censorship and distortion of dreams necessary [p. 142 ff.]. When we have interpreted a

[1] [Screen memories had been discussed by Freud in Chapter IV of *The Psychopathology of Everyday Life* (1901b), (Norton, 1965), as well as in a separate paper on the subject published earlier (1899a).]

[2] [The dream is described in Chapter I(B) of *I. of D.*, where further references will be found.]

[3] [This fact had been noted by Freud in a letter to Fliess of March 10, 1898 (Freud, 1950a, Letter 84).]

dream of this sort to the dreamer and if, to take the most favourable case, he does not actually attack the interpretation, he nevertheless regularly raises the question of where these wishes come from, since they feel alien to him and their opposite is what he is conscious of. We need have no hesitation in pointing out their origin. These evil wishful impulses arise from the past, and often from a past that is not very remote. It can be shown that there was a time when they were familiar and conscious, even if they are no longer so to-day. A woman, whose dream meant that she would like to see her daughter, now seventeen years old, dead before her eyes,[1] found under our guidance that she had indeed at one time harboured this death-wish. The child was the fruit of an unhappy marriage which was soon dissolved. Once, while she still bore her daughter in her womb, in a fit of rage after a violent scene with her husband she had beaten with her fists on her body in order to kill the child inside it. How many mothers, who love their children tenderly, perhaps over-tenderly, to-day, conceived them unwillingly and wished at that time that the living thing within them might not develop further! They may even have expressed that wish in various, fortunately harmless, actions. Thus their death-wish against someone they love, which is later so mysterious, originates from the earliest days of their relationship to that person.

In the same way, a father had a dream which justified the interpretation that he wished for the death of his favourite eldest child. He too was led to remember that there had been a time when this wish was not strange to him. When the child was still an infant in arms, the father, discontented with his choice of a wife, often thought that if the little creature, who meant nothing to him, were to die, he would be free once more and would make better use of his freedom.[2] The same origin can be shown in the case of a great number of similar impulses

[1] [This dream is described at greater length in Chapter IV of *I. of D.* In those passages the girl's age is given three times (in letters) as 'fifteen'. The '17' (in figures) in all the German editions of the present work is perhaps due to a misprint.]

[2] [What appears to be the same story as this is told in much greater detail in connection not with a dream but with a 'bungled action' near the end of Chapter VIII of *The Psychopathology of Everyday Life*, pp. 187–9.]

of hatred; they are recollections of something belonging to the past, which was once conscious and played its part in mental life. You will be inclined to conclude from this that such wishes and such dreams ought not to arise in cases where transformations of this kind in one's relation to someone never occurred, where the relation was of the same kind from the first. I am prepared to admit this; but I must remind you that what you must take into consideration is not the *wording* of the dream but its sense after it has been interpreted. It is possible that a manifest dream of the death of someone loved has merely assumed a horrifying mask and may mean something quite different, or that the loved person is intended as a misleading substitute for someone else.

But the same subject will suggest another and far more serious question. 'Even if,' you will say, 'this death-wish was present at one time and is confirmed by recollection, that is still no explanation. After all, it was superseded long ago, and can only be present to-day in the unconscious as no more than an unemotional memory, not as a powerful impulse. Nothing speaks in favour of this last possibility. Why, then, was it recollected at all in the dream?' This question may justly be raised. An attempt to answer it would lead us too far and would necessitate our taking up a position on one of the most important points in the theory of dreams. But I am obliged to keep within the framework of our discussions and to exercise restraint. So prepare yourselves for a provisional renunciation.[1] Let us content ourselves with the factual evidence that this superseded wish can be shown to be the instigator of the dream, and let us pursue our enquiry whether other evil wishes can be similarly traced back to the past.

We will keep to wishes for getting rid of someone, which may for the most part be attributed to the dreamer's unrestricted egoism. A wish of this kind can very often be pointed to as the constructor of a dream. Whenever anyone in the course of one's life gets in one's way—and how often this must happen in view of the complication of one's relationships in life!—a dream is promptly ready to kill that person, even if it be father or

[1] [Freud returns to this problem at the end of the present lecture (p. 212).]

mother, brother or sister, husband or wife. This wickedness of human nature came as a great surprise to us and we were decidedly disinclined to accept this outcome of dream-interpretation without question. But as soon as we were led to look for the origin of these wishes in the past, we discovered the period of the individual's past in which there was no longer anything strange in such egoism and such wishful impulses, directed even against his closest relatives. It is children, and precisely in those earliest years which are later veiled by amnesia, who often exhibit this egoism to an extremely marked degree and who invariably show clear rudiments or, more correctly speaking, residues of it. Children love themselves first, and it is only later that they learn to love others and to sacrifice something of their own ego to others. Even those people whom a child seems to love from the beginning are loved by him at first because he needs them and cannot do without them—once again from egoistic motives. Not until later does the impulse to love make itself independent of egoism. It is literally true that *his egoism has taught him to love.*

In this connection it will be interesting to compare the child's attitude to his brothers and sisters with that towards his parents. A small child does not necessarily love his brothers and sisters; often he obviously does not. There is no doubt that he hates them as his competitors, and it is a familiar fact that this attitude often persists for long years, till maturity is reached or even later, without interruption. Quite often, it is true, it is succeeded, or let us rather say overlaid, by a more affectionate attitude; but the hostile one seems very generally to be the earlier. This hostile attitude can be observed most easily in children between two and a half and four or five, when a new baby brother or sister appears. It usually meets with a very unfriendly reception. Such remarks as 'I don't like him; the stork can take him away again!' are quite common. After this, every opportunity is taken of disparaging the new arrival and attempts to injure him and even murderous assaults are not unknown. If the difference in age is less, by the time the child's mental activity has awakened to some degree of intensity he finds his competitor already there and adjusts himself to him. If the difference is greater, the new baby may from the first arouse a certain sympathy as an interesting object, a sort of live doll;

and where the difference in age is of eight or more years, solicitous, maternal impulses may already come into play, especially in girls. But, honestly speaking, if one comes upon a wish for the death of a brother or sister behind a dream, there is seldom need to find it puzzling and one can trace its prototype without any trouble in early childhood and often enough in later years of companionship as well.[1]

There is probably no nursery without violent conflicts between its inmates. The motives for these are rivalry for parental love, for common possessions, for living space. The hostile impulses are directed against older as well as against younger members of the family. It was, I believe, Bernard Shaw who remarked: 'As a rule there is only one person an English girl hates more than she hates her mother; and thats her eldest sister.' [2] But there is something in this remark that strikes us as strange. We might at a pinch find hatred and competition with brothers and sisters intelligible. But how can we suppose that feelings of hatred can make their way into the relation between daughter and mother, between parents and children?

This relation is undoubtedly a more favourable one, from the children's point of view as well. That is what our expectations demand; we find an absence of love far more repellent between parents and children than between brothers and sisters. In the former case we have, as it were, made something sacred which in the latter we have left profane. Yet daily observation can show us how frequently the emotional relations between parents and their grown-up children fall behind the ideal set up by society, how much hostility is ready to hand and would be expressed if it were not held back by admixtures of filial piety and affectionate impulses. The motives for this hostility are generally known and their tendency is to divide those of the same sex—the daughter from the mother and the father from the son. The daughter finds in her mother the authority which restricts her will and which is entrusted with the task of imposing on her the renunciation of sexual freedom which society demands; in a few instances she even finds in her a competitor who struggles against being supplanted. The same thing is

---

[1] [The relations between brothers and sisters are discussed with examples in Section D of Chapter V of *I. of D.*]
[2] [John Tanner in *Man and Superman*, Act II.]

repeated between the son and his father still more glaringly. In the son's eyes his father embodies every unwillingly tolerated social restraint; his father prevents him from exercising his will, from early sexual pleasure and, where there is common property in the family, from enjoying it. In the case of an heir to the throne this waiting for a father's death reaches an almost tragic height. There seems less danger to the relation between father and daughter or mother and son. This last provides the purest examples of an unchangeable affection, unimpaired by any egoistic considerations.[1]

Why am I speaking of these things, which are after all commonplaces and universally known? Because there is an unmistakable inclination to disavow their importance in life and to make out that the ideal demanded by society is fulfilled far more often than it really is. It is better, however, that the truth should be told by psychologists rather than that the task should be left to cynics. And, incidentally, this disavowal applies only to real life. Narrative and dramatic works of the imagination may freely make play with the themes that arise from a disturbance of this ideal.

There is no need to feel surprised, therefore, if, in a large number of people, dreams disclose their wish to get rid of their parents and especially of the parent of their own sex. We may assume that this wish is also present in waking life and is even conscious sometimes, if it can be masked by some other motive, as was the case with our dreamer in Example 3 [p. 189 above], where it was replaced by pity for his father's useless sufferings. It is rarely that the hostility alone dominates the relationship; far oftener it is in the background of more affectionate impulses by which it is suppressed, and it must wait until a dream isolates it, as it were. What seems to us of enormous size in a dream, on account of this isolation, shrinks up once more when our interpretation has given it its place in the context of real life (Hanns Sachs).[2] But we come upon this dream-wish, too,

---

[1] [This point is discussed at greater length in Lecture XXXIII of the *New Introductory Lectures,* p. 587.]

[2] [The actual words used by Sachs (1912, 569) were quoted by Freud in a passage which he inserted in 1914 on almost the last page of *I. of D.*]

where it has no relevance in real life, and where the adult need never confess to it in his waking life. The reason for this is that the deepest and most invariable motive for estrangement, especially between two people of the same sex, has already made itself felt in early childhood.

What I have in mind is rivalry in love, with a clear emphasis on the subject's sex. While he is still a small child, a son will already begin to develop a special affection for his mother, whom he regards as belonging to him; he begins to feel his father as a rival who disputes his sole possession. And in the same way a little girl looks on her mother as a person who interferes with her affectionate relation to her father and who occupies a position which she herself could very well fill. Observation shows us to what early years these attitudes go back. We refer to them as the 'Oedipus complex', because the legend of Oedipus realizes, with only a slight softening, the two extreme wishes that arise from the son's situation—to kill his father and take his mother to wife. I do not wish to assert that the Oedipus complex exhausts the relation of children to their parents: it can easily be far more complicated. The Oedipus complex can, moreover, be developed to a greater or less strength, it can even be reversed; but it is a regular and very important factor in a child's mental life, and there is more danger of our under-estimating rather than over-estimating its influence and that of the developments which proceed from it. Incidentally, children often react in their Oedipus attitude to a stimulus coming from their parents, who are frequently led in their preferences by difference of sex, so that the father will choose his daughter and the mother her son as a favourite, or, in case of a cooling-off in the marriage, as a substitute for a love-object that has lost its value.[1]

It cannot be said that the world has shown much gratitude to psycho-analytic research for its revelation of the Oedipus complex. On the contrary, the discovery has provoked the most violent opposition among adults; and those who had neglected to take part in the repudiation of this proscribed and tabooed emotional relationship made up for their fault later by de-priving the complex of its value through twisted re-interpreta-

[1] [Freud discusses the Oedipus complex at much greater length in Lecture XXI (p. 329 ff. below).]

tions.[1] It is my unaltered conviction that there is nothing in this to be disavowed or glossed over. We must reconcile ourselves to the fact which was recognized by the Greek legend itself as an inevitable fate. It is once again an interesting fact that the Oedipus complex, which has been rejected from real life, has been left to imaginative writing, has been placed freely, as it were, at its disposal. Otto Rank [1912b] has shown in a careful study how the Oedipus complex has provided dramatic authors with a wealth of themes in endless modifications, softenings and disguises—in distortions, that is to say, of the kind which we are already familiar with as the work of a censorship. We may therefore also ascribe this Oedipus complex to dreamers who have been fortunate enough to escape conflicts with their parents in later life. And, intimately linked with it, we find what we call the 'castration complex',[2] the reaction to the threats against the child aimed at putting a stop to his early sexual activities and attributed to his father.

What we have already learnt from our study of the mental life of children will lead us to expect to find a similar explanation of the other group of forbidden dream-wishes—the excessive sexual impulses. We are thus encouraged to make a study of the development of children's sexual life and from many sources we arrive at what follows.

First and foremost, it is an untenable error to deny that children have a sexual life and to suppose that sexuality only begins at puberty with the maturation of the genitals. On the contrary, from the very first children have a copious sexual life, which differs at many points from what is later regarded as normal. What in adult life is described as 'perverse' differs from the normal in these respects: first, by disregarding the barrier of species (the gulf between men and animals), secondly, by overstepping the barrier against disgust, thirdly that against incest (the prohibition against seeking sexual satisfaction from near blood-relations), fourthly that against members of one's own sex and fifthly the transferring of the part played by the genitals to other organs and areas of the body. None of these

---

[1] [This is of course an allusion to the secession of Adler and Jung. Cf. footnote, p. 346 below.]

[2] [This is further explained in Lecture XX, p. 317 f. below.]

barriers existed from the beginning; they were only gradually erected in the course of development and education. Small children are free from them. They recognize no frightful gulf between human beings and animals; the arrogance with which men separate themselves from animals does not emerge until later.[1] To begin with, children exhibit no disgust at excreta but acquire this slowly under the pressure of education; they attach no special importance to the distinction between the sexes, but attribute the same conformation of the genitals to both; they direct their first sexual lusts and their curiosity to those who are nearest and for other reasons dearest to them—parents, brothers and sisters, or nurses; and finally, they show (what later on breaks through once again at the climax of a love-relation) that they expect to derive pleasure not only from their sexual organs, but that many other parts of the body lay claim to the same sensitivity, afford them analogous feelings of pleasure and can accordingly play the part of genitals. Children may thus be described as 'polymorphously perverse', and if these impulses only show *traces* of activity, that is because on the one hand they are of less intensity compared with those in later life and on the other hand all a child's sexual manifestations are at once energetically suppressed by education. This suppression is, as it were, extended into theory; for adults endeavour to overlook one portion of the sexual manifestations of children and to disguise another portion by misinterpreting its sexual nature, so that they can then disavow the whole of them. It is often the very same people who in the nursery are furious with any sexual naughtinesses of children and afterwards at their writing-tables defend the sexual purity of the same children. When children are left to themselves, or under the influence of seduction, they often bring about quite considerable achievements in the way of perverse sexual activity. Adults are of course right not to take this too seriously and to regard it as 'childishness', or 'playfulness', for children are not to be condemned as fully capable or fully responsible either before the judgement-seat of morals or before the law; but nonetheless these things exist. They have their importance both as indications of a child's innate constitution and as causes and encouragements of later developments

[1] [Freud enlarged on this in a contemporary paper, 'A Difficulty in the Path of Psycho-Analysis' (1917a).]

in him; they give us information on the sexual life of children and so on human sexual life in general. If, therefore, we once more find all these perverse wishful impulses behind our distorted dreams, that only means that in this field too dreams have taken a step backwards into the state of infancy.

Among these forbidden wishes special emphasis deserves to be further laid on the incestuous ones—that is, on those aiming at sexual intercourse with parents and brothers and sisters. You know what horror is felt, or at least professed, in human society at such intercourse, and what stress is laid on the prohibitions directed against it. Tremendous efforts have been made to explain this horror of incest. Some people have supposed that breeding considerations on the part of Nature have found psychical representation in this prohibition, since inbreeding would impair racial characters. Others have maintained that, as a result of living together from early childhood onwards, sexual desire has been diverted from the people in question. In both these cases, it may be remarked, an avoidance of incest would be secured automatically, and it would not be clear why such severe prohibitions were called for, which would point rather to the presence of a strong desire for it. Psycho-analytic researches have shown unmistakably that the choice of an incestuous love-object is, on the contrary, the first and invariable one, and that it is not until later that resistance to it sets in; it is no doubt impossible to trace back this resistance to *individual* psychology.[1]

Let us now bring together what our researches into child-psychology have contributed to our understanding of dreams. We have not only found that the material of the forgotten experiences of childhood is accessible to dreams, but we have also seen that the mental life of children with all its characteristics, its egoism, its incestuous choice of love-objects, and so on, still persists in dreams—that is, in the unconscious, and that dreams carry us back every night to this infantile level. The fact is thus confirmed that *what is unconscious in mental life is also what is infantile*. The strange impression of there being so much evil in people begins to diminish. This frightful evil is simply the

[1] [The whole subject of infantile sexuality is treated again at greater length in Lectures XX and XXI.]

initial, primitive, infantile part of mental life, which we can find in actual operation in children, but which, in part, we overlook in them on account of their small size, and which in part we do not take seriously since we do not expect any high ethical standard from children. Since dreams regress to this level, they give the appearance of having brought to light the evil in us. But this is a deceptive appearance, by which we have allowed ourselves to be scared. We are not so evil as we were inclined to suppose from the interpretation of dreams.

If these evil impulses in dreams are merely infantile phenomena, a return to the beginnings of our ethical development (since dreams simply make us into children once more in our thoughts and feelings), we need not, if we are reasonable, be ashamed of these evil dreams.[1] But what is reasonable is only a *part* of mental life, a number of other things take place in the mind which are not sensible; and so it happens that we *are* ashamed of these dreams in an unreasonable way. We subject them to the dream-censorship, we are ashamed and angry if, as an exception, one of these wishes succeeds in making its way into consciousness in such an undistorted form that we are obliged to recognize it; indeed we are occasionally as ashamed of a *distorted* dream as if we understood it. Only think of the indignant judgement which the excellent elderly lady passed on her uninterpreted dream of the 'love services' [p. 137]. So the problem is not yet cleared up, and it is still possible that further consideration of the evil in dreams may lead us to form another judgement and arrive at another estimate of human nature. [Cf. p. 338 below.]

As the outcome of our whole enquiry, let us grasp two discoveries, though they only signify the beginning of fresh enigmas and fresh doubts. First, the regression of the dream-work is not only a formal but also a material one. It not only translates our thoughts into a primitive form of expression; but it also revives the characteristics of our primitive mental life—the old dominance of the ego, the initial impulses of our sexual life, and even, indeed, our old intellectual endowment, if symbolic connections may be regarded as such. And secondly, all this, which is old

---

[1] [The moral responsibility for the content of dreams was the subject of a special discussion by Freud (Section B of 1925*i*). Cf. also p. 331 below.]

and infantile and was once dominant and alone dominant, must to-day be ascribed to the unconscious, our ideas of which are now becoming altered and extended. 'Unconscious' is no longer the name of what is latent at the moment; the unconscious is a particular realm of the mind with its own wishful impulses, its own mode of expression and its peculiar mental mechanisms which are not in force elsewhere. But the latent dream-thoughts which we have discovered by interpreting dreams do not belong to this realm; they are on the contrary thoughts just as we might have thought them in waking life. Nevertheless, they are unconscious. How, then, is this contradiction to be solved? We begin to suspect that a distinction is to be drawn here. Something which is derived from our conscious life and shares its characteristics—we call it 'the day's residues'—combines with something else coming from the realm of the unconscious in order to construct a dream. The dream-work is accomplished between these two components. The influence exercised upon the day's residues by the addition of the unconscious is no doubt among the determinants of regression. This is the deepest insight that we can reach here into the essential nature of dreams—until we have investigated further regions of the mind. But the time will soon have come to provide another name for the unconscious character of the latent dream-thoughts in order to distinguish it from the unconscious which comes from the realm of the infantile.[1]

We can, of course, raise another question besides: 'What is it that forces psychical activity during sleep to make this regression? Why does it not dispose of the mental stimuli that disturb sleep without doing this? And if, for the purposes of the dream-censorship, it has to make use of disguise by means of the old and now unintelligible mode of expression, what is the point of reviving as well the old mental impulses, wishes and character-traits, which are superseded to-day—of making use of material regression in addition to the formal kind?' The only answer that could satisfy us would be that in this way alone can a dream be constructed, that it is not otherwise dynamically possible to get rid of the stimulus to the dream. But so far we have no right to give such an answer.

[1] [This question is taken up again at the end of Lecture XIV, p. 227.]

LECTURE XIV

WISH-FULFILMENT

LADIES AND GENTLEMEN,—Shall I remind you once more of the ground we have covered so far? Of how, when we began applying our technique, we came up against the distortion in dreams, of how we thought we would begin by evading it and obtained our first decisive information on the essential nature of dreams from the dreams of children? Of how, after that, armed with what we had learnt from that enquiry, we made a direct assault on dream-distortion and, as I hope, overcame it step by step? We are bound to admit, however, that the things we have discovered by the one path and by the other do not entirely correspond. It will be our task to piece the two sets of findings together and reconcile them with each other.

We found from both sources that the dream-work consists essentially in the transformation of thoughts into a hallucinatory experience. How this can happen is sufficiently mysterious; but it is a problem of general psychology with which we are not properly concerned here. We learnt from children's dreams that it is the intention of the dream-work to get rid of a mental stimulus, which is disturbing sleep, by means of the fulfilment of a wish. We were unable to say anything similar of distorted dreams till we found out how to interpret them. But it was from the first our expectation that we should be able to regard distorted dreams in the same light as those of children. The first confirmation of this expectation was brought to us by the discovery that in point of fact *all* dreams are children's dreams, that they work with the same infantile material, with the mental impulses and mechanisms of childhood. Now that we believe we have overcome dream-distortion, we must go on to enquire whether the view of dreams as the fulfilment of wishes is also valid of distorted dreams.

A short time ago we submitted a series of dreams to interpretation, but we left wish-fulfilment completely out of account. I feel sure that you must have repeatedly been driven to ask yourselves: 'But where is the wish-fulfilment, which is supposed

to be the aim of the dream-work?' The question is an important
one, for it has become the question raised by our lay critics.
Human beings, as you know, have an instinctive tendency to
fend off intellectual novelties. One of the ways in which this
tendency is manifested is by immediately reducing the novelty
to the smallest proportions, by compressing it if possible into a
single catch-word. 'Wish-fulfilment' has become the catch-
word for the new theory of dreams. The layman asks: 'Where
is the wish-fulfilment?' And instantly, having heard that dreams
are supposed to be wish-fulfilments, and in the very act of
asking the question, he answers it with a rejection. He immediately thinks of countless experiences of his own with dreams,
in which the dream has been accompanied by feelings ranging
from the unpleasurable to severe anxiety, so that the assertion
made by the psycho-analytic theory of dreams seems to him
most improbable. We have no difficulty in replying that in
distorted dreams the wish-fulfilment cannot be obvious but
must be looked for, so that it cannot be pointed out until the
dream has been interpreted. We know too that the wishes in
these distorted dreams are forbidden ones—rejected by the
censorship—whose existence was precisely the cause of the
dream's distortion, the reason for the intervention of the dream-
censorship. But it is difficult to make the lay critic understand
that before a dream has been interpreted one cannot enquire
about the fulfilment of its wish. He will keep on forgetting this.
His rejection of the theory of wish-fulfilment is actually nothing
other than a consequence of the dream-censorship, a substitute
for the rejection of the censored dream-wishes and an effluence
from it.

We too, of course, feel the need to explain to ourselves why
there are so many dreams with a distressing content and,
especially why there are anxiety-dreams. Here for the first time
we come upon the problem of affects in dreams; it would
deserve a monograph of its own, but unfortunately we cannot
enter into it. If dreams are the fulfilment of wishes, distressing
feelings should be impossible in them: the lay critics would
appear to be right there. But three kinds of complications must
be taken into account which they have not thought of.

[1] Firstly, it may be that the dream-work has not com-

pletely succeeded in creating a wish-fulfilment; so that a portion of the distressing affect in the dream-thoughts has been left over in the manifest dream. In that case analysis would have to show that these dream-thoughts were far more distressing than the dream constructed out of them. That much can always be proved. If so, we must admit that the dream-work has not achieved its aim any more than the dream of drinking, formed in response to the stimulus of thirst, succeeded in quenching the thirst [p. 133 f.]. The dreamer remains thirsty and has to wake up in order to drink. Nevertheless it was a genuine dream, and had lost nothing of a dream's essential nature. We can only say: 'Ut desint vires, tamen est laudanda voluntas.'[1] The intention, at least, which can clearly be recognized, remains praiseworthy. Such instances of failure are no rare event. This is helped by that fact that it is so much harder for the dream-work to alter the sense of a dream's *affects* than of its *content*; affects are sometimes highly resistant. What then happens is that the dream-work transforms the distressing content of the dream-thoughts into the fulfilment of a wish, while the distressing affect persists unaltered. In dreams of this kind the affect is quite inappropriate to the content, and our critics can say that dreams are so far from being wish-fulfilments that even one with a harmless content can be felt as distressing. We can answer this foolish remark by pointing out that it is precisely in dreams like this that the wish-fulfilling purpose of the dream-work appears most clearly, because in isolation. The error arises because those who are unfamiliar with the neuroses picture the link between content and affect as too intimate and therefore cannot imagine the content being altered without a simultaneous alteration of the expression of affect attached to it.[2]

[2] A second factor, which is much more important and far-reaching, but which is equally overlooked by laymen, is the following. No doubt a wish-fulfilment must bring pleasure; but

---

[1] ['Though the strength is lacking, the will deserves to be praised' (Ovid, *Ep. ex Pont.*, 3, 4, 79).]

[2] [The looseness of the connection between ideas and their accompanying affects had been insisted on by Freud from very early times. See, for instance, his first paper on 'The Neuro-Psychoses of Defence' (1894a).]

the question then arises 'To whom?' To the person who has the wish, of course. But, as we know, a dreamer's relation to his wishes is a quite peculiar one. He repudiates them and censors them—he has no liking for them, in short. So that their fulfilment will give him no pleasure, but just the opposite; and experience shows that this opposite appears in the form of anxiety, a fact which has still to be explained. Thus a dreamer in his relation to his dream-wishes can only be compared to an amalgamation of two separate people who are linked by some strong element in common. Instead of enlarging on this, I will remind you of a familiar fairy tale in which you will find the same situation repeated. A good fairy promised a poor married couple to grant them the fulfilment of their first three wishes. They were delighted, and made up their minds to choose their three wishes carefully. But a smell of sausages being fried in the cottage next door tempted the woman to wish for a couple of them. They were there in a flash; and this was the first wish-fulfilment. But the man was furious, and in his rage wished that the sausages were hanging on his wife's nose. This happened too; and the sausages were not to be dislodged from their new position. This was the second wish-fulfilment; but the wish was the man's, and its fulfilment was most disagreeable for his wife. You know the rest of the story. Since after all they were in fact one—man and wife—the third wish was bound to be that the sausages should come away from the woman's nose. This fairy tale might be used in many other connections; but here it serves only to illustrate the possibility that if two people are not at one with each other the fulfilment of a wish of one of them may bring nothing but unpleasure to the other.[1]

It will not be difficult for us now to reach a still better understanding of anxiety-dreams. We will bring up one more observation and then make up our minds to adopt a hypothesis in favour of which there is much to be said. The observation is that anxiety-dreams often have a content entirely devoid of distortion, a content which has, so to speak, evaded the censorship. An anxiety-dream is often the undisguised fulfilment of a

[1] [The whole of this paragraph was later included by Freud as a footnote to Section D of Chapter VII in the 1919 edition of *I. of D.* The same fairy tale is also quoted, but in quite a different connection, in Freud's paper on 'The "Uncanny"' (1919*h*).]

wish—not, of course, of an acceptable wish, but of a repudiated one. The generation of anxiety has taken the place of the censorship. Whereas we can say of an infantile dream that it is the open fulfilment of a permitted wish, and of an ordinary distorted dream that it is the disguised fulfilment of a repressed wish, the only formula which fits an anxiety-dream is that it is the open fulfilment of a repressed wish. The anxiety is a sign that the repressed wish has shown itself stronger than the censorship, that it has put through, or is on the point of putting through, its wish-fulfilment in spite of the censorship. We perceive that what is for it a wish-fulfilment can only be for us, who are on the side of the censorship, an occasion for distressing feelings and for fending the wish off. The anxiety that emerges in the dream is, if you like, anxiety at the strength of these wishes which are normally held down. Why this fending-off appears in the form of anxiety cannot be discovered from the study of dreams alone; anxiety must clearly be studied elsewhere.[1]

We may suppose that what is true of undistorted anxiety-dreams applies also to those which are partly distorted as well as to other unpleasurable dreams, in which the distressing feelings probably correspond to an approach to anxiety. Anxiety-dreams are as a rule also arousal dreams; we usually interrupt our sleep before the repressed wish in the dream has put its fulfilment through completely in spite of the censorship. In that case the function of the dream has failed, but its essential nature is not altered by this. We have compared dreams to the night-watchman or guardian of sleep, who tries to protect our sleep from disturbance [p. 129]. The night-watchman, too, may reach the point of waking the sleeper if he feels he is too weak alone to drive off the disturbance or the danger. Nevertheless we sometimes succeed in holding on to our sleep even when the dream begins to be precarious and to be turning into anxiety. We say to ourselves in our sleep 'after all it's only a dream', and sleep on.

When does it happen that a dream-wish is in a position to overpower the censorship? The condition necessary for this may be fulfilled equally well by the dream-wish or by the dream-censorship. The wish may for an unknown reason be excessively strong on some occasion; but one gets an impression that it is

[1] [It is the subject of Lecture XXV below.]

more often the behaviour of the dream-censorship that is responsible for this displacement of their relative strengths. We have already seen [p. 143] that the censorship acts with varying intensity in each particular case, that it treats each element of a dream with a different degree of severity. We can now add a further hypothesis to the effect that it is in general very variable and does not always employ equal severity to the same objectionable element. If things turn out so that on some occasion it feels itself powerless against a dream-wish which threatens to take it by surprise, instead of distortion, it makes use of its last remaining expedient and abandons the state of sleep, at the same time generating anxiety.

In this connection it strikes us that we are still quite ignorant of why it is that these evil, repudiated wishes become active precisely at night and disturb us during our sleep. The answer is almost bound to lie in some hypothesis going back to the nature of the state of sleep. In day-time the heavy weight of censorship rests on them and as a rule makes it impossible for them to manifest themselves in any activity. At night this censorship, like all the other interests of mental life, is probably withdrawn, or at least greatly reduced, in favour of the single wish to sleep. It is this lowering of the censorship at night that the forbidden wishes have to thank for being able to become active once more. There are some neurotic patients who are unable to sleep and who admit to us that their insomnia was originally intentional. They did not dare to sleep because they were afraid of their dreams—afraid, that is, of the results of the weakening of the censorship. You will easily see, however, that in spite of this the withdrawal of the censorship implies no gross carelessness. The state of sleep paralyses our motive powers. If our evil intentions begin to stir, they can, after all, do nothing more than precisely cause a dream, which is harmless from the practical point of view. It is this soothing consideration that is the basis of the highly sensible remark made by the sleeper—made at night, it is true, but not forming part of dream-life: 'After all it's only a dream. So let us leave it to take its course, and let us sleep on.'

[3] If, in the third place, you will recall our idea that the dreamer fighting against his own wishes is to be compared with

a summation of two separate, though in some way intimately connected, people, you will understand another possibility. For there is a possibility that the fulfilment of a wish may bring about something very far from pleasant—namely, a punishment. Here we can once more use the fairy tale of the three wishes as an illustration. The fried sausages on a plate were the direct fulfilment of the wish of the first person, the woman. The sausages on her nose were the fulfilment of the wish of the second person, the man, but were at the same time a punishment for the woman's foolish wish. (We shall discover in neuroses the motive for the third wish, the last remaining one in the fairy tale.)[1] There are many such punitive trends in the mental life of human beings; they are very powerful, and we may hold them responsible for some of the distressing dreams.[2] Perhaps you will now say that this leaves very little over of the famous wish-fulfilment. But if you look more closely you will admit that you are wrong. Compared with the multiplicity (which I shall mention later) of the things that dreams might be and according to many authorities actually are, our solution—wish-fulfilment, anxiety-fulfilment, punishment-fulfilment—is a very restricted one. We may add that the anxiety is the direct opposite of the wish, that opposites are especially close to one another in associations and that in the unconscious they coalesce [p. 178 ff.]; and further, that the punishment is also the fulfilment of a wish—of the wish of the other, censoring person.

On the whole, therefore, I have made no concession to your objection to the theory of wish-fulfilment. It is our duty, however, to be able to indicate the wish-fulfilment in any distorted dream we may come across, and we shall certainly not evade the task. Let us go back to the dream we have already interpreted of the three bad theatre-tickets for 1 florin 50 [pp. 122 and 139], from which we have already learnt so much. I hope you still recollect it. A lady, whose husband had told her during the day that her friend Elise, who was only three months her junior, had become engaged, dreamt that she was at the theatre with her husband. One side of the stalls was almost empty. Her husband said to her that Elise and her fiancé had wanted

[1] [It is not clear what is intended here.]
[2] [Punishment dreams are discussed in *I. of D.* See the Rosegger dreams in Chapter VI (H) and the discussion of wish-fulfilment in Chapter VII.]

to go to the theatre too but had not been able to, since they had
only got bad seats—three for 1 florin 50. She thought it would
not really have done any harm if they had. We found that the
dream-thoughts related to her anger at having married so
early and to her dissatisfaction with her husband. We may be
curious to discover how these gloomy thoughts were transformed into the fulfilment of a wish and where any trace of it
is to be found in the manifest content of the dream. We already
know that the element 'too early, in a hurry' was eliminated
from the dream by the censorship [p. 140]. The empty stalls
were an allusion to it. The mysterious 'three for 1 florin 50'
now becomes more intelligible to us with the help of the symbolism with which we have meanwhile become acquainted.
The '3'[1] really means a man [or husband] and the manifest
element is easy to translate: buying a husband with her dowry.
('I could have got one ten[2] times better with my dowry.')
'Marrying' is clearly replaced by 'going to the theatre'. 'Taking
the theatre tickets too early' is, indeed, an immediate substitute
for 'marrying too early'. This substitution is, however, the work
of a wish-fulfilment. Our dreamer was not always so dissatisfied with her early marriage as she was on the day when she
received the news of her friend's engagement. She had been
proud of it at one time and regarded herself as at an advantage
over her friend. Simple-minded girls, after becoming engaged,
are reputed often to express their joy that they will soon be able
to go to the theatre, to all the plays which have hitherto been
prohibited, and will be allowed to see everything. The pleasure
in looking, or curiosity, which is revealed in this was no doubt
originally a sexual desire to look [scopophilia], directed towards
sexual happenings and especially on to the girls' parents, and
hence it became a powerful motive for urging them to an early
marriage. In this way a visit to the theatre became an obvious
substitute, by way of allusion, for being married. Thus the
dreamer, in her present anger at her early marriage, harked
back to the time at which early marriage was the fulfilment of a
wish because it satisfied her scopophilia, and, under the lead of

---

[1] I have not mentioned another plausible interpretation of this '3'
in a childless woman, since this analysis brought up no material in
support of it. [Cf. p. 163 f. above.]

[2] [This is presumably a slip for 'a hundred'. Cf. above, p. 124.]

this old wishful impulse, she replaced marriage by going to the theatre.

I cannot be accused of having specially chosen out the most convenient example as evidence of a concealed wish-fulfilment. The procedure would have had to be the same in the case of other distorted dreams. I cannot demonstrate this to you now, and I will only express my conviction that it could always be successfully accomplished. I will, however, dwell a little longer on this theoretical point. Experience has taught me that it is one of those most exposed to attack in the whole theory of dreams, and that many contradictions and misunderstandings arise from it. Apart from this, you may perhaps still be under the impression that I have already withdrawn part of my assertion in saying that a dream is a fulfilled wish or the opposite of one, or a realized anxiety or punishment; and you may think this is an opportunity of forcing further qualifications out of me. I have also been reproached for putting forward things that seem to me obvious in a manner that is too concise and consequently unconvincing.

When someone has accompanied us so far in the interpretation of dreams and has accepted everything that has been brought forward up to this point, it often happens that he comes to a halt at wish-fulfilment and says: 'Granted that dreams always have a sense, and that that sense can be discovered by the technique of psycho-analysis, why must that sense, all evidence to the contrary, be invariably pushed into the formula of wish-fulfilment? Why should not the sense of this nightly thinking be of as many kinds as that of daytime thinking? Why, that is, should not a dream correspond sometimes to a fulfilled wish, sometimes, as you yourself say, to the opposite of that or to a realized fear, but sometimes express an intention, a warning, a reflection with its "pros" and "cons", or a reproach, a scruple of conscience, an attempt at preparing for a coming task, and so on? Why must it always be only a wish, or at most its opposite?'

It might be thought that a difference of opinion on this point is unimportant, if one is agreed on the rest. It is enough, it might be said, that we have discovered the sense of dreams and the way of recognizing it; it is of less importance if we seem to have defined that sense too narrowly. But that is not so. A misunderstanding on this point affects the essence of our discoveries about dreams and endangers their value for the understanding of the neuroses. Moreover, a compromise of this sort —what is highly thought of in commercial life as being 'accommodating'—is not in place, but detrimental rather, in scientific affairs.

My first answer to the question why dreams should not have a variety of meanings in the sense indicated is as usual in such cases: 'I don't know why they shouldn't. I should have no objection. As far as I'm concerned it could be so. There's only one detail in the way of this broader and more convenient view of dreams—that it isn't so in reality.' My second answer would be that the hypothesis that dreams correspond to a variety of forms of thinking and intellectual operations is not unfamiliar to me myself. I once reported a dream in one of my case histories which appeared on three nights in succession and then no more, and I explained this behaviour by the fact that the dream corresponded to an *intention*, and did not need to be repeated after the intention had been carried out.[1] Later on I published a dream which corresponded to an *admission*.[2] How, then, can I contradict myself and assert that dreams are never anything but a fulfilled wish?

I do it because I will not allow a foolish misunderstanding to pass which may rob us of the fruit of our efforts with dreams —a misunderstanding which confuses the dream with the latent dream-thoughts, and asserts of the former something that applies solely to the latter. For it is quite correct to say that a dream can represent and be replaced by everything you have just enumerated—an intention, a warning, a reflection, a preparation, an attempt at solving a problem, and so on. But if you look properly, you will see that all this only applies to the latent dream-thoughts, which have been transformed into the dream. You learn from interpretations of dreams that people's unconscious thinking is concerned with these intentions, preparations, reflections, and so on, out of which the dream-work then makes the dreams. If at the moment you are not interested

---

[1] [This was the first dream in the analysis of 'Dora' (1905e).]
[2] [Cf. 'An Evidential Dream' (1913a).]

in the dream-work, but are greatly interested in people's unconscious thought-activity, you then eliminate the dream-work and say of the dream what is in practice quite correct—that it corresponds to a warning, an intention, and so on. What often happens in psycho-analytic activity is that our efforts are chiefly directed only to doing away with the dream-form and inserting in the context instead of it the latent thoughts out of which the dream was made.

Thus, quite incidentally, we learn from our examination of the latent dream-thoughts that all these highly complicated mental acts that we have named can take place unconsciously —a discovery as imposing as it is perplexing!

But to go back, you are only correct so long as you are clearly aware that you have used an abbreviated form of expression and so long as you do not believe that the multiplicity you have been describing is to be related to the essential nature of dreams. When you speak of a 'dream', you must mean either the manifest dream—that is, the product of the dream-work—or, at most, the dream-work itself as well—that is, the psychical process which forms the manifest dream out of the latent dream-thoughts. Any other use of the word is a confusion of ideas and can only lead to mischief.[1] If you are making statements about the latent thoughts behind the dream, do so directly and do not obscure the problem of dreams by the loose manner in which you speak. The latent dream-thoughts are the material which the dream-work transforms into the manifest dream. Why should you want to confuse the material with the activity which forms it? If you do, what advantage have you over those who only knew the product of the activity and could not explain where it came from or how it was made?

The only essential thing about dreams is the dream-work that has influenced the thought-material. We have no right to ignore it in our theory, even though we may disregard it in certain practical situations. Analytic observation shows further that the dream-work never restricts itself to translating these thoughts into the archaic or regressive mode of expression that

---

[1] [Further discussions on the proper use of the term 'dream' will be found in two footnotes added in 1925 and 1914 respectively to *I. of D.* See the end of Section I in Chapter VI and Section D in Chapter VII and also at the end of Section I of 'Dreams and Telepathy' (1922a).]

is familiar to you. In addition, it regularly takes possession of something else, which is not part of the latent thoughts of the previous day, but which is the true motive force for the construction of the dream. This indispensable addition is the equally unconscious wish for the fulfilment of which the content of the dream is given its new form. A dream may thus be any sort of thing in so far as you are only taking into account the thoughts it represents—a warning, an intention, a preparation, and so on; but it is always also the fulfilment of an unconscious wish and, if you are considering it as a product of the dream-work, it is only that. A dream is therefore never simply an intention, or a warning, but always an intention, etc., translated into the archaic mode of thought by the help of an unconscious wish and transformed to fulfil that wish. [See p. 227, *n.* 2.] The one characteristic, the wish-fulfilment, is the invariable one; the other may vary. It may for its part once more be a wish, in which case the dream will, with the help of an unconscious wish, represent as fulfilled a latent wish of the previous day.

I can understand all this very clearly; but I cannot tell whether I have succeeded in making it intelligible to you as well. And I also have difficulty in proving it to you. That cannot be done without carefully analysing a great many dreams, and on the other hand this most critical and important point in our view of dreams cannot be convincingly represented without referring to what is coming later. It is impossible to suppose that, since everything is intimately interrelated, one can penetrate deeply into the nature of one thing without having concerned oneself with other things of a similar nature. Since we still know nothing of the dream's nearest relatives, neurotic symptoms, we must once more rest content at this point with what we have achieved. I will only give you one more illustrative example and lay before you one fresh consideration.

Let us once again take up the dream we have already so often returned to: the dream of the three theatre-tickets for 1 florin 50. (I can assure you that I originally chose out this example without any special purpose in view.) You know the latent dream-thoughts: anger at having been in such a hurry to get married which arose when she heard the news that her friend had only just become engaged, putting a low value on her husband and the idea that she might have got a better one if only she had waited. We already know the wish which made a dream out of these thoughts: it was the desire to look, to be able to go to the theatre, most probably an offshoot of her old curiosity to discover at long last what really happens when one is married. This curiosity is, as we know, regularly directed by children towards their parents' sexual life; it is an infantile curiosity, and, so far as it still persists later, an instinctual impulse with roots reaching back into infancy. But the news the dreamer had received during the day gave no occasion for awakening this desire to look, but only for awakening anger and regret. This wishful impulse was not in the first instance connected with the latent dream-thoughts; and we were able to include the outcome of the dream-interpretation in the analysis without taking any account of that impulse. But the anger in itself was not capable of creating a dream. A dream could not arise out of the thoughts that 'it was absurd to marry so early' until they had awakened the old wish to see at long last what happens in marriage. This wish then gave the dream-content its form by replacing marriage by going to the theatre, and the form was that of an earlier wish-fulfilment: 'There! now I may go to the theatre and look at everything that's forbidden, and you mayn't! I'm married and you must wait!' In this way the dreamer's present situation was transformed into its opposite, an old triumph was put in the place of her recent defeat. And, incidentally, a satisfaction of her scopophilia was mixed with a satisfaction of her egoistic competitive sense. This satisfaction then determined the manifest content of the dream, in which the position actually was that she was sitting in the theatre while her friend could not gain admission to it. The portions of the content of the dream behind which the latent dream-thoughts still lay concealed were superimposed on this situation of satisfaction as a misplaced and unintelligible modification of it. The dream's interpretation had to disregard everything that served to represent the wish-fulfilment and to re-establish the distressing latent dream-thoughts from these obscure remaining hints.

The fresh consideration I wish to bring before you is to draw your attention to the latent dream-thoughts which have now been put in the foreground. I beg you not to forget that in the first place they are unconscious[1] to the dreamer, and secondly that they are completely rational and coherent so that they can be understood as natural reactions to the precipitating cause of the dream, and thirdly that they can be the equivalent of any mental impulse or intellectual operation. I shall now describe these thoughts more strictly than before as the 'day's residues', whether the dreamer confesses to them or not. I shall now distinguish between the day's residues and the latent dream-thoughts, and, in conformity with our earlier usage, I shall designate as latent dream-thoughts everything we learn in interpreting the dream, whereas the day's residues are only a portion of the latent dream-thoughts. Our view is then that something is added to the day's residues, something that was also part of the unconscious, a powerful but repressed wishful impulse; and it is this alone that makes the construction of the dream possible. The influence of this wishful impulse on the day's residues creates the further portion of the latent dream-thoughts—that which need no longer appear rational and intelligible as being derived from waking life.

I have made use of an analogy for the relation of the day's residues to the unconscious wish, and I can only repeat it here. In every undertaking there must be a capitalist who covers the required outlay and an *entrepreneur* who has the idea and knows how to carry it out. In the construction of dreams, the part of the capitalist is always played by the unconscious wish alone; it provides the psychical energy for the construction of the dream. The *entrepreneur* is the day's residues, which decide how this outlay is to be employed. It is possible, of course, for the capitalist himself to have the idea and the expert knowledge or for the *entrepreneur* himself to possess capital. This simplifies the practical situation but makes its theoretical understanding more difficult. In economics the same person is constantly divided into his two aspects of capitalist and *entrepreneur* and this restores the fundamental situation on which our analogy was based. In dream-construction the same variations occur and I will leave them for you to follow out.[2]

[1] [See footnote p. 21 above.]
[2] [This analogy appeared originally in Section C of Chapter VII of *I. of D.*, where it is illustrated at greater length.]

We cannot advance any further here, for you have probably long been disturbed by a doubt which deserves to be given a hearing. 'Are the day's residues,' you will ask, 'really unconscious in the same sense as the unconscious wish which must be added to them in order to make them capable of producing a dream?' Your suspicion is correct. This is the salient point of the whole business. They are *not* unconscious in the same sense. The dream-wish belongs to a different unconscious—to the one which we have already recognized as being of infantile origin and equipped with peculiar mechanisms [p. 210]. It would be highly opportune to distinguish these two kinds of unconscious by different names. But we would prefer to wait till we have become familiar with the field of phenomena of the neuroses. People consider a single unconscious as something fantastic. What will they say when we confess that we cannot make shift without two of them?[1]

Let us break off here. Once again you have only heard something incomplete. But is it not hopeful to reflect that this knowledge has a continuation, which either we ourselves or other people will bring to light? And have not we ourselves learnt enough that is new and surprising?

[1] [The question of the uses of the term 'unconscious' was a crucial one for Freud's theories. He touched on it at several points in the course of these lectures (particularly on pp. 113, 189, 212, 227, 294 ff. and—a last brief mention—on p. 437). But he was evidently already feeling uncomfortable about it and in fact revised his views on the whole subject some years later in *The Ego and the Id* (1923*b*), (Norton, 1960).   A full account of the problem and its history will be found in the Editor's Introduction to that work.   The new solution is also explained in Lecture XXXI of the *New Introductory Lectures* (1933*a*).]

[2] [Page 224, line 14. At the end of this sentence all the German editions have the plural, '*dieser Wünsche* (those wishes)', which would seem to obscure the meaning. An examination of the original manuscript (which is not very clear) appears to show that Freud in fact wrote, or intended to write, the singular, '*dieses Wunsches*'. A shorter, though essentially similar, account of the whole process is given in 'An Evidential Dream' (1913*a*).]

LECTURE XV

UNCERTAINTIES AND CRITICISMS

LADIES AND GENTLEMEN,—We will nevertheless not leave the field of dreams without dealing with the commonest doubts and uncertainties which our novelties and our theories have given rise to so far. Attentive listeners among you will themselves have collected some of the relevant material.

(1) You may have formed an impression that, even though the technique is correctly carried out, the findings of our interpretative work on dreams admit of so many uncertainties as to defeat any secure translation of the manifest dream into the latent dream-thoughts. You will argue in support of this that in the first place one never knows whether a particular element of the dream is to be understood in its actual sense or as a symbol, since the things employed as symbols do not cease on that account to be themselves. If, however, one has no objective clue for deciding this, the interpretation must at that point be left to the arbitrary choice of the interpreter. Furthermore, as a result of the fact that in the dream-work contraries coalesce, it is always left undetermined whether a particular element is to be understood in a positive or negative sense—as itself or as its contrary [p. 178]. Here is a fresh opportunity for the interpreter to exercise an arbitrary choice. Thirdly, in consequence of the reversals of every kind of which dreams are so fond [p. 180], it is open to the interpreter to carry out a reversal like this in connection with any passage in the dream he chooses. And lastly, you will mention having heard that one is never certain whether the interpretation one has found for a dream is the only possible one. We run the risk of overlooking a perfectly admissible 'over-interpretation' of the same dream [p. 173]. In these circumstances, you will conclude, so much room is left to the interpreter's arbitrary decision as to be incompatible with objective certainty in the findings. Or alternatively you may suppose that the fault does not lie with dreams but that the inadequacies of our dream-

228

interpretation are to be attributed to errors in our views and premisses.

All your material is unimpeachable, but it does not, I think, justify your conclusions, and in two respects: namely that the interpretation of dreams is, as you insist, at the mercy of arbitrary choice and that the lack of results throws doubts on the correctness of our procedure. If instead of the interpreter's arbitrary choice you would speak of his skill, his experience and his understanding, I should agree with you. We cannot, of course, do without a personal factor of that kind, especially in the more difficult problems of dream-interpretation. But the position is no different in other scientific occupations. There is no means of preventing one person from handling a particular technique worse than another, or one person from making better use of it than another. What in other ways gives an impression of arbitrariness—in, for instance, the interpretation of symbols—is done away with by the fact that as a rule the interconnection between the dream-thoughts, or the connection between the dream and the dreamer's life, or the whole psychical situation in which the dream occurs, selects a single one from among the possible determinations presented and dismisses the rest as unserviceable. The conclusion that because of the imperfections of dream-interpretation our hypotheses are incorrect is invalidated by pointing out that on the contrary ambiguity or indefiniteness is a characteristic of dreams which was necessarily to be anticipated.

Let us recall that we have said that the dream-work makes a translation of the dream-thoughts into a primitive mode of expression similar to picture-writing [p. 175 ff.]. All such primitive systems of expression, however, are characterized by indefiniteness and ambiguity of this sort, without justifying us in casting doubts on their serviceability. The coalescence of contraries in the dream-work is, as you know, analogous to the so-called 'antithetical meaning of primal words' in the most ancient languages. Indeed, Abel (1884), the philologist to whom we owe this line of thought, implores us not to suppose that communications made by one person to another with the help of such ambivalent words were on that account ambiguous. On the contrary, intonation and gesture must have made it quite certain in the context of the speech which of the two

contraries the speaker intended to convey. In writing, where gesture is absent, its place was taken by an additional pictograph
which was not intended to be spoken—for instance by a picture
of a little man, limply squatting or stiffly erect, according to
whether the ambiguous hieroglyph '*ken*' was to mean 'weak' or
'strong'. In this way, in spite of the ambiguity of the sounds and
signs, misunderstanding was avoided. [Cf. above, p. 179.]

The old systems of expression—for instance, the scripts of the
most ancient languages—betray vagueness in a variety of ways
which we would not tolerate in our writing to-day. Thus in
some Semitic scripts only the consonants in the words are indicated. The reader has to insert the omitted vowels according
to his knowledge and the context. The hieroglyphic script behaves very similarly, though not precisely in the same way; and
for that reason the pronunciation of Ancient Egyptian remains
unknown to us. The sacred script of the Egyptians is indefinite
in yet other ways. For instance, it is left to the arbitrary decision
of the scribe whether he arranges the pictures from right to left
or from left to right. In order to be able to read it one must obey
the rule of reading towards the faces of the figures, birds, and
so on. But the scribe might also arrange the pictographs in
vertical columns, and in making inscriptions on comparatively
small objects he allowed considerations of decorativeness and
space to influence him in altering the sequence of the signs in
yet other ways. The most disturbing thing about the hieroglyphic script is, no doubt, that it makes no separation between
words. The pictures are placed across the page at equal dis-
tances apart; and in general it is impossible to tell whether a
sign is still part of the preceding word or forms the beginning
of a new word. In Persian cuneiform script, on the other hand,
an oblique wedge serves to separate words.

An extremely ancient language and script, which however is
still used by four hundred million people, is the Chinese. You
must not suppose that I at all understand it; I only obtained
some information about it because I hoped to find analogies in
it to the indefiniteness of dreams. Nor has my expectation been
disappointed. The Chinese language is full of instances of indefiniteness which might fill us with alarm. As is well known, it
consists of a number of syllabic sounds, which are spoken either
singly or combined into pairs. One of the principal dialects has

some four hundred such sounds. Since, however, the vocabulary of this dialect is reckoned at about four thousand words, it follows that each sound has on an average ten different meanings—some fewer but some correspondingly more. There are quite a number of methods of avoiding ambiguity, since one cannot infer from the context alone which of the ten meanings of the syllabic sound the speaker intends to evoke in the hearer. Among these methods are those of combining two sounds into a compound word and of using four different 'tones' in the pronunciation of the syllables. It is even more interesting from the point of view of our comparison to learn that this language has practically no grammar. It is impossible to tell of any of the monosyllabic words whether it is a noun or a verb or an adjective; and there are no verbal inflections by which one could recognize gender, number, termination, tense or mood. Thus the language consists, one might say, solely of the raw material, just as our thought-language is resolved by the dream-work into its raw material, and any expression of relations is omitted. In Chinese the decision in all cases of indefiniteness is left to the hearer's understanding and this is guided by the context. I have made a note of an example of a Chinese proverb which, literally translated, runs:

'Little what see much what wonderful.'

This is not hard to understand. It may mean: 'The less someone has seen, the more he finds to wonder at'; or: 'There is much to wonder at for him who has seen little.' There is, of course, no question of distinguishing between these two translations, which only differ grammatically. In spite of this indefiniteness, we have been assured that the Chinese language is a quite excellent vehicle for the expression of thought. So indefiniteness need not necessarily lead to ambiguity.

It must, of course, be admitted that the system of expression by dreams occupies a far more unfavourable position than any of these ancient languages and scripts. For after all they are fundamentally intended for communication: that is to say, they are always, by whatever method and with whatever assistance, meant to be understood. But precisely this characteristic is absent in dreams. A dream does not want to say anything to anyone. It is not a vehicle for communication; on the contrary, it is meant to remain ununderstood. For that reason we must not be surprised or at a loss if it turns out that a number of ambiguities and obscurities in dreams remain undecided. The one certain gain we have derived from our comparison is the discovery that these points of uncertainty which people have tried to use as objections to the soundness of our dream-interpretations are on the contrary regular characteristics of all primitive systems of expression.

The question of how far the intelligibility of dreams in fact extends can only be answered by practice and experience.[1] Very far, I believe; and my view is confirmed if we compare the results produced by correctly trained analysts. The lay public, including the scientific lay public, are well known to enjoy making a parade of scepticism when faced by the difficulties and uncertainties of a scientific achievement. I think they are wrong in this. You are perhaps not all aware that a similar situation arose in the history of the deciphering of the Babylonian–Assyrian inscriptions. There was a time when public opinion was very much inclined to regard the decipherers of cuneiform as visionaries and the whole of their researches as a 'swindle'. But in 1857 the Royal Asiatic Society made a decisive experiment. It requested four of the most highly respected experts in cuneiform, Rawlinson, Hincks, Fox Talbot and Oppert, to send it, in sealed envelopes, independent translations of a newly discovered inscription; and, after a comparison between the four productions, it was able to announce that the agreement between these experts went far enough to justify a belief in what had so far been achieved and confidence in further advances. The derision on the part of the learned lay world gradually diminished after this, and since then certainty in reading cuneiform documents has increased enormously.

(2) A second group of doubts is closely connected with the impression, which no doubt you yourselves have not escaped, that a number of the solutions to which we find ourselves driven in interpreting dreams seem to be forced, artificial, dragged in by the hair of their head—arbitrary, that is, or even comic and facetious. Remarks to this effect are so frequent that

[1] [Cf. a later paper on 'The Limits to the Possibility of Interpretation', Section A of 'Some Additional Notes on Dream-Interpretation as a Whole' (1925i).]

I will choose at random the last that has been reported to me. So listen to this. In free Switzerland the head of a training-college was recently removed from his post on account of his interest in psycho-analysis. He entered a protest, and a Berne newspaper published the report of the school authorities on his appeal. I will select a few sentences dealing with psycho-analysis from this document: 'Moreover we are surprised at the far-fetched and artificial character of many of the examples, which are also to be found in the volume by Dr. Pfister of Zurich which is quoted. . . . It is really surprising, therefore, that the head of a training-college should accept all these assertions and pretended proofs without criticism.' These sentences are represented as a decision reached by someone 'making a calm judgement'. It is rather this calmness, I think, which is 'artificial'. Let us examine these remarks more closely, in the expectation that a little reflection and a little expert knowledge can be of no disadvantage even to a calm judgement.

It is truly refreshing to see how swiftly and unerringly a person can arrive at a judgement on some delicate problem of depth-psychology after his first impression of it. The interpretations seem to him far-fetched and forced and he does not like them; so they are false and all this business of interpretation is worthless. Not even a fleeting thought is given to the other possibility—that there are good reasons why these interpretations are bound to have this appearance; after which the further question would follow of what these good reasons are.

The matter under consideration relates in essence to the results of displacement, which you have become acquainted with as the most powerful instrument of the dream-censorship. With the help of displacement the dream-censorship creates substitutive structures which we have described as allusions. But they are allusions which are not easily recognizable as such, from which the path back to the genuine thing is not easily traced, and which are connected with the genuine thing by the strangest, most unusual, external associations.[1] In all these cases it is a question, however, of things which are *meant* to be hidden, which are condemned to concealment, for that is what the dream-censorship is aiming at. But we must not expect that a

[1] [See footnote 1, p. 174 above.]

thing which has been hidden will be found in its own place, in
its proper position. The frontier-control commissions which are
operating to-day are more cunning in this respect than the
Swiss school authorities. In their search for documents and plans
they are not content with examining brief-cases and portfolios,
but they consider the possibility that spies and smugglers may
have these forbidden things in the most secret portions of their
clothing where they decidedly do not belong—for instance, between the double soles of their boots. If the hidden things are
there, it will certainly be possible to call them 'far-fetched', but
it is also true that a great deal will have been found.[1]

If we recognize that the links between a latent dream-element
and its manifest substitute can be of the most out-of-the-way
and peculiar nature, sometimes appearing comic and sometimes resembling a joke, we are basing ourselves on copious experience of examples which, as a rule, we have not solved ourselves. It is often impossible to give such interpretations on our
own account: no sensible person could guess at the connection.
The dreamer gives us the translation either all at once by a
direct association—*he* is able to, since it was he who produced
the substitute—or else he brings up so much material that the
solution no longer calls for any particular acumen, but presents
itself, so to speak, as a matter of course. If the dreamer fails to
assist in one or other of these two ways, the manifest element in
question will for ever remain unintelligible to us. I will, if I
may, give you an example which occurred to me recently. One
of my women patients lost her father in the course of the treatment. Since then she has taken every opportunity of bringing
him to life in her dreams. In one of these her father appeared
(in a particular connection of no further relevance) and said:
'*It's a quarter past eleven, it's half-past eleven, it's a quarter to twelve.*'
By way of interpretation of this oddity all that occurred to her
was that her father liked his grown-up children to appear
punctually at the family meals. No doubt this was connected
with the dream-element, but it threw no light on its origin.
There was a suspicion, based on the immediate situation in the
treatment, that a carefully suppressed critical revolt against her
beloved and honoured father played some part in the dream.
In the further course of her associations, apparently remote

[1] [There is some untranslatable punning here in the original.]

from the dream, she told how the day before there had been a lot of talk about psychology in her presence, and a relative of hers had remarked: 'The *Urmensch* [primal man] survives in all of us.' This seemed to provide us with the explanation. It had given her an excellent opportunity of bringing her dead father to life once again. She made him in the dream into an '*Uhrmensch*' ['clock-man'] by making him announce the quarterhours at midday.

You will not be able to escape the resemblance of this example to a joke; and it has in fact often happened that a joke of the dreamer's has been regarded as a joke of the interpreter's. There are other instances in which it has been far from easy to decide whether what we are dealing with is a joke or a dream. But you will recall that the same doubt arose in the case of some parapraxes—slips of the tongue [p. 43 f.]. A man reported as a dream of his that his uncle had given him a kiss while they were sitting in his *auto*(mobile).[1] He himself very quickly added the interpretation: it meant '*auto-erotism*' (a term from the theory of the libido, indicating satisfaction obtained without any outside object). Had the man set out, then, to have some fun with us and was he passing off a joke that had occurred to him as a dream? I think not; I believe he really dreamt it. But what is the origin of this puzzling similarity? This question once led me temporarily aside from my path by compelling me to make jokes themselves the subject of a detailed investigation.[2] It was there shown how jokes originate: a preconscious[3] train of thought is abandoned for a moment to be worked over in the unconscious, and from this it emerges as a joke. Under the influence of the unconscious it is subjected to the effects of the mechanisms that hold sway there—condensation and displacement—the same processes that we have found concerned in the dream-work; and it is to this common feature that is to be ascribed the similarity, when it occurs, between jokes and dreams. But the unintended 'dream-joke' brings none of the

[1] [This dream is reported in *I of D.*, in Chapter VI in Section (F).]

[2] *Jokes and their Relation to the Unconscious*(1905c),(Norton, 1960). Freud relates in *I. of D.*, VI(A), how he was led into writing that work by a critic (Wilhelm Fliess) who complained that the dreams he reported were too full of jokes. See also a passage on this point in the book on jokes itself, (p. 173).]

[3] [This term is explained in Lecture XIX, p. 296 below.]

yield of pleasure of a true joke. You can learn why if you go
more deeply into the study of jokes. A'dream-joke' strikes us as
a bad joke; it does not make us laugh, it leaves us cold.[1]

In this, however, we are treading in the footsteps of the
dream-interpretation of antiquity, which, along with much that
is unserviceable, has left us some good examples of dream-
interpretation, which we ourselves could not better. I will repeat to you a dream which was of historic importance and
which is reported of Alexander the Great, with slight variations,
by Plutarch and Artemidorus of Daldis [cf. p. 86 above].
When the king was laying siege to the obstinately defended city
of Tyre (322 B.C.), he once dreamt that he saw a dancing satyr.
Aristander, the dream-interpreter, who was present with the
army, interpreted the dream by dividing the word '*Satyros*' into
σὰ Τύρος [sa Turos] (thine is Tyre), and therefore promised
that he would triumph over the city. Alexander was led by this
interpretation to continue the siege and eventually captured
Tyre. The interpretation, which has a sufficiently artificial
appearance, was undoubtedly the right one.[2]

[3) I can well imagine that you will be especially impressed
when you hear that objections to our view of dreams have even
been made by people who have themselves, as psycho-analysts,
been engaged for a considerable time in interpreting dreams. It
would have been too much to expect that such an abundant
encouragement to fresh errors as this theory offers should have
been neglected; and so, as a result of conceptual confusions and
unjustified generalizations, assertions have been made which
are not far behind the medical view of dreams in their incorrectness. You know one of them already. It tells us that dreams are
concerned with attempts at adaptation to present conditions
and with attempts at solving future problems—that they have
a 'prospective purpose' (Maeder [1912]). We have already
shown [p. 222] that this assertion is based on a confusion
between the dream and the latent dream-thoughts and is therefore based on disregarding the dream-work. As a characteriza-

---

[1] [See the end of Chapter VI of the book on jokes. The point
has already been mentioned above on p. 174.]
[2] [This is also reported in Chapter II of *I. of D., n.*]

tion of the unconscious intellectual activity of which the latent dream-thoughts form part, it is on the one hand no novelty and on the other not exhaustive, since unconscious intellectual activity is occupied with many other things besides preparing for the future.[1] A far worse confusion seems to underlie the assurance that the idea of death will be found behind every dream [Stekel, 1911, 34]. I am not clear exactly what is meant by this formula. But I suspect that it conceals a confusion between the dream and the dreamer's whole personality. [Cf. *I. of D.*, **5**, 397.]

An unjustifiable generalization, based on a few good examples, is involved in the statement that every dream allows of two interpretations—one which agrees with our account, a 'psycho-analytic' one, and another, an 'anagogic' one, which disregards the instinctual impulses and aims at representing the higher functions of the mind (Silberer [1914]).[2] There are dreams of this kind, but you will try in vain to extend this view even to a majority of dreams. Again, after all that I have said to you, you will find quite incomprehensible an assertion that all dreams are to be interpreted bisexually, as a confluence of two currents described as a masculine and a feminine one (Adler [1910]). [Cf. *I. of D.*, **5**, 397.] There are, of course, a few dreams of this kind too; and you may learn later that they are constructed like certain hysterical symptoms. The reason why I have mentioned all these discoveries of fresh universal characteristics of dreams is in order to warn you against them or at least to leave you in no doubt as to what I think of them.

(4) One day the objective value of research into dreams seemed to be put in question by an observation that patients under analytic treatment arrange the content of their dreams in accordance with the favourite theories of their physicians— some dreaming predominantly of sexual instinctual impulses, others of the struggle for power and yet others even of

---

[1] [This theory of Maeder's was dealt with at length by Freud in two footnotes to *I. of D.*, See the end of Section I of Chapter VI and Section D of Chapter VII.]

[2] [This was fully discussed in Section A of Chapter VII in *I. of D.*, as well as in 'Dreams and Telepathy' (1922*a*), and in a footnote to 'A Metapyschological Supplement to the Theory of Dreams' (1917*d*).]

rebirth (Stekel). The weight of this observation was, however, diminished by the reflection that human beings had dreams before there was any psycho-analytic treatment which could give those dreams a direction, and that people who are now under treatment used also to dream during the period before the treatment started. What was true about this novelty could soon be seen to be self-evident and of no relevance to the theory of dreams. The day's residues which instigate dreams are left over from powerful interests in waking life. When the remarks made by the physician and the hints he gives become of significance to the patient, they enter the circle of the day's residues and can provide psychical stimuli for the construction of dreams like any other emotionally coloured interests of the previous day which have not been dealt with, and they then operate like somatic stimuli which impinge on the sleeper during his sleep. The trains of thought set going by the physician can, like these other instigators of dreams, appear in the manifest content of a dream or be discovered in its latent content. Indeed, we know that a dream can be experimentally produced, or, to put it more correctly, a part of the dream-material can be introduced into the dream. In producing these effects on his patients, an analyst is thus playing a part no different from an experimenter who, like Mourly Vold, gives particular postures to the limbs of the subjects of his experiments. [Cf. p. 87 above.]

It is often possible to influence dreamers as to what they shall dream *about*, but never as to *what* they shall dream. The mechanism of the dream-work and the unconscious dream-wish are exempt from any outside influence. In considering dreams with a somatic stimulus, we have already found [p. 96 f.] that the characteristic nature and independence of dream-life are shown in the reaction with which dreams respond to the somatic or mental stimuli that are brought to bear. The thesis which we have been discussing, and which seeks to throw doubt on the objectivity of research into dreams, is thus once again based on a confusion—this time between the dream and the dream-material.[1]

[1] [For a further discussion of this, see Section VII of 'Remarks on the Theory and Practice of Dream-Interpretation' (1923c).]

This then, Ladies and Gentlemen, is what I wanted to tell you about the problems of dreams. As you will guess, there is much that I have had to pass over, and you will have been aware that on almost every point what I have said has necessarily been incomplete. That, however, is due to the connection between the phenomena of dreaming and those of the neuroses. We have studied dreams as an introduction to the theory of the neuroses, and this was certainly a more correct procedure than if we had done the opposite. But just as dreams prepare the way to an understanding of the neuroses, so, on the other hand, a true appreciation of dreams can only be achieved after a knowledge of neurotic phenomena.[1]

I cannot tell what you will think of it, but I must assure you that I do not regret having claimed so much of your interest and of the time available to us for the problems of dreams. There is nothing else from which one can so quickly arrive at a conviction of the correctness of the theses by which psycho-analysis stands or falls. Exacting work over many months and even years is called for to show that the symptoms of a case of neurotic illness have a sense, serve a purpose and arise out of the patient's experiences in life. On the other hand, only a few hours' effort may be enough to prove that the same thing is true of a dream which is, to start with, confused to the point of being unintelligible, and thus to confirm all the premisses of psycho-analysis—the unconscious nature of mental processes, the peculiar mechanisms which they obey and the instinctual forces which are expressed in them. And when we bear in mind the sweeping analogy between the structure of dreams and that of neurotic symptoms and at the same time consider the rapidity of the transformation which makes a dreamer into a waking and reasonable man, we arrive at a certainty that neuroses too are based only on an alteration in the play of forces between the powers of mental life.[2]

[1] [There is a reference back to dreams near the end of the last lecture of the present series, p. 456 below.]

[2] [Freud dealt with the subject of dreams again in the first of his *New Introductory Lectures,* p. 471 below.]

PART III
GENERAL THEORY
OF THE NEUROSES

PSYCHO-ANALYSIS AND PSYCHIATRY

LADIES AND GENTLEMEN,—I am delighted to see you again, at the beginning of a new academic year, for a resumption of our discussions. Last year I spoke to you of the way in which psycho-analysis deals with parapraxes and dreams. This year I should like to introduce you to an understanding of the phenomena of neurosis, which, as you will soon learn, have a great deal in common with both of the others. But I must warn you in advance that I shall not be able to offer you the same position in relation to me this year as I did last year. At that time I set great store on never taking a step without remaining in agreement with your judgement; I discussed a great deal with you and gave way to your objections—in fact I recognized you and your 'common sense' as a deciding factor. But this is no longer possible and for a simple reason. Parapraxes and dreams were not unfamiliar to you as phenomena; we might say that you had as much experience or could easily obtain as much experience of them as I had. The region of the phenomena of neurosis is, however, strange to you; in so far as you are not doctors yourselves, you have no other access to them than through what I have to tell you; and of what help is the best judgement if it is not accompanied by familiarity with the material that is to be judged?

But you must not take this warning of mine to mean that I propose to give you dogmatic lectures and to insist on your unqualified belief. Such a misunderstanding would do me a grave injustice. I do not wish to arouse conviction; I wish to stimulate thought and to upset prejudices. If as a result of lack of knowledge of the material you are not in a position to form a judgement, you should neither believe nor reject. You should listen and allow what I tell you to work on you. It is not so easy to arrive at convictions, or, if they are reached easily, they soon turn out to be worthless and incapable of resistance. The only person who has a right to a conviction is someone who, like me, has worked for many years at the same material and who, in doing so, has himself had the same new and surprising experiences. What is the good, then, in the sphere of the intellect, of these sudden convictions, these lightning-like conversions, these instantaneous rejections? Is it not clear that the '*coup de foudre*', love at first sight, is derived from quite another sphere, from that of the emotions? We do not even require of our *patients* that they should bring a conviction of the truth of psycho-analysis into the treatment or be adherents of it. Such an attitude often raises our suspicions. The attitude that we find the most desirable in them is a benevolent scepticism. So you too should endeavour to allow the psycho-analytic view to grow up quietly in you alongside of the popular or psychiatric one, till opportunities arise for the two to influence each other, to compete with each other and to unite in leading to a conclusion.

On the other hand, you should not for a moment suppose that what I put before you as the psycho-analytic view is a speculative system. It is on the contrary empirical—either a direct expression of observations or the outcome of a process of working them over. Whether this working-over has been carried out in an adequate and justifiable manner will appear in the course of the further advance of the science, and indeed I may assert without boasting, after a lapse of nearly twenty-five years, and having reached a fairly advanced age,[1] that these observations are the result of particularly hard, concentrated and deep-going work. I have often had an impression that our opponents were unwilling to take any account of this origin of our theses, as though they thought what was in question were merely subjectively determined notions to which someone else might oppose others of his own choice. This behaviour of our opponents is not entirely intelligible to me. It may perhaps be due to the fact that, as a doctor, one usually makes so little contact with neurotic patients and pays so little attention to what they say that one cannot imagine the possibility that anything valuable could be derived from their communications—the possibility, that is, of carrying out any thorough observations upon them. I take this opportunity of assuring you that in the course of these lectures I shall indulge in very little controversy, especially with individuals. I have never been able to convince myself of

---

[1] [Freud was about 60 at this time.]

the truth of the maxim that strife is the father of all things. I believe it is derived from the Greek sophists and is at fault, like them, through overvaluing dialectics. It seems to me, on the contrary, that what is known as scientific controversy is on the whole quite unproductive, apart from the fact that it is almost always conducted on highly personal lines. Up to a few years ago I was able to boast that I had only once engaged in a regular scientific dispute—with one single worker (Löwenfeld of Munich).[1] It ended in our becoming friends and we have remained so to this day. But I did not repeat the experiment for a long time, as I did not feel sure that the outcome would be the same.[2]

Now you will no doubt conclude that a rejection such as this of all written discussion argues a high degree of inaccessibility to objections, of obstinacy, or, to use the polite colloquial scientific term, of pig-headedness [Verranntheit]. I should like to say in reply that when once, after such hard work, one has arrived at a conviction, one has at the same time acquired a certain right to retain that conviction with some tenacity. I may also urge that in the course of my work I have modified my views on a few important points, changed them and replaced them by fresh ones—and in each case, of course, I have made this publicly known. And the outcome of this frankness? Some people have taken no notice whatever of my self-corrections and continue to this day to criticize me for hypotheses which have long ceased to have the same meaning for me. Others reproach me precisely for these changes and regard me as untrustworthy on their account. Of course! a person who has occasionally changed his opinions is deserving of no belief at all, since he has made it all too likely that his latest assertions may also be mistaken; but a person who has unflinchingly maintained what he once asserted, or who cannot be quickly enough persuaded to give it up, must naturally be pig-headed or stubborn! What

[1] [This was on the subject of Freud's early theories on anxiety. His second paper on the question (1895f) was entirely concerned with Löwenfeld's criticisms. Löwenfeld himself, though never an adherent to Freud's views, ultimately became much more favourable to them.]

[2] [There is an allusion in this to Freud's much more recent controversies with Adler and Jung, especially in his 'History of the Psycho-Analytic Movement' (1914d), (Norton, 1966).]

can one do, in the face of these contradictory objections by the critics, but remain as one is and behave in accordance with one's own judgement? I am resolved to do that, and I shall not be deterred from modifying or withdrawing any of my theories, as my advancing experience may require. In regard to *fundamental* discoveries I have hitherto found nothing to alter, and I hope this will remain true in the future.[1]

I am to put before you, then, the psycho-analytic view of the phenomena of neurosis. In doing so, the best plan would seem to be to make a start in connection with the phenomena we have already dealt with, for the sake both of analogy and contrast; and I will begin with a symptomatic action [p. 61] which I have seen many people perform during my consulting hours. We analysts cannot do much for the people who come to us in our consulting-room to lay before us in a quarter of an hour the miseries of a long lifetime. Our deeper knowledge makes it difficult for us to give the kind of opinion another doctor would—'There's nothing wrong with you'—with the added advice: 'You should arrange for a mild hydropathic treatment.' One of my colleagues who was asked what he did with his consultation patients shrugged his shoulders and replied: 'I fine them so-and-so many *Kronen* for a frivolous waste of time.' So you will not be surprised to hear that even in the case of busy psycho-analysts their consulting hours are not apt to be very lively. I have had the ordinary door between my waiting-room and my consulting- and treatment-room doubled

---

[1] [Perhaps the chief change in Freud's views up to the time of this lecture had been his abandonment of the purely traumatic causation of the neuroses and his insistence instead on the importance of the innate instinctual forces and on the great part played by phantasies. On this see his paper on the part played by sexuality in the neuroses (1906a). Later on there were, of course, to be further important changes in his views—for instance on the nature of anxiety in *Inhibitions, Symptoms and Anxiety* (1926d), and on the sexual development of women in the Editor's Note to 'Some Psychical Consequences of the Anatomical Distinction between the Sexes' (1925j). But what lay ahead above all were a revision of the theory of the instincts in *Beyond the Pleasure Principle* (1920g) and a new structural picture of the mind in *The Ego and the Id* (1923b), (Norton, 1960). All these changes were to be discussed fifteen years later in the *New Introductory Lectures*.]

and given a baize lining. There can be no doubt about the purpose of this arrangement. Now it constantly happens that a person whom I have brought in from the waiting-room omits to shut the door behind him and almost always he leaves *both* doors open. As soon as I notice this I insist in a rather unfriendly tone on his or her going back and making good the omission— even if the person concerned is a well-dressed gentleman or a fashionable lady. This makes an impression of uncalled-for pedantry. Occasionally, too, I have put myself in a foolish position by making this request when it has turned out to be a person who cannot touch a door-handle himself and is glad if someone with him spares him the necessity. But in the majority of cases I have been right; for anyone who behaves like this and leaves the door open between a doctor's waiting-room and consulting-room is ill-mannered and deserves an unfriendly reception. But do not take sides over this till you have heard the sequel. For this carelessness on the part of the patient only occurs when he has been alone in the waiting-room and has therefore left an empty room behind him; it never happens if other people, strangers to him, have been waiting with him. In this latter case he knows quite well that it is in his interest not to be overheard while he is talking to the doctor, and he never fails to shut both the doors carefully.

Thus the patient's omission is neither accidentally nor senselessly determined; and indeed it is not unimportant, for, as we shall see, it throws light on the newcomer's attitude to the doctor. The patient is one of the great multitude who have a craving for mundane authority, who wish to be dazzled and intimidated. He may have enquired on the telephone as to the hour at which he could most easily get an appointment; he had formed a picture of a crowd of people seeking for help, like the crowd outside one of Julius Meinl's branches.[1] He now comes into an empty, and moreover extremely modestly furnished, waiting-room, and is shocked. He has to make the doctor pay for the superfluous respect which he had intended to offer him: so—he omits to shut the door between the waiting-room and the consulting-room. What he means to say to the doctor by his conduct is: 'Ah, so there's no one here and no one's likely to

---

[1] [The war-time queue outside one of the popular Austrian grocery chain-stores.]

come while I'm here.' He would behave equally impolitely and disrespectfully during the consultation if his arrogance were not given a sharp reprimand at the very beginning.

The analysis of this small symptomatic action tells you nothing you did not know before: the thesis that it was not a matter of chance but had a motive, a sense and an intention, that it had a place in an assignable mental context and that it provided information, by a small indication, of a more important mental process. But, more than anything else, it tells you that the process thus indicated was unknown to the consciousness of the person who carried out the action, since none of the patients who left the two doors open would have been able to admit that by this omission he wanted to give evidence of his contempt. Some of them would probably have been aware of a sense of disappointment when they entered the empty waiting-room; but the connection between this impression and the symptomatic action which followed certainly remained unknown to their consciousness.

Beside this small analysis of a symptomatic action we will now place an observation on a patient. I choose this one because it is fresh in my memory, but also because it can be reported comparatively briefly. A certain amount of detail is indispensable in any such account.

A young officer, home on short leave, asked me to undertake the treatment of his mother-in-law, who, though in the happiest circumstances, was embittering her own life and the lives of her relatives through an absurd idea. In this way I made the acquaintance of a well-preserved lady of fifty-three, friendly and simple in her nature, who told me the following story without any reluctance. She lived in the country, most happily married, with her husband, who was at the head of a large factory. She could not give enough praise to her husband's affectionate solicitude. It had been a love-match thirty years ago, and since then there had never been any trouble, discord or cause for jealousy. Her two children were happily married; her husband (and their father), out of a sense of duty, was not yet willing to retire. A year before, she had received an anonymous letter accusing her excellent husband of a love affair with a young girl; and the incredible—and to herself unintelligible

—result was that she immediately believed it, and since then her happiness had been destroyed. The course of events, in greater detail, was something like this. She had a housemaid with whom she used, perhaps too often, to have intimate talks. This girl pursued another one with a positively malicious hostility because she had done so much better for herself in life, though she was of no higher origin. Instead of going into service, this other girl had managed to get a commercial training, had entered the factory and, as a result of shortness of personnel, owing to members of the staff being called up for military service, she was promoted to a good position. She now lived in the factory itself, had social relations with all the gentlemen and was actually addressed as 'Fräulein'. The girl who had made less of a success in life was of course ready to repeat all kinds of bad things of her former schoolmate. One day our lady had a conversation with the housemaid about a gentleman who had been staying with them, who was well known not to be living with his wife but to be having an affair with another woman. She did not know how it happened, but she suddenly said: 'The most dreadful thing that could happen to me would be if I were to learn that my dear husband was having an affair too.' The next day she received an anonymous letter by post which, as though by magic, gave her this very information, written in a disguised hand. She decided, probably rightly, that the letter was the work of the malicious housemaid, since it specified as her husband's mistress the girl whom the servant pursued with her hatred. But although she at once saw through the intrigue and had seen enough instances where she lived of how little credence such cowardly denunciations deserved, what happened was that the letter instantly prostrated her. She became terribly excited, sent for her husband at once and reproached him violently. Her husband laughed the accusation off and did the best possible thing. He brought in the family doctor (who was also the factory doctor) who made efforts to soothe the unfortunate lady. The further conduct of both of them was also entirely sensible. The housemaid was dismissed, but the alleged rival was not. Since then the patient had repeatedly been pacified to the point of no longer believing the content of the anonymous letter, but never thoroughly and never for long. It was enough for her to hear the young lady's name mentioned or to meet her in the street and a fresh attack of distrust, pain and reproaches would burst out in her.

This, then, is the case history of this excellent woman. Not much psychiatric experience was needed to understand that, in contrast to other neurotics, she was giving too mild an account of her case—that she was, as we say, dissimulating—and that she had never really got over her belief in the accusation contained in the anonymous letter.

What attitude, then, will a psychiatrist adopt in a case of illness like this? We know already how he would behave to the symptomatic action of the patient who fails to shut the consulting-room door. He pronounces it to be a chance event of no psychological interest with which he has no further concern. But this procedure cannot be carried over to the illness of the jealous woman. The symptomatic action seems to be a matter of indifference; but the symptom forces itself on our attention as a matter of importance. It is accompanied by intense subjective suffering and, as an objective fact, it threatens the communal life of a family; it is thus an undeniable subject of psychiatric interest. The psychiatrist will start by endeavouring to characterize the symptom by some essential feature. The idea with which the woman torments herself cannot in itself be called absurd; it does, indeed, happen that elderly gentlemen have love affairs with young girls. But there is something else about it which *is* absurd and hard to understand. The patient had no other reason at all for believing that her affectionate and loyal husband belonged to this otherwise not so rare class of husbands except what was asserted in the anonymous letter. She knew that this document had no evidential value and she was able to give a satisfying explanation of its origin. She ought therefore to have been able to tell herself that she had no ground whatever for her jealousy, and she did tell herself so. But in spite of this she suffered as much as if she regarded this jealousy as completely justified. Ideas of this kind, which are inaccessible to logical arguments based on reality, are by general agreement described as *delusions*. The good lady, then, was suffering from *delusions of jealousy*. This is no doubt the essential feature of this case of illness.

After this first point has been established our psychiatric interest will become even livelier. If a delusion is not to be got

rid of by a reference to reality, no doubt it did not originate
from reality either. Where else did it originate? There are
delusions of the most varied content: why in our case is the
content of the delusion jealousy in particular? In what kind of
people do delusions, and especially delusions of jealousy, come
about? We should like to hear what the psychiatrist has to say
about this; but at this point he leaves us in the lurch. He enters
into only a single one of our enquiries. He will investigate the
woman's family history and will *perhaps* give us this reply:
'Delusions come about in people in whose families similar and
other psychical disorders have repeatedly occurred.' In other
words, if this woman developed a delusion she was predisposed
to it by hereditary transmission. No doubt that is something;
but is it all we want to know? Was this the only thing that
contributed to the causation of the illness? Must we be content
to suppose that it is a matter of indifference or caprice or is
inexplicable whether a delusion of jealousy arises rather than
any other sort? And ought we to understand the assertion of the
predominance of the hereditary influence in a negative sense as
well—that no matter what experiences this woman's mind
encountered she was destined some time or other to produce a
delusion? You will want to know why it is that scientific psychiatry will give us no further information. But my reply to you
is: 'he is a rogue who gives more than he has.' The psychiatrist
knows no way of throwing more light on a case like this one. He
must content himself with a diagnosis and a prognosis—uncertain in spite of a wealth of experience—of its future course.

But can psycho-analysis do more here? Yes, it actually can.
I hope to be able to show you that, even in a case so hard of
access as this, it can discover something which makes a first
understanding possible. And to begin with I would draw your
attention to the inconspicuous detail that the patient herself
positively provoked the anonymous letter, which now gave
support to her delusion, by informing the scheming housemaid
on the previous day that it would cause her the greatest unhappiness if her husband had a love affair with a young girl. In
this way she first put the notion of sending the anonymous
letter into the housemaid's head. Thus the delusion acquires a
certain independence of the letter; it had been present already
in the patient as a fear—or was it as a wish? Let us now add to

this the small further indications yielded by only two analytic sessions. The patient, indeed, behaved in a very unco-operative way when, after telling me her story, she was asked for her further thoughts, ideas and memories. She said that nothing occurred to her, that she had told me everything already, and after two sessions the experiment with me had in fact to be broken off because she announced that she already felt well and that she was sure the pathological idea would not come back. She only said this, of course, from resistance and from dread of the continuation of the analysis. Nevertheless, during these two sessions she let fall a few remarks which allowed of, and indeed necessitated, a particular interpretation; and this interpretation threw a clear light on the genesis of her delusion of jealousy. She herself was intensely in love with a young man, with the same son-in-law who had persuaded her to come to me as a patient. She herself knew nothing, or perhaps only a very little, of this love; in the family relationship that existed between them it was easy for this passionate liking to disguise itself as innocent affection. After all our experiences elsewhere, it is not hard for us to feel our way into the mental life of this upright wife and worthy mother, of the age of fifty-three. Being in love like this, a monstrous and impossible thing, could not become conscious; but it remained in existence and, even though it was unconscious, it exercised a severe pressure. Something had to become of it, some relief had to be looked for; and the easiest mitigation was offered, no doubt, by the mechanism of displacement which plays a part so regularly in the generating of delusional jealousy. If not only were she, the old woman, in love with a young man, but if also her old husband were having a love affair with a young girl, then her conscience would be relieved of the weight of her unfaithfulness. The phantasy of her husband's unfaithfulness thus acted as a cooling compress on her burning wound. Her own love had not become conscious to her, but its mirror-reflection, which brought her such an advantage, now became conscious as an obsession and delusion. No arguments against it could, of course, have any effect, for they were only directed against the mirror-image and not against the original which gave the other its strength and which lay hidden, inviolable, in the unconscious.

Let us now bring together what this effort at a psycho-analysis, short and impeded as it was, has brought to light for an understanding of this case—assuming, of course, that our enquiries were correctly carried out, which I cannot here submit to your judgement. Firstly, the delusion has ceased to be absurd or unintelligible; it had a sense, it had good motives and it fitted into the context of an emotional experience of the patient's. Secondly, the delusion was necessary, as a reaction to an unconscious mental process which we have inferred from other indications, and it was precisely to this connection that it owed its delusional character and its resistance to every logical and realistic attack. It itself was something desired, a kind of consolation. Thirdly, the fact that the delusion turned out to be precisely a jealous one and not one of another kind was unambiguously determined by the experience that lay behind the illness.[1] You recall of course that, the day before, she had told the scheming maid that the most dreadful thing that could happen to her would be her husband's unfaithfulness. Nor will you have overlooked the two important analogies between this case and the symptomatic action which we analysed—the explanation of its sense or intention and its relation to something unconscious that was involved in the situation.

Naturally this does not answer all the questions that we might ask in connection with this case. On the contrary, the case bristles with further problems—some that have in general not yet become soluble and others which could not be solved owing to the particular circumstances being unfavourable. For instance, why did this lady who was happily married fall in love with her son-in-law? and why did the relief, which might have been possible in other ways, take the form of this mirror-image, this projection of her state on to her husband? You must not think it is otiose or frivolous to raise such questions. We already have some material at our disposal which might possibly serve to answer them. The lady was at a critical age, at which sexual needs in women suffer a sudden and undesired increase; that alone might account for the event. Or it may further have been that her excellent and faithful husband had for some years no longer enjoyed the sexual capacity which the well-preserved woman required for her satisfaction. Experience has shown us

---

[1] [This sentence occurs in a less clear form in some of the earlier German editions.]

that it is precisely men in this position, whose faithfulness can consequently be taken for granted, who are distinguished by treating their wives with unusual tenderness, and by showing particular forbearance for their nervous troubles. Or, again, it may not be without significance that the object of this pathogenic love was precisely the young husband of one of her daughters. A powerful erotic tie with a daughter, which goes back in the last resort to the mother's sexual constitution, often finds a way of persisting in a transformation of this sort. In this connection I may perhaps remind you that the relation between mother-in-law and son-in-law has been regarded from the earliest times of the human race as a particularly awkward one and that among primitive people it has given rise to very powerful taboo regulations and 'avoidances'.[1] The relation is frequently excessive by civilized standards both in a positive and negative direction. Which of these three factors became operative in our case, or whether two of them or perhaps all three came together, I cannot, it is true, tell you; but that is only because I was not permitted to continue the analysis of the case for more than two sessions.

I notice now, Gentlemen, that I have been talking to you about a number of things which you are not yet prepared to understand. I did so in order to carry out the comparison between psychiatry and psycho-analysis. But there is one thing that I can ask you now. Have you observed any sign of a contradiction between them? Psychiatry does not employ the technical methods of psycho-analysis; it omits to make any inferences from the *content* of the delusion, and, in pointing to heredity, it gives us a very general and remote aetiology instead of indicating first the more special and proximate causes. But is there a contradiction, an opposition in this? Is it not rather a case of one supplementing the other? Does the hereditary factor contradict the importance of experience? Do not the two things rather combine in the most effective manner? You will grant that there is nothing in the nature of psychiatric work which could be opposed to psycho-analytic research. What is opposed to psycho-analysis is not psychiatry but psychiatrists. Psycho-

[1] [See first essay of *Totem and Taboo* (1912–13) (Norton, 1952.)]

analysis is related to psychiatry approximately as histology is to anatomy: the one studies the external forms of the organs, the other studies their construction out of tissues and cells. It is not easy to imagine a contradiction between these two species of study, of which one is a continuation of the other. To-day, as you know, anatomy is regarded by us as the foundation of scientific medicine. But there was a time when it was as much forbidden to dissect the human cadaver in order to discover the internal structure of the body as it now seems to be to practise psycho-analysis in order to learn about the internal mechanism of the mind. It is to be expected that in the not too distant future it will be realized that a scientifically based psychiatry is not possible without a sound knowledge of the deeper-lying unconscious processes in mental life.

Perhaps, however, the much-abused psycho-analysis has friends among you who will be pleased if it can be justified from another direction—from the therapeutic side. As you know, our psychiatric therapy is not hitherto able to influence delusions. Is it possible, perhaps, that psycho-analysis can do so, thanks to its insight into the mechanism of these symptoms? No, Gentlemen, it cannot. It is as powerless (for the time being at least) against these ailments as any other form of therapy. *We* can understand, indeed, what has happened in the patient, but we have no means of making the patient himself understand it. You have heard how I was unable to pursue the analysis of this delusion beyond a first beginning. Will you be inclined to maintain on that account that an analysis of such cases is to be rejected because it is fruitless? I think not. We have a right, or rather a duty, to carry on our research without consideration of any immediate beneficial effect. In the end—we cannot tell where or when—every little fragment of knowledge will be transformed into power, and into therapeutic power as well. Even if psycho-analysis showed itself as unsuccessful in every other form of nervous and psychical disease as it does in delusions, it would still remain completely justified as an irreplaceable instrument of scientific research. It is true that in that case we should not be in a position to practise it. The human material on which we seek to learn, which lives, has its own will and needs its motives for co-operating in our work, would hold back from us. Let me therefore end my remarks to-day by informing you that there are extensive groups of nervous disorders in which the transformation of our better understanding into therapeutic power has actually taken place, and that in these illnesses, which are difficult of access by other means, we achieve, under favourable conditions, successes which are second to no others in the field of internal medicine.[1]

[1] [Psycho-analysis as a method of psychotherapy is the subject of the last lecture of the series (XXVIII).]

LECTURE XVII

THE SENSE OF SYMPTOMS

LADIES AND GENTLEMEN,—In the last lecture I explained to you that clinical psychiatry takes little notice of the outward form or content of individual symptoms, but that psycho-analysis takes matters up at precisely that point and has established in the first place the fact that symptoms have a sense and are related to the patient's experiences. The sense of neurotic symptoms was first discovered by Josef Breuer from his study and successful cure (between 1880 and 1882) of a case of hysteria which has since become famous. It is true that Pierre Janet brought forward the same evidence independently; indeed, the French worker can claim priority of publication, for it was only a decade later (in 1893 and 1895), while he was collaborating with me, that Breuer published his observation. In any case it may seem a matter of some indifference who made the discovery, for, as you know, every discovery is made more than once and none is made all at once. And, apart from this, success does not always go along with merit: America is not named after Columbus. The great psychiatrist Leuret[1] gave it as his opinion, before Breuer and Janet, that even the delusional ideas of the insane would certainly be found to have a sense if only we understood how to translate them. I must admit that for a long time I was prepared to give Janet very great credit for throwing light on neurotic symptoms, because he regarded them as expressions of *idées inconscientes* which dominated the patients.[2] But since then he has expressed himself with exaggerated reserve, as if he wanted to admit that the unconscious had been nothing more to him than a form of words, a makeshift, *une façon de parler*—that he had meant nothing real by it.[3] Since then I have ceased to understand Janet's writings; but I think he has unnecessarily forfeited much credit.

Thus neurotic symptoms have a sense, like parapraxes and

[1] [François Leuret (1797–1851). (Leuret, 1834, 131.)]
[2] [See, for example, Janet, 1888.]
[3] [For the gist of this see Janet, 1913, 39.]

dreams, and, like them, have a connection with the life of those who produce them. I should now like to make this important discovery plainer to you by a few examples. I can indeed only assert, I cannot prove, that it is always and in every instance so. Anyone who looks for experiences himself, will find convincing evidence. But for certain reasons I shall choose these examples from cases not of hysteria but of another, highly remarkable neurosis which is fundamentally very much akin to it and about which I have a few introductory remarks to make.

This neurosis, known as 'obsessional neurosis', is not so popular as the universally familiar hysteria. It is not, if I may express myself thus, so obtrusively noisy, it behaves more like a private affair of the patient's, it dispenses almost entirely with somatic phenomena, and creates all its symptoms in the mental sphere. Obsessional neurosis and hysteria are the forms of neurotic illness upon the study of which psycho-analysis was first built, and in the treatment of which, too, our therapy celebrates its triumphs. But obsessional neurosis, in which the puzzling leap from the mental to the physical plays no part, has actually, through the efforts of psycho-analysis, become more perspicuous and familiar to us than hysteria, and we have learnt that it displays certain extreme characteristics of the nature of neurosis far more glaringly.

Obsessional neurosis is shown in the patient's being occupied with thoughts in which he is in fact not interested, in his being aware of impulses in himself which appear very strange to him and in his being led to actions the performance of which give him no enjoyment, but which it is quite impossible for him to omit. The thoughts (obsessions) may be senseless in themselves, or merely a matter of indifference to the subject; often they are completely silly, and invariably they are the starting-point of a strenuous mental activity, which exhausts the patient and to which he only surrenders himself most unwillingly. He is obliged against his will to brood and speculate as though it were a question of his most important vital problems. The impulses which the patient is aware of in himself may also make a childish and senseless impression; but as a rule they have a content of the most frightful kind, tempting him, for instance, to commit serious crimes, so that he not merely disavows them as alien to himself, but flies from them in horror and protects himself from carrying them out by prohibitions, renunciations and restrictions upon his freedom. At the same time, these impulses never—literally never—force their way through to performance; the outcome lies always in victory for the flight and the precautions. What the patient actually carries out—his so-called obsessional actions—are very harmless and certainly trivial things, for the most part repetitions or ceremonial elaborations of the activities of ordinary life. But these necessary activities (such as going to bed, washing, dressing or going for a walk) become extremely tedious and almost insoluble tasks. In different forms and cases of obsessional neurosis the pathological ideas, impulses and actions are not combined in equal proportions; it is the rule, rather, that one or other of these factors dominates the picture and gives its name to the illness, but the common element in all these forms is sufficiently unmistakable.

Certainly this is a crazy illness. The most extravagant psychiatric imagination would not, I think, have succeeded in constructing anything like it; and if one did not see it before one every day one would never bring oneself to believe in it. Do not suppose, however, that you will help the patient in the least by calling on him to take a new line, to cease to occupy himself with such foolish thoughts and to do something sensible instead of his childish pranks. He would like to do so himself, for he is completely clear in his head, shares your opinion of his obsessional symptoms and even puts it forward to you spontaneously. Only he cannot help himself. What is carried into action in an obsessional neurosis is sustained by an energy to which we probably know nothing comparable in normal mental life. There is only one thing he can do: he can make displacements, and exchanges, he can replace one foolish idea by another somewhat milder, he can proceed from one precaution or prohibition to another, instead of one ceremonial he can perform another. He can displace the obsession but not remove it. The ability to displace any symptom into something far removed from its original conformation is a main characteristic of his illness. Moreover it is a striking fact that in his condition the contradictions (polarities) with which mental life is interlaced [cf. p. 301 below] emerge especially sharply differentiated. Alongside of obsessions with a positive and negative content, *doubt* makes itself felt in the intellectual field and little by little it begins to gnaw even at what is usually most certain. The whole position ends up in an ever-increasing degree of indecision, loss of energy and restriction of freedom. At the same time, the obsessional neurotic starts off with a very energetic disposition, he is often extraordinarily self-willed and as a rule he has intellectual gifts above the average. He has usually reached a satisfactorily high level of ethical development; he exhibits over-conscientiousness, and is more than ordinarily correct in his behaviour. You can imagine that no small amount of work is needed before one can make one's way any distance into this contradictory hotchpotch of character-traits and symptoms. And to begin with we aim at nothing whatever else than understanding a few of the symptoms and being able to interpret them.

Perhaps you would like to know in advance, having in mind our earlier talks, what attitude contemporary psychiatry adopts towards the problems of obsessional neurosis. But it is a meagre chapter. Psychiatry gives names to the different obsessions but says nothing further about them. On the other hand it insists that those who suffer from these symptoms are 'degenerates'. This gives small satisfaction; in fact it is a judgement of value—a condemnation instead of an explanation. We are supposed to think that every possible sort of eccentricity may arise in degenerates. Well, it is true that we must regard those who develop such symptoms as somewhat different in their nature from other people. But we may ask: are they more 'degenerate' than other neurotics—than hysterical patients, for instance, or those who fall ill of psychoses? Once again, the characterization is evidently too general. Indeed, we may doubt whether there is any justification for it at all, when we learn that such symptoms occur too in distinguished people of particularly high capacities, capacities important for the world at large. It is true that, thanks to their own discretion and to the untruthfulness of their biographers, we learn little that is intimate about the great men who are our models; but it may nevertheless happen that one of them, like Émile Zola, may be a fanatic for the truth, and we then learn from him of the many strange obsessional habits to which he was a life-long victim.[1]

Psychiatry has found a way out by speaking of '*dégénérés*

[1] E. Toulouse, *Emile Zola, enquête médico-psychologique*, Paris, 1896.

supérieurs'. Very nice. But we have found from psycho-analysis that it is possible to get permanently rid of these strange obsessional symptoms, just as of other complaints and just as in people who are not degenerate. I myself have succeeded repeatedly in this.[1]

I shall give you only two examples of the analysis of an obsessional symptom: one an old observation which I cannot find a better one to replace, and another recently met with. I limit myself to this small number, because it is impossible in such reports to avoid being very diffuse and entering into every detail.

A lady, nearly thirty years of age, who suffered from the most severe obsessional manifestations and whom I might perhaps have helped if a malicious chance had not brought my work to nothing—I may be able to tell you more about this later on—performed (among others) the following remarkable obsessional action many times a day. She ran from her room into another neighbouring one, took up a particular position there beside a table that stood in the middle, rang the bell for her housemaid, sent her on some indifferent errand or let her go without one, and then ran back into her own room. This was certainly not a very distressing symptom, but was nevertheless calculated to excite curiosity. The explanation was reached in the most unequivocal and unobjectionable manner, free from any possible contribution on the doctor's part. I cannot see how I could possibly have formed any suspicion of the sense of this obsessional action or could have offered any suggestion on how it was to be interpreted. Whenever I asked the patient 'Why do you do that? What sense has it?' she answered: 'I don't know.' But one day, after I had succeeded in defeating a major, fundamental doubt of hers, she suddenly knew the answer and told me what it was that was connected with the obsessional action. More than ten years before, she had married a man very much older than herself, and on the wedding-night he was impotent.

---

[1] [Freud probably discussed obsessional neurosis more often than any other disorder—from the beginning of his career almost to the end of it. A list of some of the more important references will be found in an Appendix to his 'Notes upon a Case of Obsessional Neurosis' (1909*d*).]

Many times during the night he had come running from his room into hers to try once more, but every time without success. Next morning he had said angrily: 'I should feel ashamed in front of the housemaid when she makes the bed,' took up a bottle of red ink that happened to be in the room and poured its contents over the sheet, but not on the exact place where a stain would have been appropriate. I could not understand at first what this recollection had to do with the obsessional action in question; the only resemblance I could find was in the repeated running from one room into the other, and perhaps also in the entrance of the housemaid. My patient then led me up to the table in the second room and showed me a big stain on the tablecloth. She further explained that she took up her position in relation to the table in such a way that the maid who had been sent for could not fail to see the stain. There could no longer be any doubt of the intimate connection between the scene on her wedding-night and her present obsessional action, though all kinds of other things remained to be learnt.

It was clear, in the first place, that the patient was identifying herself with her husband; she was playing his part by imitating his running from one room into the other. Further, to carry on the analogy, we must agree that the bed and the sheet were replaced by the table and the tablecloth. This might seem arbitrary, but surely we have not studied dream-symbolism to no purpose. In dreams too we often find a table which has to be interpreted as a bed. Table and bed[1] together stand for marriage, so that the one can easily take the place of the other.

It already seems proved that the obsessional action had a sense; it appears to have been a representation, a repetition, of the significant scene. But we are not obliged to come to a halt here. If we examine the relation between the two more closely, we shall probably obtain information about something that goes further—about the intention of the obsessional action. Its kernel was obviously the summoning of the housemaid, before whose eyes the patient displayed the stain, in contrast to her husband's remark that he would feel ashamed in front of the maid. Thus he, whose part she was playing, did not feel ashamed in front of the maid; accordingly the stain was in the

[1] [The English phrase is 'bed and board', which is itself a translation of a law-Latin term for marriage.]

right place. We see, therefore, that she was not simply repeating the scene, she was continuing and at the same time correcting it; she was putting it right. But by this she was also correcting the other thing, which had been so distressing that night and had made the expedient with the red ink necessary—his impotence. So the obsessional action was saying: 'No, it's not true. He had no need to feel ashamed in front of the housemaid; he was not impotent.' It represented this wish, in the manner of a dream, as fulfilled in a present-day action; it served the purpose of making her husband superior to his past mishap.

Everything I could tell you about this woman fits in with this. Or, more correctly speaking, everything else we know about her points the way to this interpretation of what was in itself an unintelligible obsessional action. The woman had been living apart from her husband for years and was struggling with an intention to obtain a legal divorce. But there was no question of her being free of him; she was forced to remain faithful to him; she withdrew from the world so as not to be tempted; she exculpated and magnified his nature in her imagination. Indeed, the deepest secret of her illness was that by means of it she protected her husband from malicious gossip, justified her separation from him and enabled him to lead a comfortable separate life. Thus the analysis of a harmless obsessional action led directly to the inmost core of an illness, but at the same time betrayed to us no small part of the secret of obsessional neurosis in general. I am glad to let you dwell a little on this example because it combines conditions which we could not fairly expect to find in every case. Here the interpretation of the symptom was discovered by the patient herself at a single blow, without any prompting or intervention on the analyst's part; and it resulted from a connection with an event which did not (as is usually the case) belong to a forgotten period of childhood, but which had happened in the patient's adult life and had remained undimmed in her memory. All the objections which criticism is normally in the habit of raising against our interpretation of symptoms fall to the ground in this particular case. We cannot hope always to have such good luck.[1]

[1] [Freud had given a shorter account of this case, though with some further details, in his paper on 'Obsessive Actions and Religious Practices' (1907b).]

And one thing more. Were you not struck by the way in which this unobtrusive obsessional action has led us into the intimacies of the patient's life? A woman cannot have anything much more intimate to tell than the story of her wedding-night. Is it a matter of chance and of no further significance that we have arrived precisely at the intimacies of sexual life? No doubt it might be the result of the choice I have made on this occasion. Do not let us be too hasty in forming our judgement, and let us turn to my second example, which is of quite a different kind— a sample of a very common species, a sleep-ceremonial.

A nineteen-year-old girl, well developed and gifted, was the only child of parents to whom she was superior in education and intellectual liveliness. As a child she had been wild and high-spirited, and in the course of the last few years had changed, without any visible cause, into a neurotic. She was very irritable, particularly towards her mother, always dissatisfied and depressed, and inclined to indecisiveness and doubt; finally she admitted that she was no longer able to walk by herself across squares or along comparatively wide streets. We will not concern ourselves much with her complicated illness, which called for at least two diagnoses—agoraphobia and obsessional neurosis—but will dwell only on the fact that she also developed a sleep-ceremonial, with which she tormented her parents. In a certain sense it may be said that every normal person has his sleep-ceremonial or that he has established certain necessary conditions the non-fulfilment of which interferes with his going to sleep; he has imposed certain forms on the transition from the waking to the sleeping state and repeats them in the same manner every evening. But everything that a healthy person requires as a necessary condition for sleep can be understood rationally, and if external circumstances call for a change he will comply easily and without waste of time. A pathological ceremonial, however, is unyielding and insists on being carried through, even at the cost of great sacrifices; it too is screened by having a rational basis and at a superficial glance seems to diverge from the normal only by a certain exaggerated meticulousness. On closer examination, nevertheless, we can see that the screen is insufficient, that the ceremonial comprises some stipulations which go far beyond its rational basis and others which positively run counter to it. Our present patient put forward as a pretext for her nightly precautions that she needed quiet in order to sleep and must exclude every source of noise. With that end in view she did two kinds of things. The big clock in her room was stopped, all the other clocks or watches in the room were removed, and her tiny wrist-watch was not allowed even to be inside her bedside table. Flower-pots and vases were collected on the writing-table so that they might not fall over in the night and break, and disturb her in her sleep. She was aware that these measures could find only an *ostensible* justification in the rule in favour of quiet: the ticking of the little watch would not have been audible even if it had been left lying on the top of the bedside table, and we have all had experience of the fact that the regular ticking of a pendulum-clock never disturbs sleep but acts, rather, as a soporific. She admitted too that her fear that flower-pots and vases, if they were left in their places, might fall over and break of their own accord lacked all plausibility. In the case of other stipulations made by the ceremonial the need for quiet was dropped as a basis. Indeed, the requirement that the door between her room and her parents' bedroom should stay half-open—the fulfilment of which she ensured by placing various objects in the open doorway—seemed on the contrary to act as a source of disturbing noises. But the most important stipulations related to the bed itself. The pillow at the top end of the bed must not touch the wooden back of the bedstead. The small top-pillow must lie on this large pillow in one specific way only —namely, so as to form a diamond shape. Her head had then to lie exactly along the long diameter of the diamond. The eiderdown (or '*Duchent*' as we call it in Austria[1]) had to be shaken before being laid on the bed so that its bottom end became very thick; afterwards, however, she never failed to even out this accumulation of feathers by pressing them apart.

With your leave I will pass over the remaining, often very trivial, details of the ceremonial; they would teach us nothing new, and would lead us too far afield from our aims. But you

---

[1] [Elsewhere in Germany the French word '*duvet*' is usual. This object is normally an undivided bag of feathers, not, as in England, quilted into a number of separate compartments.]

must not overlook the fact that all this was not carried out smoothly. There was always an apprehension that things might not have been done properly. Everything must be checked and repeated, doubts assailed first one and then another of the safety measures, and the result was that one or two hours were spent, during which the girl herself could not sleep and would not allow her intimidated parents to sleep either.

The analysis of these torments did not proceed so simply as that of our earlier patient's obsessional action. I was obliged to give the girl hints and propose interpretations, which were always rejected with a decided 'no' or accepted with contemptuous doubt. But after this first reaction of rejection there followed a time during which she occupied herself with the possibilities put before her, collected associations to them, produced recollections and made connections, until by her own work she had accepted all the interpretations. In proportion as this happened, she relaxed the performance of her obsessional measures, and even before the end of the treatment she had given up the whole ceremonial. You must understand, too, that the work of analysis as we carry it out to-day quite excludes the systematic treatment of any individual symptom till it has been entirely cleared up. We are, on the contrary, obliged to keep on leaving any particular topic, in the certain expectation of coming back to it again in other connections. The interpretation of her symptoms which I am about to give you is accordingly a synthesis of findings which were arrived at, interrupted by other work, over a period of weeks and months.

Our patient gradually came to learn that it was as symbols of the female genitals that clocks were banished from her equipment for the night. Clocks and watches—though elsewhere we have found other symbolic interpretations for them[1]—have arrived at a genital role owing to their relation to periodic processes and equal intervals of time. A woman may boast that her menstruation behaves with the regularity of clockwork. Our patient's anxiety, however, was directed in particular against being disturbed in her sleep by the ticking of a clock. The ticking of a clock may be compared with the knocking or throbbing

---

[1] [Another reason for the dislike of clocks and watches felt by obsessional neurotics is mentioned in the 'Rat Man' analysis (1909d).]

in the clitoris during sexual excitement.[1] She had in fact been repeatedly woken from her sleep by this sensation, which had now become distressing to her; and she gave expression to this fear of an erection in the rule that all clocks and watches that were going should be removed from her neighbourhood at night. Flower-pots and vases, like all vessels [p. 156], are also female symbols. Taking precautions against their falling and being broken at night was thus not without its good sense. We know the widespread custom of breaking a vessel or plate at betrothal ceremonies. Each man present gets hold of a fragment, and we may regard this as a sign of his resigning the claims he had upon the bride in virtue of a marriage-regulation dating from before the establishment of monogamy.[2] In connection with this part of her ceremonial the girl produced a recollection and several associations. Once when she was a child she had fallen down while she was carrying a glass or china vase and had cut her finger and bled profusely. When she grew up and came to know the facts about sexual intercourse she formed an anxious idea that on her wedding-night she would not bleed and would thus fail to show that she was a virgin. Her precautions against vases being broken thus meant a repudiation of the whole complex concerned with virginity and bleeding at the first intercourse—a repudiation equally of the fear of bleeding and of the contrary fear of not bleeding. These precautions, which she subsumed under her avoidance of noise, had only a remote connection with it.

She found out the central meaning of her ceremonial one day when she suddenly understood the meaning of the rule that the pillow must not touch the back of the bedstead. The pillow, she said, had always been a woman to her and the upright wooden back a man. Thus she wanted—by magic, we must interpolate—to keep the man and woman apart—that is, to separate her parents from each other, not to allow them to have sexual intercourse. In earlier years, before she had established the ceremonial, she had tried to achieve the same aim in a more

[1] [Freud had reported a similar connection in his paper on a case of paranoia (1915*f*).]

[2] [Cf. a reference to 'group marriage' in *Totem and Taboo* (1912-13), (Norton, 1952), and a discussion in 'The Taboo of Virginity' (1918*a*).]

direct way. She had simulated fear (or had exploited a tendency to fear which was already present) in order that the connecting doors between her parents' bedroom and the nursery should not be shut. This rule had, indeed, been retained in her present ceremonial. In that way she gave herself the opportunity of listening to her parents, but in making use of it she brought on an insomnia which lasted for months. Not satisfied with disturbing her parents by this means, she contrived to be allowed from time to time to sleep in her parents' bed between them. The 'pillow' and the 'wooden back' were thus really unable to come together. Finally, when she was so big that it became physically uncomfortable for her to find room in the bed between her parents, she managed, by a conscious simulation of anxiety, to arrange for her mother to exchange places with her for the night and to leave her own place so that the patient could sleep beside her father. This situation no doubt became the starting-point of phantasies whose after-effect was to be seen in the ceremonial.

If a pillow was a woman, then the shaking of the eiderdown till all the feathers were at the bottom and caused a swelling there had a sense as well. It meant making a woman pregnant; but she never failed to smooth away the pregnancy again, for she had for years been afraid that her parents' intercourse would result in another child and so present her with a competitor. On the other hand, if the big pillow was a woman, the mother, then the small top-pillow could only stand for the daughter. Why did this pillow have to be placed diamond-wise and her head precisely along its centre line? It was easy to recall to her that this diamond shape is the inscription scribbled on every wall to represent the open female genitals. If so, she herself was playing the man and replacing the male organ by her head. (Cf. the symbolism of beheading for castrating.)[1]

Wild thoughts, you will say, to be running through an unmarried girl's head. I admit that is so. But you must not forget that I did not make these things but only interpreted them. A sleep-ceremonial like this is a strange thing too,[2] and you will

[1] [See Freud's paper on this subject (1916c), which includes a short reference to the present case.]

[2] [An almost equally elaborate sleep-ceremonial had been reported by Freud long before, in his second paper on the neuropsychoses of defence (1896b).]

not fail to see how the ceremonial corresponds to the phantasies which are revealed by the interpretation. But I attach more importance to your noticing that what was seen in the ceremonial was a precipitate not of a *single* phantasy but of a number of them, though they had a nodal point somewhere, and, further, that the rules laid down by the ceremonial reproduced the patient's sexual wishes at one point positively and at another negatively—in part they represented them, but in part they served as a defence against them.

More could be made, too, of the analysis of this ceremonial if it could be properly linked up with the patient's other symptoms. But our path does not lead in that direction. You must be content with a hint that the girl was in the grip of an erotic attachment to her father whose beginnings went back to her childhood. Perhaps that was why she behaved in such an unfriendly way to her mother [p. 264]. Nor can we overlook the fact that the analysis of this symptom has once again taken us back to a patient's sexual life. We shall perhaps be less surprised at this the more often we gain an insight into the sense and intention of neurotic symptoms.

I have shown you, then, on the basis of two chosen examples, that neurotic symptoms have a sense, like parapraxes and dreams, and that they have an intimate connection with the patient's experiences. Can I expect you to believe this extremely important thesis on the evidence of two examples? No. But can you require me to go on giving you further examples till you declare yourselves convinced? No, once more. For, in view of the detailed fashion in which I deal with each single case, I should have to devote a five-hour course of lectures to settling this one point in the theory of the neuroses. So I must be content with having given you a trial proof of my assertion and, for the rest, I refer you to the reports given in the literature of the subject—to the classical interpretations of symptoms in Breuer's first case (of hysteria),[1] to the striking light thrown upon the most obscure symptoms of what is known as dementia praecox by C. G. Jung [1907], at a time when he was merely a psycho-analyst and had not yet aspired to be a prophet, and all the other papers that have since than filled our periodicals.

[1] [Included in *Studies on Hysteria* (1895d), the Case of Anna O.]

There has been no lack of investigations precisely on these lines. The analysis, interpretation and translation of neurotic symptoms proved so attractive to psycho-analysts that for a time they neglected the other problems of neurosis.

If any of you undertakes exertions of this kind, he will certainly gain a powerful impression of the wealth of evidential material. But he will also come up against a difficulty. The sense of a symptom lies, as we have found, in some connection with the patient's experience. The more individual is the form of the symptom the more reason we shall have for expecting to be able to establish this connection. The task is then simply to discover, in respect to a senseless idea and a pointless action, the past situation in which the idea was justified and the action served a purpose. The obsessional action of our patient who ran to the table and rang for the housemaid is a perfect model of this kind of symptom. But there are—and they are very frequent— symptoms of quite another character. They must be described as 'typical' symptoms of an illness; they are approximately the same in all cases, individual distinctions disappear in them or at least shrink up to such an extent that it is difficult to bring them into connection with the patients' individual experience and to relate them to particular situations they have experienced. Let us look once more at obsessional neurosis. The sleep-ceremonial of our second patient already has much that is typical about it, though at the same time it has enough individual traits to make what I might call a 'historical' interpretation possible. But all these obsessional patients have a tendency to repeat, to make their performances rhythmical and to keep them isolated from other actions. The majority of them wash too much. Patients who suffer from agoraphobia (topophobia or fear of spaces), which we no longer regard as obsessional neurosis but describe as 'anxiety hysteria', often repeat the same features in their symptoms with wearisome monotony: they are afraid of enclosed spaces, of large open squares, of lengthy roads and streets. They feel protected if they are accompanied by an acquaintance or followed by a vehicle, and so on. On this similar background, however, different patients nevertheless display their individual requirements—whims, one is inclined to say—which in some cases contradict one another directly. One patient avoids only narrow streets and another only wide ones; one can go out only if there are few people in the street, another only if there are many. In the same way, hysteria, in spite of its wealth of individual traits, has a superfluity of common, typical symptoms, which seem to resist any easy historical derivation. And we must not forget that it is these typical symptoms, indeed, which give us our bearings when we make our diagnosis. Suppose, in a case of hysteria, we have really traced a typical symptom back to an experience or a chain of similar experiences—a case of hysterical vomiting, for instance, to a series of disgusting impressions—then we are at a loss when the analysis in a similar case of vomiting reveals a series of a quite different kind of ostensibly effective experiences. It looks, then, as though for unknown reasons hysterical patients are bound to produce vomiting and as though the historical precipitating causes revealed by analysis were only pretexts which, if they happen to be there, are exploited by this internal necessity.

So we are now faced by the depressing discovery that, though we can give a satisfactory explanation of the individual neurotic symptoms by their connection with experiences, our skill leaves us in the lurch when we come to the far more frequent typical symptoms. Furthermore, I am far from having made you acquainted with all the difficulties that arise when consistently pursuing the historical interpretation of symptoms. Nor do I intend to do so; for, though it is my intention not to gloss things over to you or conceal them, I cannot throw you into perplexity and confusion at the very beginning of our common studies. It is true that we have only made a beginning with our efforts at understanding the significance of symptoms; but we will hold fast to what we have achieved and pursue our way step by step to a mastery of what we have not yet understood. I will try to console you, therefore, with the reflection that any fundamental distinction between one kind of symptom and the other is scarcely to be assumed. If the individual symptoms are so unmistakably dependent on the patient's experience, it remains possible that the typical symptoms may go back to an experience which is in itself typical—common to all human beings. Other features which recur regularly in neuroses may be general reactions which are imposed on the patients by the nature of their pathological change, like the repetitions or doubts in obsessional neurosis. In short, we have no grounds for premature despair; we shall see what remains to be seen.

A quite similar difficulty faces us in the theory of dreams. I could not deal with it in our earlier discussions on dreams. The manifest content of dreams is of the greatest diversity and individual variety, and we have shown in detail what one derives from this content by means of analysis. But alongside of these there are dreams which equally deserve to be called 'typical', which happen in everyone in the same way, dreams with a uniform content, which offer the same difficulties to interpretation. They are dreams of falling, flying, floating, swimming, of being inhibited, of being naked and certain other anxiety-dreams—which lead, in different people, now to this and now to that interpretation, without any light being thrown on their monotony and typical occurrence. But in these dreams too we observe that this common background is enlivened by additions that vary individually; and it is probable that, with a widening of our knowledge, it will be possible, without constraint, to include these dreams too in the understanding of dream-life which we have acquired from other dreams.[1]

[1] [See the section on 'typical' dreams in *The Interpretation of Dreams* (1900*a*), Chapter V (D).]

LECTURE XVIII

FIXATION TO TRAUMAS—
THE UNCONSCIOUS

LADIES AND GENTLEMEN,—In my last lecture I expressed a desire that our work should go forward on the basis not of our doubts but of our discoveries. We have not yet had any discussion of two of the most interesting implications that follow from our two sample analyses.

To take the first of these. Both patients give us an impression of having been 'fixated' to a particular portion of their past, as though they could not manage to free themselves from it and were for that reason alienated from the present and the future. They then remained lodged in their illness in the sort of way in which in earlier days people retreated into a monastery in order to bear the burden there of their ill-fated lives. What had brought this fate upon our first patient was the marriage which she had in real life abandoned. By means of her symptoms she continued to carry on her dealings with her husband. We learnt to understand the voices that pleaded for him, that excused him, that put him on a pedestal and that lamented his loss. Although she was young and desirable to other men, she had taken every precaution, real and imaginary (magical), to remain faithful to him. She did not show herself to strangers and she neglected her personal appearance; furthermore, once she had sat down in a chair she was unable to get out of it quickly,[1] she refused to sign her name, and she could not make any presents, on the ground that no one ought to receive anything from her.

The same effect was produced on the life of our second patient, the young girl, by an erotic attachment to her father which had started during the years before her puberty. The conclusion she herself drew was that she could not marry as long as she was so ill. We, however, may suspect that she had become so ill in order not to have to marry and in order to remain with her father.

[1] [This symptom is further described and explained in Freud's other account of the case (1907*b*).]

We cannot dismiss the question of why, in what way and for what motive a person can arrive at such a remarkable attitude to life and one that is so inexpedient—assuming that this attitude is a general characteristic of neuroses and not a special peculiarity of these two patients. And in fact it is a general feature, of great practical importance, in every neurosis. Breuer's first hysterical patient [p. 257 above] was similarly fixated to the period when she was nursing her father in a serious illness. In spite of her recovery, in a certain respect she remained cut off from life; she remained healthy and efficient but avoided the normal course of a woman's life.[1] In every one of our patients, analysis shows us that they have been carried back to some particular period of their past by the symptoms of their illness or their consequences. In the majority of cases, indeed, a very early phase of life is chosen for the purpose—a period of their childhood or even, laughable as this may sound, of their existence as an infant at the breast.

The closest analogy to this behaviour of our neurotics is afforded by illnesses which are being produced with special frequency precisely at the present time by the war—what are described as traumatic neuroses. Similar cases, of course, appeared before the war as well, after railway collisions and other alarming accidents involving fatal risks. Traumatic neuroses are not in their essence the same thing as the spontaneous neuroses which we are in the habit of investigating and treating by analysis; nor have we yet succeeded in bringing them into harmony with our views, and I hope I shall be able at some time to explain to you the reason for this limitation.[2] But in one respect we may insist that there is a complete agreement between them. The traumatic neuroses give a clear indication that a fixation to the moment of the traumatic accident lies at their root. These patients regularly repeat the traumatic situation in their dreams;[3] where hysteriform attacks occur that admit of an analysis, we find that the attack corresponds to a

[1] [Anna O. was never married. See Jones, 1953.]

[2] [Traumatic neuroses are mentioned again on p. 381 below. Freud was later able to throw more light on the war neuroses (1919d).]

[3] [This particular point played a part in Freud's first discussion of the 'compulsion to repeat' a few years later. See *Beyond the Pleasure Principle* (1920g).]

complete transplanting of the patient into the traumatic situation.[1] It is as though these patients had not finished with the traumatic situation, as though they were still faced by it as an immediate task which has not been dealt with; and we take this view quite seriously. It shows us the way to what we may call an *economic* view of mental processes.[2] Indeed, the term 'traumatic' has no other sense than an economic one. We apply it to an experience which within a short period of time presents the mind with an increase of stimulus too powerful to be dealt with or worked off in the normal way, and this must result in permanent disturbances of the manner in which the energy operates.

This analogy is bound to tempt us to describe as traumatic those experiences too to which our neurotic patients seem to be fixated. This would promise to offer us a simple determinant for the onset of neurosis. Neurosis could then be equated with a traumatic illness and would come about owing to inability to deal with an experience whose affective colouring was excessively powerful. And this indeed was actually the first formula in which (in 1893 and 1895) Breuer and I accounted theoretically for our new observations.[3] A case like that of the first of the two patients in my last lecture—the young married woman separated from her husband—fits in very well with this view. She had not got over the failure of her marriage and remained attached to that trauma. But our second case—that of the girl with a fixation upon her father—shows us already that the formula is not sufficiently comprehensive. On the one hand, a little girl's being in love like this with her father is something so common and so frequently surmounted that the term 'traumatic' applied to it would lose all its meaning; and, on the other hand, the patient's history showed us that in the first instance her erotic fixation appeared to have passed off without doing any damage, and it was only several years later that it reappeared in the symptoms of the obsessional neurosis. Here,

---

[1] [This was already recognized in Section IV of the Breuer and Freud 'Preliminary Communication' (1893*a*).]

[2] [Freud returns to this later (p. 356).]

[3] [See, for instance, Section II of the Breuer and Freud 'Preliminary Communication' (1893*a*), and in particular its last two paragraphs.]

then, we foresee complications, a greater wealth of determinants for the onset of illness; but we may also suspect that there is no need to abandon the traumatic line of approach as being erroneous: it must be possible to fit it in and subsume it somewhere else.

Here once more, then, we must break off the course we have started on. For the moment it leads no further and we shall have to learn all kinds of other things before we can find its proper continuation.[1] But on the subject of fixation to a particular phase in the past we may add that such behaviour is far more widespread than neurosis. Every neurosis includes a fixation of that kind, but not every fixation leads to a neurosis, coincides with a neurosis or arises owing to a neurosis. A perfect model of an affective fixation to something that is past is provided by mourning, which actually involves the most complete alienation from the present and the future. But even the judgement of a layman will distinguish sharply between mourning and neurosis. There are, on the other hand, neuroses which may be described as a pathological form of mourning.[2]

It may happen, too, that a person is brought so completely to a stop by a traumatic event which shatters the foundations of his life that he abandons all interest in the present and future and remains permanently absorbed in mental concentration upon the past. But an unfortunate such as this need not on that account become a neurotic. We will not attach too much value to this one feature, therefore, in characterizing neurosis, however regularly present and however important it may usually be.

Let us turn now to the second of the discoveries which follow from our analyses; in its case we need not fear having to make a subsequent qualification of our views. I have described to you how our first patient carried out a senseless obsessional action and how she reported an intimate memory from her past life as having some connection with it: and how afterwards I

[1] [The subject is taken up again in Lecture XXII.]
[2] [See on this Freud's metapsychological paper 'Mourning and Melancholia' (1917e), actually published after the delivery of this lecture, though written two years earlier. A short reference to melancholia appears in Lecture XXVI, p. 427 f. below.]

examined the connection between the two and discovered the intention of the obsessional action from its relation to the memory. But there is one factor which I have entirely neglected, though it deserves our fullest attention. However often the patient repeated her obsessional action, she knew nothing of its being derived from the experience she had had. The connection between the two was hidden from her; she could only quite truthfully reply that she did not know what it was that was making her carry out her action. Then suddenly one day, under the influence of the treatment, she succeeded in discovering the connection and reported it to me. But she still knew nothing of the intention with which she was performing the obsessional action—the intention of correcting a distressing portion of the past and of putting her beloved husband in a better light. It took a fairly long time and called for much labour before she understood and admitted to me that such a motive alone could have been the driving force of her obsessional action.

The link with the scene after her unhappy wedding-night and the patient's affectionate motive constituted, taken together, what we have called the 'sense' of the obsessional action. But while she was carrying out the obsessional action this sense had been unknown to her in both directions—both its 'whence' and its 'whither'. [Cf. p. 284 below.] Mental processes had therefore been at work in her and the obsessional action was the effect of them; she had been aware of this effect in a normal mental fashion, but none of the mental predeterminants of this effect came to the knowledge of her consciousness. She behaved in precisely the same way as a hypnotized subject whom Bernheim had ordered to open an umbrella in the hospital ward five minutes after he woke up. The man carried out this instruction when he was awake, but he could produce no motive for his action.[1] It is a state of affairs of this sort that we have before our eyes when we speak of the existence of *unconscious mental processes*. We can challenge anyone in the world to give a more correct scientific account of this state of affairs, and if he does we will gladly renounce our hypothesis of unconscious mental processes. Till that happens, however, we will hold fast to the

---

[1] [Freud gave a much fuller account of this episode, at which he himself was present, in his last, unfinished, paper 'Some Elementary Lessons in Psycho-Analysis' (1940b [1938]). See also above, p. 103.]

hypothesis; and if someone objects that here the unconscious is nothing real in a scientific sense, is a makeshift, *une façon de parler*, we can only shrug our shoulders resignedly and dismiss what he says as unintelligible. Something not real, which produces effects of such tangible reality as an obsessional action![1]

And we meet with what is in essence the same thing in our second patient. She had made a rule that the pillow must not touch the back of the bedstead, and she had to obey this rule though she did not know where it came from, what it meant or to what motives it owed its power. Whether she herself regarded the rule as a matter of indifference, or whether she struggled against it or raged against it or decided to transgress it—none of this made any difference to her carrying it out. It had to be obeyed, and she asked herself vainly why. We must recognize, however, that these symptoms of obsessional neurosis, these ideas and impulses which emerge one knows not whence, which prove so resistant to every influence from an otherwise normal mind, which give the patient himself the impression of being all-powerful guests from an alien world, immortal beings intruding into the turmoil of mortal life—these symptoms offer the plainest indication of there being a special region of the mind, shut off from the rest. They lead, by a path that cannot be missed, to a conviction of the existence of the unconscious in the mind; and that is precisely why clinical psychiatry, which is acquainted only with a psychology of consciousness, can deal with these symptoms in no other way than by declaring them to be signs of a special sort of degeneracy. Obsessional ideas and obsessional impulses are not, of course, themselves unconscious, any more than the performance of obsessional actions escapes conscious perception. They would not have become symptoms if they had not forced their way into consciousness. But their psychical predeterminants which we infer by means of analysis, the connections into which we insert them by interpretation, are unconscious, at least until we have made them conscious to the patient by the work of analysis.

If, now, you consider further that the state of affairs which we have established in our two cases is confirmed for every symptom of every neurotic illness—that always and every-

[1] [Cf. above, p. 257.]

where the sense of the symptoms is unknown to the patient and that analysis regularly shows that these symptoms are derivatives of unconscious processes but can, subject to a variety of favourable circumstances, be made conscious—if you consider this, you will understand that in psycho-analysis we cannot do without what is at the same time unconscious and mental, and are accustomed to operate with it as though it were something palpable to the senses. But you will understand as well, perhaps, how incapable of forming a judgement on this question are all those other people, who are only acquainted with the unconscious as a concept, who have never carried out an analysis and have never interpreted dreams or found a sense and intention in neurotic symptoms. To say it for our ends once again: the possibility of giving a sense to neurotic symptoms by analytic interpretation is an unshakeable proof of the existence—or, if you prefer it, of the necessity for the hypothesis—of unconscious mental processes.

But that is not all. Thanks to a second discovery of Breuer's, which seems to me even more significant than the other [p. 257] and which he shared with no one, we learn still more of the connection between neurotic symptoms and the unconscious. Not only is the sense of the symptoms regularly unconscious, but there is an inseparable relation between this fact of the symptoms being unconscious and the possibility of their existing. You will understand me in a moment. I follow Breuer in asserting that every time we come upon a symptom we can infer that there are certain definite unconscious processes in the patient which contain the sense of the symptom. But it is also necessary for that sense to be unconscious in order that the symptom can come about. Symptoms are never constructed from conscious processes; as soon as the unconscious processes concerned have become conscious, the symptom must disappear. Here you will at once perceive a means of approach to therapy, a way of making symptoms disappear. And in this way Breuer did in fact restore his hysterical patient—that is, freed her from her symptoms; he found a technique for bringing to her consciousness the unconscious processes which contained the sense of the symptoms, and the symptoms disappeared.

This discovery of Breuer's was not the result of speculation but of a fortunate observation made possible by the patient's co-operation.[1] Nor should you torment yourselves with attempts at understanding it by tracing it back to something already known; you should recognize in it a new fundamental fact, by whose help much else will become explicable. Allow me, therefore, to repeat the same thing to you in another way.

The construction of a symptom is a substitute for something else that did not happen. Some particular mental processes should normally have developed to a point at which consciousness received information of them. This, however, did not take place, and instead—out of the interrupted processes, which had been somehow disturbed and were obliged to remain unconscious—the symptom emerged. Thus something in the nature of an exchange has taken place; if this can be reversed the therapy of the neurotic symptoms will have achieved its task.

This discovery of Breuer's is still the foundation of psychoanalytic therapy. The thesis that symptoms disappear when we have made their unconscious predeterminants conscious has been confirmed by all subsequent research, although we meet with the strangest and most unexpected complications when we attempt to carry it through in practice. Our therapy works by transforming what is unconscious into what is conscious, and it works only in so far as it is in a position to effect that transformation.

And now I must quickly make a short digression, to avoid the risk of your imagining that this therapeutic work is accomplished too easily. From what I have so far said a neurosis would seem to be the result of a kind of ignorance—a not knowing about mental events that one ought to know of. This would be a close approximation to some well-known Socratic doctrines, according to which even vices are based on ignorance. Now it would as a rule be very easy for a doctor experienced in analysis to guess what mental impulses had remained unconscious in a particular patient. So it ought not to be very difficult, either, for him to restore the patient by communicating his knowledge to him and so remedying his ignorance. One part at least of the symptom's unconscious sense could be easily dealt with in this way, though it is true that the doctor cannot guess much about the other part—the connection between the

[1] [Breuer's description of the occurrence will be found in his case history of Anna O. in *Studies on Hysteria* (1895d).]

symptoms and the patient's experiences—, since he himself does not know those experiences but must wait till the patient remembers them and tells them to him. But even for this a substitute can in some instances be found. One can make enquiries about these experiences from the patient's relatives and they will often be able to recognize which of them had a traumatic effect, and they can even sometimes report experiences of which the patient himself knows nothing because they occurred at a very early period of his life. Thus, by combining these two methods, we should have a prospect of relieving the patient of his pathogenic ignorance with little expense of time or trouble.

If only that was how things happened! We came upon discoveries in this connection for which we were at first unprepared. Knowledge is not always the same as knowledge: there are different sorts of knowledge, which are far from equivalent psychologically. 'Il y a fagots et fagots', as Molière has said.[1] The doctor's knowledge is not the same as the patient's and cannot produce the same effects. If the doctor transfers his knowledge to the patient as a piece of information, it has no result. No, it would be wrong to say that. It does not have the result of removing the symptoms, but it has another one—of setting the analysis in motion, of which the first signs are often expressions of denial. The patient knows after this what he did not know before—the sense of his symptom; yet he knows it just as little as he did. Thus we learn that there is more than one kind of ignorance. We shall need to have a somewhat deeper understanding of psychology to show us in what these differences consist.[2] But our thesis that the symptoms vanish when their sense is known remains true in spite of this. All we have to add is that the knowledge must rest on an internal change in the patient such as can only be brought about by a piece of psychical work with a particular aim. We are faced here by problems which will presently be brought together into the *dynamics* of the construction of symptoms.

I must ask now, Gentlemen, whether what I am saying to you is not too obscure and complicated. Am I not confusing you by so often taking back what I have said or qualifying it— by starting up trains of thought and then dropping them? I

[1] [*Le médecin malgré lui*, I, 6.]
[2] [Freud returns to this question in Lecture XXVII, p. 436 below.]

should be sorry if that were so. But I have a strong dislike of simplifying things at the expense of truthfulness. I have no objection to your receiving the full impact of the many-sidedness and complexity of our subject; and I think, too, that it does no harm if I tell you more on every point than you can at the moment make use of. I am aware, after all, that every listener or reader puts what is presented to him into shape in his mind, shortens it and simplifies it, and selects from it what he would like to retain. Up to a certain point it is no doubt true that the more there is at one's disposal the more one is left with. Permit me to hope that, in spite of all the trimmings, you have clearly grasped the essential part of what I have told you—about the sense of symptoms, about the unconscious and about the relation between them. No doubt you have also understood that our further efforts will lead in two directions: first towards discovering how people fall ill and how they can come to adopt the neurotic attitude to life—which is a clinical problem; and secondly towards learning how the pathological symptoms develop from the determinants of the neurosis—which remains a problem of mental dynamics. There must moreover be a point somewhere at which the two problems converge.

I will not go into this any further to-day. But since we still have some time to spare, I should like to direct your attention to another characteristic of our two analyses, which, once again, it will only be possible to appreciate fully later on—to the gaps in the patients' memories, their amnesias. As you have heard [p. 201], the task of a psycho-analytic treatment can be expressed in this formula: its task is to make conscious everything that is pathogenically unconscious. You will perhaps be surprised to learn, then, that this formula can be replaced by another one: its task is to fill up all the gaps in the patient's memory, to remove his amnesias. This would amount to the same thing. We are thus implying that the amnesias of neurotic patients have an important connection with the origin of their symptoms. If, however, you consider the case of our first analysis you will not find this view of amnesia justified. The patient had *not* forgotten the scene from which her obsessive action was derived; on the contrary, she had a vivid recollection of it; nor did anything else forgotten play a part in the origin of the symptom. The position with our second patient (the girl with the obsessional ceremonial), though less clear, was on the whole analogous. She had not really forgotten her behaviour in earlier years—the fact that she had insisted on the door between her parents' bedroom and her own being left open and that she had driven her mother out of her place in her parents' bed; she remembered this very plainly, even though with hesitation and unwillingly. The only thing we can consider striking is that the first patient, in carrying out her obsessional action on countless occasions, had never *once* noticed its resemblance to her experience on her wedding-night, and that the memory of it did not occur to her when she was directly asked to look for the motives of her obsessional action. And the same thing applies to the girl, whose ceremonial and its causes were moreover connected with a situation which was identically repeated every evening.[1] In both these cases there was no true amnesia, no missing memory; but a connection had been broken which ought to have led to the reproduction or re-emergence of the memory.

A disturbance of memory of this kind is enough for obsessional neurosis; but the case is different with hysteria. As a rule the latter neurosis is marked by amnesias on a really large scale. In analysing each separate hysterical symptom one is usually led to a whole chain of impressions of events, which, when they recur, are expressly described by the patient as having been till then forgotten. On the one hand, this chain reaches back to the earliest years of life, so that the hysterical amnesia can be recognized as an immediate continuation of the infantile amnesia which, for us normal people, conceals the beginnings of our mental life. [Cf. p. 199 f. above.] On the other hand, we learn with astonishment that even the patient's most recent experiences can be subject to forgetting, and that the occasions which precipitated the outbreak of the illness or led to its intensification are in particular encroached upon, if not completely swallowed up, by amnesia. It regularly happens that important details have disappeared from the total picture of a recent recollection of this sort or that they have been replaced by falsifications of memory. Indeed it happens with

[1] [I.e. her father and mother sleeping together.]

almost equal regularity that certain memories of recent experiences only emerge shortly before the end of an analysis—memories which had been held back till that late moment and had left perceptible gaps in the continuity of the case.

Such restrictions upon the faculty of memory are, as I have said, characteristic of hysteria, in which, indeed, states also arise as symptoms—hysterical attacks—which need leave no trace behind them in the memory . If things are different in obsessional neurosis, you may conclude that what we are dealing with in these amnesias is a psychological characteristic of the change that occurs in hysteria and is not a universal feature of neuroses in general. The importance of this distinction is reduced by the following consideration. We have comprised two things as the 'sense' of a symptom: its 'whence' and its 'whither' or 'what for' [p. 277]—that is, the impressions and experiences from which it arose and the intentions which it serves. Thus the 'whence' of a symptom resolves itself into impressions which came from outside, which were necessarily once conscious and may have since become unconscious through forgetting. The 'whither' of a symptom, its purpose, is invariably, however, an endopsychic process, which may possibly have been conscious at first but may equally well never have been conscious and may have remained in the unconscious from the very start. Thus it is not of great importance whether the amnesia has laid hold on the 'whence' as well—the experiences on which the symptom is supported—as happens in hysteria; it is on the 'whither', the purpose of the symptom, which may have been unconscious from the beginning, that its dependence on the unconscious is founded—and no less firmly in obsessional neurosis than in hysteria.

But in thus emphasizing the unconscious in mental life we have conjured up the most evil spirits of criticism against psycho-analysis. Do not be surprised at this, and do not suppose that the resistance to us rests only on the understandable difficulty of the unconscious or the relative inaccessibility of the experiences which provide evidence of it. Its source, I think, lies deeper. In the course of centuries the *naïve* self-love of men has had to submit to two major blows at the hands of science. The first was when they learnt that our earth was not the centre of the universe but only a tiny fragment of a cosmic system of scarcely imaginable vastness. This is associated in our minds with the name of Copernicus, though something similar had already been asserted by Alexandrian science. The second blow fell when biological research destroyed man's supposedly privileged place in creation and proved his descent from the animal kingdom and his ineradicable animal nature. This revaluation has been accomplished in our own days by Darwin, Wallace and their predecessors, though not without the most violent contemporary opposition. But human megalomania will have suffered its third and most wounding blow from the psychological research of the present time which seeks to prove to the ego that it is not even master in its own house, but must content itself with scanty information of what is going on unconsciously in its mind. We psycho-analysts were not the first and not the only ones to utter this call to introspection; but it seems to be our fate to give it its most forcible expression and to support it with empirical material which affects every individual. Hence arises the general revolt against our science, the disregard of all considerations of academic civility and the releasing of the opposition from every restraint of impartial logic.[1] And beyond all this we have yet to disturb the peace of this world in still another way, as you will shortly hear.

[1] [Freud had developed this theme at greater length in a paper on 'A Difficulty in the Path of Psycho-Analysis' (1917a).]

LECTURE XIX

RESISTANCE AND REPRESSION[1]

LADIES AND GENTLEMEN,—Before we can make any further progress in our understanding of the neuroses, we stand in need of some fresh observations. Here we have two such, both of which are very remarkable and at the time when they were made were very surprising. Our discussions of last year will, it is true, have prepared you for both of them.[2]

In the first place, then, when we undertake to restore a patient to health, to relieve him of the symptoms of his illness, he meets us with a violent and tenacious resistance, which persists throughout the whole length of the treatment. This is such a strange fact that we cannot expect it to find much credence. It is best to say nothing about it to the patient's relatives, for they invariably regard it as an excuse on our part for the length or failure of our treatment. The patient, too, produces all the phenomena of this resistance without recognizing it as such, and if we can induce him to take our view of it and to reckon with its existence, that already counts as a great success. Only think of it! The patient, who is suffering so much from his symptoms and is causing those about him to share his sufferings, who is ready to undertake so many sacrifices in time, money, effort and self-discipline in order to be freed from those symptoms—we are to believe that this same patient puts up a struggle in the interest of his illness against the person who is helping him. How

[1] [The essence of Freud's views on repression is already given in his contribution to *Studies on Hysteria* (1895*d*). He gave a similar description of his discovery in the first section of his history of the psycho-analytic movement (1914*d*), (Norton, 1966). An account of the development of Freud's theory of repression will be found in the Editor's Note to his metapsychological paper on the subject (1915*d*)–a paper which, together with Section IV of the paper on 'The Unconscious' (1915*e*), contains Freud's deepest reflections on the question.]

[2] [The concept of resistance had been introduced in Lecture VII, p. 116 above. The second observation is described on p. 298 below.]

improbable such an assertion must sound! Yet it is true; and when its improbability is pointed out to us, we need only reply that it is not without analogies. A man who has gone to the dentist because of an unbearable toothache will nevertheless try to hold the dentist back when he approaches the sick tooth with a pair of forceps.

The patient's resistance is of very many sorts, extremely subtle and often hard to detect; and it exhibits protean changes in the forms in which it manifests itself. The doctor must be distrustful and remain on his guard against it.

In psycho-analytic therapy we make use of the same technique that is familiar to you from dream-interpretation. We instruct the patient to put himself into a state of quiet, unreflecting self-observation, and to report to us whatever internal perceptions he is able to make—feelings, thoughts, memories— in the order in which they occur to him. At the same time we warn him expressly against giving way to any motive which would lead him to make a selection among these associations or to exclude any of them, whether on the ground that it is too *disagreeable* or too *indiscreet* to say, or that it is too *unimportant* or *irrelevant*, or that it is *nonsensical* and need not be said. We urge him always to follow only the surface of his consciousness and to leave aside any criticism of what he finds, whatever shape that criticism may take; and we assure him that the success of the treatment, and above all its duration, depends on the conscientiousness with which he obeys this fundamental technical rule of analysis.[1] We already know from the technique of

[1] [Freud had already stated the rule in connection with the interpreting of dreams in Lecture VII, p. 115 above. He first laid it down in Chapter II of *The Interpretation of Dreams* (1900a) and again in his contribution to Löwenfeld's book on obsessional phenomena (Freud, 1904a [1903]). The actual term 'fundamental rule' was first used in the technical paper on 'The Dynamics of Transference' (1912b), where an Editor's footnote gives some other early references. Perhaps the fullest account is in another technical paper, 'On Beginning the Treatment' (1913c). Among later mentions may be noted a passage near the beginning of Chapter IV of the *Autobiographical Study* (1925d), (Norton, 1963), and an interesting allusion to the deeper reasons for the obstacles to obeying the rule, towards the end of Chapter VI of *Inhibitions, Symptoms and Anxiety* (1926d). In the latter passage, in the course of a discussion of the part

dream-interpretation that the associations giving rise to the doubts and objections I have just enumerated are precisely the ones that invariably contain the material which leads to the uncovering of the unconscious. [Cf. Lecture VII, p. 116.]

The first thing we achieve by setting up this fundamental technical rule is that it becomes the target for the attacks of the resistance. The patient endeavours in every sort of way to extricate himself from its provisions. At one moment he declares that nothing occurs to him, at the next that so many things are crowding in on him that he cannot get hold of anything. Presently we observe with pained astonishment that he has given way first to one and then to another critical objection: he betrays this to us by the long pauses that he introduces into his remarks. He then admits that there is something he really cannot say—he would be ashamed to; and he allows this reason to prevail against his promise. Or he says that something has occurred to him, but it concerns another person and not himself and is therefore exempt from being reported. Or, what has now occurred to him is really too unimportant, too silly and senseless: I cannot possibly have meant him to enter into thoughts like that. So it goes on in innumerable variations, and one can only reply that 'to say everything' really does mean 'to say everything'.

One hardly comes across a single patient who does not make an attempt at reserving some region or other for himself so as to prevent the treatment from having access to it. A man, whom I can only describe as of the highest intelligence, kept silence in this way for weeks on end about an intimate love-affair, and, when he was called to account for having broken the sacred rule, defended himself with the argument that he thought this particular story was his private business. Analytic treatment does not, of course, recognize any such right of asylum. Suppose that in a town like Vienna the experiment was made of treating a square such as the Hohe Markt, or a church like St. Stephen's, as places where no arrests might be made, and suppose we then wanted to catch a particular criminal. We could be quite sure of finding him in the sanctuary. I once decided to allow a man, on whose efficiency much depended in the external world, the

played by the defensive process of 'isolation' in ordinary directed thinking, Freud mentions especially the difficulties felt by obsessional neurotics in this connection. See below, p. 289.]

right to make an exception of this kind because he was bound under his oath of office not to make communications about certain things to another person. He, it is true, was satisfied with the outcome; but I was not. I determined not to repeat an attempt under such conditions.

Obsessional neurotics understand perfectly how to make the technical rule almost useless by applying their over-conscientiousness and doubts to it.[1] Patients suffering from anxiety hysteria occasionally succeed in carrying the rule *ad absurdum* by producing only associations which are so remote from what we are in search of that they contribute nothing to the analysis. But it is not my intention to induct you into the handling of these technical difficulties. It is enough to say that in the end, through resolution and perseverance, we succeed in extorting a certain amount of obedience to the fundamental technical rule from the resistance—which thereupon jumps over to another sphere.

It now appears as an *intellectual* resistance, it fights by means of arguments and exploits all the difficulties and improbabilities which normal but uninstructed thinking finds in the theories of analysis. It is now our fate to hear from this single voice all the criticisms and objections which assail our ears in a chorus in the scientific literature of the subject. And for this reason none of the shouts that reach us from outside sound unfamiliar. It is a regular storm in a tea-cup. But the patient is willing to be argued with; he is anxious to get us to instruct him, teach him, contradict him, introduce him to the literature, so that he can find further instruction. He is quite ready to become an adherent of psycho-analysis—on condition that analysis spares him personally. But we recognize this curiosity as a resistance, as a diversion from our particular tasks, and we repel it. In the case of an obsessional neurotic we have to expect special tactics of resistance. He will often allow the analysis to proceed on its way uninhibited, so that it is able to shed an ever-increasing light upon the riddle of his illness. We begin to wonder in the end, however, why this enlightenment is accompanied by no practical advance, no diminution of the symptoms. We are then able to realize that resistance has withdrawn on to the doubt belonging to the obsessional neurosis and from that position is successfully defying us. It is as though the

[1] [Cf. the end of the last footnote.]

patient were saying: 'Yes, that's all very nice and interesting, and I'll be very glad to go on with it further. It would change my illness a lot if it were true. But I don't in the least believe that it *is* true; and, so long as I don't believe it, it makes no difference to my illness.' Things can proceed like this for a long time, till finally one comes up against this uncommitted attitude itself, and the decisive struggle then breaks out.[1]

Intellectual resistances are not the worst: one always remains superior to them. But the patient also knows how to put up resistances, without going outside the framework of the analysis, the overcoming of which is among the most difficult of technical problems. Instead of remembering, he *repeats* attitudes and emotional impulses from his early life which can be used as a resistance against the doctor and the treatment by means of what is known as 'transference'.[2] If the patient is a man, he usually extracts this material from his relation to his father, into whose place he fits the doctor, and in that way he makes resistances out of his efforts to become independent in himself and in his judgements, out of his ambition, the first aim of which was to do things as well as his father or to get the better of him, or out of his unwillingness to burden himself for the second time in his life with a load of gratitude. Thus at times one has an impression that the patient has entirely replaced his better intention of making an end to his illness by the alternative one of putting the doctor in the wrong, of making him realize his impotence and of triumphing over him. Women have a masterly gift for exploiting an affectionate, erotically tinged transference to the doctor for the purposes of resistance. If this attachment reaches a certain height, all their interest in the immediate situation in the treatment and all the obligations they undertook at its commencement vanish; their jealousy, which is never absent, and their exasperation at their inevitable rejection, however considerately expressed, are bound to have a damaging effect on their personal understanding with the

---

[1] [The part played by doubt in cases of obsessional neurosis is referred to above in Lecture XVII, p. 259. The necessity for special technical methods in dealing with such cases was mentioned by Freud a little later in his Budapest Congress paper (1919a).]

[2] [Lecture XXVII, p. 431 below, is devoted to a full discussion of this phenomenon.]

doctor and so to put out of operation one of the most powerful motive forces of the analysis.

Resistances of this kind should not be one-sidedly condemned. They include so much of the most important material from the patient's past and bring it back in so convincing a fashion that they become some of the best supports of the analysis if a skilful technique knows how to give them the right turn. Nevertheless, it remains a remarkable fact that this material is always in the service of the resistance to begin with and brings to the fore a *façade* that is hostile to the treatment. It may also be said that what is being mobilized for fighting against the alterations we are striving for are character-traits, attitudes of the ego. In this connection we discover that these character-traits were formed in relation to the determinants of the neurosis and in reaction against its demands, and we come upon traits which cannot normally emerge, or not to the same extent, and which may be described as latent. Nor must you get an impression that we regard the appearance of these resistances as an unforeseen risk to analytic influence. No, we are aware that these resistances are bound to come to light; in fact we are dissatisfied if we cannot provoke them clearly enough and are unable to demonstrate them to the patient. Indeed we come finally to understand that the overcoming of these resistances is the essential function of analysis[1] and is the only part of our work which gives us an assurance that we have achieved something with the patient.

If you further consider that the patient makes all the chance events that occur during his analysis into interferences with it, that he uses as reasons for slackening his efforts every diversion outside the analysis, every comment by a person of authority in his environment who is hostile to analysis, any chance organic illness or any that complicates his neurosis and, even, indeed, every improvement in his condition—if you consider all this, you will have obtained an approximate, though still incomplete, picture of the forms and methods of the resistance, the struggle against which accompanies every analysis.[2]

[1] [That this was a relatively late development in analytic technique is shown, for instance, by a paragraph in Freud's Nuremberg Congress paper (1910*d*).]

[2] [The present description of the forms taken by resistance in general is as full as any by Freud. But the special case of transference-resistance is discussed in greater detail in his paper on 'The Dynamics of Transference' (1912*b*).]

I have treated this point in such great detail because I must now inform you that this experience of ours with the resistance of neurotics to the removal of their symptoms became the basis of our dynamic view of the neuroses. Originally Breuer and I myself carried out psychotherapy by means of hypnosis; Breuer's first patient[1] was treated throughout under hypnotic influence, and to begin with I followed him in this. I admit that at that period the work proceeded more easily and pleasantly, and also in a much shorter time. But results were capricious and not lasting; and for that reason I finally dropped hypnosis.[2] And I then understood that an insight into the dynamics of these illnesses had not been possible so long as hypnosis was employed.[3] That state was precisely able to withhold the existence of the resistance from the doctor's perception. It pushed the resistance back, making a certain area free for analytic work, and dammed it up at the frontiers of that area in such a way as to be impenetrable, just as doubt does in obsessional neurosis. For that reason I have been able to say that psycho-analysis proper began when I dispensed with the help of hypnosis.[4]

If, however, the recognition of resistance has become so important, we should do well to find room for a cautious doubt whether we have not been too light-heartedly assuming resistances. Perhaps there really are cases of neurosis in which associations fail for other reasons, perhaps the arguments against our hypotheses really deserve to have their content examined, and perhaps we are doing patients an injustice in so conveniently setting aside their intellectual criticisms as resistance. But, Gentlemen, we did not arrive at this judgement

is as full as any by Freud. But the special case of transference-resistance is discussed in greater detail in his paper on 'The Dynamics of Transference' (1912b).]

[1] [See Lecture XVIII, p. 279 f. above.]

[2] [Fairly exact dates for Freud's use of hypnotism (1887–1896) will be found in an Editor's footnote to the case of Lucy R. in *Studies on Hysteria* (1895d).]

[3] [Freud tells us that he first realized the great importance of resistance during his analysis of Elisabeth von R. He was at that time using the 'pressure' technique, without hypnosis. See *Studies on Hysteria* (1895d).]

[4] [Cf. Freud's statement in very similar words in the first section of his history of the psycho-analytic movement (1914d), (Norton, 1966). Earlier he had not been inclined to draw such a clear-cut line.]

lightly. We have had occasion to observe all these critical patients at the moment of the emergence of a resistance and after its disappearance. For resistance is constantly altering its intensity during the course of a treatment; it always increases when we are approaching a new topic, it is at its most intense while we are at the climax of dealing with that topic, and it dies away when the topic has been disposed of. Nor do we ever, unless we have been guilty of special clumsiness in our technique, have to meet the full amount of resistance of which a patient is capable. We have therefore been able to convince ourselves that on countless occasions in the course of his analysis the same man will abandon his critical attitude and then take it up again. If we are on the point of bringing a specially distressing piece of unconscious material to his consciousness, he is extremely critical; he may previously have understood and accepted a great deal, but now it is just as though those acquisitions have been swept away; in his efforts for opposition at any price, he may offer a complete picture of someone who is an emotional imbecile. But if we succeed in helping him to overcome this new resistance, he recovers his insight and understanding. Thus his critical faculty is not an independent function, to be respected as such, it is the tool of his emotional attitudes and is directed by his resistance. If there is something he does not like, he can put up a shrewd fight against it and appear highly critical; but if something suits his book, he can, on the contrary, show himself most credulous. Perhaps none of us are very different; a man who is being analysed only reveals this dependence of the intellect upon emotional life so clearly because in analysis we are putting such great pressure on him.

How, then, do we account for our observation that the patient fights with such energy against the removal of his symptoms and the setting of his mental processes on a normal course? We tell ourselves that we have succeeded in discovering powerful forces here which oppose any alteration of the patient's condition; they must be the same ones which in the past brought this condition about. During the construction of his symptoms something must have taken place which we can now reconstruct from our experiences during the *resolution* of his symptoms. We already know from Breuer's observation that there is a precondition for the existence of a symptom: some mental process must not have been brought to an end normally —so that it could become conscious. The symptom is a substitute for what did not happen at that point [p. 280 above]. We now know the point at which we must locate the operation of the force which we have surmised. A violent opposition must have started against the entry into consciousness of the questionable mental process, and for that reason it remained unconscious. As being something unconscious, it had the power to construct a symptom. This same opposition, during psycho-analytic treatment, sets itself up once more against our effort to transform what is unconscious into what is conscious. This is what we perceive as resistance. We have proposed to give the pathogenic process which is demonstrated by the resistance the name of *repression*.

We must now form more definite ideas about this process of repression. It is the precondition for the construction of symptoms; but it is also something to which we know nothing similar. Let us take as our model an impulse, a mental process that endeavours to turn itself into an action. We know that it can be repelled by what we term a rejection or condemnation. When this happens, the energy at its disposal is withdrawn from it; it becomes powerless, though it can persist as a memory. The whole process of coming to a decision about it runs its course within the knowledge of the ego. It is a very different matter if we suppose that the same impulse is subjected to repression. In that case it would retain its energy and no memory of it would remain behind; moreover the process of repression would be accomplished unnoticed by the ego. This comparison, therefore, brings us no nearer to the essential nature of repression.

I will put before you the only theoretical ideas which have proved of service for giving a more definite shape to the concept of repression. It is above all essential for this purpose that we should proceed from the purely descriptive meaning of the word 'unconscious' to the systematic meaning of the same word.[1] That is, we will decide to say that the fact of a psychical

[1] [See footnote 1, p. 227 above. The spatial analogy to resistance and repression, which follows here, is similar to the one in the second of his *Five Lectures* (1910a).]

process being conscious or unconscious is only one of its attributes and not necessarily an unambiguous one. If a process of this kind has remained unconscious, its being kept away from consciousness may perhaps only be an indication of some vicissitude it has gone through, and not that vicissitude itself. In order to form a picture of this vicissitude, let us assume that every mental process—we must admit one exception, which we shall mention at a later stage[1]—exists to begin with in an unconscious stage or phase and that it is only from there that the process passes over into the conscious phase, just as a photographic picture begins as a negative and only becomes a picture after being turned into a positive. Not every negative, however, necessarily becomes a positive; nor is it necessary that every unconscious mental process should turn into a conscious one. This may be advantageously expressed by saying that an individual process belongs to begin with to the system of the unconscious and can then, in certain circumstances, pass over into the system of the conscious.

The crudest idea of these systems is the most convenient for us—a spatial one. Let us therefore compare the system of the unconscious to a large entrance hall, in which the mental impulses jostle one another like separate individuals. Adjoining this entrance hall there is a second, narrower, room—a kind of drawing-room—in which consciousness, too, resides. But on the threshold between these two rooms a watchman performs his function: he examines the different mental impulses, acts as a censor, and will not admit them into the drawing-room if they displease him. You will see at once that it does not make much difference if the watchman turns away a particular impulse at the threshold itself or if he pushes it back across the threshold after it has entered the drawing-room. This is merely a question of the degree of his watchfulness and of how early he carries out his act of recognition. If we keep to this picture, we shall be able to extend our nomenclature further. The impulses in the entrance hall of the unconscious are out of sight of the conscious, which is in the other room; to begin with they must remain unconscious. If they have already pushed their way forward to the threshold and have been turned back by the watchman,

[1] [The exception, which seems to have escaped mention, must no doubt be the case of external perception.]

then they are inadmissible to consciousness;[1] we speak of them as *repressed*. But even the impulses which the watchman has allowed to cross the threshold are not on that account necessarily conscious as well; they can only become so if they succeed in catching the eye of consciousness. We are therefore justified in calling this second room the system of the *preconscious*. In that case becoming conscious retains its purely descriptive sense. For any particular impulse, however, the vicissitude of repression consists in its not being allowed by the watchman to pass from the system of the unconscious into that of the preconscious. It is the same watchman whom we get to know as resistance when we try to lift the repression by means of the analytic treatment.

Now I know you will say that these ideas are both crude and fantastic and quite impermissible in a scientific account. I know that they are crude: and, more than that, I know that they are incorrect, and, if I am not very much mistaken, I already have something better to take their place.[2] Whether it will seem to you equally fantastic I cannot tell. They are preliminary working hypotheses, like Ampère's manikin swimming in the electric current,[3] and they are not to be despised in so far as they are of service in making our observations intelligible. I should like to assure you that these crude hypotheses of the two rooms, the watchman at the threshold between them and consciousness as a spectator at the end of the second room, must nevertheless be very far-reaching approximations to the real facts. And I should like to hear you admit that our terms, 'unconscious', 'preconscious' and 'conscious', prejudge things far less and are far easier to justify than others which have been proposed or are in use, such as 'subconscious', 'paraconscious', 'intraconscious' and the like.[4]

---

[1] ['*Bewusstseinsunfähig*.' The term is due to Breuer, who constructed it on the model of '*hoffähig*' ('admissible to Court', 'having the *entrée*'). See Section 5 of his contribution to *Studies on Hysteria* (1895d).

[2] [What Freud had in mind is not obvious.]

[3] [A.-M. Ampere (1775–1836), one of the founders of the science of electro-magnetism, made use of a magnetic metal manikin in one of his early experiments establishing the relation between electricity and magnetism.]

[4] [Freud gives an explanation of his objection to the term 'sub-

It will therefore be of greater importance to me if you warn me that an arrangement of the mental apparatus, such as I have here assumed in order to explain neurotic symptoms, must necessarily claim general validity and must give us information about normal functioning as well. You will, of course, be quite right in this. At the moment we cannot pursue this implication further; but our interest in the psychology of the forming of symptoms cannot but be increased to an extraordinary extent if there is a prospect, through the study of pathological conditions, of obtaining access to the normal mental events which are so well concealed.

Perhaps you recognize, moreover, what it is that supports our hypotheses of the two systems, and their relation to each other and to consciousness? After all, the watchman between the unconscious and the preconscious is nothing else than the *censorship*, to which, as we found, the form taken by the manifest dream is subject. [Cf. Lecture IX, p. 139 above.] The day's residues, which we recognized as the instigators of the dream, were preconscious material which, at night-time and in the state of sleep, had been under the influence of unconscious and repressed wishful impulses; they had been able, in combination with those impulses and thanks to their energy, to construct the latent dream. Under the dominance of the unconscious system this material had been worked over (by condensation and displacement) in a manner which is unknown or only exceptionally permissible in normal mental life—that is, in the preconscious system. We came to regard this difference in their manner of operating as what characterizes the two systems; the relation which the preconscious has to consciousness was regarded by us merely as an indication of its belonging to one of the two systems.[1] Dreams are not pathological phenomena; they can appear in any healthy person under the conditions of a state of sleep. Our hypothesis about the structure of the mental apparatus, which allows us to understand the formation alike of dreams and of neurotic symptoms, has an incontrovertible

conscious' near the end of Chapter II of his work on lay analysis (1926*e*), (Norton, 1950). See also an Editor's footnote to Section I of 'The Unconscious' (1915*e*).

[1] [Cf. the discussions at the end of Lectures XIII and XIV, pp. 212 and 227.]

claim to being taken into account in regard to normal mental life as well.

That much is what we have to say for the moment about repression. But it is only the *precondition* for the construction of symptoms. Symptoms, as we know, are a substitute for something that is held back by repression. It is a long step further, however, from repression to an understanding of this substitutive structure. On this other side of the problem, these questions arise out of our observation of repression: what kind of mental impulses are subject to repression? by what forces is it accomplished? and for what motives? So far we have only one piece of information on these points. In investigating resistance we have learnt that it emanates from forces of the ego, from known and latent character traits [p. 291 above]. It is these too, therefore, that are responsible for repression, or at any rate they have a share in it. We know nothing more at present.

At this point the second of the two observations which I mentioned to you earlier [at the opening of this Lecture] comes to our help. It is quite generally the case that analysis allows us to arrive at the intention of neurotic symptoms. This again will be nothing new to you. I have already demonstrated it to you in two cases of neurosis.[1] But, after all, what do two cases amount to? You are right to insist on its being demonstrated to you in two hundred cases—in countless cases. The only trouble is that I cannot do that. Once again, your own experience must serve instead, or your belief, which on this point can appeal to the unanimous reports of all psycho-analysts.

You will recollect that, in the two cases whose symptoms we submitted to a detailed investigation, the analysis initiated us into these patients' most intimate sexual life. In the first case we further recognized with particular clarity the intention or purpose of the symptom we were examining; in the second case this was perhaps somewhat concealed by a factor which will be mentioned later [p. 300 below]. Well, every other case that we submit to analysis would show us the same thing that we have found in these two examples. In every instance we should be introduced by the analysis into the patient's sexual experiences and wishes; and in every instance we should be bound to see

[1] [In Lecture XVII, p. 261 ff. above.]

that the symptoms served the same intention. We find that this intention is the satisfaction of sexual wishes; the symptoms serve for the patients' sexual satisfaction; they are a substitute for satisfaction of this kind, which the patients are without in their lives.

Think of our first patient's obsessional action. The woman was without her husband, whom she loved intensely but with whom she could not share her life on account of his deficiencies and weaknesses. She had to remain faithful to him; she could not put anyone else in his place. Her obsessional symptom gave her what she longed for, set her husband on a pedestal, denied and corrected his weaknesses and above all his impotence. This symptom was fundamentally a wish-fulfilment, just like a dream—and moreover, what is not always true of a dream, an *erotic* wish-fulfilment. In the case of our second patient you could at least gather that her ceremonial sought to obstruct intercourse between her parents or prevent it from producing a new baby. You will also probably have guessed that it was at bottom endeavouring to put her herself in her mother's place. Once again, therefore, a setting-aside of interferences with sexual satisfaction and a fulfilment of the patient's own sexual wishes. I shall soon come to the complication I have hinted at.

I should like to anticipate, Gentlemen, the qualifications which I shall have to make later in the universal validity of these statements. I will therefore point out to you that all I have said here about repression and the formation and meaning of symptoms was derived from three forms of neurosis—anxiety hysteria, conversion hysteria and obsessional neurosis—and that in the first instance it is also valid only for these forms. These three disorders, which we are accustomed to group to-gether as '*transference neuroses*',[1] also circumscribe the region in which psycho-analytic therapy can function. The other neuroses have been far less thoroughly studied by psycho-analysis; in one group of them the impossibility of therapeutic influence has been a reason for this neglect. Nor should you forget that psycho-analysis is still a very young science, that preparing for it costs much trouble and time, and that not at all long ago it

[1] [The explanation of this term is given in a later lecture, p. 445 below.]

was being practised single-handed. Nevertheless, we are everywhere on the point of penetrating to an understanding of these other disorders which are not transference neuroses. I hope later to be able to introduce you to the extensions of our hypotheses and findings which result from adaptation to this new material, and to show you that these further studies have not led to contradictions but to the establishment of higher unities.[1] If, then, everything I am saying here applies to the transference neuroses, let me first increase the value of symptoms by a new piece of information. For a comparative study of the determining causes of falling ill leads to a result which can be expressed in a formula: these people fall ill in one way or another of *frustration*, when reality prevents them from satisfying their sexual wishes.[2] You see how excellently these two findings tally with each other. It is only thus that symptoms can be properly viewed as substitutive satisfactions for what is missed in life.

No doubt all kinds of objections can still be raised to the assertion that neurotic symptoms are substitutes for sexual satisfactions. I will mention two of them to-day. When you yourselves have carried out analytic examinations of a considerable number of neurotics, you will perhaps tell me, shaking your head, that in a lot of cases my assertion is simply not true; the symptoms seem rather to have the contrary purpose of excluding or of stopping sexual satisfaction. I will not dispute the correctness of your interpretation. The facts in psycho-analysis have a habit of being rather more complicated than we like. If they were as simple as all that, perhaps it might not have needed psycho-analysis to bring them to light. Indeed, some of the features of our second patient's ceremonial show signs of this ascetic character with its hostility to sexual satisfaction: when, for instance, she got rid of the clocks and watches [p. 265], which had the magical meaning of avoiding erections during the night [p. 267], or when she tried to guard against flower-pots falling and breaking [p. 265], which was equivalent to protecting her virginity [p. 267]. In some other cases of bed-ceremonials, which I have been able to analyse, this negative character was far more outspoken; the ceremonial might con-

---

[1] [See the discussion of narcissism in Lecture XXVI.]

[2] [This is discussed in greater detail in Lecture XXII, p. 344 ff. below.]

sist exclusively of defensive measures against sexual memories and temptations. However, we have already found often enough that in psycho-analysis opposites imply no contradiction.[1] We might extend our thesis and say that symptoms aim either at a sexual satisfaction or at fending it off, and that on the whole the positive, wish-fulfilling character prevails in hysteria and the negative, ascetic one in obsessional neurosis. If symptoms can serve the purpose both of sexual satisfaction and of its opposite, there is an excellent basis for this double-sidedness or polarity in a part of their mechanism which I have so far not been able to mention. For, as we shall hear, they are the products of a compromise and arise from the mutual interference between two opposing currents; they represent not only the repressed but also the repressing force which had a share in their origin. One side or the other may be more strongly represented; but it is rarely that one influence is entirely absent. In hysteria a convergence of both intentions in the same symptom is usually achieved. In obsessional neurosis the two portions are often separated; the symptom then becomes diphasic [falls into two stages] and consists in two actions, one after the other, which cancel each other out.[2]

We shall not be able to dismiss a second objection so easily. If you survey a fairly long series of interpretations of symptoms, you will probably start by judging that the concept of a substitutive sexual satisfaction has been stretched to its extreme limits in them. You will not fail to emphasize the fact that these symptoms offer nothing real in the way of satisfaction, that often enough they are restricted to the revival of a sensation or the representation of a phantasy derived from a sexual complex. And you will further point out that these supposed sexual satisfactions often take on a childish and discreditable form, approximate to an act of masturbation perhaps, or recall dirty kinds of naughtiness which are forbidden even to children—habits of which they have been broken. And, going on from this, you will also express surprise that we are representing as a sexual satisfaction what would rather have to be described as the

---

[1] [E.g. in Lecture XI, p. 178 above.]

[2] [Examples of this will be found, with a discussion, in Section E of Part I of the 'Rat Man' case history (1909d).]

satisfaction of lusts that are cruel or horrible or would even have to be called unnatural. We shall come to no agreement, Gentlemen, on this latter point till we have made a thorough investigation of the sexual life of human beings and till, in doing so, we have decided what it is that we are justified in calling 'sexual'.

LECTURE XX

THE SEXUAL LIFE OF HUMAN BEINGS[1]

LADIES AND GENTLEMEN,—One would certainly have supposed that there could be no doubt as to what is to be understood by 'sexual'. First and foremost, what is sexual is something improper, something one ought not to talk about. I have been told that the pupils of a celebrated psychiatrist made an attempt once to convince their teacher of how frequently the symptoms of hysterical patients represent sexual things. For this purpose they took him to the bedside of a female hysteric, whose attacks were an unmistakable imitation of the process of childbirth. But with a shake of his head he remarked: 'Well, there's nothing sexual about childbirth.' Quite right. Childbirth need not in every case be something improper.

I see that you take offence at my joking about such serious things. But it is not altogether a joke. Seriously, it is not easy to decide what is covered by the concept 'sexual'. Perhaps the only suitable definition would be 'everything that is related to the distinction between the two sexes'. But you will regard that as colourless and too comprehensive. If you take the fact of the sexual act as the central point, you will perhaps define as sexual everything which, with a view to obtaining pleasure, is concerned with the body, and in particular with the sexual organs, of someone of the opposite sex, and which in the last resort aims at the union of the genitals and the performance of the sexual act. But if so you will really not be very far from the equation of what is sexual with what is improper, and childbirth will really not be anything sexual. If, on the other hand, you take the reproductive function as the nucleus of sexuality, you risk excluding a whole number of things which are not aimed at

[1] [Freud's principal work on this subject was, of course, his *Three Essays on the Theory of Sexuality* (1905d), to which he made a large number of additions and corrections in a succession of editions over the subsequent twenty years. A list of his chief other contributions to the subject is given in an appendix to that work. The material in this and the following lecture is mainly derived from the *Three Essays*.]

303

reproduction but which are certainly sexual, such as masturbation and perhaps even kissing. But we are already prepared to find that attempts at a definition always lead to difficulties; so let us renounce the idea of doing better in this particular case. We may suspect that in the course of the development of the concept 'sexual' something has happened which has resulted in what Silberer has aptly called an 'error of superimposition'.[1]

On the whole, indeed, when we come to think of it, we are not quite at a loss in regard to what it is that people call sexual. Something which combines a reference to the contrast between the sexes, to the search for pleasure, to the reproductive function and to the characteristic of something that is improper and must be kept secret—some such combination will serve for all practical purposes in everyday life. But for science that is not enough. By means of careful investigations (only made possible, indeed, by disinterested self-discipline) we have come to know groups of individuals whose 'sexual life' deviates in the most striking way from the usual picture of the average. Some of these 'perverse' people have, we might say, struck the distinction between the sexes off their programme. Only members of their own sex can rouse their sexual wishes; those of the other sex, and especially their sexual parts, are not a sexual object for them at all, and in extreme cases are an object of disgust. This implies, of course, that they have abandoned any share in reproduction. We call such people homosexuals or inverts. They are men and women who are often, though not always, irreproachably fashioned in other respects, of high intellectual and ethical development, the victims only of this one fatal deviation. Through the mouth of their scientific spokesmen they represent themselves as a special variety of the human species—a 'third sex' which has a right to stand on an equal footing beside the other two. We shall perhaps have an opportunity of examining their claims critically. [Cf. p. 307 f. below.] Of course they are not, as they also like to assert, an '*élite*' of man-

---

[1] ['*Überdeckungsfehler*.' See Silberer, 1914, 161. What Silberer seems to have in mind is mistakenly thinking that you are looking at a single thing, when in fact you are looking at two different things superimposed on each other.]

kind; there are at least as many inferior and useless individuals among them as there are among those of a different sexual kind.

This class of perverts at any rate behave to their sexual objects in approximately the same way as normal people do to theirs. But we now come to a long series of abnormal people whose sexual activity diverges more and more widely from what seems desirable to a sensible person. In their multiplicity and strangeness they can only be compared to the grotesque monsters painted by Breughel for the temptation of St. Anthony or to the long procession of vanished gods and believers which Flaubert leads past, before the eyes of his pious penitent.[1] Such a medley calls for some kind of arrangement if it is not to confuse our senses. We accordingly divide them into those in whom, like the homosexuals, the sexual *object* has been changed, and others in whom the sexual *aim* is what has primarily been altered. The first group includes those who have renounced the union of the two genitals and who replace the genitals of one of the couple engaged in the sexual act by some other part or region of the body; in this they disregard the lack of suitable organic arrangements as well as any impediment offered by feelings of disgust. (They replace the vulva, for instance, by the mouth or anus.) Others follow, who, it is true, still retain the genitals as an object—not, however, on account of their sexual function but of other functions in which the genital plays a part either for anatomical reasons or because of its propinquity. We find from them that the excretory functions, which have been put aside as improper during the upbringing of children, retain the ability to attract the whole of sexual interest. Then come others again, who have abandoned the genital as an object altogether, and have taken some other part of the body as the object they desire—a woman's breast, a foot or a plait of hair. After them come others for whom parts of the body are of no importance but whose every wish is satisfied by a piece of clothing, a shoe, a piece of underclothing—the fetishists. Later in the procession come people who require the whole object indeed, but make quite definite demands of it—strange or horrible—even that it must have become a defenceless corpse,

[1] [Flaubert's *La tentation de Saint Antoine*, Part V of the final version (1874).]

and who, using criminal violence, make it into one so that they may enjoy it. But enough of this kind of horror!

The second group is led by perverts who have made what is normally only an introductory or preparatory act into the aim of their sexual wishes. They are people whose desire it is to look at the other person or to feel him or to watch him in the performance of his intimate actions, or who expose parts of their own bodies which should be covered, in the obscure expectation that they may be rewarded by a corresponding action in return. Next come the sadists, puzzling people whose tender endeavours have no other aim than to cause pain and torment to their object, ranging from humiliation to severe physical injuries; and, as though to counterbalance them, their counterparts, the masochists, whose only pleasure it is to suffer humiliations and torments of every kind from their loved object either symbolically or in reality. There are still others in whom several of these abnormal preconditions are united and intertwined; and lastly, we must learn that each of these groups is to be found in two forms: alongside of those who seek their sexual satisfaction in reality are those who are content merely to *imagine* that satisfaction, who need no real object at all, but can replace it by their phantasies.

Now there cannot be the slightest doubt that all these crazy, eccentric and horrible things really constitute the sexual activity of these people. Not only do they themselves regard them as such and are aware that they are substitutes for each other, but we must admit that they play the same part in their lives as normal sexual satisfaction does in ours; they make the same, often excessive sacrifices for them, and we can trace both in the rough and in finer detail the points at which these abnormalities are based on what is normal and the points at which they diverge from it. Nor can you fail to notice that here once again you find the characteristic of being improper, which clings to sexual activity, though here it is for the most part intensified to the point of being abominable.

Well, Ladies and Gentlemen, what attitude are we to adopt to these unusual kinds of sexual satisfaction? Indignation, an expression of our personal repugnance and an assurance that we ourselves do not share these lusts will obviously be of no help. Indeed, that is not what we have been asked for. When all is said and done, what we have here is a field of phenomena like any other. A denial in the form of an evasive suggestion that after all these are only rarities and curiosities would be easy to refute. On the contrary, we are dealing with quite common and widespread phenomena. If, however, it is argued that we need not allow our views of sexual life to be misled by them because they are one and all aberrations and deviations of the sexual instinct, a serious answer is called for. Unless we can understand these pathological forms of sexuality and can co-ordinate them with normal sexual life, we cannot understand normal sexuality either. In short, it remains an unavoidable task to give a complete theoretical account of how it is that these perversions can occur and of their connection with what is described as normal sexuality.

We shall be helped in this by a piece of information and two fresh observations. We owe the former to Iwan Bloch [1902–3]. It corrects the view that all these perversions are 'signs of degeneracy' by showing that aberrations of this kind from the sexual aim, loosenings like these of the tie with the sexual object, have occurred from time immemorial, in all periods known to us, among all peoples, the most primitive and the most civilized, and have occasionally obtained toleration and general recognition. The two observations were derived from the psycho-analytic investigation of neurotics; they are bound to have a decisive influence on our view of the sexual perversions.

I have said that neurotic symptoms are substitutes for sexual satisfaction [p. 299], and I indicated to you that the confirmation of this assertion by the analysis of symptoms would come up against a number of difficulties. For it can only be justified if under 'sexual satisfaction' we include the satisfaction of what are called perverse sexual needs, since an interpretation of symptoms of that kind is forced upon us with surprising frequency. The claim made by homosexuals or inverts to being exceptions collapses at once when we learn that homosexual impulses are invariably discovered in every single neurotic, and that a fair number of symptoms give expression to this latent inversion. Those who call themselves homosexuals are only the conscious and manifest inverts, whose number is nothing compared to that of the *latent* homosexuals. We are compelled, however, to regard choice of an object of one's own sex as a divergence in erotic life which is of positively habitual occurrence, and we are learning more and more to ascribe an especially high importance to it. No doubt this does not do away with the differences between manifest homosexuality and a normal attitude; their practical significance remains, but their theoretical value is greatly diminished. We have even found that a particular disease, paranoia, which is not to be counted among the transference neuroses, regularly arises from an attempt to fend off excessively strong homosexual impulses.[1] You will perhaps recall that one of our patients (p. 262) behaved in her obsessional action like a man, her own husband whom she had left; neurotic women very commonly produce symptoms in this way in the character of a man. Even if this is not actually to be regarded as homosexuality, it is closely related to its preconditions.

As you probably know, the hysterical neurosis can produce its symptoms in any system of organs and so disturb any function. Analysis shows that in this way all the so-called perverse impulses which seek to replace the genital by some other organ manifest themselves: these organs are then behaving like substitutive genitals. The symptoms of hysteria have actually led us to the view that the bodily organs, besides the functional part they play, must be recognized as having a sexual (erotogenic) significance, and that the execution of the first of these tasks is disturbed if the second of them makes too many claims.[2] Countless sensations and innervations which we come across as symptoms of hysteria in organs that have no apparent connection with sexuality are in this way revealed to us as being in the nature of fulfilments of perverse sexual impulses in relation to which other organs have acquired the significance of the sexual parts. We learn too to what a large extent the organs for the intake of nourishment and for excretion can in particular become the vehicles of sexual excitation. Here, then, we have the same thing that we were shown by the perversions; only in their case it was visible easily and unmistakably, whereas in

[1] [Paranoia is further discussed in Lecture XXVI, p. 423 ff. below.]

[2] [This point is discussed at greater length in a paper on psychogenic disturbance of vision (1910*i*).]

hysteria we have to take a circuitous path by way of the interpretation of symptoms, and do not then ascribe the perverse sexual impulses concerned to the subject's consciousness but locate them in his unconscious.

Of the many symptomatic pictures in which obsessional neurosis appears, the most important turn out to be those provoked by the pressure of excessively strong sadistic sexual impulses (perverse, therefore, in their aim). The symptoms, indeed, in accordance with the structure of an obsessional neurosis, serve predominantly as a *defence* against these wishes or give expression to the struggle between satisfaction and defence. But satisfaction does not come off too badly either; it succeeds in roundabout ways in putting itself into effect in the patients' behaviour and is preferably directed against themselves and makes them into self-tormentors. Other forms of the neurosis, the brooding kinds, correspond to an excessive sexualization of actions which ordinarily have their place on the path to normal sexual satisfaction—an excessive sexualization of wanting to look or to touch or to explore. Here we have the explanation of the great importance of the fear of touching and of the obsession for washing. An unsuspectedly large proportion of obsessional actions may be traced back to masturbation, of which they are disguised repetitions and modifications;[1] it is a familiar fact that masturbation, though a single and uniform action, accompanies the most various forms of sexual phantasying.

I should not have much difficulty in giving you a far more intimate picture of the relations between perversion and neurosis; but I think what I have already said will serve our purpose. We must however guard against being misled by what I have told you of the meaning of symptoms into over-estimating the frequency and intensity of people's perverse inclinations. It is possible, as you have heard [p. 300], to fall ill of a neurosis as a result of a frustration of normal sexual satisfaction. But when a real frustration like this occurs, the need moves over on to abnormal methods of sexual excitation. You will later learn the way in which this happens [p. 344 ff.]. But in any case you

[1] [The mechanism of the development of obsessional actions is described in detail in the paper on obsessions and religion (1907*b*).]

will realize that as a result of this 'collateral' damming-back [of the normal sexual current] the perverse impulses must emerge more strongly than they would have if normal sexual satisfaction had met with no obstacle in the real world.[1] More- over a similar influence is to be recognized also as affecting the *manifest* perversions. In some cases they are provoked or made active if the normal satisfaction of the sexual instinct encounters too great difficulties for temporary reasons or because of per- manent social regulations.[2] In other cases, it is true, the inclina- tion to perversions is quite independent of such favouring conditions; they are, we might say, the normal species of sexual life for those particular individuals.

For the moment, perhaps, you may have an impression that I have confused rather than explained the relation between normal and perverse sexuality. But you must bear the following consideration in mind. If it is true that increased difficulty in obtaining normal sexual satisfaction in real life, or deprivation of that satisfaction, brings out perverse inclinations in people who had not shown any previously, we must suppose that there was something in these people which came half-way to meet the perversions; or, if you prefer it, the perversions must have been present in them in a latent form.

And this brings us to the second novelty that I announced to you [p. 307].[3] For psycho-analytic research has had to concern itself, too, with the sexual life of children, and this is because the memories and associations arising during the analysis of symp- toms [in adults] regularly led back to the early years of child- hood. What we inferred from these analyses was later confirmed point by point by direct observations of children.[4] And it then

[1] [This analogy of a collateral flow through intercommunica- ting channels is more clearly explained in Section 6 of the first of Freud's *Three Essays on Sexuality* (1905d). Cf. also below, p. 345.]
[2] [This last point is discussed at length in Freud's paper on ' "Civilized" Sexual Morality and Modern Nervous Illness' (1908d).]
[3] [The first was the important part played in the neuroses by perverse sexuality. What follows was touched on more briefly in Lecture XIII, p. 208 ff. above.]
[4] [The earliest of these direct observations were made in the case of 'Little Hans' (1909b).]

turned out that all these inclinations to perversion had their roots in childhood, that children have a predisposition to all of them and carry them out to an extent corresponding to their immaturity—in short, that perverse sexuality is nothing else than a magnified infantile sexuality split up into its separate impulses.

At all events you will now see the perversions in a new light and no longer fail to realize their connection with the sexual life of human beings: but at the price of what surprises and of what feelings of distress over these incongruities! No doubt you will feel inclined at first to deny the whole business: the fact that children have anything that can be described as sexual life, the correctness of our observations and the justification for finding any kinship between the behaviour of children and what is later condemned as perversion. So allow me to begin by explaining to you the motives for your opposition, and then to present you with the sum of our observations. To suppose that children have no sexual life—sexual excitations and needs and a kind of satisfaction—but suddenly acquire it between the ages of twelve and fourteen, would (quite apart from any observations) be as improbable, and indeed senseless, biologically as to suppose that they brought no genitals with them into the world and only grew them at the time of puberty. What *does* awaken in them at this time is the reproductive function, which makes use for its purposes of physical and mental material already present. You are committing the error of confusing sexuality and reproduction and by doing so you are blocking your path to an understanding of sexuality, the perversions and the neuroses. This error is, however, a tendentious one. Strangely enough, it has its source in the fact that you yourselves were once children and, while you were children, came under the influence of education. For society must undertake as one of its most important educative tasks to tame and restrict the sexual instinct when it breaks out as an urge to reproduction, and to subject it to an individual will which is identical with the bidding of society. It is also concerned to postpone the full development of the instinct till the child shall have reached a certain degree of intellectual maturity, for, with the complete irruption of the sexual instinct, educability is for practical purposes at an end. Otherwise, the instinct would break down every dam and wash away the laboriously erected work of civilization. Nor is the task of taming it ever an easy one; its success is sometimes too small, sometimes too great. The motive of human society is in the last resort an economic one; since it does not possess enough provisions to keep its members alive unless they work, it must restrict the number of its members and divert their energies from sexual activity to work. It is faced, in short, by the eternal, primaeval exigencies of life, which are with us to this day.[1]

Experience must no doubt have taught the educators that the task of making the sexual will of the new generation tractable could only be carried out if they began to exercise their influence very early, if they did not wait for the storm of puberty but intervened already in the sexual life of children which is preparatory to it. For this reason almost all infantile sexual activities were forbidden to children and frowned upon; an ideal was set up of making the life of children asexual, and in course of time things came to the point at which people really believed they were asexual and thereafter science pronounced this as its doctrine. To avoid contradicting their belief and their intentions, people since then overlook the sexual activities of children (no mean achievement) or are content in science to take a different view of them. Children are pure and innocent, and anyone who describes them otherwise can be charged with being an infamous blasphemer against the tender and sacred feelings of mankind.

Children are alone in not falling in with these conventions. They assert their animal rights with complete *naïveté* and give constant evidence that they have still to travel the road to purity. Strangely enough, the people who deny the existence of sexuality in children do not on that account become milder in their educational efforts but pursue the manifestations of what they deny exists with the utmost severity—describing them as 'childish naughtinesses'. It is also of the highest theoretical interest that the period of life which contradicts the prejudice of an asexual childhood most glaringly—the years of a child's life up to the age of five or six—is afterwards covered in most people by the veil of amnesia which is only completely torn away by an analytic enquiry, though it has been per-

[1] [See p. 22 f. above.]

meable earlier for the construction of a few dreams. [Cf. p. 201 above.]

I will now set out before you what is most definitely known about the sexual life of children. Let me at the same time, for convenience sake, introduce the concept of 'libido'. On the exact analogy of 'hunger', we use 'libido' as the name of the force (in this case that of the sexual instinct, as in the case of hunger that of the nutritive instinct) by which the instinct manifests itself. Other concepts, such as sexual 'excitation' and 'satisfaction', call for no explanation. You yourselves will easily perceive that the sexual activities of infants in arms are mostly a matter of interpretation, or you will probably use that as a ground of objection. These interpretations are arrived at on the basis of analytic examinations made by tracing from the symptoms backwards. In an infant the first impulses of sexuality make their appearance attached to other vital functions. His main interest is, as you know, directed to the intake of nourishment; when children fall asleep after being sated at the breast, they show an expression of blissful satisfaction which will be repeated later in life after the experience of a sexual orgasm. This would be too little on which to base an inference. But we observe how an infant will repeat the action of taking in nourishment without making a demand for further food; here, then, he is not actuated by hunger. We describe this as sensual sucking,[1] and the fact that in doing this he falls asleep once more with a blissful expression shows us that the act of sensual sucking has in itself alone brought him satisfaction. Soon, as we know, things come to a point at which he cannot go to sleep without having sucked. A paediatrician in Budapest, Dr. Lindner [1879], was the first to point out long ago the sexual nature of this activity. Those who are in charge of children, and who have no theoretical views on the subject, seem to form a similar judgement of sucking. They have no doubt of its only purpose being to obtain pleasure, class it as one of a child's 'naughtinesses' and compel him to abandon it by causing him distress, if he will not give it up of his own accord. Thus we learn that infants perform actions which have no purpose other

[1] [The German nursery terms here used are *'lutschen'* or *'ludeln'*, for which there is no obvious English equivalent.]

than obtaining pleasure. It is our belief that they first experience this pleasure in connection with taking nourishment but that they soon learn to separate it from that accompanying condition. We can only refer this pleasure to an excitation of the areas of the mouth and lips; we call those parts of the body 'erotogenic zones' and describe the pleasure derived from sucking as a sexual one. We shall no doubt have to discuss further whether this description is justifiable.

If an infant could speak, he would no doubt pronounce the act of sucking at his mother's breast by far the most important in his life. He is not far wrong in this, for in this single act he is satisfying at once the two great vital needs. We are therefore not surprised to learn from psycho-analysis how much psychical importance the act retains all through life. Sucking at the mother's breast is the starting-point of the whole of sexual life, the unmatched prototype of every later sexual satisfaction, to which phantasy often enough recurs in times of need. This sucking involves making the mother's breast the first object of the sexual instinct. I can give you no idea of the important bearing of this first object upon the choice of every later object, of the profound effects it has in its transformations and substitutions in even the remotest regions of our sexual life. But at first the infant, in his sucking activity, gives up this object and replaces it by a part of his own body. He begins to suck his thumbs or his own tongue. In this way he makes himself independent of the consent of the external world as regards gaining pleasure, and besides this he increases it by adding the excitation of a second area of his body. The erotogenic zones are not all equally generous in yielding pleasure; it is therefore an important experience when the infant, as Lindner reports, discovers, in the course of feeling around, the specially excitable regions afforded by his genitals and so finds his way from sucking to masturbation.

In forming this opinion of sensual sucking we have already become acquainted with two decisive characteristics of infantile sexuality. It makes its appearance attached to the satisfaction of the major organic needs, and it behaves *auto-erotically* —that is, it seeks and finds its objects in the infant's own body. What has been shown most clearly in connection with the intake of nourishment is repeated in part with the excretions.

We conclude that infants have feelings of pleasure in the process of evacuating urine and faeces and that they soon contrive to arrange those actions in such a way as to bring them the greatest possible yield of pleasure through the corresponding excitations of the erotogenic zones of the mucous membrane. It is here for the first time (as Lou Andreas-Salomé [1916] has subtly perceived) that they encounter the external world as an inhibiting power, hostile to their desire for pleasure, and have a glimpse of later conflicts both external and internal. An infant must not produce his excreta at whatever moment he chooses, but when other people decide that he shall. In order to induce him to forgo these sources of pleasure, he is told that everything that has to do with these functions is improper and must be kept secret. This is where he is first obliged to exchange pleasure for social respectability. To begin with, his attitude to his excreta themselves is quite different. He feels no disgust at his faeces, values them as a portion of his own body with which he will not readily part, and makes use of them as his first 'gift', to distinguish people whom he values especially highly. Even after education has succeeded in its aim of making these inclinations alien to him, he carries on his high valuation of faeces in his estimate of 'gifts' and 'money'. On the other hand he seems to regard his achievements in urinating with peculiar pride.[1]

I know you have been wanting for a long time to interrupt me and exclaim: 'Enough of these atrocities! You tell us that defaecating is a source of sexual satisfaction, and already exploited in infancy! that faeces is a valuable substance and that the anus is a kind of genital! We don't believe all that—but we do understand why paediatricians and educationists have given a wide berth to psycho-analysis and its findings.' No, Gentlemen. You have merely forgotten that I have been trying to introduce the facts of infantile sexual life to you in connection with the facts of the sexual perversions. Why should you

---

[1] [The relations between faeces and money were discussed by Freud in a paper on 'Character and Anal Erotism' (1908b) and in a later one, almost contemporary with the present lecture, 'On Transformations of Instinct as Exemplified in Anal Erotism' (1917c). The connection between micturition and pride had been shown in a dream-analysis in *The Interpretation of Dreams* (1900a). See example IV of Section H in Chapter VI.]

not be aware that for a large number of adults, homosexual and heterosexual alike, the anus does really take over the role of the vagina in sexual intercourse? And that there are many people who retain a voluptuous feeling in defaecating all through their lives and describe it as being far from small? As regards interest in the act of defaecation and enjoyment in watching someone else defaecating, you can get children themselves to confirm the fact when they are a few years older and able to tell you about it. Of course, you must not have systematically intimidated them beforehand, or they will quite understand that they must be silent on the subject. And as to the other things that you are anxious not to believe, I will refer you to the findings of analysis and of the direct observation of children and will add that it calls for real ingenuity not to see all this or to see it differently. Nor do I complain if you find the kinship between infantile sexual activity and sexual perversions something very striking. But it is in fact self-evident: if a child has a sexual life at all it is bound to be of a perverse kind; for, except for a few obscure hints, children are without what makes sexuality into the reproductive function. On the other hand, the abandonment of the reproductive function is the common feature of all perversions. We actually describe a sexual activity as perverse if it has given up the aim of reproduction and pursues the attainment of pleasure as an aim independent of it. So, as you will see, the breach and turning-point in the development of sexual life lies in its becoming subordinate to the purposes of reproduction. Everything that happens before this turn of events and equally everything that disregards it and that aims solely at obtaining pleasure is given the uncomplimentary name of 'perverse' and as such is proscribed.

Allow me, therefore, to proceed with my brief account of infantile sexuality. What I have already reported of two systems of organs [nutritional and excretory] might be confirmed in reference to the others. A child's sexual life is indeed made up entirely of the activities of a number of component instincts which seek, independently of one another, to obtain pleasure, in part from the subject's own body and in part already from an external object. Among these organs the genitals come into prominence very soon. There are people in whom obtaining pleasure from their own genitals, without the assistance of any other genitals or of an object, continues uninterruptedly from infantile masturbation to the unavoidable masturbation[1] of puberty and persists for an indefinite length of time afterwards. Incidentally, the topic of masturbation is not one that can be so easily disposed of: it is something that calls for examination from many angles.[2]

Though I am anxious to cut short this discussion still further, I must nevertheless tell you a little about the sexual researches of children: they are too characteristic of infantile sexuality and of too great significance for the symptomatology of the neuroses to be passed over.[3] Infantile sexual researches begin very early, sometimes before the third year of life. They do not relate to the distinction between the sexes,[4] for this means nothing to children, since they (or at any rate boys) attribute the same male genital to both sexes. If, afterwards, a boy makes the discovery of the vagina from seeing his little sister or a girl playmate, he tries, to begin with, to disavow the evidence of his senses, for he cannot imagine a human creature like himself who is without such a precious portion. Later on, he takes fright at the possibility thus presented to him; and any threats that may have been made to him earlier, because he took too intense an interest in his little organ, now produce a deferred effect. He comes under the sway of the castration complex,[5] the

---

[1] ['Notonanie.' Literally, masturbation by necessity, i.e. forced on the subject by circumstances.]

[2] Freud's fullest remarks on the subject are in his 'Contribution to a Discussion on Masturbation' (1912f), where an Editor's Note gives further references.]

[3] [See 'On the Sexual Theories of Children' (1908c).]

[4] [This statement and the related one at the beginning of the next paragraph were corrected by Freud later, in a footnote to his paper on the anatomical distinction between the sexes (1925j). He there argues that the problem of sex-distinction came first and that of the origin of babies afterwards, at any rate in girls.]

[5] [This has already been mentioned above (on p. 208), and appears again below (on p. 368 ff.). The first published discussions on the castration complex appeared in Freud's case history of 'Little Hans' (1909b), though it had been referred to in an earlier paper on the sexual theories of children (1908c). Its relation to the Oedipus complex was fully examined in later years, more particularly in Freud's papers on 'The Dissolution of the Oedipus Complex' (1924d) and on the anatomical distinction between the sexes (1925j).]

form taken by which plays a great part in the construction of his character if he remains normal, in his neurosis if he falls ill, and in his resistances if he comes into analytic treatment. As regards little girls, we can say of them that they feel greatly at a disadvantage owing to their lack of a big, visible penis, that they envy boys for possessing one and that, in the main for this reason, they develop a wish to be a man—a wish that re-emerges later on, in any neurosis that may arise if they meet with a mishap in playing a feminine part. In her childhood, moreover, a girl's clitoris takes on the role of a penis entirely: it is characterized by special excitability and is the area in which auto-erotic satisfaction is obtained. The process of a girl's becoming a woman depends very much on the clitoris passing on this sensitivity to the vaginal orifice in good time and completely. In cases of what is known as sexual anaesthesia in women the clitoris has obstinately retained its sensitivity.

The sexual interest of children begins by turning, rather, to the problem of where babies come from[1]—the same problem which underlies the question put by the Theban Sphinx—and it is most often raised by egoistic fears on the arrival of a new baby. The reply which is ready to hand in the nursery, that babies are brought by the stork [p. 160], comes up against disbelief on the part even of small children far oftener than we are aware. The sense of being defrauded of the truth by the grown-ups contributes much to making children feel lonely and to developing their independence. But a child is not in a position to solve this problem by his own means. His undeveloped sexual constitution sets definite limits to his power of perception. He begins by supposing that babies come from people taking in something special in their food, nor does he know that only women can have babies. Later he becomes aware of this limitation and ceases to regard eating as the origin of babies—though the theory persists in fairy tales. When the child has grown bigger, he soon notices that his father must play some part in getting babies, but he cannot guess what. If he happens to witness a sexual act, he regards it as an attempt at subjugation, a struggle, and this is the sadistic misunderstanding of coition. But at first he does not connect this act with the coming into being of a baby. So, too, if he finds traces of blood on his

[1] [See the last footnote but one.]

mother's bed or on her underclothes, he takes it as a sign that she has been injured by his father. Still later in childhood, he no doubt suspects that the man's sexual organ has an essential share in producing babies, but the only function he can attribute to that part of the body is micturition.

From the very first, children are at one in thinking that babies must be born through the bowel; they must make their appearance like lumps of faeces. This theory is not abandoned until all anal interests have been deprived of their value, and it is then replaced by the hypothesis that the navel comes open or that the area of the breast between the nipples is where birth takes place. In this way the child in the course of his researches comes nearer to the facts about sex, or, feeling at a loss owing to his ignorance, he passes them by till, usually in the years before puberty, he is given what is as a rule a depreciatory and incomplete explanation, which often produces traumatic effects.

You will no doubt have heard, Gentlemen, that in psycho-analysis the concept of what is sexual has been unduly extended in order to support the theses of the sexual causation of the neuroses and the sexual meaning of symptoms. You are now in a position to judge for yourselves whether this extension is unjustified. We have only extended the concept of sexuality far enough to be able to comprise the sexual life of perverts and of children. We have, that is to say, given it back its true compass. What is called sexuality outside psycho-analysis relates only to a restricted sexual life, which serves the purpose of reproduction and is described as normal.

LECTURE XXI

THE DEVELOPMENT OF THE LIBIDO
AND THE SEXUAL ORGANIZATIONS

GENTLEMEN,—I am under the impression that I have not succeeded in bringing home to you quite convincingly the importance of the perversions for our view of sexuality, and I should therefore like so far as I can to improve and supplement what I have said.

It is not the case that the perversions alone would have obliged us to make the change in the concept of sexuality which has brought such violent contradictions down on us. The study of infantile sexuality had even more to do with it and it was the concurrence of the two which was decisive for us. But the manifestations of infantile sexuality, however unmistakable they may be in later childhood, seem to melt into indefiniteness towards their beginnings. Anyone who chooses to disregard the history of their development and their analytic context will deny that they are of a sexual character and will attribute some undifferentiated character to them instead. You must not forget that at the moment we are not in possession of any generally recognized criterion of the sexual nature of a process, apart, once again, from a connection with the reproductive function which we must reject as being too narrow-minded. The biological criteria, such as the periodicities of twenty-three and twenty-eight days postulated by Wilhelm Fliess [1906], are still highly debatable; the chemical characteristics of the sexual process, which we may suspect, are still awaiting discovery. On the other hand, the sexual perversions of adults are something tangible and unambiguous. As is already shown by the name by which they are universally known, they are unquestionably sexual. Whether they are described as indications of degeneracy or in any other way, no one has yet had the courage to class them as anything but phenomena of sexual life. On their account alone we are justified in asserting that sexuality and reproduction do not coincide, for it is obvious that all of them disavow the aim of reproduction.

320

I find a parallel here which is not uninteresting. Whereas for most people 'conscious' and 'psychical' are the same, we have been obliged to extend the concept of 'psychical' and to recognize something 'psychical' that is not 'conscious'. And in just the same way, whereas other people declare that 'sexual' and 'connected with reproduction' (or, if you prefer to put it more shortly, 'genital') are identical, we cannot avoid postulating something 'sexual' that is not 'genital'—has nothing to do with reproduction. The similarity here is only a formal one, but it is not without a deeper foundation.

But if the existence of sexual perversions is such a decisive argument in this question, why has it not long since had its effect and settled the matter? I really cannot say. I think it is connected with the fact that these sexual perversions are subject to a quite special ban, which has even affected theory and has stood in the way of the scientific consideration of them. It is as though no one could forget that they are not only something disgusting but also something monstrous and dangerous—as though people felt them as seductive, and had at bottom to fight down a secret envy of those who were enjoying them. One is reminded of the admission made by the condemnatory Landgraf in the famous *Tannhäuser* parody:

> 'Im Venusberg vergass er Ehr und Pflicht!
> —Merkwürdig, unser einem passiert
> so etwas nicht.'[1]

In reality perverts are poor wretches, rather, who have to pay extremely dear for their hard-won satisfaction.

What makes the activity of perverts so unmistakably sexual in spite of all the strangeness of its objects and aims is the fact that as a rule an act of perverse satisfaction nevertheless ends in complete orgasm and voidance of the genital products. This is of course only the result of the people concerned being adults. In children orgasm and genital excretion are scarcely possible; their place is taken by hints which are once more not recognized as being clearly sexual.

[1] ['The Venusberg made him forget
Honour and Duty thus!—
Strange how these things don't happen
To people such as us.'—By Nestroy (cf. p. 352*n*.).]

There is something else that I must add in order to complete our view of sexual perversions. However infamous they may be, however sharply they may be contrasted with normal sexual activity, quiet consideration will show that some perverse trait or other is seldom absent from the sexual life of normal people. Even a kiss can claim to be described as a perverse act, since it consists in the bringing together of two oral erotogenic zones instead of the two genitals. Yet no one rejects it as perverse; on the contrary, it is permitted in theatrical performances as a softened hint at the sexual act. But precisely kissing can easily turn into a complete perversion—if, that is to say, it becomes so intense that a genital discharge and orgasm follow upon it directly, an event that is far from rare. We can learn, too, that for one person feeling and looking at the object are indispensable preconditions of sexual enjoyment, that another person will pinch or bite at the climax of sexual excitation, that the highest pitch of excitement in lovers is not always provoked by the genitals but by some other region of the object's body, and any number of similar things besides. There is no sense in excluding people with individual traits of this kind from the class of the normal and putting them among the perverts. On the contrary, we shall recognize more and more clearly that the essence of the perversions lies not in the extension of the sexual aim, not in the replacement of the genitals, not even always in the variant choice of the object, but solely in the exclusiveness with which these deviations are carried out and as a result of which the sexual act serving the purpose of reproduction is put on one side. In so far as the perverse actions are inserted in the performance of the normal sexual act as preparatory or intensifying contributions, they are in reality not perversions at all. The gulf between normal and perverse sexuality is of course very much narrowed by facts of this kind. It is an easy conclusion that normal sexuality has emerged out of something that was in existence before it, by weeding out certain features of that material as unserviceable and collecting together the rest in order to subordinate them to a new aim, that of reproduction.

Before we make use of our familiarity with the perversions to plunge once again into the study of infantile sexuality on the basis of clearer premisses, I must draw your attention to an important difference between them. Perverse sexuality is as a rule excellently centred: all its actions are directed to an aim—usually to a single one; one component instinct has gained the upper hand in it and is either the only one observable or has subjected the others to its purposes. In that respect there is no distinction between perverse and normal sexuality other than the fact that their dominating component instincts and consequently their sexual aims are different. In both of them, one might say, a well-organized tyranny has been established, but in each of the two a different family has seized the reins of power. Infantile sexuality, on the other hand, lacks, speaking generally, any such centring and organization; its separate component instincts have equal rights, each of them goes its own way to obtaining pleasure. Both the absence and the presence of centring harmonize well, of course, with the fact that both perverse and normal sexuality have arisen out of infantile sexuality. Incidentally, there are also cases of perverse sexuality which have a much greater resemblance to the infantile kind, since in them numerous component instincts have put through (or, more correctly, have persisted in) their aims independently of one another. It is better in such cases to speak of infantilism in sexual life rather than of a perversion.

Thus forearmed we can proceed to the consideration of a suggestion which we shall certainly not be spared. 'Why', we shall be asked, 'are you so obstinate in describing as being already sexuality what on your own evidence are indefinable manifestations in childhood out of which sexual life will later develop? Why should you not be content instead with giving them a physiological description and simply say that in an infant at the breast we already observe activities, such as sensual sucking or holding back the excreta, which show us that he is striving for "organ-pleasure"?[1] In that way you would have avoided the hypothesis, so repugnant to every feeling, of the smallest babies having a sexual life.'—Indeed, Gentlemen, I have no objection at all to organ-pleasure. I know that even the supreme pleasure

---

[1] ['*Organlust.*' The term occurs in 'Instincts and their Vicissitudes' (1915c), where Freud seems to have used it for the first time. He uses it again below in the *New Introductory Lectures,* p. 562. The *concept,* of course, is familiar from the time of the *Three Essays* (1905d), Essay II.]

of sexual union is only an organ-pleasure attached to the activity of the genitals. But can you tell me when this originally indifferent organ-pleasure acquires the sexual character which it undoubtedly possesses in the later phases of development? Do we know any more about 'organ-pleasure' than about sexuality? You will reply that it gains its sexual character precisely when the genitals begin to play their part; 'sexual' coincides with 'genital'. You will even reject the objection raised by the perversions by pointing out to me that in the majority of perversions a genital orgasm is after all aimed at, even if it is arrived at by a method other than the union of the genitals. You are certainly taking up a much stronger position in determining the characteristics of what is sexual if you knock out of it the relation to reproduction which is made untenable by the perversions and put genital activity in its place. But, if so, we are no longer far apart: it is only a question of the genital organs versus the other organs. What are you going to do, however, about the numerous experiences which show you that the genitals can be represented as regards their yield of pleasure by other organs, as in the case of kissing or of the perverse practices of voluptuaries or of the symptoms of hysteria? In that neurosis it is quite usual for signs of stimulation, sensations and innervations, and even the processes of erection, which belong properly to the genitals, to be displaced on to other, remote regions of the body—as, for instance, by transposition upwards, to the head and face. Being thus convinced that you have nothing to catch hold of for your characterization of what is sexual, you will no doubt have to make up your minds to follow my example and extend the description of being 'sexual' to the activities of early childhood, too, which strive for organ-pleasure.

And now, for my justification, there are two other considerations which I must ask you to take into account. As you know, we call the dubious and indefinable pleasurable activities of earliest childhood sexual because, in the course of analysis, we arrive at them from the symptoms after passing through indisputably sexual material. They need not necessarily themselves be sexual on that account—agreed! But take an analogous case. Suppose we had no means of observing the development from their seed of two dicotyledonous plants, the apple-tree and the bean, but that it was possible in both cases for us to trace their development backwards from the fully developed individual plant to the first seedling with two seed-leaves. The two seed-leaves have a neutral appearance; they are just alike in both cases. Am I then to suppose that they are really alike, and that the specific difference between an apple-tree and a bean is only introduced into the plants later? Or is it biologically more correct to believe that this difference is already there in the seedling, although I cannot observe any distinction in the seed-leaves? But we are doing the same thing when we call the pleasure in the activities of an infant-in-arms a sexual one. I cannot discuss here whether each and every organ-pleasure should be called a sexual one or whether, alongside of the sexual one, there is another which does not deserve to be so called. I know too little about organ-pleasure and its determinants; and, in view of the retrogressive character of analysis in general, I cannot feel surprised if at the very end I arrive at what are for the time being indefinable factors.

And one thing more! On the whole you will have gained very little for what you want to assert—the sexual purity of children —even if you succeed in convincing me that it would be better to regard the activities of infants-in-arms as non-sexual. For the sexual life of children is already free from all these doubts from the third year of life onwards: at about that time the genitals already begin to stir, a period of infantile masturbation—of genital satisfaction, therefore—sets in, regularly perhaps. The mental and social phenomena of sexual life need no longer be absent; the choice of an object, an affectionate preference for particular people, a decision, even, in favour of one of the two sexes, jealousy—all these have been established by impartial observations made independently of psycho-analysis and before its time, and they can be confirmed by any observer who cares to see them. You will object that you have never doubted the early awakening of affection; you have only doubted whether this affection bears a 'sexual' character. It is true that children have already learnt to conceal this between the ages of three and eight. But if you are attentive you will be able nevertheless to collect enough evidence of the 'sensual' aims of this affection, and whatever you still lack after that can easily be supplied in plenty by the investigations of analysis. The sexual aims at this period of life are intimately connected with the child's contemporary sexual researches, of which I have given you some instances [p. 317]. The perverse character of some of these aims is of course dependent on the child's constitutional immaturity, for he has not yet discovered the aim that consists in the act of copulation.

From about the sixth to the eighth year of life onwards, we can observe a halt and retrogression in sexual development, which, in cases where it is most propitious culturally, deserves to be called a period of latency. The latency period may also be absent: it need not bring with it any interruption of sexual activity and sexual interests along the whole line. The majority of experiences and mental impulses before the start of the latency period now fall victim to infantile amnesia—the forgetting (already discussed by us [p. 199 ff.]) which veils our earliest youth from us and makes us strangers to it. The task is set us in every psycho-analysis of bringing this forgotten period back into memory. It is impossible to avoid a suspicion that the beginnings of sexual life which are included in that period have provided the motive for its being forgotten—that this forgetting, in fact, is an outcome of repression.

From the third year of life a child's sexual life shows much agreement with an adult's. It differs from the latter, as we already know, in lacking a firm organization under the primacy of the genitals, in its inevitable traits of perversion and also, of course, in the far lesser intensity of the whole trend. But from the point of view of theory the most interesting phases of sexual, or, as we will say, of libidinal, development lie earlier than this point of time. This course of development takes place so rapidly that we should probably never have succeeded in getting a firm hold of its fleeting pictures by direct observation. It was only with the help of the psycho-analytic investigation of the neuroses that it became possible to discern the still earlier phases of the development of the libido. These are nothing but constructions, to be sure, but, if you carry out psycho-analyses in practice, you will find that they are necessary and useful constructions. You will soon learn how it comes about that pathology can here put us in possession of conditions which we should inevitably overlook in a normal subject.

Accordingly, I can now describe to you the form taken by a child's sexual life before the establishment of the primacy of the genitals, preparations for which are made in the first period of infancy preceding the latency period and which is permanently organized from puberty onwards. A kind of loose organization which may be called 'pregenital' exists during this early period. During this phase what stand in the forefront are not the genital component instincts but the sadistic and anal ones. The contrast between 'masculine' and 'feminine' plays no part here as yet. Its place is taken by the contrast between 'active' and 'passive', which may be described as a precursor of the sexual polarity and which later on is soldered to that polarity. What appears to us as masculine in the activities of this phase, when we look at it from the point of view of the genital phase, turns out to be an expression of an instinct for mastery which easily passes over into cruelty. Trends with a passive aim are attached to the erotogenic zone of the anal orifice, which is very important at this period. The instincts for looking and for gaining knowledge [the scopophilic and epistemophilic instincts] are powerfully at work; the genitals actually play a part in sexual life only as organs for the excretion of urine. The component instincts of this phase are not without objects, but those objects do not necessarily converge into a single object. The sadistic-anal organization is the immediate forerunner of the phase of genital primacy. Detailed study shows how much of it is retained in the later definitive shape of things and shows too the way in which its component instincts are compelled to take their place in the new genital organization.[1] Behind the sadistic-anal phase of libidinal development we get a glimpse of a still earlier and more primitive stage of organization, in which the erotogenic zone of the mouth plays the chief part. As you will guess, the sexual activity of sensual sucking [p. 313] belongs to it. We must admire the understanding of the Ancient Egyptians who, in their art, represented children, including the God Horus, with a finger in their mouth. Only recently Abraham [1916] has given examples of the traces which this primitive oral phase leaves behind it in later sexual life.

I can well suppose, Gentlemen, that this last account of the

[1] [Freud afterwards interposed a 'phallic' phase between the sadistic-anal and genital organizations (Freud, 1923e).]

sexual organizations has obstructed rather than instructed you, and it may be that I have once more entered too much into details. But you must have patience. What you have just heard will derive increased value for you from its later application. For the present you should keep firmly in mind that sexual life (or, as we put it, the libidinal function) does not emerge as something ready-made and does not even develop further in its own likeness, but passes through a series of successive phases which do not resemble one another; its development is thus several times repeated—like that of a caterpillar into a butterfly. The turning-point of this development is the subordination of all the component sexual instincts under the primacy of the genitals and along with this the subjection of sexuality to the reproductive function. This is preceded by a sexual life that might be described as distracted—the independent activity of the different component instincts striving for organ-pleasure. This anarchy is mitigated by abortive beginnings of 'pregenital' organizations—a sadistic-anal phase preceded by an oral one, which is perhaps the most primitive. In addition, there are the various, still incompletely known, processes which lead one stage of organization over to the subsequent and next higher one. We shall learn later[1] what an important light is thrown on the neuroses by the fact that the libido passes through such a long course of development and one which has so many breaks in it.

To-day we will follow yet another side of this development—namely the relation of the component sexual instincts to their object. Or rather, we will make a hasty survey of this development and dwell somewhat longer on one of its rather late consequences. A few of the components of the sexual instinct, then, have an object from the first and hold fast to it—for instance, the instinct for mastery (sadism) and the scopophilic and epistemophilic instincts. Others, more definitely linked to particular erotogenic zones of the body, have one to begin with only, so long as they are still attached to the non-sexual functions [cf. p. 313 above], and give it up when they become separated from them. Thus the first object of the oral component of the sexual instinct is the mother's breast which satisfies the infant's

[1] [Actually in the next lecture.]

need for nourishment. The erotic component, which is satisfied simultaneously during the [nutritive] sucking, makes itself independent with the act of *sensual* sucking [*lutschen*]; it gives up the outside object and replaces it by an area of the subject's own body. The oral instinct becomes *auto-erotic*, as are the anal and other erotogenic instincts from the first. Further development, to put the matter as concisely as possible, has two aims: firstly, the abandonment of auto-erotism, the replacement of the subject's own body once more by an outside object, and secondly, the unification of the various objects of the separate instincts and their replacement by a single object. This can, of course, only be achieved if the object is again a whole body, similar to the subject's own. Nor can it be effected unless a number of the auto-erotic instinctual impulses are left behind as being unserviceable.

The processes of finding an object are fairly complex and no comprehensive account has hitherto been given of them. For our purposes it may be specially pointed out that when, in the years of childhood before puberty, the process has in some respects reached a conclusion, the object that has been found turns out to be almost identical with the first object of the oral pleasure-instinct, which was reached by attachment [to the nutritional instinct].[1] Though it is not actually the mother's breast, at least it is the mother. We call the mother the first *love*-object. For we speak of love when we bring the mental side of the sexual trends into the foreground and want to force back the underlying physical or 'sensual' instinctual demands or to forget them for a moment. At the time at which the child's mother becomes his love-object the psychical work of repression has already begun in him, which is withdrawing from his knowledge awareness of a part of his sexual aims. To his choice of his mother as a love-object everything becomes attached which, under the name of the 'Oedipus complex', has attained so much importance in the psycho-analytic explanation of the neuroses and has played no less a part, perhaps, in the resistance to psycho-analysis. [Cf. p. 207 above.][2]

[1] [This is further explained in Lecture XXVI, p. 426 below.]
[2] [Freud's first published account of the Oedipus complex was given in Section D of Chapter V in *The Interpretation of Dreams* (1900a), though he had put it forward earlier in a letter to Fliess

Listen to this episode which occurred in the course of the present war. One of the stout disciples of psycho-analysis was stationed as medical officer on the German front somewhere in Poland. He attracted his colleagues' attention by the fact that he occasionally exercised an unexpected influence on a patient. When he was questioned, he acknowledged that he was employing the methods of psycho-analysis and declared his readiness to convey his knowledge to his colleagues. Every evening thereafter the medical officers of the corps, his colleagues and his superiors, came together in order to learn the secret doctrines of analysis. All went well for a while; but when he spoke to his audience about the Oedipus complex, one of his superiors rose, declared he did not believe it, that it was a vile act on the part of the lecturer to speak of such things to them, honest men who were fighting for their country and fathers of a family, and that he forbade the continuance of the lectures. That was the end of the matter. The analyst got himself transferred to another part of the front. It seems to me a bad thing, however, if a German victory requires that science shall be 'organized' in this way, and German science will not respond well to organization of such a kind.

And now you will be eager to hear what this terrible Oedipus complex contains. Its name tells you. You all know the Greek legend of King Oedipus, who was destined by fate to kill his father and take his mother to wife, who did everything possible to escape the oracle's decree and punished himself by blinding when he learned that he had none the less unwittingly committed both these crimes. I hope many of you may yourselves have felt the shattering effect of the tragedy in which Sophocles has treated the story. The work of the Athenian dramatist exhibits the way in which the long-past deed of Oedipus is gradually brought to light by an investigation ingeniously protracted and fanned into life by ever fresh relays of evidence. To this extent it has a certain resemblance to the progress of a psychoanalysis. In the course of the dialogue Jocasta, the deluded mother and wife, declares herself opposed to the continuance of

of October 15, 1897 (Freud, 1950a, Letter 71). The actual term 'Oedipus complex' was first introduced much later, in a paper on a special type of object-choice (1910h).]

the enquiry. She appeals to the fact that many people have dreamt of lying with their mothers, but that dreams should be despised. We do not despise dreams—least of all, typical dreams which occur to many people; and we do not doubt that the dream referred to by Jocasta has an intimate connection with the strange and terrifying content of the legend.

It is a surprising thing that the tragedy of Sophocles does not call up indignant repudiation in his audience—a reaction similar to that of our simple-minded army doctor but far better justified. For fundamentally it is an amoral work: it absolves men from moral responsibility, exhibits the gods as promoters of crime and shows the impotence of the moral impulses of men which struggle against crime. It might easily be supposed that the material of the legend had in view an indictment of the gods and of fate; and in the hands of Euripides, the critic and enemy of the gods, it would probably have become such an indictment. But with the devout Sophocles there is no question of an application of that kind. The difficulty is overcome by the pious sophistry that to bow to the will of the gods is the highest morality even when it promotes crime. I cannot think that this morality is a strong point of the play, but it has no influence on its effect. It is not to it that the auditor reacts but to the secret sense and content of the legend. He reacts as though by self-analysis he had recognized the Oedipus complex in himself and had unveiled the will of the gods and the oracle as exalted disguises of his own unconscious. It is as though he was obliged to remember the two wishes—to do away with his father and in place of him to take his mother to wife—and to be horrified at them. And he understands the dramatist's voice as though it were saying to him: 'You are struggling in vain against your responsibility and are protesting in vain of what you have done in opposition to these criminal intentions. You are guilty, for you have not been able to destroy them; they still persist in you unconsciously.' And there is psychological truth contained in this. Even if a man has repressed his evil impulses into the unconscious and would like to tell himself afterwards that he is not responsible for them, he is nevertheless bound to be aware of this responsibility as a sense of guilt whose basis is unknown to him.[1]

There can be no doubt that the Oedipus complex may be

[1] [Cf. a paragraph near the end of Lecture XIII, p. 211 above.]

looked upon as one of the most important sources of the sense of guilt by which neurotics are so often tormented. But more than this: in a study of the beginnings of human religion and morality which I published in 1913 under the title of *Totem and Taboo* [Freud, 1912–13] I put forward a suggestion that mankind as a whole may have acquired its sense of guilt, the ultimate source of religion and morality, at the beginning of its history, in connection with the Oedipus complex. I should be very glad to tell you more about this, but I had better leave it on one side. Once one has begun on that topic it is hard to break off; and we must go back to individual psychology.

What, then, can be gathered about the Oedipus complex from the direct observation of children at the time of their making their choice of an object before the latency period? Well, it is easy to see that the little man wants to have his mother all to himself, that he feels the presence of his father as a nuisance, that he is resentful if his father indulges in any signs of affection towards his mother and that he shows satisfaction when his father has gone on a journey or is absent. He will often express his feelings directly in words and promise his mother to marry her. It will be thought that this amounts to little compared to the deeds of Oedipus; but in fact it is enough, it is the same thing at root. Observation is often obscured by the circumstance that on other occasions the same child will simultaneously give evidence of great affection for his father. But contrary—or, as it is better to say, 'ambivalent'[1]—emotional attitudes, which in adults would lead to a conflict, remain compatible with each other for a long time in children, just as later they find a permanent place beside each other in the unconscious. It will also be objected that the little boy's conduct arises from egoistic motives and gives no grounds for postulating an erotic complex: the child's mother attends to all his needs, so that he has an interest in preventing her from looking after anyone else. This also is true; but it will soon become clear that in this situation as in similar ones the egoistic interest[2] is merely affording a point of support to which the erotic

[1] [See below, p. 427 f.]

[2] [This term recurs many times in Lecture XXVI, where some editorial comment is made on it (p. 414).]

trend is attached. The little boy may show the most undisguised sexual curiosity about his mother, he may insist upon sleeping beside her at night, he may force his presence on her while she is dressing or may even make actual attempts at seducing her, as his mother will often notice and report with amusement—all of which puts beyond doubt the erotic nature of his tie with his mother. Nor must it be forgotten that the mother devotes the same attention to a little daughter without producing the same result[1] and that the father often competes with her in looking after the boy and yet fails to gain the same significance as she does. In short, the factor of sexual preference cannot be eliminated from the situation by any criticism. From the standpoint of egoistic interest it would be simply foolish of the little man not to prefer to put up with having two people in his service rather than only one of them.

As you see, I have only described the relation of a *boy* to his father and mother. Things happen in just the same way with little girls, with the necessary changes:[2] an affectionate attachment to her father, a need to get rid of her mother as superfluous and to take her place, a coquetry which already employs the methods of later womanhood—these offer a charming picture, especially in small girls, which makes us forget the possibly grave consequences lying behind this infantile situation. We must not omit to add that the parents themselves often exercise a determining influence on the awakening of a child's Oedipus attitude by themselves obeying the pull of sexual attraction, and that where there are several children the father will give the plainest evidence of his greater affection for his little daughter and the mother for her son. But the spontaneous nature of the Oedipus complex in children cannot be seriously shaken even by this factor.

When other children appear on the scene the Oedipus complex is enlarged into a family complex. This, with fresh support

[1] [See, however, the next footnote.]

[2] [It was not till many years later that Freud became fully aware of the lack of symmetry in the Oedipus relations of the two sexes. This emerged in his paper on 'Some Psychical Consequences of the Anatomical Distinction between the Sexes' (1925*j*) and was elaborated in the later one on 'Female Sexuality' (1931*b*). He discusses the question again in Lecture XXXIII of the *New Introductory Lectures*, p. 576 ff., and lastly in Chapter VII of his posthumous *Outline of Psycho-Analysis* (1940a [1938]), (Norton, 1949).]

from the egoistic sense of injury, gives grounds for receiving the new brothers or sisters with repugnance and for unhesitatingly getting rid of them by a wish. It is even true that as a rule children are far readier to give verbal expression to *these* feelings of hate than to those arising from the parental complex. If a wish of this kind is fulfilled and the undesired addition to the family is removed again shortly afterwards by death, we can discover from a later analysis what an important experience this death has been to the child, even though it need not have remained fixed in his memory. A child who has been put into second place by the birth of a brother or sister, and who is now for the first time almost isolated from his mother, does not easily forgive her this loss of place; feelings which in an adult would be described as greatly embittered arise in him and are often the basis of a permanent estrangement. We have already mentioned [p. 318] that the child's sexual researches, with all their consequences, usually follow from this vital experience of his. As these brothers and sisters grow up, the boy's attitude to them undergoes very significant transformations. He may take his sister as a love-object by way of substitute for his faithless mother. Where there are several brothers, all of them courting a younger sister, situations of hostile rivalry, which are so important for later life, arise already in the nursery. A little girl may find in her elder brother a substitute for her father who no longer takes an affectionate interest in her as he did in her earliest years. Or she may take a younger sister as a substitute for the baby she has vainly wished for from her father.

This and very much else of a similar nature will be shown to you by the direct observation of children and by the consideration of clearly retained memories from childhood uninfluenced by analysis. From this you will conclude among other things that the position of a child in the family order is a factor of extreme importance in determining the shape of his later life and should deserve consideration in every life-history. But, what is more important, in view of this information which can be so easily obtained, you will not be able to recall without a smile the pronouncements of science in explanation of the prohibition of incest. [Cf. p. 210 above.] There is no end to what has been invented on the subject. It has been said that sexual inclination is diverted from members of the same family who are of the opposite sex by the fact of having lived together from childhood; or, again, that a biological purpose of avoiding inbreeding is represented psychically by an innate horror of incest. In all this the fact is entirely overlooked that such an inexorable prohibition of it in law and custom would not be needed if there were any reliable natural barriers against the temptation to incest. The truth is just the opposite. A human being's first choice of an object is regularly an incestuous one, aimed, in the case of the male, at his mother and sister; and it calls for the severest prohibitions to deter this persistent infantile tendency from realization. Among the primitive races still living to-day, among savages, the prohibitions against incest are even very much stricter than among ourselves, and Theodor Reik has only recently shown in a brilliant work [Reik, 1915–16] that the puberty rites of savages, which represent a re-birth, have the sense of releasing the boy from his incestuous bond with his mother and of reconciling him with his father.

Mythology will teach you that incest, which is supposed to be so much detested by humans, is unhesitatingly allowed to the gods. And you may learn from ancient history that incestuous sister-marriage was a sanctified injunction upon the person of the Ruler (among the Egyptian Pharaohs and the Incas of Peru). What was in question was thus a privilege forbidden to the common herd.

Mother-incest was one of the crimes of Oedipus, parricide was the other. It may be remarked in passing that they are also the two great crimes proscribed by totemism, the first socio-religious institution of mankind.[1]

But let us now turn from the direct observation of children to the analytic examination of adults who have become neurotic. What help does analysis give towards a further knowledge of the Oedipus complex? That can be answered in a word. Analysis confirms all that the legend describes. It shows that each of these neurotics has himself been an Oedipus or, what comes to the same thing, has, as a reaction to the complex, become a Hamlet.[2] The analytic account of the Oedipus complex is, of

---

[1] [Cf. Freud's *Totem and Taboo* (1912–13), (Norton, 1952).]

[2] [Freud's earliest published commentary on *Hamlet* (as well as on *Oedipus Rex)* appeared in *The Interpretation of Dreams* (1900a), Chapter V(D).]

course, a magnification and coarsening of the infantile sketch. The hatred of the father, the death-wishes against him, are no longer hinted at timidly, the affection for the mother admits that its aim is to possess her as a woman. Should we really attribute such blatant and extreme emotional impulses to the tender years of childhood, or is analysis deceiving us by an admixture of some new factor? It is not hard to find one. Whenever someone gives an account of a past event, even if he is a historian, we must take into account what he unintentionally puts back into the past from the present or from some intermediate time, thus falsifying his picture of it. In the case of a neurotic it is even a question whether this putting back is an entirely unintentional one; later on we shall have to discover reasons for this and have to do justice in general to the fact of 'retrospective phantasying'.[1] We can easily see, too, that hatred of the father is reinforced by a number of factors arising from later times and circumstances and that the sexual desires towards the mother are cast into forms which must have been alien as yet to a child. But it would be a vain effort to seek to explain the whole Oedipus complex by retrospective phantasying and to attach it to later times. Its infantile core and more or less of its accessories remain as they were confirmed by the direct observation of children.

The clinical fact which meets us behind the form of the Oedipus complex as it is established by analysis is of the highest practical significance. We learn that at puberty, when the sexual instinct first makes its demands in full strength, the old familiar incestuous objects are taken up again and freshly cathected[2] with libido. The infantile object-choice was only a feeble one, but it was a prelude, pointing the direction for the object-choice at puberty. At this point, then, very intense emotional processes come into play, following the direction of the Oedipus complex or reacting against it, processes which, however, since their premises have become intolerable, must

---

[1] [See the latter part of Lecture XXIII.]

[2] ['Besetzt', charged with energy. The concept of 'Besetzungen' (cathexes), charges of psychical energy, is fundamental to Freud's theories. A discussion of it will be found in an Editor's Appendix to Freud's early paper on The Neuro-Psychoses of Defense, (1894a). The term reappears frequently below.]

to a large extent remain apart from consciousness. From this time onwards, the human individual has to devote himself to the great task of detaching himself from his parents, and not until that task is achieved can he cease to be a child and become a member of the social community. For the son this task consists in detaching his libidinal wishes from his mother and employing them for the choice of a real outside love-object, and in reconciling himself with his father if he has remained in opposition to him, or in freeing himself from his pressure if, as a reaction to his infantile rebelliousness, he has become subservient to him. These tasks are set to everyone; and it is remarkable how seldom they are dealt with in an ideal manner —that is, in one which is correct both psychologically and socially. By neurotics, however, no solution at all is arrived at: the son remains all his life bowed beneath his father's authority and he is unable to transfer his libido to an outside sexual object. With the relationship changed round, the same fate can await the daughter. In this sense the Oedipus complex may justly be regarded as the nucleus of the neuroses.[1]

As you may imagine, Gentlemen, I have passed very cursorily over a great number of considerations of both practical and theoretical importance connected with the Oedipus complex. Nor shall I enter into its variations or its possible reversal.[2] Among its remoter connections I will only give you a further hint that it has turned out to have a highly important effect on literary production. In a valuable work Otto Rank [1912b] has shown that dramatists of every period have chosen their material in the main from the Oedipus and incest complex and its variations and disguises. Nor should it be allowed to pass unnoticed that the two criminal wishes of the Oedipus complex were recognized as the true representatives of the uninhibited life of the instincts long before the time of psycho-analysis. Among the writings of the Encyclopaedist Diderot you will find a celebrated dialogue, *Le neveu de Rameau*, which was rendered

[1] [Freud had been using this phrase frequently for several years previously. It appears already in a footnote to Section G of his 'Rat Man' case history (1909d).]

[2] [This last point is most fully dealt with in Chapter III of *The Ego and the Id* (1923b), (Norton, 1960).]

into German by no less a person than Goethe. There you may read this remarkable sentence: 'Si le petit sauvage était aban-donné à lui-même, qu'il conservât toute son imbécillité, et qu'il réunît au peu de raison de l'enfant au berceau la violence des passions de l'homme de trente ans, il tordrait le col à son père et coucherait avec sa mère.'[1]

But there is something else that I cannot pass by. The re-minder of dreams given to us by the mother and wife of Oedipus must not be allowed to remain fruitless. Do you recall the out-come of our dream-analyses—how the wishes that construct dreams are so often of a perverse or incestuous nature or reveal an unsuspected hostility to those who are nearest and dearest to the dreamer? At that time [p. 142] we gave no explanation of the origin of these evil impulses. Now you can find it for yourselves. They are allocations of the libido and object-cathexes[2] which date from early infancy and have long since been abandoned as far as conscious life is concerned, but which prove still to be present at night-time and to be capable of func-tioning in a certain sense. Since, however, everyone, and not only neurotics, experiences these perverse, incestuous and mur-derous dreams, we may conclude that people who are normal to-day have passed along a path of development that has led through the perversions and object-cathexes of the Oedipus complex, that that is the path of normal development and that neurotics merely exhibit to us in a magnified and coarsened form what the analysis of dreams reveals to us in healthy people as well. And this is one of the reasons why I dealt with the study of dreams before that of neurotic symptoms.

[1] ['If the little savage were left to himself, preserving all his foolishness and adding to the small sense of a child in the cradle the violent passions of a man of thirty, he would strangle his father and lie with his mother.' Freud quoted this passage again (in Goethe's German version) in his note on 'The Expert Opinion in the Halsmann Case' (1931d) and again (in French) at the end of Part II of his posthumous Outline of Psycho-Analysis (1940a [1938]), (Norton, 1949).]

[2] [I.e. charges of psychical energy concentrated upon objects. See footnote 2, p. 336 above.]

SOME THOUGHTS ON DEVELOPMENT
AND REGRESSION—AETIOLOGY

Ladies and Gentlemen,—You have heard that the libidinal function goes through a lengthy development before it can, in what is described as the normal manner, be enlisted in the service of reproduction. I should now like to bring to your attention the significance of this fact in the causation of the neuroses.

We are, I think, in agreement with the theories of general pathology in assuming that a development of this kind involves two dangers—first, of *inhibition*, and secondly, of *regression*. That is to say, in view of the general tendency of biological processes to variation, it is bound to be the case that not every preparatory phase will be passed through with equal success and completely superseded: portions of the function will be permanently held back at these early stages, and the total picture of development will be qualified by some amount of developmental inhibition.

Let us look for some analogies to these processes in other fields of knowledge. When, as often happened at early periods of human history, a whole people left their place of domicile and sought a new one, we may be certain that the whole of them did not arrive at the new location. Apart from other losses, it must regularly have happened that small groups or bands of the migrants halted on the way and settled at these stopping-places while the main body went further. Or, as you know, to turn to a nearer comparison, in the highest mammals the male sex-glands, which are originally situated deep in the abdominal cavity, start upon a migration at a particular stage of intra-uterine life, which brings them almost directly under the skin of the pelvic extremity. As a consequence of this migration, we find in a number of male individuals that one of these paired organs has remained behind in the pelvic cavity, or that it has become permanently lodged in what is known as the inguinal canal, through which both organs must pass in the course of their migration, or at least that this canal has remained open, though it should normally close up after the sex-glands have completed their change of situation. Or again, when as a young student I was engaged under von Brücke's direction on my first piece of scientific work, I was concerned with the origin of the posterior nerve-roots in the spinal cord of a small fish of very archaic structure;[1] I found that the nerve-fibres of these roots have their origin in large cells in the posterior horn of the grey matter, which is no longer the case in other vertebrates. But I also discovered soon afterwards that nerve-cells of this kind are present outside the grey matter the whole way to what is known as the spinal ganglion of the posterior root; and from this I inferred that the cells of these masses of ganglia had migrated from the spinal cord along the roots of the nerves. This is also shown by their evolutionary history. But in this small fish the whole path of their migration was demonstrated by the cells that had remained behind.[2]

If you go into the matter more closely, you will have no difficulty in detecting the weak points in these comparisons. I will therefore declare without more ado that I regard it as possible in the case of every particular sexual trend that some portions of it have stayed behind at earlier stages of its development, even though other portions may have reached their final goal. You will recognize here that we are picturing every such trend as a current which has been continuous since the beginning of life but which we have divided up, to some extent artificially, into separate successive advances. Your impression that these ideas stand in need of greater clarification is justified; but to attempt it would take us too far afield. Let me further make it clear that we propose to describe the lagging behind of a part trend at an earlier stage as a *fixation*—a fixation, that is, of the instinct.

The second danger in a development by stages of this sort lies in the fact that the portions which have proceeded further may also easily return retrogressively to one of these earlier stages—what we describe as a *regression*. The trend will find itself led into a regression of this kind if the exercise of its function—

---

[1] [The larval form of the brook lamprey.]

[2] [This is a summary of the findings of two of Freud's very first papers (1877a and 1878a). Cf. his own earlier abstracts of them (1897b, Nos. II and III).]

that is, the attainment of its aim of satisfaction—is met, in its later or more highly developed form, by powerful external obstacles. It is plausible to suppose that fixation and regression are not independent of each other. The stronger the fixations on its path of development, the more readily will the function evade external difficulties by regressing to the fixations—the more incapable, therefore, does the developed function turn out to be of resisting external obstacles in its course. Consider that, if a people which is in movement has left strong detachments behind at the stopping-places on its migration, it is likely that the more advanced parties will be inclined to retreat to these stopping-places if they have been defeated or have come up against a superior enemy. But they will also be in the greater danger of being defeated the more of their number they have left behind on their migration.

It is important for your understanding of the neuroses that you should not leave this relation between fixation and regression out of sight. This will give you a firmer footing in facing the question of how the neuroses are caused—the question of the aetiology of the neuroses which we shall shortly have to meet.

For the moment we will dwell a little longer on regression. After what you have learnt of the development of the libidinal function, you will be prepared to hear that there are regressions of two sorts: a return to the objects first cathected by the libido, which, as we know, are of an incestuous nature, and a return of the sexual organization as a whole to earlier stages. Both sorts are found in the transference neuroses [p. 299] and play a great part in their mechanism. In particular, a return to the first incestuous objects of the libido is a feature that is found in neurotics with positively fatiguing regularity. There is much more to be said about regressions of the libido itself when we take into account as well another group of neuroses, the narcissistic ones, which for the time being we do not intend to do.[1] These disorders give us access to other developmental processes of the libidinal function which we have not yet mentioned, and show us correspondingly new sorts of regression as well. But above all I think I ought to warn you now not to confuse *regression* with *repression* and help you to form a clear idea

[1] [They are discussed in Lecture XXVI.]

of the relations between the two processes.[1] Repression, as you will recall [p. 294 ff.], is the process by which an act which is admissible to consciousness, one, therefore, which belongs to the system *Pcs.*, is made unconscious—is pushed back, therefore, into the system *Ucs.*[2] And we equally speak of repression if the unconscious mental act is altogether forbidden access to the neighbouring preconscious system and is turned back at the threshold by the censorship. Thus the concept of repression involves no relation to sexuality: I must ask you to take special note of that. It indicates a purely psychological process, which we can characterize still better if we call it a 'topographical' one. By this we intend to say that it is concerned with the psychical regions which we have assumed to exist, or, if we drop this clumsy working hypothesis, with the construction of the mental apparatus out of distinct psychical systems.

The comparison we have proposed has drawn our attention for the first time to the fact that we have not hitherto been using the word 'regression' in its general sense but in a quite special one. If we give it its general sense—of a return from a higher to a lower stage of development—then repression too can be subsumed under the concept of regression, for it too can be described as a return to an earlier and deeper stage in the development of a psychical act. In the case of repression, however, this retrogressive movement does not concern us, since we also speak of repression, in the *dynamic* sense, when a psychical act is held back at the lower, unconscious, stage. The fact is that repression is a topographico-dynamic concept, while regression is a purely descriptive one. What we have hitherto spoken of as regression, however, and have related to fixation, has meant exclusively a return of the libido to earlier stopping-places in its development—something, that is, entirely different in its nature from repression and entirely independent of it. Nor can we call regression of the libido a purely psychical process and we cannot tell where we should localize it in the

[1] [The extremely close resemblance of the two words to each other is an added misfortune peculiar to English. In German no such similarity exists between *'Regression'* and *'Verdrängung'*.]

[2] [*'Pcs.'* and *'Ucs.'* are the abbreviations first introduced by Freud in the seventh chapter of *The Interpretation of Dreams* (1900a), for the preconscious and unconscious mental systems.]

mental apparatus. And though it is true that it exercises the most powerful influence on mental life, yet the most prominent factor in it is the organic one.

Discussions like this, Gentlemen, are bound to become somewhat arid. So let us turn to clinical material in order to find applications of it that will be a little more impressive. Hysteria and obsessional neurosis are, as you know, the two chief representatives of the group of transference neuroses. Now it is true that in hysteria there is a regression of the libido to the primary incestuous sexual objects and that this occurs quite regularly; but there is as good as no regression to an earlier stage of the sexual organization. To offset this, the chief part in the mechanism of hysteria is played by repression. If I might venture to complete what we already know for certain about this neurosis by making a construction, I might explain the position thus. The unification of the component instincts under the primacy of the genitals has been accomplished; but its results come up against the resistance of the preconscious system which is linked with consciousness. Thus the genital organization holds good for the unconscious, but not in the same way for the preconscious; and this rejection on the part of the preconscious brings about a picture which has certain resemblances to the state of things before genital primacy. But it is nevertheless something quite different.

Of the two kinds of regression of the libido, that to an earlier phase of the sexual organization is by far the more striking. Since this is absent in hysteria, and since our whole view of the neuroses is still far too much under the influence of the study of hysteria, which was chronologically the first, the significance of libidinal regression also became clear to us far later than that of repression. We must be prepared to find that our views will be subjected to still further extensions and revaluations when we are able to take into consideration not only hysteria and obsessional neurosis but also the other, narcissistic neuroses.

In obsessional neurosis, on the contrary, it is the regression of the libido to the preliminary stage of the sadistic-anal organization that is the most striking fact and the one which is decisive for what is manifested in symptoms. The love-impulse is obliged, when this has happened, to disguise itself as a sadistic impulse. The obsessional idea 'I should like to kill you', when it has been freed from certain additions which are not a matter of chance but are indispensable, means at bottom nothing other than 'I should like to enjoy you in love'. If you consider further that there has been a simultaneous regression in regard to the object, so that these impulses apply only to those who are nearest and dearest to the patient, you can form some idea of the horror which these obsessions arouse in him and at the same time of the alien appearance which they present to his conscious perception. But repression, too, plays a great part in the mechanism of these neuroses, though in a cursory introduction like ours this is not easily demonstrated. A regression of the libido without repression would never produce a neurosis but would lead to a perversion. From this you can see that repression is the process which is most peculiar to neuroses and is most characteristic of them. Perhaps I may have an opportunity later of telling you what we know of the mechanism of the perversions, and you will see that in their case too things are not so simple as we should be glad to make them out.[1]

I think, Gentlemen, that you will best come to terms with what you have just been told about fixation and regression of the libido if you will regard it as a preparation for research into the aetiology of the neuroses. Hitherto I have only given you one piece of information about this: namely that people fall ill of a neurosis if they are deprived of the possibility of satisfying their libido—that they fall ill owing to 'frustration', as I put it —and that their symptoms are precisely a substitute for their frustrated satisfaction. [Cf. p. 300.] This is not supposed to mean, of course, that every frustration of a libidinal satisfaction makes the person it affects neurotic, but merely that the factor of frustration could be discerned in every case of neurosis that has been examined. Thus [as logicians would say] the proposition is not convertible. No doubt, too, you will have understood that this assertion does not claim to reveal the whole secret of the aetiology of neuroses but is only bringing into prominence one important and indispensable determinant.

In further pursuing the discussion of this thesis, are we to

[1] [This seems to be one of the points to which, as he remarks at the end of these lectures (p. 463), he had no opportunity of returning.]

consider the nature of the frustration or the peculiar character of those who are affected by it? It is extremely seldom, after all, that frustration is universal and absolute. In order to operate pathogenically it must no doubt affect the mode of satisfaction which alone the subject desires, of which alone he is capable. There are in general very many ways of tolerating deprivation of libidinal satisfaction without falling ill as a result. In the first place, we know people who are able to put up with a deprivation of this kind without being injured: they are not happy, they suffer from longing, but they do not fall ill. Next, we must bear in mind that the sexual instinctual impulses in particular are extraordinarily *plastic*, if I may so express it. One of them can take the place of another, one of them can take over another's intensity; if the satisfaction of one of them is frustrated by reality, the satisfaction of another can afford complete compensation. They are related to one another like a network of intercommunicating channels filled with a liquid;[1] and this is so in spite of their being subject to the primacy of the genitals —a state of affairs that is not at all easily combined in a single picture. Further, the component instincts of sexuality, as well as the sexual current which is compounded from them, exhibit a large capacity for changing their object, for taking another in its place—and one, therefore, that is more easily attainable. This displaceability and readiness to accept a substitute must operate powerfully against the pathogenic effect of a frustration. Among these protective processes against falling ill owing to deprivation there is one which has gained special cultural significance. It consists in the sexual trend abandoning its aim of obtaining a component or a reproductive pleasure and taking on another which is related genetically to the abandoned one but is itself no longer sexual and must be described as social. We call this process 'sublimation', in accordance with the general estimate that places social aims higher than the sexual ones, which are at bottom self-interested. Sublimation is, incidentally, only a special case of the way in which sexual trends are attached to other, non-sexual ones [cf. p. 313]. We shall have to discuss it again in another connection.[2]

You may now have an impression that deprivation has been

[1] [Cf. footnote 1 above, p. 310.]
[2] [See the end of the next lecture, p. 376.]

reduced to insignificance owing to all these methods of tolerating it. But no, it retains its pathogenic power. The countermeasures are on the whole insufficient. There is a limit to the amount of unsatisfied libido that human beings on the average can put up with. The plasticity or free mobility of the libido is by no means fully preserved in everyone, and sublimation is never able to deal with more than a certain fraction of libido, quite apart from the fact that many people are gifted with only a small amount of capacity to sublimate. The most important of these limitations is evidently that upon the mobility of the libido, since it makes a person's satisfaction depend on the attainment of only a very small number of aims and objects. You have only to recall that an imperfect development of the libido leaves behind it very fertile and perhaps, too, very numerous libidinal fixations to early phases of the organization and of the finding of objects, which are for the most part incapable of real satisfaction, and you will recognize in libidinal fixation the second powerful factor which combines with frustration as the cause of illness. You can declare, as a schematic abbreviation, that libidinal fixation represents the predisposing, internal factor in the aetiology of the neuroses, while frustration represents the accidental, external one.

I take the opportunity here of warning you against taking sides in a quite unnecessary dispute. In scientific matters people are very fond of selecting one portion of the truth, putting it in the place of the whole and of then disputing the rest, which is no less true, in favour of this one portion. In just this way a number of schools of opinion have already split off from the psycho-analytic movement, some of which recognize the egoistic instincts while disavowing the sexual ones, and others attribute importance to the influence of the real tasks of life while overlooking the individual's past[1]—and others besides. Now here we have a similar occasion for pointing a contrast and starting a controversy. Are neuroses *exogenous* or *endogenous* illnesses? Are they the inevitable result of a particular constitution or the product of certain detrimental (traumatic) experiences in life? More particularly, are they brought about by fixation of the

[1] [The schools of Adler and Jung had been discussed at some length by Freud in Section III of his 'History of the Psycho-Analytic Movement' (1914d), (Norton, 1966).]

libido (and the other features of the sexual constitution) or by the pressure of frustration? This dilemma seems to me no more sensible on the whole than another that I might put to you: does a baby come about through being begotten by its father or conceived by its mother? Both determinants are equally indispensable, as you will justly reply. In the matter of the causation of the neuroses the relation, if not precisely the same, is very similar. As regards their causation, instances of neurotic illness fall into a series within which the two factors—sexual constitution and experience, or, if you prefer it, fixation of the libido and frustration—are represented in such a manner that if there is more of the one there is less of the other. At one end of the series are the extreme cases of which you could say with conviction: these people, in consequence of the singular development of their libido, would have fallen ill in any case, whatever they had experienced and however carefully their lives had been sheltered. At the other end there are the cases, as to which, on the contrary, you would have had to judge that they would certainly have escaped falling ill if their lives had not brought them into this or that situation. In the cases lying within the series a greater or lesser amount of predisposition in the sexual constitution is combined with a lesser or greater amount of detrimental experience in their lives. Their sexual constitution would not have led them into a neurosis if they had not had these experiences, and these experiences would not have had a traumatic effect on them if their libido had been otherwise disposed. In this series I can perhaps allow a certain preponderance in significance to the predisposing factors; but even that admission depends on how far you choose to extend the frontiers of neurotic illness.

I propose, Gentlemen, that we should name a series of this kind a 'complemental series', and I forewarn you that we shall have occasion to construct others of the same kind.[1]

[1] [This seems to be Freud's first use of the actual term 'complemental series'. The concept goes back a long way. It appears in a somewhat different form as an 'aetiological equation' in the second paper on anxiety neurosis (1895f), where some discussion of the history of the notion will be found in an Editor's Note. It reappears at two points below (pp. 362 and 364), and turns up again in the New Introductory Lectures and in Essay III, Part I (C), of Moses and Monotheism (1939a).]

The tenacity with which the libido adheres to particular trends and objects—what may be described as the 'adhesiveness' of the libido—makes its appearance as an independent factor, varying from individual to individual, whose determinants are quite unknown to us, but whose significance for the aetiology of the neuroses we shall certainly no longer underestimate.[1] We should not, on the other hand, over-estimate the intimacy of this connection. For a similar 'adhesiveness' of the libido occurs (for unknown reasons) under numerous conditions in normal people, and it is found as a determining factor in people who are in one sense the contrary of neurotics—in perverts. It was known even before the days of psycho-analysis (cf. Binet [1888]) that in the anamnesis of perverts a very early impression of an abnormal instinctual trend or choice of object was quite often found, to which the subject's libido remained attached all through his life. It is often impossible to say what it is that enabled this impression to exercise such an intense attraction on the libido. I will describe a case of this sort which I myself observed.

The subject was a man who is to-day quite indifferent to the genitals and other attractions of women, but who can be plunged into irresistible sexual excitement only by a foot of a particular form wearing a shoe. He can recall an event from his sixth year which was decisive for the fixation of his libido. He was sitting on a stool beside the governess who was to give him lessons in English. The governess, who was an elderly, dried-up, plain-looking spinster, with pale-blue eyes and a snub nose, had something wrong with her foot that day, and on that account kept it, wearing a velvet slipper, stretched out on a cushion. Her leg itself was most decently concealed. A thin, scraggy foot, like the one he had then seen belonging to his governess, thereupon became (after a timid attempt at normal sexual activity at puberty) his only sexual object; and the man was irresistibly attracted if a foot of this kind was associated with other features besides which recalled the type of the English governess. This fixation of his libido, however, made him, not

[1] [This factor, under various names, was discussed by Freud at least as early as in the first edition of the *Three Essays* (1905d). A number of references are given in an Editor's footnote to the paper on a case of paranoia (1915f).]

into a neurotic, but into a pervert—what we call a foot-fetishist.[1] You see, then, that although an excessive, and more-over premature, fixation of the libido is indispensable for the causation of neuroses, the area of its effects extends far beyond the field of the neuroses. This determinant, too, is as little decisive in itself as is the frustration which we have already talked about.

Thus the problem of the causation of the neuroses seems to grow more complicated. In fact, psycho-analytic investigation makes us acquainted with a fresh factor, which is not taken into account in our aetiological series and which we can recognize easiest in cases in which what has hitherto been a healthy condition is suddenly disturbed by an onset of neurotic illness. In such people we regularly find indications of a contention between wishful impulses or, as we are in the habit of saying, a psychical conflict. One part of the personality champions certain wishes while another part opposes them and fends them off. Without such a conflict there is no neurosis. There would not seem to be anything peculiar in this. Our mental life is, as you know, perpetually agitated by conflicts which we have to settle. No doubt, therefore, special conditions must be fulfilled if such a conflict is to become pathogenic. We must ask what these conditions are, between what mental powers these patho-genic conflicts are played out, and what the relation is between the conflict and the other causative factors.

I hope to be able to give you adequate replies to these ques-tions, even though the replies may be reduced to schematic dimensions. The conflict is conjured up by frustration, as a result of which the libido, deprived of satisfaction, is driven to look for other objects and paths. The necessary precondition of the conflict is that these other paths and objects arouse dis-pleasure in one part of the personality, so that a veto is imposed which makes the new method of satisfaction impossible as it stands. From this point the construction of symptoms pursues

[1] [Two or three years earlier Freud had read a paper to the Vienna Psycho-Analytical Society on a similar case—possibly, even, the same one. The paper has not yet been published, but is summarized by Ernest Jones in the second volume of his Freud biography (1955, 342–3). An account of Freud's many dis-cussions of fetishism is given in the Editor's Note to the paper bearing that title (1927e).]

its course, which we shall follow later.[1] The repudiated libidinal trends nevertheless succeed in getting their way by certain roundabout paths, though not, it is true, without taking the objection into account by submitting to some distortions and mitigations. The roundabout paths are those taken by the construction of symptoms; the symptoms are the fresh or substitute satisfaction which has become necessary owing to the fact of frustration.

The meaning of psychical conflict can be adequately expressed in another way by saying that for an *external* frustration to become pathogenic an *internal* frustration must be added to it. In that case, of course, the external and internal frustration relate to different paths and objects. The external frustration removes one possibility of satisfaction and the internal frustration seeks to exclude *another* possibility, about which the conflict then breaks out. I prefer this way of representing the matter because it has a secret content. For it hints at the probability that the internal impediments arose from real external obstacles during the prehistoric periods of human development.[2]

But what are the powers from which the objection to the libidinal trend arises? What is the other party to the pathogenic conflict? These powers, to put it quite generally, are the non-sexual instinctual forces. We class them together as the 'ego-instincts'.[3] The psycho-analysis of the transference-neuroses gives us no easy access to a further dissecting of them; at most we come to know them to some extent by the resistances which oppose analysis. The pathogenic conflict is thus one between the ego-instincts and the sexual instincts. In a whole number of cases, it looks as though there might also be a conflict between different purely sexual trends. But in essence that is the same thing; for, of the two sexual trends that are in conflict, one is always, as we might say, 'ego-syntonic',[4] while the other provokes the ego's defence. It therefore still remains a conflict between the ego and sexuality.

[1] [In the following lecture.]

[2] [Cf. p. 371 below. The whole question of frustration as a cause of neurosis was discussed by Freud in a paper on 'Types of Onset of Neurosis' (1912c).]

[3] [An account of Freud's use of this term is given in the Editor's Note to 'Instincts and their Vicissitudes' (1915c).]

[4] ['*Ichgerecht*', i.e. in consonance with the ego.]

Over and over again, Gentlemen, when psycho-analysis has claimed that some mental event is the product of the sexual instincts, it has been angrily pointed out to it by way of defence that human beings do not consist only of sexuality, that there are instincts and interests in mental life other than sexual ones, that it ought not to derive 'everything' from sexuality, and so on. Well, it is most gratifying for once in a way to find ourselves in agreement with our opponents. Psycho-analysis has never forgotten that there are instinctual forces as well which are not sexual. It was based on a sharp distinction between the sexual instincts and the ego-instincts, and, in spite of all objections, it has maintained not that the neuroses are derived from sexuality but that their origin is due to a conflict between the ego and sexuality. Nor has it any conceivable reason for disputing the existence or significance of the ego-instincts while it pursues the part played by the sexual instincts in illness and in ordinary life. It has simply been its fate to begin by concerning itself with the sexual instincts because the transference neuroses made them the most easily accessible to examination and because it was incumbent on it to study what other people had neglected.

Nor is it a fact that psycho-analysis has paid no attention whatever to the non-sexual part of the personality. It is precisely the distinction between the ego and sexuality which has enabled us to recognize with special clarity that the ego-instincts pass through an important process of development—a development which is neither completely independent of the libido nor without a counter-effect upon it. Nevertheless, we are far less well acquainted with the development of the ego than of the libido, since it is only the study of the narcissistic neuroses[1] that promises to give us an insight into the structure of the ego. We already have before us, however, a notable attempt by Ferenczi [1913] to make a theoretical construction of the stages of development of the ego, and there are at least two points at which we have a solid basis for judging that development. It is not our belief that a person's libidinal interests are from the first in opposition to his self-preservative interests; on the contrary, the ego endeavours at every stage to remain in harmony with its sexual organization as it is at the time and to fit itself into it. The succession of the different phases of libidinal

[1] [Discussed in Lecture XXVI.]

development probably follows a prescribed programme. But the possibility cannot be rejected that this course of events can be influenced by the ego, and we may expect equally to find a certain parallelism, a certain correspondence, between the developmental phases of the ego and the libido; indeed a disturbance of that correspondence might provide a pathogenic factor. We are now faced by the important consideration of how the ego behaves if its libido leaves a strong fixation behind at some point in its (the libido's) development. The ego may accept this and consequently become to that extent perverse or, what is the same thing, infantile. It may, however, adopt a non-compliant attitude to the libido's settling down in this position, in which case the ego experiences a *repression* where the libido has experienced a *fixation*.

Thus we discover that the third factor in the aetiology of the neuroses, the *tendency to conflict*, is as much dependent on the development of the ego as on that of the libido. Our insight into the causation of the neuroses is thus made more complete. First there is the most general precondition—frustration; next, fixation of the libido which forces it into particular directions; and thirdly, the tendency to conflict, arising from the development of the ego, which rejects these libidinal impulses. The situation, then, is not so very confused and hard to penetrate as it probably seemed to you during the course of my remarks. It is true, however, that we shall find we have not yet finished with it. There is something new to be added and something already familiar to be further examined.

In order to demonstrate to you the influence which the development of the ego has upon the construction of conflicts and upon the causation of neuroses, I should like to put an example before you—one which, it is true, is a complete invention but which is nowhere divorced from probability. I shall describe it (on the basis of the title of one of Nestroy's farces[1]) as 'In the Basement and on the First Floor'. The caretaker of the house inhabits the basement and its landlord, a

[1] [Johann Nestroy (1801–62), famous in Vienna for his comedies and farces. The literal translation of Nestroy's title would be 'On the Ground Floor and on the First Floor': the difference in the social habits of nineteenth-century Vienna and London calls for the alteration.]

wealthy and respectable gentleman, the first floor. Both have children, and we may suppose that the landlord's little daughter is allowed to play, without any supervision, with the proletarian girl. It might very easily happen, then, that the children's games would take on a 'naughty'—that is to say, a sexual—character, that they would play at 'father and mother', that they would watch each other at their most private business and excite each other's genitals. The caretaker's girl, though only five or six years old, would have had an opportunity of observing a good deal of adult sexuality, and she might well play the part of seductress in all this. These experiences, even if they were not continued over a long period, would be enough to set certain sexual impulses to work in the two children; and, after their games together had ceased, these impulses would for several years afterwards find expression in masturbation. So much for their experiences in common; the final outcome in the two children will be very different. The caretaker's daughter will continue her masturbation, perhaps, till her menstrual periods begin and she will then give it up with no difficulty. A few years later she will find a lover and perhaps have a baby. She will take up some occupation or other, possibly become a popular figure on the stage and end up as an aristocrat. Her career is more likely to be less brilliant, but in any case she will go through her life undamaged by the early exercise of her sexuality and free from neurosis. With the landlord's little girl things will be different. At an early stage and while she is still a child she will get an idea that she has done something wrong; after a short time, but perhaps only after a severe struggle, she will give up her masturbatory satisfaction, but she will nevertheless still have some sense of oppression about her. When in her later girlhood she is in a position to learn something of human sexual intercourse, she will turn away from it with unexplained disgust and prefer to remain in ignorance. And now she will probably be subject to a fresh emergence of an irresistible pressure to masturbate of which she will not dare to complain. During the years in which she should exercise a feminine attraction upon some man, a neurosis breaks out in her which cheats her of marriage and her hopes in life. If after this an analysis succeeds in gaining an insight into her neurosis, it will turn out that the well-brought-up, intelligent and high-minded girl has completely repressed her sexual impulses, but that these, unconscious to her, are still attached to her petty experiences with her childhood friend.

The difference between the lives of these two, in spite of their having had the same experience, rests on the fact that the ego of one of them underwent a development with which the other never met. Sexual activity seemed to the caretaker's daughter just as natural and harmless in later life as it had in childhood. The landlord's daughter came under the influence of education and accepted its demands. From the suggestions offered to it, her ego constructed ideals of feminine purity and abstinence which are incompatible with sexual activity; her intellectual education reduced her interest in the feminine part which she was destined to play. Owing to this higher moral and intellectual development of her ego she came into conflict with the demands of her sexuality.

I will dwell for a little to-day on yet another point in ego-development, partly because I have some remoter aims in view, but also because what follows is precisely calculated to justify the sharp separation between the ego-instincts and the sexual instincts which we favour but which is not self-evident. In forming our judgement of the two courses of development— both of the ego and of the libido—we must lay emphasis on a consideration which has not often hitherto been taken into account. For both of them are at bottom heritages, abbreviated recapitulations of the development which all mankind has passed through from its primaeval days over long periods of time. In the case of the development of the libido, this *phylogenetic* origin is, I venture to think, immediately obvious. Consider how in one class of animals the genital apparatus is brought into the closest relation to the mouth, while in another it cannot be distinguished from the excretory apparatus, and in yet others it is linked to the motor organs—all of which you will find attractively set out in W. Bölsche's valuable book [1911–13]. Among animals one can find, so to speak in petrified form, every species of perversion of the sexual organization. In the case of human beings, however, this phylogenetic point of view is partly veiled by the fact that what is at bottom inherited is nevertheless freshly acquired in the development of the individual,[1] probably because the same conditions which originally necessitated its acquisition persist and continue to operate upon each individual. I should like to add that originally the operation of these conditions was creative but that it is now evocative. Besides this, there is no doubt that the prescribed course of development can be disturbed and altered in each individual by recent external influences. But we know the power which forced a development of this kind upon humanity and maintains its pressure in the same direction to-day. It is, once again, frustration by reality, or, if we are to give it its true, grand name, the pressure of vital needs—Necessity ('Aνάγκη [Ananke]). She has been a strict educator and has made much out of us. The neurotics are among those of her children to whom her strictness has brought evil results; but that is a risk with all education. This appreciation of the necessities of life need not, incidentally, weigh against the importance of 'internal developmental trends', if such can be shown to be present.

Now it is a very noteworthy fact that the sexual instincts and the self-preservative instincts do not behave in the same way towards real necessity.[2] The self-preservative instincts, and everything to do with them, are much easier to educate: they learn early to comply with necessity and to arrange their developments in accordance with the instructions of reality. This is intelligible, since they could not obtain the objects they need in any other way; and without those objects the individual would inevitably perish. The sexual instincts are harder to educate, for at first they have no need of an object. Since they are attached like parasites, as it were, to the other bodily functions, and find their satisfaction auto-erotically on the subject's own body, they are to begin with withdrawn from the educative influence of real necessity, and they retain this characteristic of being self-willed and inaccessible to influence (what we

---

[1] [This is an echo of a couplet from Goethe's *Faust,* which was a favourite quotation of Freud's. See, for instance, *Totem and Taboo* (1912–13), (Norton, 1952), p. 158, and the closing sentences of his unfinished *Outline of Psycho-Analysis* (1940a [1938]), (Norton, 1949).]

[2] ['*Reale Not*', i.e. the exigencies imposed by reality. For what follows, cf. paragraph (3) of 'Formulations on the Two Principles of Mental Functioning' (1911b).]

describe as being 'unreasonable') in most people in some respect all through their lives. Moreover, as a rule the educability of a youthful individual is at an end when his sexual needs arise in their full strength. Educators are aware of this and act accordingly; but the findings of psycho-analysis may perhaps also induce them to shift the main impact of education on to the earliest years of childhood, from infancy onwards. The little creature is often completed by the fourth or fifth year of life, and after that merely brings gradually to light what is already within him.

In order to appreciate the full significance of the difference which I have pointed out between the two groups of instincts, we shall have to go back a long way and introduce one of those considerations which deserve to be described as *economic* [p. 275 above]. This leads us to one of the most important, but unluckily also one of the most obscure, regions of psycho-analysis. We may ask whether in the operation of our mental apparatus a main purpose can be detected, and we may reply as a first approximation that that purpose is directed to obtaining pleasure. It seems as though our total mental activity is directed towards achieving pleasure and avoiding unpleasure —that it is automatically regulated by the *pleasure principle*.[1] We should of all things like to know, then, what determines the generation of pleasure and unpleasure; but that is just what we are ignorant of. We can only venture to say this much: that pleasure is *in some way* connected with the diminution, reduction or extinction of the amounts of stimulus prevailing in the mental apparatus, and that similarly unpleasure is connected with their increase. An examination of the most intense pleasure which is accessible to human beings, the pleasure of accomplishing the sexual act, leaves little doubt on this point. Since in such processes related to pleasure it is a question of what happens to *quantities* of mental excitation or energy, we call considerations of this kind economic. It will be noticed that we can describe the tasks and achievements of the mental apparatus in another and more general way than by stressing the acquisition of pleasure. We can say that the mental apparatus serves the purpose of mastering and disposing of the amounts of stimulus and sums of excitation that impinge on it from outside and

[1] [See the next footnote.]

inside.[1] It is immediately obvious that the sexual instincts, from beginning to end of their development, work towards obtaining pleasure; they retain their original function unaltered. The other instincts, the ego-instincts, have the same aim to start with. But under the influence of the instructress Necessity, they soon learn to replace the pleasure principle by a modification of it. For them the task of avoiding unpleasure turns out to be almost as important as that of obtaining pleasure. The ego discovers that it is inevitable for it to renounce immediate satisfaction, to postpone the obtaining of pleasure, to put up with a little unpleasure and to abandon certain sources of pleasure altogether. An ego thus educated has become 'reasonable'; it no longer lets itself be governed by the pleasure principle, but obeys the *reality principle*,[2] which also at bottom seeks to obtain pleasure, but pleasure which is assured through taking account of reality, even though it is pleasure postponed and diminished.

The transition from the pleasure principle to the reality principle is one of the most important steps forward in the ego's development. We know already that it is only late and unwillingly that the sexual instincts join in this piece of development, and we shall hear later the consequences for human beings of the fact that their sexuality is content with such a loose connection with external reality. And now in conclusion one last remark on this subject. If man's ego has its process of development like the libido, you will not be surprised to hear that there are also 'regressions of the ego', and you will be anxious to know too what part may be played in neurotic illnesses by this return of the ego to earlier phases of its development.[3]

[1] [This is sometimes referred to as the 'principle of constancy'. It, and the related 'pleasure principle', are discussed in an Editor's Appendix to Freud's first paper on the neuro-psychoses of defence (1894*a*). See also the footnote on p. 375 below.]

[2] [The term appears first in 'Formulations on the Two Principles of Mental Functioning' (1911*b*), the Editor's Note to which traces the origin of the concept.]

[3] [Some account of the development of Freud's views on regression and of his various uses of the term will be found in an Editor's note at the end of Part I of the 'Project' of 1895.]

THE PATHS TO THE FORMATION
OF SYMPTOMS

LADIES AND GENTLEMEN,—For laymen the symptoms constitute the essence of a disease and its cure consists in the removal of the symptoms. Physicians attach importance to distinguishing the symptoms from the disease and declare that getting rid of the symptoms does not amount to curing the disease. But the only tangible thing left of the disease after the symptoms have been got rid of is the capacity to form new symptoms. For that reason we will for the moment adopt the layman's position and assume that to unravel the symptoms means the same thing as to understand the disease.

Symptoms—and of course we are dealing now with psychical (or psychogenic) symptoms and psychical illness—are acts detrimental, or at least useless, to the subject's life as a whole, often complained of by him as unwelcome and bringing unpleasure or suffering to him. The main damage they do resides in the mental expenditure which they themselves involve and in the further expenditure that becomes necessary for fighting against them. Where there is an extensive formation of symptoms, these two sorts of expenditure can result in an extraordinary impoverishment of the subject in regard to the mental energy available to him and so in paralysing him for all the important tasks of life. Since this outcome depends mainly on the *quantity* of the energy which is thus absorbed, you will easily see that 'being ill' is in its essence a practical concept. But if you take up a theoretical point of view and disregard this matter of quantity, you may quite well say that we are *all* ill— that is, neurotic—since the preconditions for the formation of symptoms can also be observed in normal people.

We already know that neurotic symptoms are the outcome of a conflict which arises over a new method of satisfying the libido [p. 349]. The two forces which have fallen out meet once again in the symptom and are reconciled, as it were, by the compromise of the symptom that has been constructed. It is for that reason, too, that the symptom is so resistant: it is supported from both sides. We also know that one of the two partners to the conflict is the unsatisfied libido which has been repulsed by reality and must now seek for other paths to its satisfaction. If reality remains relentless even though the libido is ready to take another object in place of the one that has been refused to it, then it will finally be compelled to take the path of regression and strive to find satisfaction either in one of the organizations which it has already outgrown or from one of the objects which it has earlier abandoned. The libido is lured into the path of regression by the fixation which it has left behind it at these points in its development.

The path to perversion branches off sharply from that to neurosis. If these regressions rouse no objection from the ego, no neurosis will come about either; and the libido will arrive at some real, even though no longer normal, satisfaction. But if the ego, which has under its control not only consciousness but also the approaches to motor innervation and accordingly to the realization of mental desires, does not agree with these regressions, conflict will follow. The libido is, as it were, cut off and must try to escape in some direction where, in accordance with the requirements of the pleasure principle, it can find a discharge for its cathexis of energy. It must withdraw from the ego. An escape of this kind is offered it by the fixations on the path of its development which it has now entered on regressively—fixations from which the ego had protected itself in the past by repressions. By cathecting these repressed positions as it flows backward, the libido has withdrawn from the ego and its laws, and has at the same time renounced all the education it has acquired under the ego's influence. It was docile so long as satisfaction beckoned to it; but under the double pressure of external and internal frustration it becomes refractory, and recalls earlier and better times. Such is the libido's fundamentally unchangeable character. The ideas to which it now transfers its energy as a cathexis belong to the system of the unconscious and are subject to the processes which are possible there, particularly to condensation and displacement. In this way conditions are established which completely resemble those in dream-construction. The dream proper,

which has been completed in the unconscious and is the fulfilment of an unconscious wishful phantasy, is brought up against
a portion of (pre)conscious activity which exercises the office of
censorship and which, when it has been indemnified, permits
the formation of the manifest dream as a compromise. In the
same way, what represents[1] the libido in the unconscious has
to reckon with the power of the preconscious ego. The opposition which had been raised against it in the ego pursues it as an
'anticathexis'[2] and compels it to choose a form of expression
which can at the same time become an expression of the opposition itself. Thus the symptom emerges as a many-times-distorted
derivative of the unconscious libidinal wish-fulfilment, an ingeniously chosen piece of ambiguity with two meanings in
complete mutual contradiction. In this last respect, however,
there is a distinction between the construction of a dream and of
a symptom. For in dream-formation the preconscious purpose
is merely concerned to preserve sleep, to allow nothing that
would disturb it to make its way into consciousness; it does not
insist upon calling out sharply 'No! on the contrary!' to the
unconscious wishful impulse. It can afford to be more tolerant
because the situation of someone sleeping is less perilous. The
state of sleep in itself bars any outlet into reality.

You see, then, that the libido's escape under conditions of
conflict is made possible by the presence of fixations. The
regressive cathexis of these fixations leads to the circumvention
of the repression and to a discharge (or satisfaction) of the
libido, subject to the conditions of a compromise being observed. By the roundabout path *viâ* the unconscious and the old
fixations, the libido finally succeeds in forcing its way through
to real satisfaction—though to one which is extremely restricted
and scarcely recognizable as such. Let me add two comments
to this conclusion. First, I should like you to notice how closely
here the libido and the unconscious on one side and the ego,
consciousness and reality on the other are shown to be inter-

---

[1] ['*Vertretung*', i.e. the representative in psychical terms of the
libido regarded as something somatic. A fuller discussion of this
notion will be found in the Editor's Note to 'Instincts and their
Vicissitudes' (1915*c*).]

[2] [That is, a force acting in a sense contrary to the primary
instinctual energy. See Section IV of 'The Unconscious' (1915*e*).]

linked, although to begin with they did not belong together at all. And secondly, I must ask you to bear in mind that everything I have said about this and what is still to follow relates only to the formation of symptoms in the neurosis of hysteria.

Where, then, does the libido find the fixations which it requires in order to break through the repressions? In the activities and experiences of infantile sexuality, in the abandoned component trends, in the objects of childhood which have been given up. It is to them, accordingly, that the libido returns. The significance of this period of childhood is twofold: on the one hand, during it the instinctual trends which the child has inherited with his innate disposition first become manifest, and secondly, others of his instincts are for the first time awakened and made active by external impressions and accidental experiences. There is no doubt, I think, that we are justified in making this twofold division. The manifestation of the innate disposition is indeed not open to any critical doubts, but analytic experience actually compels us to assume that purely chance experiences in childhood are able to leave fixations of the libido behind them. Nor do I see any theoretical difficulty in this. Constitutional dispositions are also undoubtedly after-effects of experiences by ancestors in the past; they too were once acquired. Without such acquisition there would be no heredity. And is it conceivable that acquisition such as this, leading to inheritance, would come to an end precisely with the generation we are considering? The significance of infantile experiences should not be totally neglected, as people like doing, in comparison with the experiences of the subject's ancestors and of his own maturity; on the contrary, they call for particular consideration. They are all the more momentous because they occur in times of incomplete development and are for that very reason liable to have traumatic effects. The studies on developmental mechanics by Roux[1] and others have shown that the prick of a needle into an embryonic germinal layer in the act of cell-division results in a severe disturbance of development. The same injury inflicted on a larval or fully grown animal would do no damage.

[1] [Wilhelm Roux (1850–1924) was one of the founders of experimental embryology.]

Thus fixation of the libido in the adult, which we introduced into the aetiological equation of neurosis as representing the constitutional factor [p. 346], now falls, for our purposes, into two further parts: the inherited constitution and the disposition acquired in early childhood. As we all know, a diagram is certain of a sympathetic reception from students. So I will summarize the position diagrammatically:[1]

Causation of Neurosis = Disposition due + Accidental [Adult]
                        to Fixation of   Experience
                        Libido   (Traumatic)

Sexual Constitution   Infantile Experience
(Prehistoric Experience)

The hereditary sexual constitution presents us with a great variety of dispositions, according as one component instinct or another, alone or in combination with others, is inherited in particular strength. The sexual constitution forms once again, together with the factor of infantile experience, a 'complemental series' exactly similar to the one we first came to know between disposition and the accidental experience of the adult [p. 347]. In both of them we find the same extreme cases and the same relations between the two factors concerned. And here the question suggests itself of whether the most striking kinds of libidinal regressions—those to earlier stages of the sexual organization—may not be predominantly determined by the hereditary constitutional factor. But it is best to postpone answering this question till we have been able to take a wider range of forms of neurotic illness into account.

Let us dwell now on the fact that analytic research shows the libido of neurotics tied to their infantile sexual experiences. It

[1] [Readers may find this diagram easier to follow in the form of a genealogical tree:
    Sexual Constitution   + Infantile Experience
    (Prehistoric Experience)

                Disposition due to + Accidental [Adult]
                Fixation of Libido   Experience (Traumatic)

                        [Neurosis]

thus lends these the appearance of an enormous importance for the life and illness of human beings. They retain this importance undiminished so far as the work of therapeutics is concerned. But if we turn away from that task we can nevertheless easily see that there is a danger here of a misunderstanding which might mislead us into basing our view of life too one-sidedly on the neurotic situation. We must after all subtract from the importance of infantile experiences the fact that the libido has returned to them *regressively*, after being driven out of its later positions. In that case the contrary conclusion becomes very tempting—that these libidinal experiences had no importance at all at the time they occurred but only acquired it regressively. You will recall that we have already considered a similar alternative in our discussion of the Oedipus complex [p. 336].

Once again we shall not find it hard to reach a decision. The assertion that the libidinal cathexis (and therefore the pathogenic significance) of the infantile experiences has been largely intensified by the regression of the libido is undoubtedly correct, but it would lead to error if we were to regard it alone as decisive. Other considerations must be allowed weight as well.

In the first place observation shows, in a manner that excludes all doubt, that the infantile experiences have an importance of their own and give evidence of it already in childhood. Children too have their neuroses, in which the factor of displacement backwards in time is necessarily very much reduced or is even completely absent, since the onset of the illness follows the traumatic experiences immediately. The study of these infantile neuroses protects us from more than one dangerous misunderstanding of the neuroses of adults, just as the dreams of children gave us the key to an understanding of adult dreams.[1] Children's neuroses are very common, much commoner than is supposed. They are often overlooked, regarded as signs of a bad or naughty child, often, too, kept under by the nursery authorities; but they can always be easily recognized in retrospect. They usually appear in the form of *anxiety*

[1] [See Lecture VIII. Freud was no doubt thinking here of his analysis of the 'Wolf Man', which he had already completed though it was not yet published: 'From the History of an Infantile Neurosis' (1918*b*).]

hysteria. We shall learn on a later occasion what that means [p. 400 below]. If a neurosis breaks out in later life, analysis regularly reveals it as a direct continuation of the infantile illness which may have emerged as no more than a veiled hint. As I have said, however, there are cases in which these signs of neurosis in childhood proceed uninterruptedly into a lifelong illness. We have been able to analyse a few examples of these children's neuroses in childhood itself—when they were actually present;[1] but far more often we have had to be content with someone who has fallen ill in adult life enabling us to obtain a deferred insight into his childhood neurosis. In such cases we must not fail to make certain corrections and take certain precautions.

In the second place, we must reflect that it would be inconceivable for the libido to regress so regularly to the period of childhood unless there were something there to exercise an attraction on it. The fixation which we have supposed to be present at particular points in the course of development can only have a meaning if we regard it as consisting in the retention of a certain quota of libidinal energy. And finally I may point out to you that between the intensity and pathogenic importance of infantile and of later experiences a complemental relationship exists similar to the series we have already discussed. There are cases in which the whole weight of causation falls on the sexual experiences of childhood, cases in which those impressions exert a definitely traumatic effect and call for no other support than can be afforded them by an average sexual constitution and the fact of its incomplete development. Alongside of these cases there are others in which the whole accent lies on the later conflicts and the emphasis we find in the analysis laid on the impressions of childhood appears entirely as the work of regression. Thus we have extremes of 'developmental inhibition' and 'regression' and between them every degree of co-operation between the two factors.

These facts have a certain interest from the point of view of education, which plans the prevention of neuroses by intervening at an early stage in children's sexual development. So long as one focuses attention principally on infantile sexual experiences, one must suppose that one has done everything for the

[1] [Cf. the case history of 'Little Hans' (1909*b*).]

prophylaxis of nervous illnesses by taking care that the child's development is delayed and that it is spared experiences of the sort. We already know, however, that the preconditions for the causation of neuroses are complex and cannot be influenced in general if we take account of only a single factor. Strict protection of the young loses value because it is powerless against the constitutional factor. Besides, it is more difficult to carry out than educationists imagine and it brings with it two fresh dangers which must not be underestimated: the fact that it may achieve too much—that it may encourage an excess of sexual repression, with damaging results, and the fact that it may send the child out into life without any defence against the onrush of sexual demands that is to be looked for at puberty.[1] Thus it remains extremely doubtful how far prophylaxis in childhood can be carried with advantage and whether an altered attitude to the immediate situation may not offer a better angle of approach for the prevention of neuroses.

Let us now go back to the symptoms. They create a substitute, then, for the frustrated satisfaction by means of a regression of the libido to earlier times, with which a return to earlier stages of object-choice or of the organization is inseparably bound up. We discovered some time ago that neurotics are anchored somewhere in their past;[2] we know now that it is at a period of their past in which their libido did not lack satisfaction, in which they were happy. They search about in the history of their life till they find a period of that sort, even if they have to go back as far as the time when they were infants in arms—as they remember it or as they imagine it from later hints. In some way the symptom repeats this early infantile kind of satisfaction, distorted by the censorship arising from the conflict, turned as a rule to a feeling of suffering, and mingled with elements from the precipitating cause of the illness. The kind of satisfaction which the symptom brings has much that is strange about it.

We may disregard the fact that it is unrecognizable to the subject, who, on the contrary, feels the alleged satisfaction as

[1] [Freud elaborated this difficulty in Lecture XXXIV of the *New Introductory Lectures,* p. 613.]

[2] [See for instance the beginning of Lecture XVIII, p. 273 above.]

suffering and complains of it. This transformation is a function of the psychical conflict under pressure of which the symptom had to be formed. What was once a satisfaction to the subject is, indeed, bound to arouse his resistance or his disgust to-day. We are familiar with a trivial but instructive model of this change of mind. The same child who once eagerly sucked the milk from his mother's breast is likely a few years later to display a strong dislike to drinking milk, which his upbringing has difficulties in overcoming. This dislike increases to disgust if a skin forms on the milk or the drink containing it. We cannot exclude the possibility, perhaps, that the skin conjures up a memory of the mother's breast, once so ardently desired. Between the two situations, however, there lies the experience of weaning, with its traumatic effects.

It is something else besides that makes symptoms seem strange to us and incomprehensible as a means of libidinal satisfaction. They do not remind us in the very least of anything from which we are in the habit of normally expecting satisfaction. Usually they disregard objects and in so doing abandon their relation to external reality. We can see that this is a consequence of turning away from the reality principle and of returning to the pleasure principle. But it is also a return to a kind of extended auto-erotism, of the sort that offered the sexual instinct its first satisfactions. In place of a change in the external world these substitute a change in the subject's own body: they set an internal act in place of an external one, an adaptation in place of an action—once again, something that corresponds, phylogenetically, to a highly significant regression. We shall only understand this in connection with something new that we have still to learn from the analytic researches into the formation of symptoms. We must further remember that the same processes belonging to the unconscious play a part in the formation of symptoms as in the formation of dreams— namely, condensation and displacement. A symptom, like a dream, represents something as fulfilled: a satisfaction in the infantile manner. But by means of extreme condensation that satisfaction can be compressed into a single sensation or inner-vation, and by means of extreme displacement it can be restric-ted to one small detail of the entire libidinal complex. It is not to be wondered at if we, too, often have difficulty in recognizing in a symptom the libidinal satisfaction whose presence we suspect and which is invariably confirmed.

I have warned you that we still have something new to learn; it is indeed something surprising and perplexing. By means of analysis, as you know, starting from the symptoms, we arrive at a knowledge of the infantile experiences to which the libido is fixated and out of which the symptoms are made. Well, the surprise lies in the fact that these scenes from infancy are not always true. Indeed, they are not true in the majority of cases, and in a few of them they are the direct opposite of the historical truth. As you will see, this discovery is calculated more than any other to discredit either analysis, which has led to this result, or the patients, on whose statements the analysis and our whole understanding of the neuroses are founded. But there is something else remarkably perplexing about it. If the infantile experiences brought to light by analysis were invariably real, we should feel that we were standing on firm ground; if they were regularly falsified and revealed as inventions, as phantasies of the patient, we should be obliged to abandon this shaky ground and look for salvation elsewhere. But neither of these things is the case: the position can be shown to be that the childhood experiences constructed or remembered in analysis are sometimes indisputably false and sometimes equally certainly correct, and in most cases compounded of truth and falsehood. Sometimes, then, symptoms represent events which really took place and to which we may attribute an influence on the fixation of the libido, and sometimes they represent phantasies of the patient's which are not, of course, suited to playing an aetiological role. It is difficult to find one's way about in this. We can make a first start, perhaps, with a similar discovery—namely, that the isolated childhood memories that people have possessed consciously from time immemorial and before there was any such thing as analysis [p. 200 above] may equally be falsified or at least may combine truth and falsehood in plenty. In their case there is seldom any difficulty in showing their incorrectness; so we at least have the reassurance of knowing that the responsibility for this unexpected disappointment lies, not with analysis, but in some way with the patients.

After a little reflection we shall easily understand what it is about this state of things that perplexes us so much. It is the low valuation of reality, the neglect of the distinction between it and phantasy. We are tempted to feel offended at the patient's having taken up our time with invented stories. Reality seems to us something worlds apart from invention, and we set a very different value on it. Moreover the patient, too, looks at things in this light in his normal thinking. When he brings up the material which leads from behind his symptoms to the wishful situations modelled on his infantile experiences, we are in doubt to begin with whether we are dealing with reality or phantasies. Later, we are enabled by certain indications to come to a decision and we are faced by the task of conveying it to the patient. This, however, invariably gives rise to difficulties. If we begin by telling him straight away that he is now engaged in bringing to light the phantasies with which he has disguised the history of his childhood (just as every nation disguises its forgotten prehistory by constructing legends), we observe that his interest in pursuing the subject further suddenly diminishes in an undesirable fashion. He too wants to experience realities and despises everything that is merely 'imaginary'. If, however, we leave him, till this piece of work is finished, in the belief that we are occupied in investigating the real events of his childhood, we run the risk of his later on accusing us of being mistaken and laughing at us for our apparent credulity. It will be a long time before he can take in our proposal that we should equate phantasy and reality and not bother to begin with whether the childhood experiences under examination are the one or the other. Yet this is clearly the only correct attitude to adopt towards these mental productions. They too possess a reality of a sort. It remains a fact that the patient has created these phantasies for himself, and this fact is of scarcely less importance for his neurosis than if he had really experienced what the phantasies contain. The phantasies possess *psychical* as contrasted with *material* reality, and we gradually learn to understand that *in the world of the neuroses it is psychical reality which is the decisive kind.*

Among the occurrences which recur again and again in the youthful history of neurotics—which are scarcely ever absent —there are a few of particular importance, which also deserve on that account, I think, to be brought into greater prominence than the rest. As specimens of this class I will enumerate these: observation of parental intercourse, seduction by an adult and threat of being castrated. It would be a mistake to suppose that they are never characterized by material reality; on the contrary, this is often established incontestably through enquiries from older members of the patient's family. It is by no means a rare thing, for instance, for a little boy, who is beginning to play with his penis in a naughty way and is not yet aware that one must conceal such activities, to be threatened by a parent or nurse with having his penis or his sinful hand cut off. Parents will often admit this when they are asked, since they think they have done something useful in making such a threat; a number of people have a correct conscious memory of such a threat, especially if it was made at a somewhat later period. If the threat is delivered by the mother or some other female she usually shifts its performance on to the father—or the doctor. In *Struwwelpeter*, the famous work of the Frankfurt paediatrician Hoffmann (which owes its popularity precisely to an understanding of the sexual and other complexes of childhood), you will find castration softened into a cutting-off of the thumbs as a punishment for obstinate sucking. But it is highly improbable that children are threatened with castration as often as it appears in the analyses of neurotics. We shall be satisfied by realizing that the child puts a threat of this kind together in his imagination on the basis of hints, helped out by a knowledge that auto-erotic satisfaction is forbidden and under the impression of his discovery of the female genitals. [Cf. p. 317 above.] Nor is it only in proletarian families that it is perfectly possible for a child, while he is not yet credited with possessing an understanding or a memory, to be a witness of the sexual act between his parents or other grown-up people; and the possibility cannot be rejected that he will be able to understand and react to the impression *in retrospect*. If, however, the intercourse is described with the most minute details, which would be difficult to observe, or if, as happens most frequently, it turns out to have been intercourse from behind, *more ferarum* [in the manner of animals], there can be no remaining doubt that the phantasy is based on an observation of intercourse between animals (such as dogs) and that its motive was the child's unsatisfied scopophilia during puberty. The extreme achievement on these lines is a phantasy of observing parental intercourse while one is still an unborn baby in the womb. Phantasies of being seduced are of particular interest, because so often they are not phantasies but real memories. Fortunately, however, they are nevertheless not real as often as seemed at first to be shown by the findings of analysis. Seduction by an older child or by one of the same age is even more frequent than by an adult; and if in the case of girls who produce such an event in the story of their childhood their father figures fairly regularly as the seducer, there can be no doubt either of the imaginary nature of the accusation or of the motive that has led to it.[1] A phantasy of being seduced when no seduction has occurred is usually employed by a child to screen the auto-erotic period of his sexual activity. He spares himself shame about masturbation by retrospectively phantasying a desired object into these earliest times. You must not suppose, however, that sexual abuse of a child by its nearest male relatives belongs entirely to the realm of phantasy. Most analysts will have treated cases in which such events were real and could be un-impeachably established; but even so they related to the later years of childhood and had been transposed into earlier times.

The only impression we gain is that these events of childhood are somehow demanded as a necessity, that they are among the essential elements of a neurosis. If they have occurred in reality, so much to the good; but if they have been withheld by reality, they are put together from hints and supplemented by phantasy. The outcome is the same, and up to the present we have not succeeded in pointing to any difference in the consequences, whether phantasy or reality has had the greater share in these events of childhood. Here we simply have once again one of the complemental relations that I have so often mentioned; more-over it is the strangest of all we have met with. Whence comes the need for these phantasies and the material for them? There can be no doubt that their sources lie in the instincts; but it has still to be explained why the same phantasies with the same content are created on every occasion. I am prepared with an

[1] [Cf. a later reference to this, with a further explanation, in Section III of Freud's paper on 'Female Sexuality' (1931b). A full history of Freud's views on this subject is given in an Editor's footnote to the New Introductory Lectures, pp. 120-1.]

answer which I know will seem daring to you. I believe these *primal phantasies*, as I should like to call them, and no doubt a few others as well, are a phylogenetic endowment. In them the individual reaches beyond his own experience into primaeval experience at points where his own experience has been too rudimentary. It seems to me quite possible that all the things that are told to us to-day in analysis as phantasy—the seduction of children, the inflaming of sexual excitement by observing parental intercourse, the threat of castration (or rather castration itself)—were once real occurrences in the primaeval times of the human family, and that children in their phantasies are simply filling in the gaps in individual truth with prehistoric truth. I have repeatedly been led to suspect that the psychology of the neuroses has stored up in it more of the antiquities of human development than any other source.[1]

The things I have just been discussing, Gentlemen, compel me to enter more closely into the origin and significance of the mental activity which is described as 'phantasy' [or 'imagination'].[2] As you are aware, it enjoys a universally high reputation, without its position in mental life having become clear. I have the following remarks to make about it. The human ego is, as you know, slowly educated by the pressure of external necessity to appreciate reality and obey the reality principle; in the course of this process it is obliged to renounce, temporarily or permanently, a variety of the objects and aims at which its striving for pleasure, and not only for sexual pleasure, is directed. But men have always found it hard to renounce pleasure; they cannot bring themselves to do it without some kind of compensation. They have therefore retained a mental

[1] [This discussion of 'primal phantasies' and the possibility of their being inherited was based to a considerable extent on Freud's findings in his 'Wolf Man' case history (1918*b*), which he had completed two or three years earlier. When he came to publish it (in the year following that in which this lecture was delivered), he added two long passages to his original draft, referring back to the present discussion. Cf. Chapters V and VIII of *An Infantile Neurosis*.]

[2] [Freud's main earlier discussions of phantasy will be found in 'Creative Writers and Day-Dreaming' (1908*e*) and 'Hysterical Phantasies and their Relation to Bisexuality' (1908*a*).]

activity in which all these abandoned sources of pleasure and methods of achieving pleasure are granted a further existence —a form of existence in which they are left free from the claims of reality and of what we call 'reality-testing'.[1] Every desire takes before long the form of picturing its own fulfilment; there is no doubt that dwelling upon imaginary wish-fulfilments brings satisfaction with it, although it does not interfere with a knowledge that what is concerned is not real. Thus in the activity of phantasy human beings continue to enjoy the freedom from external compulsion which they have long since renounced in reality. They have contrived to alternate between remaining an animal of pleasure and being once more a creature of reason. Indeed, they cannot subsist on the scanty satisfaction which they can extort from reality. 'We cannot do without auxiliary constructions', as Theodor Fontane once said.[2] The creation of the mental realm of phantasy finds a perfect parallel in the establishment of 'reservations' or 'nature reserves' in places where the requirements of agriculture, communications and industry threaten to bring about changes in the original face of the earth which will quickly make it unrecognizable. A nature reserve preserves its original state which everywhere else has to our regret been sacrificed to necessity. Everything, including what is useless and even what is noxious, can grow and proliferate there as it pleases. The mental realm of phantasy is just such a reservation withdrawn from the reality principle.

The best-known productions of phantasy are the so-called 'day-dreams', which we have already come across [p. 98], imagined satisfactions of ambitious, megalomanic, erotic wishes, which flourish all the more exuberantly the more reality counsels modesty and restraint. The essence of the happiness of phantasy—making the obtaining of pleasure free once more from the assent of reality—is shown in them unmistakably. We know that such day-dreams are the nucleus and prototype of

---

[1] [I.e. the process of judging whether things are real or not. The deeper implications of this are discussed in Freud's metapsychological paper on dreams (1917d); for full references see the Editor's Note to that paper.]

[2] [Freud quoted this again in a similar connection in Chapter II of *Civilization and its Discontents* (1930a), (Norton, 1962).]

night-dreams. A night-dream is at bottom nothing other than a day-dream that has been made utilizable owing to the liberation of the instinctual impulses at night, and that has been distorted by the form assumed by mental activity at night. We have already become familiar with the idea that even a day-dream is not necessarily conscious—that there are unconscious day-dreams, as well [p. 368]. Such unconscious day-dreams are thus the source not only of night-dreams but also of neurotic symptoms.[1]

The importance of the part played by phantasy in the formation of symptoms will be made clear to you by what I have to tell you. I have explained [p. 359] how in the case of frustration the libido cathects regressively the positions which it has given up but to which some quotas of it have remained adhering. I shall not withdraw this or correct it, but I have to insert a connecting link. How does the libido find its way to these points of fixation? All the objects and trends which the libido has given up have not yet been given up in every sense. They or their derivatives are still retained with a certain intensity in phantasies. Thus the libido need only withdraw on to phantasies in order to find the path open to every repressed fixation. These phantasies have enjoyed a certain amount of toleration: they have not come into conflict with the ego, however sharp the contrasts between them may have been, so long as a particular condition is observed. This condition is of a *quantitative* nature and it is now upset by the backward flow of libido on to the phantasies. As a result of this surplus, the energic cathexis of the phantasies is so much increased that they begin to raise claims, that they develop a pressure in the direction of becoming realized. But this makes a conflict between them and the ego inevitable. Whether they were previously preconscious or conscious, they are now subjected to repression from the direction of the ego and are at the mercy of attraction from the direction of the unconscious. From what are now unconscious phantasies the libido travels back to their origins in the unconscious—to its own points of fixation.

The libido's retreat to phantasy is an intermediate stage on the path to the formation of symptoms and it seems to call for a

[1] [Cf. a long footnote added by Freud in 1920 to the third of his *Three Essays* (1905*d*).]

special name. C. G. Jung coined the very appropriate one of 'introversion', but then most inexpediently gave it another meaning as well.[1] We will continue to take it that introversion denotes the turning away of the libido from the possibilities of real satisfaction and the hypercathexis[2] of phantasies which have hitherto been tolerated as innocent. An introvert is not yet a neurotic, but he is in an unstable situation: he is sure to develop symptoms at the next shift of forces, unless he finds some other outlets for his dammed-up libido. The unreal character of neurotic satisfaction and the neglect of the distinction between phantasy and reality are on the other hand already determined by the fact of lingering at the stage of introversion.

You will no doubt have observed that in these last discussions I have introduced a fresh factor into the structure of the aetiological chain—namely the quantity, the magnitude, of the energies concerned. We have still to take this factor into account everywhere. A purely qualitative analysis of the aetiological determinants is not enough. Or, to put it another way, a merely *dynamic* view of these mental processes is insufficient; an *economic* line of approach is also needed. We must tell ourselves that the conflict between two trends does not break out till certain intensities of cathexis have been reached, even though the determinants for it have long been present so far as their subject-matter is concerned. In the same way, the pathogenic significance of the constitutional factors must be weighed according to how much *more* of one component instinct than of another is present in the inherited disposition. It may even be

[1] [This had been discussed by Freud earlier, in a footnote to his paper on 'The Dynamics of Transference' (1912*b*), in which he stated that Jung seemed to be applying the term 'introversion' exclusively to dementia praecox. In that footnote further references are given.]

[2] [I.e. charging with an extra amount of psychical energy. Freud generally used the term in this sense: e.g. in 'The Unconscious' (1915*e*), *Beyond the Pleasure Principle* (1920*g*), and 'Humour' (1927*d*). On the other hand he sometimes applied it more specially to the distinction between unconscious and preconscious ideas: once more in Chapter VI of 'The Unconscious', and in Chapter IV of the *Outline* (1940*a* [1938]), (Norton, 1949). Cf. also Part III, Section 1, of the 'Project' of 1895 (Freud, 1950*a*).]

supposed that the disposition of all human beings is qualitatively alike and that they differ only owing to these quantitative conditions. The quantitative factor is no less decisive as regards capacity to resist neurotic illness. It is a matter of *what quota* of unemployed libido a person is able to hold in suspension and of *how large a fraction* of his libido he is able to divert from sexual to sublimated aims. The ultimate aim of mental activity, which may be described qualitatively as an endeavour to obtain pleasure and avoid unpleasure, emerges, looked at from the economic point of view, as the task of mastering the amounts of excitation (mass of stimuli) operating in the mental apparatus and of keeping down their accumulation which creates unpleasure.[1]

This, then, is what I wanted to tell you about the formation of symptoms in the neuroses. But I must not fail to lay emphasis expressly once again on the fact that everything I have said here applies only to the formation of symptoms in hysteria. Even in obsessional neurosis there is much—apart from fundamentals, which remain unaltered—that will be found different. The anticathexes opposing the demands of the instincts (which we have already spoken of in the case of hysteria as well [p. 360]) become prominent in obsessional neurosis and dominate the clinical picture in the form of what are known as 'reaction-formations'. We discover similar and even more far-reaching divergences in the other neuroses, where our researches into the mechanisms of symptom-formation are not yet concluded at any point.

Before I let you go to-day, however, I should like to direct your attention a little longer to a side of the life of phantasy which deserves the most general interest. For there is a path that leads back from phantasy to reality—the path, that is, of

---

[1] [Here Freud appears to be equating the 'pleasure principle' and 'the principle of constancy', though in the earlier passage above (p. 356f.), where this subject is touched on, there is a hint at a doubt about this. At a later date he drew a clear distinction between the two: (see Freud), *The Economic Problem of Masochism* (1924c). A full discussion of the development of Freud's views on these principles is given in an Editor's footnote to 'Instincts and their Vicissitudes' (1915c).]

art. An artist is once more in rudiments an introvert, not far removed from neurosis. He is oppressed by excessively powerful instinctual needs. He desires to win honour, power, wealth, fame and the love of women; but he lacks the means for achieving these satisfactions. Consequently, like any other unsatisfied man, he turns away from reality and transfers all his interest, and his libido too, to the wishful constructions of his life of phantasy, whence the path might lead to neurosis. There must be, no doubt, a convergence of all kinds of things if this is not to be the complete outcome of his development; it is well known, indeed, how often artists in particular suffer from a partial inhibition of their efficiency owing to neurosis. Their constitution probably includes a strong capacity for sublimation and a certain degree of laxity in the repressions which are decisive for a conflict. An artist, however, finds a path back to reality in the following manner. To be sure, he is not the only one who leads a life of phantasy. Access to the half-way region of phantasy is permitted by the universal assent of mankind, and everyone suffering from privation expects to derive alleviation and consolation from it. But for those who are not artists the yield of pleasure to be derived from the sources of phantasy is very limited. The ruthlessness of their repressions forces them to be content with such meagre day-dreams as are allowed to become conscious. A man who is a true artist has more at his disposal. In the first place, he understands how to work over his day-dreams in such a way as to make them lose what is too personal about them and repels strangers, and to make it possible for others to share in the enjoyment of them. He understands, too, how to tone them down so that they do not easily betray their origin from proscribed sources. Furthermore, he possesses the mysterious power of shaping some particular material until it has become a faithful image of his phantasy; and he knows, moreover, how to link so large a yield of pleasure to this representation of his unconscious phantasy that, for the time being at least, repressions are outweighed and lifted by it. If he is able to accomplish all this, he makes it possible for other people once more to derive consolation and alleviation from their own sources of pleasure in their unconscious which have become inaccessible to them; he earns their gratitude and admiration and he has thus achieved *through* his phantasy what originally he had achieved only *in* his phantasy—honour, power and the love of women.[1]

[1] [Cf. 'Creative Writers and Day-Dreaming' (1908*e*), the fifth of Freud's *Five Lectures* (1910*a*), 'Two Principles of Mental Functioning' (1911*b*), and Section II (F) of his contribution to *Scientia* (1913*j*).]

LECTURE XXIV

THE COMMON NEUROTIC STATE

LADIES AND GENTLEMEN,—Now that we have disposed of such a difficult piece of work in our last discussions, I propose for a time to leave the subject and turn to you yourselves.

For I am aware that you are dissatisfied. You pictured an 'Introduction to Psycho-Analysis' [1] very differently. What you expected to hear were lively examples, not theory. On one occasion, you say, when I told you the parable of 'In the Basement and on the First Floor' [p. 352], you grasped something of the way in which neuroses are caused; the observations should have been real ones, however, and not made-up stories. Or when at the start I described two symptoms to you (not invented ones this time, let us hope) and described their solution and their relation to the patients' lives [p. 261], the 'sense' of symptoms dawned on you. You hoped I should go on along those lines. But instead I gave you long-winded theories, hard to grasp, which were never complete but were always having something fresh added to them; I worked with concepts which I had not yet explained to you; I went from a descriptive account of things to a dynamic one and from that to what I called an 'economic' one; I made it hard for you to understand how many of the technical terms I used meant the same thing and were merely being interchanged for reasons of euphony; I brought up such far-reaching conceptions as those of the pleasure and reality principles and of phylogenetically inherited endowments; and, far from introducing you to anything, I paraded something before your eyes which constantly grew more and more remote from you.

Why did I not begin my introduction to the theory of neuroses with what you yourselves know of the neurotic state and what has long aroused your interest—with the peculiar characteristics of neurotic people, their incomprehensible reactions to human intercourse and external influences, their irritability, their incalculable and inexpedient behaviour? Why

[1] [See p. 9 above.]

did I not lead you step by step from an understanding of the simpler, everyday forms of the neurotic state to the problems of its enigmatic, extreme manifestations?

Indeed, Gentlemen, I cannot even disagree with you. I am not so enamoured of my skill in exposition that I can declare each of its artistic faults to be a peculiar charm. I think myself that it might have been more to your advantage if I had proceeded otherwise; and that was, indeed, my intention. But one cannot always carry out one's reasonable intentions. There is often something in the material itself which takes charge of one and diverts one from one's first intentions. Even such a trivial achievement as the arrangement of a familiar piece of material is not entirely subject to an author's own choice; it takes what line it likes and all one can do is to ask oneself after the event why it has happened in this way and no other.

One reason is probably that the title 'Introduction to Psycho-Analysis' is no longer applicable to the present section, which is supposed to deal with the neuroses. An introduction to psycho-analysis is provided by the study of parapraxes and dreams; the theory of the neuroses is psycho-analysis itself. It would not, I believe, have been possible to give you a knowledge of the subject-matter of the theory of the neuroses in so short a time except in this concentrated form. It was a question of presenting you with a connected account of the sense and significance of symptoms and of the external and internal determinants and mechanism of their formation. That is what I have tried to do; it is more or less the nucleus of what psycho-analysis has to teach to-day. It involved saying a great deal about the libido and its development and a little, too, about that of the ego. Our introduction had already prepared you in advance for the premises of our technique and for the major considerations of the unconscious and of repression (of resistance). You will discover from one of the next lectures [Lecture XXVI] the points from which the work of psycho-analysis makes its further organic advance. For the time being I have made no secret of the fact that everything I have said is derived from the study of a single group of nervous disorders— what are termed the 'transference neuroses'. Indeed, I have traced the mechanism of symptom-formation in the case only of the hysterical neurosis. Even if you have acquired no thorough knowledge and have not retained every detail, yet I hope that you have formed some picture of the methods by which psycho-analysis works, of the problems which it attacks and of the results at which it has arrived.

I have credited you with a wish that I might have started my description of the neuroses from the behaviour of neurotic people, from an account of the manner in which they suffer under their neurosis, of how they defend themselves against it and how they come to terms with it. No doubt that is an interesting topic, worth investigating; nor would it be very difficult to handle. But it would be of debatable wisdom to start with it. There would be a risk of not discovering the unconscious and at the same time of overlooking the great importance of the libido and of judging everything as it appears to the ego of the neurotic subject. It is obvious that this ego is not a trustworthy or impartial agency. The ego is indeed the power which disavows the unconscious and has degraded it into being repressed; so how can we trust it to be fair to the unconscious? The most prominent elements in what is thus repressed are the repudiated demands of sexuality, and it is quite self-evident that we should never be able to guess their extent and importance from the ego's conceptions. From the moment the notion of repression dawns on us, we are warned against making one of the two contesting parties (and the victorious one, at that) into being judge in the dispute. We are prepared to find that the ego's assertions will lead us astray. If we are to believe the ego, it was active at every point and itself willed and created its symptoms. But we know that it puts up with a good amount of passivity, which it afterwards tries to disguise and gloss over. It is true that it does not always venture on such an attempt; in the symptoms of obsessional neurosis it is obliged to admit that there is something alien which is confronting it and against which it can only defend itself with difficulty.

Anyone whom these warnings do not deter from taking the ego's counterfeits as sterling coin will have an easy time of it and will avoid all the resistances which oppose the psychoanalytic emphasis upon the unconscious, sexuality and the passivity of the ego. He will be able to declare like Alfred Adler that the 'neurotic character'[1] is the cause of neuroses instead of their consequence; but neither will he be in a position to explain a single detail of symptom-formation or a single dream.

You will ask whether it may not be possible, however, to do justice to the part played by the ego in neurotic states and in the formation of symptoms without at the same time grossly neglecting the factors revealed by psycho-analysis. My reply is that that must certainly be possible and will sooner or later be done; but the road followed by the work of psycho-analysis does not admit of actually *beginning* with this. It is of course possible to foresee when psycho-analysis will be confronted by this task. There are neuroses in which the ego plays a far more intensive part than in those we have studied hitherto; we call them the 'narcissistic' neuroses. The investigation of these disorders will enable us to form an impartial and trustworthy judgement of the share taken by the ego in the onset of neuroses.[2]

One of the ways in which the ego is related to its neuroses is, however, so obvious that it was possible to take it into account from the first. It seems never to be absent; but it is most clearly recognizable in a disorder which we are even to-day far from understanding—*traumatic neurosis*. For you must know that the same factors always come into operation in the causation and mechanism of every possible form of neurosis; but the chief importance in the construction of the symptoms falls now upon one and now upon another of these factors. The position is like that among the members of a theatrical company. Each of them is regularly cast for his own stock role—hero, confidant, villain, and so on; but each of them will choose a different piece for his benefit performance. In the same way phantasies which turn into symptoms are nowhere more obvious than in hysteria; the anticathexes or reaction-formations of the ego dominate the picture in obsessional neurosis; what in the case of dreams we have termed 'secondary revision' [p. 182] stands in the forefront in paranoia in the shape of delusions, and so on.

---

[1] [*Über den nervösen Charakter* (1912) was the title of one of Adler's earlier works. The title of its English translation is *The Neurotic Constitution.*]

[2] [Freud deals further with this in Lecture XXVI below.]

Thus in traumatic neuroses, and particularly in those brought about by the horrors of war, we are unmistakably presented with a self-interested motive on the part of the ego, seeking for protection and advantage—a motive which cannot, perhaps, create the illness by itself but which assents to it and maintains it when once it has come about. This motive tries to preserve the ego from the dangers the threat of which was the precipitating cause of the illness and it will not allow recovery to occur until a repetition of these dangers seems no longer possible or until compensation has been received for the danger that has been endured.[1]

The ego takes a similar interest, however, in the development and maintenance of the neurosis in every other case. I have already shown [p. 359] that symptoms are supported by the ego, too, because they have a side with which they offer satisfaction to the repressing purpose of the ego. Moreover, settling the conflict by constructing a symptom is the most convenient way out and the one most agreeable to the pleasure principle: it unquestionably spares the ego a large amount of internal work which is felt as distressing. Indeed there are cases in which even the physician must admit that for a conflict to end in neurosis is the most harmless and socially tolerable solution. You must not be surprised to hear that even the physician may occasionally take the side of the illness he is combating. It is not his business to restrict himself in every situation in life to being a fanatic in favour of health. He knows that there is not only neurotic misery in the world but real, irremovable suffering as well, that necessity may even require a person to sacrifice his health; and he learns that a sacrifice of this kind made by a single person can prevent immeasurable unhappiness for many others. If we may say, then, that whenever a neurotic is faced by a conflict he takes flight into illness,[2] yet we must allow that in some cases that flight is fully justified, and a physician who has recognized how the situation lies will silently and solicitously withdraw.

[1] [Cf. Freud's studies on the war neuroses (1919*d* and 1955*c* [1920]).]

[2] [This phrase appeared first in Freud's paper on hysterical attacks (1909*a*), where some further references will be found.]

But let us disregard these exceptional cases and proceed with our discussion. In average circumstances we recognize that by escaping into a neurosis the ego obtains a certain internal 'gain from illness'. In some circumstances of life this is further accompanied by an appreciable *external* advantage bearing a greater or less real value. Consider the commonest example of this sort. A woman who is roughly treated and ruthlessly exploited by her husband will fairly regularly find a way out in neurosis, if her constitution makes it possible, if she is too cowardly or too moral to console herself secretly with another man, if she is not strong enough to separate from her husband in the face of every external deterrent, if she has no prospect of supporting herself or obtaining a better husband and if in addition she is still attached to this brutal husband by her sexual feelings. Her illness now becomes a weapon in her battle with her dominating husband —a weapon which she can use for her defence and misuse for her revenge. To complain of her illness is allowable, though to lament her marriage was probably not. She finds a helper in her doctor, she forces her usually inconsiderate husband to look after her, to spend money on her, to allow her at times to be away from home and so free from her married oppression. When an external or accidental gain from illness like this is really considerable and no real substitute for it is available, you must not reckon very high the chances of influencing the neurosis by your treatment.

You will now protest that what I have told you about the gain from illness argues entirely in favour of the view I have rejected—that the ego itself wills and creates the neurosis [p. 380]. Not too fast, Gentlemen! It may perhaps mean nothing more than that the ego puts up with the neurosis, which it cannot, after all, prevent, and that it makes the best of it, if anything can be made of it at all. That is only one side of the business, the pleasant side, it is true. So far as the neurosis has advantages the ego no doubt accepts it; but it does not only have advantages. As a rule it soon turns out that the ego has made a bad bargain by letting itself in for the neurosis. It has paid too dearly for an alleviation of the conflict, and the sufferings attached to the symptoms are perhaps an equivalent substitute for the torments of the conflict, but they probably involve an increase in unpleasure. The ego would like to free itself from this unpleasure of the symptoms without giving up the gain from illness, and this is just what it cannot achieve. This shows, then, that it was not so entirely active as it thought it was; and we shall bear this well in mind.

In your contact as doctors with neurotics, Gentlemen, you will soon give up expecting that the ones who raise the most lamentations and complaints about their illness will be the most eager to co-operate and will offer you the least resistance. It is rather the opposite. But of course you will easily realize that everything that contributes to the gain from illness will intensify the resistance due to repression and will increase the therapeutic difficulties. But to the portion of gain from illness which is, so to say, born with the illness we have to add another portion which arises later. When a psychical organization like an illness has lasted for some time, it behaves eventually like an independent organism; it manifests something like a self-preservative instinct; it establishes a kind of *modus vivendi* between itself and other parts of the mind, even with those which are at bottom hostile to it; and there can scarcely fail to be occasions when it proves once again useful and expedient and acquires, as it were, a *secondary function* which strengthens its stability afresh. Instead of an example from pathology, let us take a glaring instance from daily life. A capable working-man, who earns his living, is crippled by an accident in the course of his occupation. The injured man can no longer work, but eventually he obtains a small disablement pension, and he learns how to exploit his mutilation by begging. His new, though worsened, means of livelihood is based precisely on the very thing that deprived him of his former means of livelihood. If you could put an end to his injury you would make him, to begin with, without means of subsistence; the question would arise of whether he was still capable of taking up his earlier work again. What corresponds in the case of neuroses to a secondary exploitation like this of an illness may be described as the *secondary* gain from illness in contrast to the primary one.[1]

[1] [The distinction between the two different kinds of gain from illness had been indicated by Freud in a letter to Fliess of November 18, 1897 (Freud, 1950a, Letter 76), though it was first made explicit in the paper (1909a) quoted in the last footnote. The question had already been discussed at some length in the 'Dora'

In general, however, I should like to recommend that, while not under-estimating the *practical* importance of the gain from illness, you should not let yourselves be impressed by it theoretically. After all, apart from the exceptions I recognized earlier [p. 382], it always calls to mind the examples of 'animal intelligence' illustrated by Oberländer in *Fliegende Blätter*.[1] An Arab was riding his camel along a narrow path cut in the steep face of a mountain. At a turn in the path he suddenly found himself face to face with a lion, which prepared to make a spring. He saw no way out: on one side a perpendicular cliff and on the other a precipice; retreat and flight were impossible. He gave himself up for lost. But the animal thought otherwise. He took one leap with his rider into the abyss—and the lion was left in the lurch. The help provided by a neurosis has as a rule no better success with the patient. This may be because dealing with a conflict by forming symptoms is after all an automatic process which cannot prove adequate to meeting the demands of life, and in which the subject has abandoned the use of his best and highest powers. If there were a choice, it would be preferable to go down in an honourable struggle with fate.

But I still owe you further enlightenment, Gentlemen, on my reasons for not starting my account of the theory of the neuroses with the common neurotic state. You may perhaps suppose that it was because in that case I should have had greater difficulty in proving the sexual causation of the neuroses. But you would be wrong there. In the case of the transference neuroses one must work one's way through the interpretation of symptoms before one can arrive at that discovery. In the common forms of what are known as the 'actual neuroses'[2] the aetiological significance of sexual life is a crude fact that springs to the

case history (1905*e*), where the instances of the crippled beggar and of the ill-treated wife appear again. But the analysis there was later considered incorrect by Freud, who added a long footnote in 1923, which gives perhaps the clearest account of the matter.]

[1] [See footnote 2, p. 28.]

[2] ['*Aktualneurosen*'. '*Aktual*', like the French '*actuel*', has the sense of 'contemporary', 'of the present moment'. The epithet is applied to this group of neuroses because their causes are purely contemporary and do not, as in the case of the psychoneuroses, have their origin in the patient's past life. 'Actual neuroses' is the accepted translation.]

observer's eyes. I came upon it more than twenty years ago when one day I asked myself the question of why in the examination of neurotics their sexual activities were so regularly excluded from consideration. At that time I sacrificed my popularity with my patients for the sake of these enquiries; but after only a brief effort I was able to declare that 'if the *vita sexualis* is normal, there can be no neurosis'—and by this I meant no 'actual neurosis'.[1] No doubt this statement passes too lightly over people's individual differences; it suffers, too, from the indefiniteness inseparable from the judgement of what is 'normal'. But as a rough guide it retains its value to this day. I had by then reached the point of establishing specific relations between particular forms of neurosis and particular sexual noxae; and I have no doubt that I could repeat the same observations to-day if similar pathological material were still at my disposal. I found often enough that a man who indulged in a certain kind of incomplete sexual satisfaction (for instance, manual masturbation) had fallen ill of a particular form of 'actual neurosis', and that this neurosis promptly gave place to another if he replaced this sexual *régime* by another equally far from being irreproachable. I was then in a position to infer the change in a patient's sexual mode of life from an alteration in his condition.[2] I also learnt then to stand obstinately by my suspicions till I had overcome the patients' disingenuousness and compelled them to confirm my views. It is true that thereafter they preferred to go to other doctors who did not make such keen enquiries about their sexual life.

Even at that time I could not fail to notice that the causation of the illness did not always point to sexual life. One person, it was true, fell ill directly from a sexual noxa; but another did so because he had lost his fortune or had been through an exhausting organic illness. The explanation of these varieties came later, when we gained an insight into the suspected interrela-

---

[1] [This is quoted from a paper on sexuality in the aetiology of the neuroses contributed by Freud to a volume of Löwenfeld's (Freud, 1906a). But he had reached the conclusion more than ten years earlier, and expressed it in almost the same words, in his two papers on anxiety neurosis (1895b and f), where a large part of what follows is already to be found.]

[2] [Cf. an example of this in 'Sexuality in the Aetiology of the Neuroses' (1898a).]

tions between the ego and the libido, and the explanation became the more satisfactory the deeper that insight extended. A person only falls ill of a neurosis if his ego has lost the capacity to allocate his libido in some way. The stronger is his ego, the easier will it be for it to carry out that task. Any weakening of his ego from whatever cause must have the same effect as an excessive increase in the claims of the libido and will thus make it possible for him to fall ill of a neurosis. There are other and more intimate relations between the ego and the libido;[1] but these have not yet come within our scope, so I will not bring them up as part of my present explanation. What remains essential and makes things clear to us is that, in every case and no matter how the illness is set going, the symptoms of the neurosis are sustained by the libido and are consequently evidence that it is being employed abnormally.

Now, however, I must draw your attention to the decisive difference between the symptoms of the 'actual' neuroses and those of the psychoneuroses, the first group of which, the transference neuroses, have occupied us so much hitherto. In both cases the symptoms originate from the libido, and are thus abnormal employments of it, substitutive satisfactions. But the symptoms of the 'actual' neuroses—intracranial pressure, sensations of pain, a state of irritation in an organ, weakening or inhibition of a function—have no 'sense', no psychical meaning. They are not only manifested predominantly in the body (as are hysterical symptoms, for instance, as well), but they are also themselves entirely somatic processes, in the generating of which all the complicated mental mechanisms we have come to know are absent. Thus they really are what psychoneurotic symptoms were so long believed to be. But if so, how can they correspond to employments of the libido, which we have recognized as a force operating in the *mind*? Well, Gentlemen, that is a very simple matter. Let me remind you of one of the very first objections that were brought up against psycho-analysis. It was said then that it was occupied in finding a purely psychological theory of neurotic phenomena and this was quite hopeless, since psychological theories could never explain an illness. People had chosen to forget that the sexual function is not a

[1] [No doubt an allusion to the subject of narcissism, which is discussed in Lecture XXVI.]

purely psychical thing any more than it is a purely somatic one. It influences bodily and mental life alike. If in the symptoms of the psychoneuroses we have become acquainted with manifestations of disturbances in the *psychical* operation of the sexual function, we shall not be surprised to find in the 'actual' neuroses the direct *somatic* consequences of sexual disturbances.

Clinical medicine has given us a valuable pointer towards an interpretation of these disturbances, and one that has been taken into account by various enquirers. The 'actual' neuroses, in the details of their symptoms and also in their characteristic of influencing every organic system and every function, exhibit an unmistakable resemblance to the pathological states which arise from the chronic influence of external toxic substances and from a sudden withdrawal of them—to intoxications and conditions of abstinence. The two groups of disorders are brought together still more closely by intermediate conditions such as Grave's disease which we have learnt to recognize as equally due to the operation of toxic substances, but of toxins which are not introduced into the body from outside but originate in the subject's own metabolism. In view of these analogies, we cannot, I think, avoid regarding the neuroses as results of disturbances in the sexual metabolism, whether because more of these sexual toxins is produced than the subject can deal with, or whether because internal and even psychical conditions restrict the proper employment of these substances. The popular mind has from time immemorial paid homage to hypotheses of this kind on the nature of sexual desire, speaking of love as an 'intoxication' and believing that falling in love is brought about by love-philtres—though here the operative agent is to some extent externalized. And for us this would be an occasion for recalling the erotogenic zones and our assertion that sexual excitation can be generated in the most various organs [p. 324]. But for the rest the phrase 'sexual metabolism' or 'chemistry of sexuality' is a term without content; we know nothing about it and cannot even decide whether we are to assume two sexual substances, which would then be named 'male' and 'female',[1] or whether we could be satisfied with *one* sexual toxin which we should have to recognize as the vehicle of all the stimulant

[1] [Elsewhere, e.g. in the *New Introductory Lectures*, p. 131, Freud strongly rejects such a notion.]

effects of the libido. The theoretical structure of psycho-analysis that we have created is in truth a superstructure, which will one day have to be set upon its organic foundation. But we are still ignorant of this.

What characterizes psycho-analysis as a science is not the material which it handles but the technique with which it works. It can be applied to the history of civilization, to the science of religion and to mythology, no less than to the theory of the neuroses, without doing violence to its essential nature. What it aims at and achieves is nothing other than the uncovering of what is unconscious in mental life. The problems of the 'actual' neuroses, whose symptoms are probably generated by direct toxic damage, offer psycho-analysis no points of attack. It can do little towards throwing light on them and must leave the task to biologico-medical research.

And now perhaps you understand better why I did not choose to arrange my material differently. If I had promised you an 'Introduction to the Theory of the Neuroses' the correct path would certainly have led from the simple forms of the 'actual' neuroses to the more complicated psychical illnesses due to disturbance of the libido. As regards the former I should have had to collect from various sources what we have learnt or believe we know, and in connection with the psychoneuroses psychoanalysis would have come up for discussion as the most important technical aid in throwing light on those conditions. But what I intended to give and what I announced was an 'Introduction to Psycho-Analysis'. It was more important for me that you should gain an idea of psycho-analysis than that you should obtain some pieces of knowledge about the neuroses; and for that reason the 'actual' neuroses, unproductive so far as psycho-analysis is concerned, could no longer have a place in the foreground. I believe, too, that I have made the better choice for you. For, on account of the profundity of its hypotheses and the comprehensiveness of its connections, psychoanalysis deserves a place in the interest of every educated person, while the theory of the neuroses is a chapter in medicine like any other.

Nevertheless you will rightly expect that we should devote some interest to the 'actual' neuroses as well. Their intimate clinical connection with the psychoneuroses would alone compel us to do so. I may inform you, then, that we distinguish three pure forms of 'actual' neuroses: neurasthenia, anxiety neurosis and hypochondria.[1] Even this assertion is not uncontradicted. All the names are in use, it is true, but their content is indefinite and fluctuating. There are even doctors who oppose any dividing lines in the chaotic world of neurotic phenomena, any segregation of clinical entities or individual diseases, and who do not even recognize the distinction between the 'actual' neuroses and the psychoneuroses. I think they are going too far and have not chosen the path which leads to progress. The forms of neurosis which I have mentioned occur occasionally in their pure form; more often, however, they are intermixed with each other and with a psychoneurotic disorder. This need not lead us to abandon the distinction between them. Consider the difference between the study of minerals and of rocks in mineralogy. The minerals are described as individuals, no doubt on the basis of the fact that they often occur as crystals, sharply separated from their environment. Rocks consist of aggregations of minerals, which, we may be sure, have not come together by chance but as a result of what determined their origin. In the theory of the neuroses we still know too little of the course of their development to produce anything resembling petrology. But we are certainly doing the right thing if we start by isolating from the mass the individual clinical entities which we recognize and which are comparable to the minerals.

A noteworthy relation between the symptoms of the 'actual' neuroses and of the psychoneuroses makes a further important contribution to our knowledge of the formation of symptoms in the latter. For a symptom of an 'actual' neurosis is often the nucleus and first stage of a psychoneurotic symptom. A relation of this kind can be most clearly observed between neurasthenia and the transference neurosis known as 'conversion hysteria', between anxiety neurosis and anxiety hysteria, but also between hypochondria and the forms of disorder which will be mentioned later [p. 423 ff.] under the name of paraphrenia (dementia praecox and paranoia). Let us take as an example a

[1] [A discussion of hypochondria as a third 'actual' neurosis appears in Section II of Freud's paper on 'Narcissism' (1914c).]

case of hysterical headache or lumbar pain. Analysis shows us that, by condensation and displacement, it has become a substitutive satisfaction for a whole number of libidinal phantasies or memories. But this pain was also at one time a real one and it was then a direct sexual-toxic symptom, the somatic expression of a libidinal excitation. We are far from asserting that *all* hysterical symptoms contain a nucleus of this kind. But it remains a fact that this is especially often the case and that whatever somatic influences (whether normal or pathological) are brought about by libidinal excitation are preferred for the construction of hysterical symptoms. In such cases they play the part of the grain of sand which a mollusc coats with layers of mother-of-pearl. In the same way, the passing indications of sexual excitement which accompany the sexual act are employed by the psychoneurosis as the most convenient and appropriate material for the construction of symptoms.

A similar course of events affords peculiar diagnostic and therapeutic interest. It not at all infrequently happens in the case of a person who is disposed to a neurosis without actually suffering from a manifest one, that a pathological somatic change (through inflammation or injury perhaps) sets the activity of symptom-formation going; so that this activity hastily turns the symptom which has been presented to it by reality into the representative of all the unconscious phantasies which have only been lying in wait to seize hold of some means of expression. In such a case the physician will adopt sometimes one and sometimes another line of treatment. He will either endeavour to remove the organic basis, without bothering about its noisy neurotic elaboration; or he will attack the neurosis which has taken this favourable opportunity for arising and will pay little attention to its organic precipitating cause. The outcome will prove the one or the other line of approach right or wrong; it is impossible to make general recommendations to meet such mixed cases.[1]

[1] [It will be clear from what Freud says in this lecture that the aetiology of the 'actual' neuroses and the distinction between them and the psychoneuroses were established by him at a very early date. The term appears first in a paper on 'Sexuality in the Aetiology of the Neuroses' (1898*a*), though the notion goes back at least to 1895. A full list of references is given in an Editor's footnote to the paper on ' "Wild" Psycho-Analysis' (1910*k*).]

LECTURE XXV

ANXIETY[1]

LADIES AND GENTLEMEN,—What I said to you in my last lecture about the general[2] neurotic state will no doubt have struck you as the most incomplete and inadequate of all my pronouncements. I know that is true, and nothing will have surprised you more, I expect, than that there was nothing in it about anxiety,[3] of which most neurotics complain, which they themselves describe as their worst suffering and which does in fact attain enormous intensity in them and may result in their adopting the craziest measures. But there at least I had no intention of giving you short measure. On the contrary, it was my intention to attack the problem of anxiety in neurotics particularly keenly and to discuss it at length with you.

I have no need to introduce anxiety itself to you. Every one of us has experienced that sensation, or, to speak more correctly,

---

[1] [The problem of anxiety occupied Freud's mind throughout his life, and his views on it went through a number of changes. His first major discussion of it was in his two early papers on anxiety neurosis (1895b and f); his last major discussion of it was in *Inhibitions, Symptoms and Anxiety* (1926d). In an Editor's Introduction to the latter, some account will be found of the development of his views. It should be borne in mind that what he says in the present lecture was subjected later to some important—in one case, fundamental—revisions; these changes were summarized by him in Addendum A to *Inhibitions, Symptoms and Anxiety*. At a still later date, in Lecture XXXII of his *New Introductory Lectures*, p. 81 ff., he restated his final position in a particularly clear form. It must be remembered, however, that, as Freud himself indicates in his Preface (pp. 9–10), the present lecture was his most complete treatment of the subject at the time of its delivery.]

[2] ['*Allgemeine*' in the original. Throughout the last lecture Freud had used the word '*gemeine*' (common).]

[3] ['*Angst*'. Some remarks on the English rendering of this word will be found in an Editor's Appendix to Freud's first paper on anxiety neurosis. Though 'anxiety', in a sense quite different from the colloquial one, is the technical translation, we often find it necessary to render it by such words as 'fear', being 'frightened' or 'afraid', and so on.]

that affective state, at one time or other on our own account. But I think the question has never been seriously enough raised of why neurotics in particular suffer from anxiety so much more and so much more strongly than other people. Perhaps it has been regarded as something self-evident: the words '*nervös*' and '*ängstlich*'[1] are commonly used interchangeably, as though they meant the same thing. But we have no right to do so: there are '*ängstlich*' people who are otherwise not at all '*nervös*' and, moreover, '*nervös*' people who suffer from many symptoms, among which a tendency to '*Angst*' is not included.

However that may be, there is no question that the problem of anxiety is a nodal point at which the most various and important questions converge, a riddle whose solution would be bound to throw a flood of light on our whole mental existence. I will not assert that I can give you this complete solution; but you will certainly expect psycho-analysis to approach this subject too in quite a different way from academic medicine. Interest there seems mainly to be centred on tracing the anatomical paths along which the state of anxiety is brought about. We are told that the medulla oblongata is stimulated, and the patient learns that he is suffering from a neurosis of the vagus nerve. The medulla oblongata is a very serious and lovely object. I remember quite clearly how much time and trouble I devoted to its study many years ago. To-day, however, I must remark that I know nothing that could be of less interest to me for the psychological understanding of anxiety than a knowledge of the path of the nerves along which its excitations pass.[2]

It is possible at the start to work upon the subject of anxiety for quite a time without thinking at all of neurotic states. You will understand me at once when I describe this kind of anxiety as 'realistic' anxiety in contrast to 'neurotic' anxiety. Realistic anxiety strikes us as something very rational and intelligible.

[1] [These words are by no means equivalent to the colloquial English 'nervous' and 'anxious'. '*Nervös*' might be rendered by 'nervy' or 'jumpy' and '*ängstlich*' by 'nervous' in its colloquial sense. 'Anxious' in its ordinary usage is more like the German '*bekümmert*' or '*besorgt*'.]

[2] [At the age of about thirty Freud had worked for two years at the histology of the medulla oblongata and published three papers on the subject: 1885*d*, 1886*b* and 1886*c*. His own abstracts of these (1897*b*) are included in Vol. III of the *Standard Edition*.]

We may say of it that it is a reaction to the perception of an external danger—that is, of an injury which is expected and foreseen. It is connected with the flight reflex and it may be regarded as a manifestation of the self-preservative instinct. On what occasions anxiety appears—that is to say, in the face of what objects and in what situations—will of course depend to a large extent on the state of a person's knowledge and on his sense of power *vis-à-vis* the external world. We can quite understand how a savage is afraid of a cannon and frightened by an eclipse of the sun, while a white man, who knows how to handle the instrument and can foretell the eclipse, remains without anxiety in these circumstances. On other occasions it is actually superior knowledge that promotes anxiety, because it makes an early recognition of the danger possible. Thus the savage will be terrified at a trail in the jungle that tells an uninformed person nothing, because it warns him of the proximity of a wild animal; and an experienced sailor will look with terror at a small cloud in the sky that seems trivial to a passenger, because it tells him of an approaching hurricane.

On further consideration we must tell ourselves that our judgement that realistic anxiety is rational and expedient calls for drastic revision. For the only expedient behaviour when a danger threatens would be a cool estimate of one's own strength in comparison with the magnitude of the threat and, on the basis of that, a decision as to whether flight or defence, or possibly even attack, offers the best prospect of a successful issue. But in this situation there is no place at all for anxiety; everything that happens would be achieved just as well and probably better if no anxiety were generated. And you can see, indeed, that if the anxiety is excessively great it proves in the highest degree inexpedient; it paralyses all action, including even flight. Usually the reaction to danger consists in a mixture of the affect of anxiety and defensive action. A terrified animal is afraid and flees; but the expedient part of this is the 'flight' and not the 'being afraid'.

Thus one feels tempted to assert that the generation of anxiety is never an expedient thing. It may perhaps help us to see more clearly if we dissect the situation of anxiety more carefully. The first thing about it is *preparedness* for the danger, which manifests itself in increased sensory attention and motor tension. This expectant preparedness can be unhesitatingly recognized as an advantage; indeed, its absence may be made responsible for serious consequences. From it there then proceeds on the one hand motor action—flight in the first instance and at a higher level active defence—and on the other hand what we feel as a state of anxiety. The more the generation of anxiety is limited to a mere abortive beginning—to a signal[1]—the more will the preparedness for anxiety transform itself without disturbance into action and the more expedient will be the shape taken by the whole course of events. Accordingly, the *preparedness* for anxiety seems to me to be the expedient element in what we call anxiety, and the *generation* of anxiety the inexpedient one.

I shall avoid going more closely into the question of whether our linguistic usage means the same thing or something clearly different by '*Angst* [anxiety]', '*Furcht* [fear]' and '*Schreck* [fright]'. I will only say that I think '*Angst*' relates to the state and disregards the object, while '*Furcht*' draws attention precisely to the object. It seems that '*Schreck*', on the other hand, does have a special sense; it lays emphasis, that is, on the effect produced by a danger which is not met by any preparedness for anxiety. We might say, therefore, that a person protects himself from fright by anxiety.[2]

A certain ambiguity and indefiniteness in the use of the word '*Angst*' will not have escaped you. By 'anxiety' we usually understand the subjective state into which we are put by perceiving the 'generation of anxiety' and we call this an affect. And what is an affect in the dynamic sense? It is in any case something highly composite. An affect includes in the first place particular motor innervations or discharges and secondly certain feelings; the latter are of two kinds—perceptions of the motor actions that have occurred and the direct feelings of pleasure and unpleasure which, as we say, give the affect its keynote. But I do not think that with this enumeration we have arrived at the essence of an affect. We seem to see deeper in the

[1] [This notion of anxiety serving as a 'signal' was to play a central part in Freud's later accounts of anxiety, in *Inhibitions, Symptoms and Anxiety* (1926d) and in the *New Introductory Lectures*. It appears again below on p. 405.]

[2] [Cf. similar later discussions in Chapter II of *Beyond the Pleasure Principle* (1920g), and in Addendum B to *Inhibitions, Symptoms and Anxiety* (1926d).]

case of some affects and to recognize that the core which holds the combination we have described together is the repetition of some particular significant experience. This experience could only be a very early impression of a very general nature, placed in the prehistory not of the individual but of the species. To make myself more intelligible—an affective state would be constructed in the same way as a hysterical attack and, like it, would be the precipitate of a reminiscence. A hysterical attack may thus be likened to a freshly constructed individual affect, and a normal affect to the expression of a general hysteria which has become a heritage.[1]

Do not suppose that the things I have said to you here about affects are the recognized stock-in-trade of normal psychology. They are on the contrary views that have grown up on the soil of psycho-analysis and are native only to it. What you may gather about affects from psychology—the James-Lange theory, for example—is quite beyond understanding or discussion to us psycho-analysts. But we do not regard our knowledge about affects as very assured either; it is a first attempt at finding our bearings in this obscure region. I will proceed, however. We believe that in the case of the affect of anxiety we know what the early impression is which it repeats. We believe that it is in the *act of birth* that there comes about the combination of unpleasurable feelings, impulses of discharge and bodily sensations which has become the prototype of the effects of a mortal danger and has ever since been repeated by us as the state of anxiety. The immense increase of stimulation owing to the interruption of the renovation of the blood (internal respiration) was at the time the cause of the experience of anxiety; the first anxiety was thus a toxic one. The name *'Angst'*— *'angustiae'*, *'Enge'*[2]—emphasizes the characteristic of restriction

---

[1] [This account of hysterical attacks had been suggested by Freud in a paper on that subject many years earlier (1909a). The view of affects in general which is expressed here may possibly be based on Darwin's explanation of them as relics of actions which originally had a meaning (Darwin, 1872)—an explanation quoted from him by Freud near the end of the Case of Elisabeth von R. (1895d). Freud repeats the present argument in *Inhibitions, Symptoms and Anxiety* (1926d).]

[2] [These Latin and German words, meaning 'narrow place', 'straits', are from the same root as *'Angst'* (and 'anxiety').]

in breathing which was then present as a consequence of the real situation and is now almost invariably reinstated in the affect. We shall also recognize it as highly relevant that this first state of anxiety arose out of separation from the mother.[1] It is, of course, our conviction that the disposition to repeat the first state of anxiety has been so thoroughly incorporated into the organism through a countless series of generations that a single individual cannot escape the affect of anxiety even if, like the legendary Macduff, he 'was from his mother's womb untimely ripped' and has therefore not himself experienced the act of birth. We cannot say what has become the prototype of the state of anxiety in the case of creatures other than mammals. And in the same way we do not know either what complex of feelings is in such creatures the equivalent to our anxiety.

It may perhaps interest you to learn how anyone could have formed such an idea as that the act of birth is the source and prototype of the affect of anxiety. Speculation had a very small share in it; what I did, rather, was to borrow from the *naïve* popular mind. Long years ago, while I was sitting with a number of other young hospital doctors at our mid-day meal in an inn, a house physician from the midwifery department told us of a comic thing that had happened at the last examination for midwives. A candidate was asked what it meant if meconium (excreta) made its appearance at birth in the water coming away, and she promptly replied: 'it means the child's frightened.' She was laughed at and failed in the examination. But silently I took her side and began to suspect that this poor woman from the humbler classes had laid an unerring finger on an important correlation.[2]

If we now pass over to consider neurotic anxiety, what fresh forms and situations are manifested by anxiety in neurotics?

---

[1] [See below, p. 407.]

[2] [The episode must have occurred in the early eighties, and this is the only record of it. A full history of Freud's belief in a connection between anxiety and birth was given in the Editor's Introduction to *Inhibitions, Symptoms and Anxiety*. From this it seemed that the first known reference to it was in a footnote appearing in the 1909 edition of *The Interpretation of Dreams*, and probably written in the summer of 1908. Since the publication of this Introduction, however, an earlier reference has come to light in the *Minutes of the Vienna Psychoanalytic Society* (1962). At a meeting on April 24, 1907, at which Stekel read a

There is much to be described here. In the first place we find a general apprehensiveness, a kind of freely floating anxiety which is ready to attach itself to any idea that is in any way suitable, which influences judgement, selects what is to be expected, and lies in wait for any opportunity that will allow it to justify itself. We call this state 'expectant anxiety' or 'anxious expectation'. People who are tormented by this kind of anxiety always foresee the most frightful of all possibilities, interpret every chance event as a premonition of evil and exploit every uncertainty in a bad sense. A tendency to an expectation of evil of this sort is to be found as a character trait in many people whom one cannot otherwise regard as sick; one calls them over-anxious or pessimistic. A striking amount of expectant anxiety, however, forms a regular feature of a nervous disorder to which I have given the name of 'anxiety neurosis' and which I include among the 'actual' neuroses.[1]

A second form of anxiety, in contrast to the one I have just described, is bound psychically[2] and attached to particular objects or situations. This is the anxiety of the extremely multifarious and often very strange 'phobias'. Stanley Hall [1914], the respected American psychologist, has recently taken the trouble to present us with a whole series of these phobias in all the magnificence of Greek names. This sounds like a list of the ten Plagues of Egypt, though their number goes far beyond ten.[3] Listen to all the things that can become the object or content of a phobia: darkness, open air, open spaces, cats,

paper on 'The Psychology and Pathology of the Anxiety Neurosis', Adler is reported to have made the following remark: 'One need not venture so far as Freud, who sees anxiety in the process of birth; but anxiety can be traced back into childhood.' Neither in Freud's contribution to the discussion, which was subsequent to Adler's, nor in any other, is the matter referred to again. It would appear from this, however, that Freud's hypothesis was familiarly known in the Vienna Society at least a couple of years before its first publication.]

[1] [Cf. Freud's original account of the anxiety neurosis (1895b).]
[2] [Instead of being freely floating.]
[3] [Actually, Stanley Hall enumerates 132 of them. See a review of his paper by Ernest Jones (1916). Stanley Hall (1846–1924) was originally a supporter of Freud's and it was he who invited Freud to lecture in America in 1909, though he later became a follower of Adler.]

spiders, caterpillars, snakes, mice, thunderstorms, sharp points, blood, enclosed spaces, crowds, solitude, crossing bridges, sea voyages and railway journeys, etc., etc. A first attempt at finding one's way about in this confusion suggests a division into three groups. Some of the dreaded objects and situations have something uncanny about them for normal people as well, some relation to danger; and such phobias, therefore, do not strike us as unintelligible, though their strength is greatly exaggerated. Thus most of us have a sense of repulsion if we meet with a snake. Snake phobia, we might say, is a universal human characteristic; and Darwin [1889, 40] has described most impressively how he could not avoid feeling fear of a snake that struck at him, even though he knew that he was protected from it by a thick sheet of glass. We may refer to a second group the cases in which a relation to a danger is still present, though we are accustomed to minimize the danger and not to anticipate it. The majority of situation phobias belong to this group. We know that there is more chance of an accident when we are on a railway-journey than when we stay at home—the chance of a collision; we know, too, that a ship may go down, in which case there is a probability of being drowned; but we do not think about these dangers, and travel by rail and ship without anxiety. It cannot be disputed that we should fall into the river if the bridge collapsed at the moment we were crossing it; but that happens so exceedingly seldom that it does not arise as a danger. Solitude, too, has its dangers and in certain circumstances we avoid it; but there is no question of our not being able to tolerate it under any condition even for a moment. Much the same is true of crowds, of enclosed spaces, of thunderstorms and so on. What in general appears to us strange in these phobias of neurotics is not so much their content as their intensity. The anxiety of phobias is positively overwhelming. And sometimes we get an impression that what neurotics are afraid of are not at all the same things and situations which may in certain circumstances cause anxiety in us too and which they describe by the same names.

We are left with a third group of phobias, which is quite beyond our comprehension. When a strong, grown-up man is unable owing to anxiety to walk along a street or cross a square in his own familiar home-town, when a healthy, well-developed woman is thrown into insensate anxiety because a cat has brushed against the edge of her dress or because a mouse has run across the room, how are we to relate these things to the danger which they obviously constitute for the phobic subject? In the case of such animal phobias there can be no question of an exaggeration of universal human antipathies, since, as though to demonstrate the contrary, there are numerous people who cannot pass by a cat without coaxing it and stroking it. The mouse of which these women are so much afraid of is also [in German] one of the chief terms of affection; a girl who is delighted when her lover calls her one will often scream with terror when she sees the pretty creature which bears that name. In the case of the man with agoraphobia the only explanation that we can reach is that he is behaving like a small child. A child is actually taught as part of his education to avoid such situations as dangerous; and our agoraphobic will in fact be saved from his anxiety if we accompany him across the square.

The two forms of anxiety that I have just described—the freely floating expectant anxiety and the sort which is bound to phobias—are independent of each other. One is not a higher stage, as it were, of the other; and they only appear simultaneously in exceptional cases and, so to speak, accidentally. The most powerful general apprehensiveness need not be expressed in phobias; people whose whole existence is restricted by agoraphobia may be entirely free from pessimistic expectant anxiety. Some phobias—for instance, agoraphobia and railway phobia—are demonstrably acquired at a fairly mature age, while others—such as fear of darkness, thunderstorms and animals—seem to have been present from the first. Those of the former kind have the significance of severe illnesses; the latter make their appearance rather as eccentricities or whims. If a person exhibits one of these latter, one may suspect as a rule that he will have other similar ones. I must add that we class all these phobias as *anxiety hysteria*; that is to say, we regard them as a disorder closely related to the familiar conversion hysteria[1] [p. 390].

[1] [Freud's first long discussion of anxiety hysteria was in the case history of 'little Hans' (1909b). Some account of his changing views on phobias is given in an Editor's Appendix to his early paper on 'Obsessions and Phobias' (1895c).]

The third of the forms of neurotic anxiety faces us with the puzzling fact that here the connection between anxiety and a threatening danger is completely lost to view. For instance, anxiety may appear in hysteria as an accompaniment to hysterical symptoms, or in some chance condition of excitement in which, it is true, we should expect some manifestation of affect but least of all one of anxiety; or it may make its appearance, divorced from any determinants and equally incomprehensible to us and to the patient, as an unrelated attack of anxiety. Here there is no sign whatever of any danger or of any cause that could be exaggerated into one. We next learn from these spontaneous attacks that the complex which we describe as a state of anxiety is capable of fragmentation. The total attack can be represented by a single, intensely developed symptom, by a tremor, a vertigo, by palpitation of the heart, or by dyspnoea; and the general feeling by which we recognize anxiety may be absent or have become indistinct. Yet these conditions, which we describe as 'anxiety-equivalents', have to be equated with anxiety in all clinical and aetiological respects.

Two questions now arise. Can we relate neurotic anxiety, in which danger plays little or no part, to realistic anxiety, which is invariably a reaction to danger? And how are we to understand neurotic anxiety? We shall certainly be inclined in the first instance to hold fast to our expectation that where there is anxiety there must be something that one is afraid of.

Clinical observation affords us a number of hints towards understanding neurotic anxiety, and I will give you their tenor:—

(a) It is not difficult to establish the fact that expectant anxiety or general apprehensiveness is closely dependent on certain happenings in sexual life, or, let us say, certain employments of the libido. The simplest and most instructive case of this sort occurs in people who expose themselves to what is known as unconsummated excitation—that is, people in whom violent sexual excitations meet with no sufficient discharge, cannot be brought to a satisfying conclusion—men, for instance, while they are engaged to be married, and women whose husbands are insufficiently potent or, as a precaution, perform the sexual act in an incomplete or curtailed fashion. In such circumstances the libidinal excitation vanishes and anxiety appears in its place whether in the form of expectant anxiety or in attacks and anxiety-equivalents. Interruption of the sexual act as a precaution, if it is practised as a sexual *régime*, is such a regular cause of anxiety neurosis in men, but more particularly in women, that in medical practice it is advisable in such cases to begin by investigating this aetiology. It will then be found on countless occasions that the anxiety neurosis disappears when the sexual abuse is discontinued.

The fact of there being a connection between sexual restraint and anxiety states is, so far as I know, no longer disputed even by physicians who have no contact with psycho-analysis. But I can well believe that an attempt is made to reverse the relation and to put forward the view that the people concerned are such as are already inclined to apprehensiveness and for that reason practise restraint in sexual matters as well. This, however, is decisively contradicted by the behaviour of women, whose sexual activity is essentially of a passive nature—is determined, that is to say, by their treatment by the man. The more passionate a woman is—the more inclined, therefore, to sexual intercourse and the more capable of being satisfied—the more certain she is to react with manifestations of anxiety to a man's impotence or to coitus interruptus, whereas in the case of anaesthetic women or those without much libido such ill-treatment plays a far smaller part.

Of course, the sexual abstinence now so warmly recommended by doctors only has the same importance in generating anxiety states when the libido which is prevented from finding a satisfying discharge is correspondingly strong and has not been dealt with for the greater part by sublimation. Indeed, the decision on whether the outcome is to be illness or not always lies with quantitative factors. Even where what is in question is not illness but the form assumed by a person's character, it is easy to recognize that sexual restriction goes hand in hand with some kind of anxiousness and hesitancy, while intrepidity and impudent daring bring along with them a free indulgence of sexual needs. However much these relations are altered and complicated by a variety of cultural influences, it nevertheless remains true of the average of mankind that anxiety has a close connection with sexual limitation.

I am far from having told you of all the observations that

speak in favour of the genetic relation I have asserted to exist between libido and anxiety. Among them, for instance, is the influence on anxiety disorders of certain phases of life to which, as in the case of puberty and the time of the menopause, a considerable increase in the production of libido may be attributed. In some states of excitement, too, it is possible to observe directly a mixture of libido and anxiety and the final replacement of libido by anxiety. The impression one gains from all these facts is twofold: first, that what is in question is an accumulation of libido which is kept away from its normal employment, and secondly, that here we are entirely in the sphere of somatic processes. How anxiety arises from libido is not at first discernible; we can only recognize that libido is absent and that anxiety is observed in its place.[1]

(b) A second pointer is to be found in the analysis of the psychoneuroses, and especially of hysteria. We have seen that in this illness anxiety often appears in company with the symptoms, but that unbound anxiety appears, too, manifested as an attack or as a chronic condition. The patients cannot say what it is they are afraid of, and, by the help of an unmistakable secondary revision [p. 182], link it to the first phobias that come to hand—such as dying, going mad, or having a stroke. If the situation out of which the anxiety (or the symptoms accompanied by anxiety) arose is subjected to analysis, we can as a rule discover what normal course of psychical events has failed to occur and has been replaced by phenomena of anxiety. To express it in another way: we construct the unconscious process as it would have been if it had not experienced any repression and had proceeded unhindered into consciousness. [Pp. 293–4.] This process would have been accompanied by a particular affect, and we now learn to our surprise that this affect accompanying the normal course of events is invariably replaced by anxiety after repression has occurred, no matter what its own quality may be. Thus, when we have a hysterical anxiety-state before us, its unconscious correlate may be an impulse of a similar character—anxiety, shame, embarrassment—or, just as easily, a positive libidinal excitation or a hostile aggressive one, such as rage or anger. Anxiety is therefore the universally

[1] [The last four paragraphs are to a large extent a summary of Freud's first paper on anxiety neurosis (1895b).]

current coinage for which *any* affective impulse is or can be exchanged if the ideational content attached to it is subjected to repression.[1]

(*c*) We make a third discovery when we come to patients suffering from obsessional actions, who seem in a remarkable way exempt from anxiety. If we try to hinder their carrying out of their obsessional action—their washing or their ceremonial—or if they themselves venture upon an attempt to give up one of their compulsions, they are forced by the most terrible anxiety to yield to the compulsion. We can see that the anxiety was screened by the obsessional action, and that the latter was only performed in order to avoid the anxiety. In an obsessional neurosis, therefore, anxiety which would otherwise inevitably set in is replaced by the formation of a symptom, and if we turn to hysteria we find a similar relation: the result of the process of repression is either a generating of anxiety pure and simple, or anxiety accompanied by the formation of a symptom, or a more complete formation of a symptom without anxiety. It would thus seem not to be wrong in an abstract sense to assert that in general symptoms are only formed to escape an otherwise unavoidable generating of anxiety. If we adopt this view, anxiety is placed, as it were, in the very centre of our interest in the problems of neurosis.

Our observations on anxiety neurosis led us to conclude that the deflection of the libido from its normal employment, which causes the development of anxiety, takes place in the region of somatic processes [p. 403]. Analyses of hysteria and obsessional neurosis yield the additional conclusion that a similar deflection with the same outcome may also be the result of a refusal on the part of the *psychical* agencies. This much, therefore, we know about the origin of neurotic anxiety. It still sounds fairly indefinite; but for the moment I see no path that would lead us further. The second problem we set ourselves—of establishing a connection between neurotic anxiety, which is libido put to an abnormal employment, and realistic anxiety, which corresponds to a reaction to danger—seems even harder to solve. One might suppose that these were two quite disparate

[1] [See the metapsychological paper on 'Repression' (1915*d*).]

things; and yet we have no means of distinguishing in our feelings between realistic anxiety and neurotic anxiety.

We finally arrive at the connection we are in search of, if we take as our starting-point the opposition we have so often asserted between the ego and the libido. As we know, the generation of anxiety is the ego's reaction to danger and the signal for taking flight. [Cf. p. 395.] If so, it seems plausible to suppose that in neurotic anxiety the ego is making a similar attempt at flight from the demand by its libido, that it is treating this internal danger as though it were an external one. This would therefore fulfil our expectation [p. 401] that where anxiety is shown there is something one is afraid of. But the analogy could be carried further. Just as the attempt at flight from an external danger is replaced by standing firm and the adoption of expedient measures of defence, so too the generation of neurotic anxiety gives place to the formation of symptoms, which results in the anxiety being bound.

The difficulty in understanding now lies elsewhere. The anxiety which signifies a flight of the ego from its libido is after all supposed to be derived from that libido itself. This is obscure and it reminds us not to forget that after all a person's libido is fundamentally something of his and cannot be contrasted with him as something external. It is the topographical dynamics of the generation of anxiety which are still obscure to us—the question of what mental energies are produced in that process and from what mental systems they derive. This is once more a question which I cannot promise to answer: but there are two other tracks which we must not fail to follow and in doing so we shall once more be making use of direct observation and analytic enquiry as a help to our speculations. We will turn to the genesis of anxiety in children and to the source of the neurotic anxiety which is attached to phobias.

Apprehensiveness in children is something very usual, and it seems most difficult to distinguish whether it is neurotic or realistic anxiety. Indeed the value of making the distinction is put in question by the behaviour of children. For on the one hand we are not surprised if a child is frightened of all strangers, or of new situations and things; and we account for this reaction very easily as being due to his weakness and ignorance. Thus we attribute to children a strong inclination to realistic anxiety and we should regard it as quite an expedient arrangement if this apprehensiveness were an innate heritage in them. Children would merely be repeating in this the behaviour of prehistoric men and of modern primitive peoples who as a result of their ignorance and helplessness are afraid of every novelty and of many familiar things which no longer cause us any anxiety to-day. And it would fit in perfectly with our expectation if children's phobias, in part at least, were the same as those which we may attribute to the primaeval periods of human development.

On the other hand we cannot overlook the fact that not all children are anxious to the same degree, and that precisely children who exhibit a special timidity towards objects and in situations of every kind turn out later to be neurotic. Thus the neurotic disposition betrays itself also by an outspoken tendency to realistic anxiety; apprehensiveness appears to be the primary thing and we reach the conclusion that the reason why children and, later, growing youths and girls are afraid of the height of their libido is because in fact they are afraid of everything. The genesis of anxiety from libido would in this way be denied; and if one examined into the determinants of realistic anxiety, consistency would lead one to the view that consciousness of one's own weakness and helplessness—inferiority, according to Adler's terminology,—if it can be prolonged from childhood into adult life, is the final basis of neuroses.

This sounds so simple and seductive that it has a claim on our attention. It is true that it would involve a displacement of the riddle of the neurotic state. The continued existence of the sense of inferiority—and thus, of what determines anxiety and the formation of symptoms—seems so well assured that what calls for an explanation is rather how, as an exception, what we know as health can come about. But what is revealed by a careful examination of apprehensiveness in children? At the very beginning, what children are afraid of is strange *people*; situations only become important because they include people, and impersonal things do not come into account at all until later. But a child is not afraid of these strangers because he attributes evil intentions to them and compares his weakness with their strength, and accordingly assesses them as dangers to his existence, safety and freedom from pain. A child who is mistrustful in this way and terrified of the aggressive instinct which dominates the world is a theoretical construction that has quite miscarried. A child is frightened of a strange face because he is adjusted to the sight of a familiar and beloved figure— ultimately of his mother. It is his disappointment and longing that are transformed into anxiety—his libido, in fact, which has become unemployable, which cannot at that time be held in suspense and is discharged as anxiety. And it can scarcely be a matter of chance, either, that in this situation which is the prototype of the anxiety of children there is a repetition of the determinant of the first state of anxiety during the act of birth—namely, separation from the mother.[1]

In children the first phobias relating to situations are those of darkness and solitude. The former of these often persists throughout life; both are involved when a child feels the absence of some loved person who looks after it—its mother, that is to say. While I was in the next room, I heard a child who was afraid of the dark call out: 'Do speak to me, Auntie! I'm frightened!' 'Why, what good would that do? You can't see me.' To this the child replied: 'If someone speaks, it gets lighter.'[2] Thus a *longing* felt in the dark is transformed into a *fear* of the dark. Far from its being the case that neurotic anxiety is only secondary and a special case of realistic anxiety, we see on the contrary that in a small child something that behaves like realistic anxiety shares its essential feature—origin from unemployed libido—with neurotic anxiety. Innately, children seem to have little true realistic anxiety. In all the situations which can later become determinants of phobias (on heights, on narrow bridges over water, on railway journeys, on ships) children exhibit no anxiety; and, to be sure, the greater

[1] [This was Freud's first explicit insistence on the primary importance of separation from the mother as a factor in the origin of anxiety, though it had been suggested above (p. 397) and implied in earlier writings. References to these will be found in the Editor's Introduction to *Inhibitions, Symptoms and Anxiety* (1926d). In the latter work the matter was discussed at greater length in Chapter VIII. It had also been briefly mentioned at the end of Chapter V in *The Ego and the Id* (1923b), (Norton, 1960).]

[2] [This anecdote had appeared (in a slightly different form) in a footnote to Section 5 of the third of Freud's *Three Essays* (1905d).]

their ignorance the less their anxiety. It would have been a very good thing if they had inherited more of such life-preserving instincts,[1] for that would have greatly facilitated the task of watching over them to prevent their running into one danger after another. The fact is that children, to begin with, over-estimate their strength and behave fearlessly because they are ignorant of dangers. They will run along the brink of the water, climb on to the window-sill, play with sharp objects and with fire—in short, do everything that is bound to damage them and to worry those in charge of them. When in the end realistic anxiety is awakened in them, that is wholly the result of educa-tion; for they cannot be allowed to make the instructive experiences themselves.

If, then, there are children who come some way to meet this education in anxiety, and who go on to find dangers themselves that they have not been warned against, this is sufficiently explained by the fact that they have a greater amount of innate libidinal need in their constitution or have been prematurely spoiled by libidinal satisfaction. It is not to be wondered at if such children include, too, the later neurotics: as we know, what most facilitates the development of a neurosis is an in-capacity to tolerate a considerable damming-up of libido over any great length of time. You will observe that here once more the constitutional factor comes into its rights—and these, in-deed, we have never sought to dispute. We are only on our guard against those who in its favour neglect all other claims, and who introduce the constitutional factor at points at which the combined results of observation and analysis show that it does not belong or must take the last place.

Let me sum up what we have learnt from our observations of the apprehensiveness of children. Infantile anxiety has very little to do with realistic anxiety, but, on the other hand, is closely related to the neurotic anxiety of adults. Like the latter, it is derived from unemployed libido and it replaces the missing love-object by an external object or by a situation.

You will be glad to hear that the analysis of phobias has not much more that is new to teach us. For the same thing happens

[1] [This is one of the extremely few occasions on which Freud uses the word '*Instinkt*' instead of his usual '*Trieb*'.]

with them as with children's anxiety: unemployable libido is being constantly transformed into an apparently realistic anxiety and thus a tiny external danger is introduced to represent the claims of the libido. There is nothing to be wondered at in this agreement [between phobias and children's anxiety], for the infantile phobias are not only the prototype of the later ones which we class as 'anxiety hysteria' but are actually their precondition and the prelude to them. Every hysterical phobia goes back to an infantile anxiety and is a continuation of it, even if it has a different content and must thus be given another name. The difference between the two disorders lies in their mechanism. In order that libido shall be changed into anxiety, it no longer suffices in the case of adults for the libido to have become momentarily unemployable in the form of a longing. Adults have long since learnt how to hold such libido in suspense or to employ it in some other way. If, however, the libido belongs to a psychical impulse which has been subjected to repression, then circumstances are re-established similar to those in the case of a child in whom there is still no distinction between conscious and unconscious; and by means of regression to the infantile phobia a passage is opened, as it were, through which the transformation of libido into anxiety can be comfortably accomplished.

As you will recall, we have dealt with repression at great length,[1] but in doing so we have always followed the vicissitudes only of the idea that is to be repressed—naturally, since this was easier to recognize and describe. We have always left on one side the question of what happens to the affect that was attached to the repressed idea; and it is only now that we learn [p. 403] that the immediate vicissitude of that affect is to be transformed into anxiety, whatever quality it may have exhibited apart from this in the normal course of events. This transformation of affect is, however, by far the more important part of the process of repression. It is not so easy to speak of this, since we cannot assert the existence of unconscious affects in the same sense as that of unconscious ideas.[2] An idea remains

[1] [In Lecture XIX.]
[2] [For more information on what follows, see the third section of the metapsychological paper on 'The Unconscious' (1915e), and the second chapter of *The Ego and the Id* (1923b), (Norton, 1960).]

the same, except for the one difference, whether it is conscious or unconscious; we can state what it is that corresponds to an unconscious idea. But an affect is a process of discharge and must be judged quite differently from an idea; what corresponds to it in the unconscious cannot be declared without deeper reflection and a clarification of our hypotheses about psychical processes. And that we cannot undertake here. We will, however, emphasize the impression we have now gained that the generation of anxiety is intimately linked to the system of the unconscious.

I have said that transformation into anxiety—it would be better to say discharge in the form of anxiety—is the immediate vicissitude of libido which is subjected to repression. I must add that that vicissitude is not the only or the definitive one. In the neuroses processes are in action which endeavour to bind this generating of anxiety and which even succeed in doing so in various ways. In phobias, for instance, two phases of the neurotic process can be clearly distinguished. The first is concerned with repression and the changing of libido into anxiety, which is then bound to an external danger. The second consists in the erection of all the precautions and guarantees by means of which any contact can be avoided with this danger, treated as it is like an external thing. Repression corresponds to an attempt at flight by the ego from libido which is felt as a danger. A phobia may be compared to an entrenchment against an external danger which now represents the dreaded libido. The weakness of the defensive system in phobias lies, of course, in the fact that the fortress which has been so greatly strengthened towards the outside remains assailable from within. A projection outwards of the danger of libido can never succeed thoroughly.[1] For that reason, in other neuroses other systems of defence are in use against the possible generation of anxiety. That is a most interesting part of the psychology of the neuroses; but unluckily it would lead us too far and it presupposes a deeper specialized knowledge. I will only add one thing more. I have already spoken to you [p. 360] of the 'anticathexis' which is employed by the ego in the process of repression and

---

[1] [More technical accounts of the structure of phobias will be found in 'Repression' (1915d), and 'The Unconscious' (1915e).]

which must be permanently maintained in order that the repression may have stability. This anticathexis has the task of carrying through the various forms of defence against the generating of anxiety after repression.

Let us return to the phobias. I can safely say that you now see how inadequate it is merely to seek to explain their content, to take no interest in anything but how it comes about that this or that object or some particular situation or other has been made into the object of the phobia. The content of a phobia has just about as much importance in relation to it as the manifest façade of a dream has in relation to the dream. It must be admitted, subject to the necessary qualifications, that among the contents of phobias there are a number which, as Stanley Hall [1914, see p. 398] insists, are adapted to serve as objects of anxiety owing to phylogenetic inheritance. It tallies with this, indeed, that many of these anxiety-objects can only establish their connection with danger by a symbolic tie.

We thus find ourselves convinced that the problem of anxiety occupies a place in the question of the psychology of the neuroses which may rightly be described as central. We have received a strong impression of the way in which the generation of anxiety is linked to the vicissitudes of the libido and the system of the unconscious. There is only a single point that we have found disconnected—a gap in our views: the single, yet scarcely disputable, fact that realistic anxiety must be regarded as a manifestation of the ego's self-preservative instincts.[1]

[1] [This difficulty is met at the end of the next lecture, p. 430.]

THE LIBIDO THEORY AND NARCISSISM

LADIES AND GENTLEMEN,—We have repeatedly (and only recently once again [p. 350]) had to deal with the distinction between the ego-instincts and the sexual instincts. In the first place, repression showed us that the two can come into opposition to each other, that the sexual instincts are then ostensibly subdued and are obliged to find satisfaction for themselves along regressive and roundabout paths, and that in doing so they are able to find compensation for their defeat in their indomitability. We next learnt that the two kinds of instincts are from the first differently related to Necessity the educator [p. 355], so that their course of development is not the same and they do not enter into the same connection with the reality principle. Lastly, we seem to have found that the sexual instincts are linked by much closer bonds than the ego-instincts to the affective state of anxiety—a conclusion which seems incomplete in only one important respect. In order to establish it more firmly, therefore, I will bring forward the further noteworthy fact that if hunger and thirst (the two most elementary self-preservative instincts) are unsatisfied, the result is never their transformation into anxiety, whereas the changing of unsatisfied libido into anxiety is, as we have seen, among the best known and most frequently observed of phenomena.

Our right to separate the ego-instincts from the sexual ones cannot, no doubt, be shaken: it is implied in the existence of sexual life as a distinct activity of the individual. The only question is what importance we attribute to this separation, how deep-going we wish to consider it. The answer to this question, however, will be guided by how far we are able to establish the extent to which the sexual instincts behave differently in their somatic and mental manifestations from the others which we are contrasting with them, and how important the consequences are which arise from those differences. Moreover, we have, of course, no motive for asserting an essential difference between the two groups of instincts which is not plainly appreciable. Both of them come before us merely as designations of sources of energy in the individual, and the discussion as to whether they are fundamentally one or essentially different and as to when, if they are one, they became separate from each other—this discussion cannot be conducted on the basis of the connotation of the terms but must keep to the biological facts lying behind them. At the moment we know too little about these, and even if we knew more it would have no relevance for our analytic task.

It is obvious, too, that we shall profit very little if, following Jung's example, we insist upon the original unity of all the instincts and give the name of 'libido' to the energy manifested in all of them. Since no device whatever will make it possible to eliminate the sexual function from mental life, we shall in that case find ourselves obliged to speak of sexual and asexual libido. But the name of libido is properly reserved for the instinctual forces of sexual life, as has hitherto been our practice.

In my opinion, therefore, the question of how far we are to carry the undoubtedly justifiable separation between the sexual and self-preservative instincts is not of much importance for psycho-analysis. Nor is psycho-analysis competent to answer the question. Biology, however, offers a number of suggestive possibilities which speak in favour of the distinction having some importance. Sexuality is, indeed, the single function of the living organism which extends beyond the individual and is concerned with his relation to the species. It is an unmistakable fact that it does not always, like the individual organism's other functions, bring it advantages, but, in return for an unusually high degree of pleasure, brings dangers which threaten the individual's life and often enough destroy it. It is probable, too, that quite special metabolic processes are necessary, differing from all others, in order to maintain a portion of the individual life as a disposition for its descendants. And finally, the individual organism, which regards itself as the main thing and its sexuality as a means, like any other, for its own satisfaction, is from the point of view of biology only an episode in a succession of generations, a short-lived appendage to a germ-plasm endowed with virtual immortality—like the temporary holder of an entail which will outlast him.[1]

The psycho-analytic explanation of the neuroses does not, however, call for such far-ranging considerations. The separate following-up of the sexual and ego-instincts has helped us to find the key to an understanding of the group of transference neuroses. We have been able to trace them back to the basic situation in which the sexual instincts have come into a dispute with the self-preservative instincts, or, to put it in biological (though less precise) terms, a situation in which one aspect of the ego, as an independent individual organism, comes into conflict with its other aspect, as a member of a succession of generations. A dissension of this kind may perhaps only occur in human beings, and on that account neurosis may, generally speaking, constitute their prerogative over the animals. The excessive development of their libido and—what is perhaps made possible precisely by that—their development of a richly articulated mental life seem to have created the determinants for the occurrence of such a conflict. It is at once obvious that these are also the determinants for the great advances that human beings have made beyond what they have in common with the animals; so that their susceptibility to neurosis would only be the reverse side of their other endowments. But these too are only speculations, which are diverting us from our immediate task.

Hitherto it has been a premiss of our work that we can distinguish the ego-instincts from the sexual ones by their manifestations. With the transference neuroses this could be done without difficulty. We termed the cathexes of energy which the ego directs towards the objects of its sexual desires 'libido'; all the others, which are sent out by the self-preservative instincts, we termed 'interest'.[2] By tracing the course of the

[1] [Freud developed this biological argument further in *Beyond the Pleasure Principle* (1920g), particularly in Chapter VI.]

[2] [The term 'ego-interest', sometimes in the alternative forms of 'egoistic interest' or simply 'interest', occurs frequently in this lecture. Freud had first used the term in his paper on narcissism (1914c), and it also appears several times in the metapsychological papers of 1915. The term is used regularly in those passages (as it is in the present one) to distinguish self-preservative forces from the libido. The introduction of the concept of narcissism made this distinction less clear-cut; but it is evident that all through

libidinal cathexes, their transformations and final vicissitudes, we were able to obtain a first insight into the machinery of the mental forces. For this purpose the transference neuroses offered us the most favourable material. But the ego, its composition out of various organizations and their construction and mode of functioning, remained hidden from us; and we were driven to suspect that only the analysis of other neurotic disorders would be able to bring us the necessary insight.

We began at an early date to extend psycho-analytic observations to these other illnesses. Already in 1908 Karl Abraham, after an exchange of thoughts with me, pronounced the main characteristic of dementia praecox (which was reckoned among the psychoses) to be that *in it the libidinal cathexis of objects was lacking*. But the question then arose of what happened to the libido of dementia praecox patients which had turned away from objects. Abraham did not hesitate to give the answer: it is turned back on to the ego and *this reflexive turning-back is the source of the megalomania* in dementia praecox. Megalomania is in every way comparable to the familiar sexual overvaluation of the object in [normal] erotic life.[1] In this way for the first time we learnt to understand a trait in a psychotic illness by relating it to normal erotic life.

I may tell you at once that these first explanations of Abraham's have been accepted in psycho-analysis and have become the basis of our attitude to the psychoses. We thus slowly became familiar with the notion that the libido, which we find attached to objects and which is the expression of an effort to obtain satisfaction in connection with those objects,

this lecture (see, in particular, its last paragraph) Freud was at pains to keep ego-libido (or narcissistic libido) separate from ego-interest (or the self-preservative instinct). Not long afterwards, however, he abandoned this attempt and declared in *Beyond the Pleasure Principle* (1920g), that narcissistic libido 'had necessarily to be identified with the "self-preservative instinct" '. He continued to believe, nevertheless, that there were object-instincts other than libidinal ones—namely those which he described as destructive or death instincts. But after the present work the term 'interest' ceased to appear. A fuller account of this is given in the Editor's Note to 'Instincts and their Vicissitudes' (1915c).]

[1] [This is discussed in the first of Freud's *Three Essays* (1905d).]

can also leave the objects and set the subject's own ego in their place; and this notion was gradually built up more and more consistently. The name for this way of allocating the libido—'narcissism'—was borrowed by us from a perversion described by Paul Näcke [1899] in which an adult treats his own body with all the caresses that are usually devoted to an outside sexual object.[1]

Reflection will quickly suggest that if any such fixation of the libido to the subject's own body and personality instead of to an object does occur, it cannot be an exceptional or a trivial event. On the contrary it is probable that this narcissism is the universal and original state of things, from which object-love is only later developed, without the narcissism necessarily disappearing on that account. Indeed we had to recall from the history of the development of object-libido that many sexual instincts begin by finding satisfaction in the subject's own body —*auto-erotically*, as we say [p. 314]—and that this capacity for auto-erotism is the basis of the lagging-behind of sexuality in the process of education in the reality principle [p. 355]. Auto-erotism would thus be the sexual activity of the narcissistic stage of allocation of the libido.

To put the matter shortly, we pictured the relation of ego-libido to object-libido in a way which I can make plain to you by an analogy from zoology. Think of those simplest of living organisms [the amoebas] which consist of a little-differentiated globule of protoplasmic substance. They put out protrusions, known as pseudopodia, into which they cause the substance of their body to flow over. They are able, however, to withdraw the protrusions once more and form themselves again into a globule. We compare the putting-out of these protrusions, then, to the emission of libido on to objects while the main mass of libido can remain in the ego; and we suppose that in normal circumstances ego-libido can be transformed unhindered into object-libido and that this can once more be taken back into the ego.[2]

[1] [The term is in part due to Havelock Ellis. See a full discussion in an Editor's first footnote to Freud's paper on narcissism (1914c), which is Freud's main exposition of the whole subject.]

[2] [Some discussion of this analogy will be found in the Editor's Appendix B to *The Ego and the Id* (1923b), (Norton, 1960).]

With the help of these ideas we are now able to explain a whole number of mental states or, to express it more modestly, to describe them in terms of the libido theory—states which we must reckon as belonging to normal life, such as the psychical behaviour of a person in love, during an organic illness or when asleep. As regards the state of sleep, we assumed that it was based on turning-away from the external world and adopting a wish to sleep [p. 88]. The mental activity during the night which is manifested in dreams takes place, we found, in obedience to a wish to sleep and is moreover dominated by purely egoistic motives [p. 142].We may now add, on the lines of the libido theory, that sleep is a state in which all object-cathexes, libidinal as well as egoistic, are given up and withdrawn into the ego. May not this throw a fresh light on the recuperating effect of sleep and on the nature of fatigue in general? The picture of the blissful isolation of intra-uterine life which a sleeper conjures up once more before us every night is in this way completed on its psychical side as well. In a sleeper the primal state of distribution of the libido is restored —total narcissism, in which libido and ego-interest, still united and indistinguishable, dwell in the self-sufficing ego.

This is the place for two remarks. First, how do we differenti-ate between the concepts of narcissism and egoism? Well, narcissism, I believe, is the libidinal complement to egoism. When we speak of egoism, we have in view only the individual's *advantage*; when we talk of narcissism we are also taking his libidinal satisfaction into account. As practical motives the two can be traced separately for quite a distance. It is possible to be absolutely egoistic and yet maintain powerful object-cathexes, in so far as libidinal satisfaction in relation to the object forms part of the ego's needs. In that case, egoism will see to it that striving for the object involves no damage to the ego. It is possible to be egoistic and at the same time to be excessively narcissistic—that is to say, to have very little need for an object, whether, once more, for the purpose of direct sexual satisfaction, or in connection with the higher aspirations, derived from sexual need, which we are occasionally in the habit of contrasting with 'sensuality' under the name of 'love'. In all these connections egoism is what is self-evident and constant, while narcissism is the variable element. The opposite to egoism, *altruism*, does not, as a concept, coincide with libidinal object-cathexis, but is distinguished from it by the absence of longings for sexual satisfaction. When someone is completely in love, however, altruism converges with libidinal object-cathexis. As a rule the sexual object attracts a portion of the ego's narcissism to itself, and this becomes noticeable as what is known as the 'sexual overvaluation' of the object. [See above, p. 415.] If in addition there is an altruistic transposition of egoism on to the sexual object, the object becomes supremely powerful; it has, as it were, absorbed the ego.

You will find it refreshing, I believe, if, after what is the essentially dry imagery of science, I present you with a poetic representation of the economic[1] contrast between narcissism and being in love. Here is a quotation from Goethe's *West-östlicher Diwan*:[2]

ZULEIKA

The slave, the lord of victories,
    The crowd, when'er you ask, confess
In sense of personal being lies
    A child of earth's chief happiness.

There's not a life we need refuse
    If our true self we do not miss,
There's not a thing we may not lose
    If one remain the man one is.

HATEM

So it is held, so well may be;
    But down a different track I come;
Of all the bliss earth holds for me
    I in Zuleika find the sum.

Does she expend her being on me,
    Myself grows to myself of cost;
Turns she away, then instantly
    I to my very self am lost.

[1] [I.e. the quantitative factor in the energies concerned. See p. 374 above.]

[2] [The translation is from Ernest Dowden, *West Eastern Divan*, 1914. The word 'divan' in its original Persian sense, which was adopted by Goethe, meant 'a collection of poems'.]

That day with Hatem all were over;
    And yet I should but change my state;
Swift, should she grace some happy lover,
    In him I were incorporate.

My second remark is a supplement to the theory of dreams. We cannot explain the origin of dreams unless we adopt the hypothesis that the repressed unconscious has achieved some degree of independence of the ego, so that it does not acquiesce in the wish to sleep and retains its cathexes even when all the object-cathexes depending on the ego have been withdrawn in order to encourage sleep. Only if that is so can we understand how the unconscious can make use of the lifting or reduction of the censorship which occurs at night, and can succeed in obtaining control over the day's residues so as to construct a forbidden dream-wish out of their material. On the other hand, it may be that these day's residues have to thank an already existing connection with the repressed unconscious for some of their resistance to the withdrawal of libido commanded by the wish to sleep. We will, then, insert this dynamically important feature into our view of the formation of dreams by way of supplement.[1]

Organic illness, painful stimulation or inflammation of an organ, creates a condition which clearly results in a detachment of the libido from its objects. The libido which is withdrawn is found in the ego once more, as an increased cathexis of the diseased part of the body. One may venture to assert, indeed, that the withdrawal of the libido from its objects in these circumstances is more striking than the diversion of egoistic interest from the external world. This seems to offer us a path to an understanding of hypochondria, in which an organ excites the ego's attention in the same way, without being ill so far as we can perceive.

But I shall resist the temptation of going further here or of discussing other situations which can be understood or pictured if we adopt the hypothesis that the object-libido may withdraw into the ego—for I am obliged to meet two objections which, as I know, are now attracting your attention. In the first place

[1] [This had been discussed by Freud at greater length in his 'Metapsychological Supplement to the Theory of Dreams' (1917d [1915]).]

you want to call me to account because in talking of sleep, illness and similar situations I invariably try to separate libido from interest, sexual from ego-instincts, where observations can be fully satisfied by the hypothesis of a single and uniform energy which, being freely mobile, cathects now the object and now the ego, in obedience to one or the other instinct. And in the second place you want to know how I can venture to treat the detaching of the libido from the object as the source of a pathological state, when a transposition of this kind of object-libido into ego-libido (or, more generally, into ego-energy) is among the normal processes of mental dynamics which are repeated daily and every night.

Here is my reply. Your first objection sounds well enough. Consideration of the states of sleep, of illness and of being in love in themselves would probably never have led us to distinguish an ego-libido from an object-libido or libido from interest. But there you are neglecting the investigations from which we started and in the light of which we now look at the mental situations under discussion. The differentiation between libido and interest—that is to say, between the sexual and the self-preservative instincts—was forced upon us by our discovery of the conflict out of which the transference neuroses arise. Since then we cannot give it up. The hypothesis that object-libido can be transformed into ego-libido, that we must therefore take an ego-libido into account, seems to us the only one which is able to resolve the enigma of what are termed the narcissistic neuroses—dementia praecox, for instance—and to account for the resemblances and dissimilarities between them and hysteria or obsessions. We are now applying to illness, sleep and being in love what we have elsewhere found inescapably established. We should proceed further with applications of this kind and see where they will take us to. The only thesis which is not an immediate precipitate of our analytic experience is to the effect that libido remains libido, whether it is directed to objects or to one's own ego, and never turns into egoistic interest, and the converse is also true. This thesis, however, is equivalent to the separation between the sexual and ego-instincts which we have already considered critically and to which we shall continue to hold for heuristic reasons until its possible collapse.

Your second observation, too, raises a justifiable question, but it is aimed in the wrong direction. It is true that a withdrawal of the object-libido into the ego is not directly pathogenic; it takes place, indeed, as we know, every time before we go to sleep, only to be reversed when we wake up. The amoeba withdraws its protrusions only to send them out again at the first opportunity. But it is quite a different thing when a particular, very energetic process forces a withdrawal of libido from objects. Here the libido that has become narcissistic cannot find its way back to objects, and this interference with the libido's mobility certainly becomes pathogenic. It seems that an accumulation of narcissistic libido beyond a certain amount is not tolerated. We may even imagine that it was for that very reason that object-cathexes originally came about, that the ego was obliged to send out its libido so as not to fall ill as a result of its being dammed up. If it lay within our plan to go more deeply into dementia praecox, I would show you that the process which detaches the libido from objects and cuts off its return to them is closely related to the process of repression and is to be looked at as its counterpart. But you would, first and foremost, find yourselves on familiar ground when you learnt that the determinants of this process are almost identical—so far as we know at present—with those of repression. The conflict seems to be the same and to be carried on between the same forces. If the outcome is so different from, for instance, that in hysteria, the reason can only depend on a difference in innate disposition. The weak spot in the libidinal development of these patients lies in a different phase; the determining fixation, which, as you will recollect [p. 346], permits the irruption that leads to the formation of symptoms, lies elsewhere, probably in the stage of primitive narcissism to which dementia praecox returns in its final outcome. It is very remarkable that in the case of all the narcissistic neuroses we have to assume fixation points for the libido going back to far earlier phases of development than in hysteria or obsessional neurosis. As you heard, however, the concepts which we arrived at during our study of the transference neuroses are adequate in helping us to find our way about in the narcissistic neuroses which are so much more severe in practice. The conformities go very far; at bottom the field of phenomena is the same. And you can imagine how small a prospect anyone has of explaining these disorders (which belong within the sphere of psychiatry) who is not forearmed for his task with an analytic knowledge of the transference neuroses.

The clinical picture of dementia praecox (which, incidentally, is very changeable) is not determined exclusively by the symptoms arising from the forcing away of the libido from objects and its accumulation in the ego as narcissistic libido. A large part, rather, is played by other phenomena, which are derived from efforts of the libido to attain objects once more and which thus correspond to an attempt at restitution or recovery. These latter symptoms are indeed the more striking and noisy; they exhibit an undeniable resemblance to those of hysteria or, less frequently, of obsessional neurosis, but nevertheless differ from them in every respect. It seems as though in dementia praecox the libido, in its efforts once more to reach objects (that is, the presentations of objects), does in fact snatch hold of something of them, but, as it were, only their shadows—I mean the word-presentations belonging to them. I cannot say more about this now, but I believe that this behaviour of the libido as it strives to find its way back has enabled us to obtain an insight into what really constitutes the difference between a conscious and an unconscious idea.[1]

I have now led you into the region in which the next advances in the work of analysis are to be expected [p. 379]. Since we have ventured to operate with the concept of ego-libido the narcissistic neuroses have become accessible to us; the task before us is to arrive at a dynamic elucidation of these disorders and at the same time to complete our knowledge of mental life by coming to understand the ego. The ego-psychology after which we are seeking must not be based on the data of our self-perceptions but (as in the case of the libido) on the analysis of disturbances and disruptions of the ego. It is likely that we shall have a low opinion of our present knowledge of the vicissitudes

[1] [The view that some of the symptoms in the psychoses represent attempts at recovery was first expressed by Freud in his Schreber analysis (1911c), where an Editor's footnote gives a number of further references. The point, only hinted at here, as to the basic distinction between conscious and unconscious ideas, had been discussed at length in Section VII of the metapsychological paper on the unconscious (1915e).]

of the libido, which we have gained from a study of the transference neuroses, when we have achieved this greater task. But hitherto we have not made much progress with it. The narcissistic neuroses can scarcely be attacked with the technique that has served us with the transference neuroses. You will soon learn why. [Cf. p. 447 below.] What always happens with them is that, after proceeding for a short distance, we come up against a wall which brings us to a stop. Even with the transference neuroses, as you know, we met with barriers of resistance, but we were able to demolish them bit by bit. In the narcissistic neuroses the resistance is unconquerable; at the most, we are able to cast an inquisitive glance over the top of the wall and spy out what is going on on the other side of it. Our technical methods must accordingly be replaced by others; and we do not know yet whether we shall succeed in finding a substitute. Nevertheless, we have no lack of material with these patients either. They make a large number of remarks, even if they do not answer our questions, and for the time being it is our business to interpret these remarks with the help of the understanding we have gained from the symptoms of the transference neuroses. The agreement is great enough to guarantee us some initial advantage. It remains to be seen how far this technique will take us.

There are difficulties in addition which hold up our advance. The narcissistic disorders and the psychoses related to them can only be deciphered by observers who have been trained through the analytic study of the transference neuroses. But our psychiatrists are not students of psycho-analysis and we psycho-analysts see too few psychiatric cases. A race of psychiatrists must first grow up who have passed through the school of psycho-analysis as a preparatory science. A start in that direction is now being made in America, where very many leading psychiatrists lecture to students on the theories of psycho-analysis and where the proprietors of institutions and the directors of insane asylums endeavour to observe their patients in conformity with those theories. Nevertheless we too, over here, have succeeded sometimes in casting a glance over the narcissistic wall, and in what follows I shall tell you a little of what we think we have detected.

The form of disease known as paranoia, chronic systematic insanity, occupies an unsettled position in the attempts at

classification made by present-day psychiatry. There is, however, no doubt of its close affinity to dementia praecox. I once
ventured to suggest that paranoia and dementia praecox should
be brought together under the common designation of 'paraphrenia'.[1] The forms of paranoia are described according to
their content as megalomania, persecution mania, erotomania,
delusions of jealousy, and so on. We shall not expect anything
much in the way of an attempt at an explanation from
psychiatry. Here is an example of one, though, it is true, one
that is out of date and does not carry much weight—an attempt
to derive one symptom from another by means of an intellectual
rationalization: it is suggested that the patient, who, owing to
a primary disposition, believes that he is being persecuted,
infers from his persecution that he must be someone of quite
particular importance and so develops megalomania. According
to our analytic view the megalomania is the direct result of a
magnification of the ego due to the drawing in of the libidinal
object-cathexes—a secondary narcissism which is a return of the
original early infantile one. We have, however, made a few
observations of persecution mania which have induced us to
follow a particular track. The first thing that struck us was that
in the large majority of cases the persecutor was of the same sex
as the persecuted patient. This was still open to an innocent
explanation; but in a few cases that were thoroughly studied
it was clear that the person of the same sex whom the patient
loved most had, since his illness, been turned into his persecutor.
This made a further development possible: namely, the replacement of the beloved person, along the line of familiar resemblances, by someone else—for instance, a father by a schoolmaster
or by some superior. Experiences of this kind in ever increasing
numbers led us to conclude that *paranoia persecutoria* is the
form of the disease in which a person is defending himself
against a homosexual impulse which has become too powerful.[2]
The change over from affection to hatred, which, it is well
known, may become a serious threat to the life of the loved and

---

[1] [Some comments on Freud's use of this term will be found in
a footnote to his first introduction of it in the last section of the
Schreber analysis (1911c).]

[2] [Cf. the third section of Freud's Schreber analysis (1911c).]

hated object, corresponds in such cases to the transformation of libidinal impulses into anxiety which is a regular outcome of the process of repression. Listen, for instance, to what is, once again, the most recent instance of my observations in this connection.

A young doctor had to be expelled from the town in which he lived because he had threatened the life of the son of a university professor residing there, who had up till then been his greatest friend. He attributed really fiendish intentions and demonic power to this former friend, whom he regarded as responsible for all the misfortunes that had befallen his family in recent years, for every piece of ill-luck whether in his home or in his social life. But that was not all. He believed that this bad friend and the friend's father, the Professor, had caused the war, too, and brought the Russians into the country. His friend had forfeited his life a thousand times, and our patient was convinced that the criminal's death would put an end to every evil. Yet his affection for him was still so strong that it had paralysed his hand when, on one occasion, he had an opportunity of shooting down his enemy at close range. In the course of the short conversations I had with the patient, it came to light that their friendship went back far into their schooldays. Once at least it had overstepped the bounds of friendship: a night which they had spent together had been an occasion for complete sexual intercourse. Our patient had never acquired the emotional relation to women which would have corresponded to his age and his attractive personality. He had once been engaged to a beautiful young girl of good social position; but she had broken off the engagement because she found that her *fiancé* was without any affection. Years later, his illness broke out just at the moment when he had succeeded for the first time in satisfying a woman completely. When this woman embraced him in gratitude and devotion, he suddenly had a mysterious pain that went round the top of his head like a sharp cut. Later on he interpreted this sensation as though an incision were being made at an autopsy for exposing the brain. And as his friend had become a pathological anatomist, it slowly dawned on him that he alone could have sent this last woman to him to seduce him. From that point onwards his eyes were opened to the other persecutions to which he believed he had been made a victim by the machinations of his one-time friend.

But what about the cases in which the persecutor is not of the same sex as the patient and which appear, therefore, to contradict our explanation of their being a defence against homosexual libido? A little time ago I had an opportunity of examining such a case and was able to derive a confirmation from the apparent contradiction. A girl, who believed she was being persecuted by a man with whom she had had affectionate assignations on two occasions, had in fact first had a delusion that was directed against a woman who could be looked on as a substitute for her mother. It was only after her second assignation that she took the step of detaching the delusion from the woman and transferring it to the man. To begin with, therefore, the precondition of the persecutor being of the same sex as the patient was fulfilled in this case too. In making a complaint to a lawyer and to a doctor, the patient made no mention of this preliminary stage of her delusion and thus gave rise to an appearance of there being a contradiction of our explanation of paranoia.[1]

Homosexual object-choice originally lies closer to narcissism than does the heterosexual kind. When it is a question, therefore, of repelling an undesirably strong homosexual impulse, the path back to narcissism is made particularly easy. Hitherto I have had very little opportunity of talking to you about the foundations of erotic life so far as we have discovered them, and it is too late now to catch up on the omission. This much, however, I can emphasize to you. Object-choice, the step forward in the development of the libido which is made after the narcissistic stage, can take place according to two different types: either according to the *narcissistic type*, where the subject's own ego is replaced by another one that is as similar as possible, or according to the *attachment type*,[2] where people who have become precious through satisfying the other vital needs are chosen as objects by the libido as well. A strong libidinal

---

[1] [The case had been reported in full by Freud not long before (1915*f*).]

[2] ['*Anlehnungstypus*.' This has sometimes been translated '*anaclitic type*'. This is fully discussed in the second section of Freud's paper on narcissism (1914*c*), Cf. above, p. 329.]

fixation to the narcissistic type of object-choice is to be included in the predisposition to manifest homosexuality.

You will recall that at our first meeting of the present academic year I described a case to you of a woman suffering from delusions of jealousy [p. 248]. Now that we are so near its end you would no doubt like to hear how delusions are explained by psycho-analysis. But I have less to tell you about that than you expect. The fact that a delusion cannot be shaken by logical arguments or real experiences is explained in the same way as in the case of an obsession—by its relation to the unconscious, which is represented and held down by the delusion or by the obsession. The difference between the two is based on the difference between the topography and dynamics of the two illnesses.

As with paranoia, so also with melancholia (of which, incidentally, many different clinical forms have been described) we have found a point at which it has become possible to obtain some insight into the internal structure of the disease. We have discovered that the self-reproaches, with which these melancholic patients torment themselves in the most merciless fashion, in fact apply to another person, the sexual object which they have lost or which has become valueless to them through its own fault. From this we can conclude that the melancholic has, it is true, withdrawn his libido from the object, but that, by a process which we must call 'narcissistic identification', the object has been set up in the ego itself, has been, as it were, projected on to the ego. (Here I can only give you a pictorial description and not an ordered account on topographical and dynamic lines.)[1] The subject's own ego is then treated like the object that has been abandoned, and it is subjected to all the acts of aggression and expressions of vengefulness which have been aimed at the object. A melancholic's propensity to suicide is also made more intelligible if we consider that the patient's embitterment strikes with a single blow at his own ego and at the loved and hated object. In melancholia, as well as in other narcissistic disorders, a particular trait in the patient's emotional life emerges with peculiar emphasis—what, since Bleuler, we have been accustomed to describe as 'ambivalence'. By this

[1] [A full account is given in 'Mourning and Melancholia' (1917e [1915]).]

we mean the direction towards the same person of contrary—affectionate and hostile—feelings.[1] Unluckily I have been unable in the course of these lectures to tell you more about this emotional ambivalence. [Cf. p. 443.]

In addition to narcissistic identification, there is a hysterical kind, which has been familiar to us very much longer.[2] I wish it were possible to illustrate for you the differences between the two forms by a few clear specifications. There is something I can tell you about the periodic and cyclical forms of melancholia which I am sure you will be glad to hear. For in favourable circumstances—I have experienced this twice—it is possible by analytic treatment in the lucid intervals to prevent the return of the condition in the same or the opposite emotional mood. We learn from such cases that in melancholia and mania we are concerned once more with a special method of dealing with a conflict whose underlying determinants agree precisely with those of the other neuroses. You can imagine how much more there is for psycho-analysis to learn in this field of knowledge.

I told you too [p. 415] that we hoped that the analysis of the narcissistic disorders would give us an insight into the way in which our ego is put together and built up out of different agencies. We have already made a start with this at one point.[3] From the analysis of delusions of observation we have drawn the conclusion that there actually exists in the ego an agency which unceasingly observes, criticizes and compares, and in that way sets itself over against the other part of the ego. We believe, therefore, that the patient is betraying a truth to us which is not yet sufficiently appreciated when he complains that he is spied upon and observed at every step he takes and that every one of his thoughts is reported and criticized. His

[1] [Some discussion of Freud's use of the term will be found in an Editor's footnote to 'Instincts and their Vicissitudes' (1915c).]
[2] [An early account of hysterical identification occurs in the course of the fourth chapter of *The Interpretation of Dreams* (1900a). The distinction between the two kinds of identification is explained in the early part of 'Mourning and Melancholia'.]
[3] [For what follows see the third section of 'On Narcissism' (1914c). The later development of these ideas is discussed in the Editor's Introduction to *The Ego and the Id* (1923b), (Norton, 1960).]

only mistake is in regarding this uncomfortable power as something alien to him and placing it outside himself. He senses an agency holding sway in his ego which measures his actual ego and each of its activities by an *ideal ego* that he has created for himself in the course of his development. We believe, too, that this creation was made with the intention of re-establishing the self-satisfaction which was attached to primary infantile narcissism but which since then has suffered so many disturbances and mortifications. We know the self-observing agency as the ego-censor,[1] the conscience; it is this that exercises the dream-censorship during the night, from which the repressions of inadmissible wishful impulses proceed. When in delusions of observation it becomes split up, it reveals to us its origin from the influences of parents, educators and social environment— from an identification with some of these model figures.

These are a few of the findings which have hitherto been reached from the application of psycho-analysis to the narcissistic disorders. No doubt there are not yet enough of them and they still lack the precision which can only be attained from established familiarity with a new field. We owe all of them to a use of the concept of ego-libido or narcissistic libido, by whose help we can extend to the narcissistic neuroses the views which have proved their value with the transference neuroses. Now, however, you will ask whether it is possible that we shall succeed in subsuming all the disturbances of the narcissistic illnesses and of the psychoses under the libido theory, whether we look upon the libidinal factor in mental life as universally guilty of the causation of illness, and need never attribute the responsibility for it to changes in the functioning of the self-preservative instinct. Well, Ladies and Gentlemen, this question seems to me to call for no urgent reply, and, above all, not to be ripe for judgement. We can confidently leave it over in expectation of the progress of our scientific work. I should not be surprised if it turned out that the power to produce pathogenic

---

[1] [The German form used here is the personal *'Zensor'* in contrast to the impersonal *'Zensur'* in the next part of the sentence, which is the form almost invariably adopted by Freud. Other instances of this very exceptional form occur in the 'Secondary Revision' of Chapter VI of *The Interpretation of Dreams* (1900a), in the paper on narcissism (1914c), and in the *New Introductory Lectures,* p. 479.]

effects was in fact a prerogative of the libidinal instincts, so that the libido theory could celebrate its triumph all along the line from the simplest 'actual' neurosis to the most severe alienation of the personality. We after all know that it is a characteristic feature of the libido that it struggles against submitting to the reality of the universe—to Ananke [p. 355]. But I regard it as extremely probable that the ego-instincts are carried along secondarily by the pathogenic instigation of the libido and forced into functional disturbances. Nor can I think that it would be a disaster to the trend of our researches, if what lies before us is the discovery that in severe psychoses the ego-instincts themselves have gone astray as a primary fact. The future will give the answer—to you, at any rate.

Let me once more, however, return for a moment to anxiety, to throw light on a last obscurity that we left there. I have said [p. 411] that there is something that does not tally with the relation (so thoroughly recognized apart from this) between anxiety and libido: the fact, namely, that realistic anxiety in face of a danger seems to be a manifestation of the self-preservative instinct—which, after all, can scarcely be disputed. How would it be, though, if what was responsible for the affect of anxiety was not the egoistic ego-instincts but the ego-libido? After all, the state of anxiety is in every instance inexpedient, and its inexpedience becomes obvious if it reaches a fairly high pitch. In such cases it interferes with action, whether flight or defence, which alone is expedient and alone serves the cause of self-preservation. If, therefore, we attribute the affective portion of realistic anxiety to ego-libido and the accompanying action to the self-preservative instinct, we shall have got rid of the theoretical difficulty. After all, you do not seriously believe that one runs away because one feels anxiety? No. One feels anxiety and one runs away for a common motive, which is roused by the perception of danger. People who have been through a great mortal danger tell us that they were not at all afraid but merely acted—for instance, that they aimed their rifle at the wild beast—and that is unquestionably what was most expedient.

LECTURE XXVII

TRANSFERENCE[1]

LADIES AND GENTLEMEN,—Since we are now drawing towards
the end of our discussions, there is a particular expectation
which will be in your minds and which should not be disappointed. You no doubt suppose that I would not have led you
through thick and thin of the subject-matter of psycho-analysis
only to dismiss you at the end without saying a word about
therapy, on which, after all, the possibility of practising psychoanalysis at all is based. The subject, moreover, is one that I
cannot withhold from you, since what you learn in connection
with it will enable you to make the acquaintance of a new fact
in whose absence your understanding of the illnesses investigated by us will remain most markedly incomplete.

You do not, I know, expect me to initiate you into the technique by which analysis for therapeutic ends should be carried
out. You only want to know in the most general way the method
by which psycho-analytic therapy operates and what, roughly,
it accomplishes. And you have an indisputable right to learn
this. I shall not, however, tell it you but shall insist on your
discovering it for yourselves.

Think it over! You have learnt all that is essential about the
determinants of falling ill as well as all the factors that come into
effect *after* the patient has fallen ill. Where do these leave room
for any therapeutic influence? In the first place there is hereditary disposition. We have not talked about it very often because
it is emphatically stressed from other directions and we have

[1] [Freud first broached the idea of transference in his technical
contribution to the Breuer and Freud *Studies on Hysteria* (1895*d*).
He returned to it in his 'Dora' analysis (1905*e*). But his main discussions of the subject before the present one will be found in his
papers on technique: in particular 'The Dynamics of Transference' (1912*b*) deals with the theoretical side of the phenomenon,
while 'Observations on Transference-Love' (1915*a*) is concerned
with the technical difficulties raised by the positive transference.
Towards the end of his life Freud approached the subject once
more in 'Analysis Terminable and Interminable' (1937*c*).]

nothing new to say about it. But do not suppose that we under-estimate it; precisely as therapists we come to realize its power clearly enough. In any case we can do nothing to alter it; we too must take it as something given, which sets a limit to our efforts. Next there is the influence of early experiences in child-hood, to which we are in the habit of giving prominence in analysis: they belong to the past and we cannot undo them. Then comes everything that we have summarized as 'real frustration'—the misfortunes of life from which arise depriva-tion of love, poverty, family quarrels, ill-judged choice of a partner in marriage, unfavourable social circumstances, and the strictness of the ethical standards to whose pressure the individual is subject. Here, to be sure, there would be handles enough for a very effective therapy, but it would have to be of the kind which Viennese folklore attributes to the Emperor Joseph[1]—the benevolent interference of a powerful personage before whose will people bow and difficulties vanish. But who are we, that we should be able to adopt benevolence of this kind as an instrument of our therapy? Poor ourselves and socially powerless, and compelled to earn our livelihood from our medical activity, we are not even in a position to extend our efforts to people without means, as other doctors with other methods of treatment are after all able to do. Our therapy is too time-consuming and too laborious for that to be possible. Perhaps, however, you are clutching at one of the factors I have mentioned and believe that there you have found the point at which our influence can make its attack. If the ethical restrictions demanded by society play a part in the deprivation imposed on the patient, treatment can, after all, give him the courage, or perhaps a direct injunction, to disregard those barriers and achieve satisfaction and recovery while forgoing the fulfilment of an ideal that is exalted, but so often not adhered to, by society. The patient will thus become healthy by 'living a full life' sexually. This, it is true, casts a shadow on analytic treatment for not serving general morality. What it has given to the individual it will have taken from the community.

But, Ladies and Gentlemen, who has so seriously misin-formed you? A recommendation to the patient to 'live a full life'

[1] [Joseph II, whose unconventional methods of distributing charity were notorious.]

sexually could not possibly play a part in analytic therapy—if only because we ourselves have declared that an obstinate conflict is taking place in him between a libidinal impulse and sexual repression, between a sensual and an ascetic trend. This conflict would not be solved by our helping one of these trends to victory over its opponent. We see, indeed, that in neurotics asceticism has the upper hand; and the consequence of this is precisely that the suppressed sexual tendency finds a way out in symptoms. If, on the contrary, we were to secure victory for sensuality, then the sexual repression that had been put on one side would necessarily be replaced by symptoms. Neither of these two alternative decisions could end the internal conflict; in either case one party to it would remain unsatisfied. There are only a few cases in which the conflict is so unstable that a factor such as the doctor's taking sides could decide it; and such cases do not in fact stand in need of analytic treatment. Anyone on whom the doctor could have so much influence would have found the same way out without the doctor. You must be aware that if an abstinent young man decides in favour of illicit sexual intercourse or if an unsatisfied wife seeks relief with another man, they have not as a rule waited for permission from a doctor or even from their analyst.

In this connection people usually overlook the one essential point—that the pathogenic conflict in neurotics is not to be confused with a normal struggle between mental impulses both of which are on the same psychological footing. In the former case the dissension is between two powers, one of which has made its way to the stage of what is preconscious or conscious while the other has been held back at the stage of the unconscious. For that reason the conflict cannot be brought to an issue; the disputants can no more come to grips than, in the familiar simile, a polar bear and a whale. A true decision can only be reached when they both meet on the same ground. To make this possible is, I think, the sole task of our therapy.

Moreover, I can assure you that you are misinformed if you suppose that advice and guidance in the affairs of life play an integral part in analytic influence. On the contrary, so far as possible we avoid the role of a mentor such as this, and there is nothing we would rather bring about than that the patient should make his decisions for himself. With this purpose, too, we require him to postpone for the term of his treatment any vital decisions on choice of a profession, business undertakings, marriage or divorce, and only to put them in practice when the treatment is finished. You must admit that all this is different from what you pictured. Only in the case of some very youthful or quite helpless or unstable individuals are we unable to put the desired limitation of our role into effect. With them we have to combine the functions of a doctor and an educator; but when this is so we are quite conscious of our responsibility and behave with the necessary caution.[1]

But you must not conclude from my eagerness in defending myself against the charge that neurotics are encouraged in analytic treatment to live a full life—you must not conclude from this that we influence them in favour of conventional virtue. That is at least as far from being the case. It is true that we are not reformers but merely observers; nevertheless, we cannot help observing with a critical eye and we have found it impossible to side with conventional sexual morality or to form a very high opinion of the manner in which society attempts the practical regulation of the problems of sexual life. We can present society with a blunt calculation that what is described as its morality calls for a bigger sacrifice than it is worth and that its proceedings are not based on honesty and do not display wisdom. We do not keep such criticisms from our patients' ears, we accustom them to giving unprejudiced consideration to sexual matters no less than to any others; and if, having grown independent after the completion of their treatment, they decide on their own judgement in favour of some midway position between living a full life and absolute asceticism, we feel our conscience clear whatever their choice. We tell ourselves that anyone who has succeeded in educating himself to truth about himself is permanently defended against the danger of immorality, even though his standard of morality may differ in some respect from that which is customary in society. Moreover, we must guard against over-estimating the importance of the part played by the question of abstinence in influencing neuroses. Only in a minority of cases can the pathogenic situation of frustration and the subsequent damming-up of libido be

[1] [Freud discusses this further in the *New Introductory Lectures*, p. 148.]

brought to an end by the sort of sexual intercourse that can be procured without much trouble.

Thus you cannot explain the therapeutic effect of psycho-analysis by its permitting a full sexual life. Look around, then, for something else. I fancy that, while I was rejecting this suggestion of yours, one remark of mine put you on the right track. What we make use of must no doubt be the replacing of what is unconscious by what is conscious, the translation of what is unconscious into what is conscious. Yes, that is it. By carrying what is unconscious on into what is conscious, we lift the repressions, we remove the preconditions for the formation of symptoms, we transform the pathogenic conflict into a normal one for which it must be possible somehow to find a solution. All that we bring about in a patient is this single psychical change: the length to which it is carried is the measure of the help we provide. Where no repressions (or analogous psychical processes) can be undone, our therapy has nothing to expect.

We can express the aim of our efforts in a variety of formulas: making conscious what is unconscious, lifting repressions, filling gaps in the memory—all these amount to the same thing. But perhaps you will be dissatisfied by this admission. You had formed a different picture of the return to health of a neurotic patient—that, after submitting to the tedious labours of a psycho-analysis, he would become another man; but the total result, so it seems, is that he has rather less that is unconscious and rather more that is conscious in him than he had before. The fact is that you are probably under-estimating the import-ance of an internal change of this kind. The neurotic who is cured has really become another man, though at bottom, of course, he has remained the same; that is to say, he has become what he might have become at best under the most favourable conditions. But that is a very great deal. If you now hear all that has to be done and what efforts it needs to bring about this apparently trivial change in a man's mental life, you will no doubt begin to realize the importance of this difference in psychical levels.

I will digress for a moment to ask if you know what is meant by a causal therapy. That is how we describe a procedure which does not take the symptoms of an illness as its point of attack but sets about removing its *causes*. Well, then, is our psycho-analytic method a causal therapy or not? The reply is not a simple one, but it may perhaps give us an opportunity of realizing the worthlessness of a question framed in this way. In so far as analytic therapy does not make it its first task to remove the symptoms, it is behaving like a causal therapy. In another respect, you may say, it is not. For we long ago traced the causal chain back through the repressions to the instinctual dispositions, their relative intensities in the constitution and the deviations in the course of their development. Supposing, now, that it was possible, by some chemical means, perhaps, to interfere in this mechanism, to increase or diminish the quantity of libido present at a given time or to strengthen one instinct at the cost of another—this then would be a causal therapy in the true sense of the word, for which our analysis would have carried out the indispensable preliminary work of reconnaissance. At present, as you know, there is no question of any such method of influencing libidinal processes; with our psychical therapy we attack at a different point in the combination—not exactly at what we know are the roots of the phenomena, but nevertheless far enough away from the symptoms, at a point which has been made accessible to us by some very remarkable circumstances.

What, then, must we do in order to replace what is unconscious in our patients by what is conscious? There was a time when we thought this was a very simple matter: all that was necessary was for us to discover this unconscious material and communicate it to the patient. But we know already that this was a short-sighted error [p. 281]. *Our* knowledge about the unconscious material is not equivalent to *his* knowledge; if we communicate our knowledge to him, he does not receive it *instead of* his unconscious material but *beside* it; and that makes very little change in it. We must rather picture this unconscious material topographically, we must look for it in his memory at the place where it became unconscious owing to a repression. The repression must be got rid of—after which the substitution of the conscious material for the unconscious can proceed smoothly. How, then, do we lift a repression of this kind? Here our task enters a second phase. First, the search for the repression and then the removal of the resistance which maintains the repression.

How do we remove the resistance? In the same way: by discovering it and showing it to the patient. Indeed, the resistance too is derived from a repression—from the same one that we are endeavouring to resolve, or from one that took place earlier. It was set up by the anticathexis which arose in order to repress the objectionable impulse. Thus we now do the same thing that we tried to do to begin with: interpret, discover and communicate; but now we are doing it at the right place. The anticathexis or the resistance does not form part of the unconscious but of the ego, which is our collaborator, and is so even if it is not conscious. As we know, the word 'unconscious' is being used here in two senses: on the one hand as a phenomenon and on the other as a system. This sounds very difficult and obscure; but is it not only repeating what we have already said in earlier passages?[1] We have long been prepared for it. We expect that this resistance will be given up and the anticathexis withdrawn when our interpretation has made it possible for the ego to recognize it. What are the motive forces that we work with in such a case? First with the patient's desire for recovery, which has induced him to take part with us in our joint work, and secondly with the help of his intelligence, to which we give support by our interpretation. There is no doubt that it is easier for the patient's intelligence to recognize the resistance and to find the translation corresponding to what is repressed if we have previously given him the appropriate anticipatory ideas. If I say to you: 'Look up at the sky! There's a balloon there!' you will discover it much more easily than if I simply tell you to look up and see if you can see anything. In the same way, a student who is looking through a microscope for the first time is instructed by his teacher as to what he will see; otherwise he does not see it at all, though it is there and visible.

And now for the fact![2] In a whole number of nervous diseases—in hysteria, anxiety states, obsessional neurosis—our

---

[1] [See the Editor's footnote 1 on p. 227 above, where these earlier passages are enumerated and references are given to Freud's later, revised views on the subject.]

[2] [See the opening paragraph of the lecture, p. 431.]

expectation is fulfilled. By searching for the repression in this way, by uncovering the resistances, by pointing out what is re-pressed, we really succeed in accomplishing our task—that is, in overcoming the resistances, lifting the repression and transform-ing the unconscious material into conscious. In doing so we gain the clearest impression of the way in which a violent struggle takes place in the patient's mind about the overcoming of each resistance—a *normal* mental struggle, on the same psychological ground, between the motives which seek to maintain the anti-cathexis and those which are prepared to give it up. The former are the old motives which in the past put the repression into effect; among the latter are the newly arrived ones which, we may hope, will decide the conflict in our favour. We have suc-ceeded in reviving the old conflict which led to repression and in bringing up for revision the process that was then decided. The new material that we produce includes, first, the reminder that the earlier decision led to illness and the promise that a different path will lead to recovery, and, secondly, the enor-mous change in all the circumstances that has taken place since the time of the original rejection. Then the ego was feeble, in-fantile, and may perhaps have had grounds for banning the demands of the libido as a danger. To-day it has grown strong and experienced, and moreover has a helper at hand in the shape of the doctor. Thus we may expect to lead the revived conflict to a better outcome than that which ended in re-pression, and, as I have said, in hysteria and in the anxiety and obsessional neuroses success proves us in general to be correct.

There are, however, other forms of illness in which, in spite of the conditions being the same, our therapeutic procedure is never successful. In them, too, it had been a question of an original conflict between the ego and the libido which led to repression—though this may call for a different topographical description; in them, too, it is possible to trace the points in the patient's life at which the repressions occurred; we make use of the same procedure, are ready to make the same promises and give the same help by the offer of anticipatory ideas; and once again the lapse of time between the repressions and the present day favours a different outcome to the conflict. And yet we do not succeed in lifting a single resistance or getting rid of a single repression. These patients, paranoics, melancholics,

sufferers from dementia praecox, remain on the whole un-
affected and proof against psycho-analytic therapy. What can
be the reason for this? Not any lack of intelligence. A certain
amount of intellectual capacity is naturally required in our
patients; but there is certainly no lack of it in, for instance, the
extremely shrewd combinatory paranoics [cf. p. 66 f.]. Nor do
any of the other motives seem to be absent. Thus the melancholics have a very high degree of consciousness, absent in
paranoics, that they are ill and that that is why they suffer so
much; but this does not make them more accessible. We are
faced here by a fact which we do not understand and which
therefore leads us to doubt whether we have really understood
all the determinants of our possible success with the other
neuroses.

If we continue to concern ourselves only with our hysterics
and obsessional neurotics, we are soon met by a second fact for
which we were not in the least prepared. For after a while we
cannot help noticing that these patients behave in a quite
peculiar manner to us. We believed, to be sure, that we had
reckoned with all the motives concerned in the treatment, that
we had completely rationalized the situation between us and
the patients so that it could be looked over at a glance like a
sum in arithmetic; yet, in spite of all this, something seems to
creep in which has not been taken into account in our sum.
This unexpected novelty itself takes many shapes, and I will
begin by describing to you the commoner and more easily
understandable of the forms in which it appears.

We notice, then, that the patient, who ought to want nothing
else but to find a way out of his distressing conflicts, develops a
special interest in the person of the doctor. Everything connected with the doctor seems to be more important to him than
his own affairs and to be diverting him from his illness. For a
time, accordingly, relations with him become very agreeable;
he is particularly obliging, tries wherever possible to show his
gratitude, reveals refinements and merits in his nature which we
should not, perhaps, have expected to find in him. The doctor,
too, thereupon forms a favourable opinion of the patient and
appreciates the good fortune which has enabled him to give his
assistance to such a particularly valuable personality. If the
doctor has an opportunity of talking to the patient's relatives,

he learns to his satisfaction that the liking is a mutual one. The patient never tires in his home of praising the doctor and of extolling ever new qualities in him. 'He's enthusiastic about you,' say his relatives, 'he trusts you blindly; everything you say is like a revelation to him.' Here and there someone in this chorus has sharper eyes and says: 'It's becoming a bore, the way he talks of nothing else but you and has your name on his lips all the time.'

Let us hope that the doctor is modest enough to attribute his patient's high opinion of him to the hopes he can rouse in him and to the widening of his intellectual horizon by the surprising and liberating enlightenment that the treatment brings with it. Under these conditions the analysis makes fine progress too. The patient understands what is interpreted to him and becomes engrossed in the tasks set him by the treatment; the material of memories and associations floods in upon him in plenty, the certainty and appositeness of his interpretations are a surprise to the doctor, and the latter can only take note with satisfaction that here is a patient who readily accepts all the psychological novelties which are apt to provoke the most bitter contradiction among healthy people in the outside world. Moreover the cordial relations that prevail during the work of analysis are accompanied by an objective improvement, which is recognized on all sides, in the patient's illness.

But such fine weather cannot last for ever. One day it clouds over. Difficulties arise in the treatment; the patient declares that nothing more occurs to him. He gives the clearest impression of his interest being no longer in the work and of his cheerfully disregarding the instructions given him to say everything that comes into his head and not to give way to any critical obstacle to doing so. He behaves as though he were outside the treatment and as though he had not made this agreement with the doctor. He is evidently occupied with something, but intends to keep it to himself. This is a situation that is dangerous for the treatment. We are unmistakably confronted by a formidable resistance. But what has happened to account for it?

If we are able once more to clarify the position, we find that the cause of the disturbance is that the patient has transferred on to the doctor intense feelings of affection which are justified neither by the doctor's behaviour nor by the situation that has developed during the treatment. The form in which this affection is expressed and what its aims are depend of course on the personal relation between the two people involved. If those concerned are a young girl and a youngish man, we shall get the impression of a normal case of falling in love; we shall find it understandable that a girl should fall in love with a man with whom she can be much alone and talk of intimate things and who has the advantage of having met her as a helpful superior; and we shall probably overlook the fact that what we should expect from a neurotic girl would rather be an impediment in her capacity for love. The further the personal relations between doctor and patient diverge from this supposed case, the more we shall be surprised to find nevertheless the same emotional relationship constantly recurring. It may still pass muster if a woman who is unhappy in her marriage appears to be seized with a serious passion for a doctor who is still unattached, if she is ready to seek a divorce in order to be his, or if, where there are social obstacles, she even expresses no hesitation about entering into a secret *liaison* with him. Such things come about even outside psycho-analysis. But in these circumstances we are astonished to hear declarations by married women and girls which bear witness to a quite particular attitude to the therapeutic problem: they had always known, they say, that they could only be cured by love, and before the treatment began they had expected that through this relation they would at last be granted what life had hitherto withheld from them; it had only been in this hope that they had taken so much trouble over the treatment and overcome all the difficulties in communicating their thoughts—and we on our part can add: and had so easily understood what is otherwise so hard to believe. But an admission of this sort surprises us: it throws all our calculations to the winds. Can it be that we have left the most important item out of our account?

And indeed, the greater our experience the less we are able to resist making this correction, though having to do so puts our scientific pretensions to shame. On the first few occasions one might perhaps think that the analytic treatment had come up against a disturbance due to a chance event—an event, that is, not intended and not provoked by it. But when a similar affectionate attachment by the patient to the doctor is repeated regularly in every new case, when it comes to light again and again, under the most unfavourable conditions and where there are positively grotesque incongruities, even in elderly women and in relation to grey-bearded men, even where, in our judgement, there is nothing of any kind to entice—then we must abandon the idea of a chance disturbance and recognize that we are dealing with a phenomenon which is intimately bound up with the nature of the illness itself.

This new fact, which we thus recognize so unwillingly, is known by us as *transference*. We mean a transference of feelings on to the person of the doctor, since we do not believe that the situation in the treatment could justify the development of such feelings. We suspect, on the contrary, that the whole readiness for these feelings is derived from elsewhere, that they were already prepared in the patient and, upon the opportunity offered by the analytic treatment, are transferred on to the person of the doctor. Transference can appear as a passionate demand for love or in more moderate forms; in place of a wish to be loved, a wish can emerge between a girl and an old man to be received as a favourite daughter; the libidinal desire can be toned down into a proposal for an inseparable, but ideally non-sensual, friendship. Some women succeed in sublimating the transference and in moulding it till it achieves a kind of viability; others must express it in its crude, original, and for the most part, impossible form. But at bottom it is always the same, and never allows its origin from the same source to be mistaken.

Before we enquire where we are to find a place for this new fact, I will complete my description of it. What happens with male patients? There at least one might hope to escape the troublesome interference caused by difference of sex and by sexual attraction. Our answer, however, must be much the same as in the case of women. There is the same attachment to the doctor, the same overvaluation of his qualities, the same absorption in his interests, the same jealousy of everyone close to him in real life. The sublimated forms of transference are more frequent between one man and another and straightforward sexual demands are rarer, in proportion as manifest homosexuality is unusual as compared with the other ways in which these instinctual components are employed. With his male patients, again, more often than with women, the doctor comes across a form of expression of the transference which seems at first sight to contradict all our previous descriptions— a hostile or *negative* transference.

I must begin by making it clear that a transference is present in the patient from the beginning of the treatment and for a while is the most powerful motive in its advance. We see no trace of it and need not bother about it so long as it operates in favour of the joint work of analysis. If it then changes into a resistance, we must turn our attention to it and we recognize that it alters its relation to the treatment under two different and contrary conditions: firstly, if as an affectionate trend it has become so powerful, and betrays signs of its origin in a sexual need so clearly, that it inevitably provokes an internal opposition to itself, and, secondly, if it consists of hostile instead of affectionate impulses. The hostile feelings make their appearance as a rule later than the affectionate ones and behind them; their simultaneous presence gives a good picture of the emotional ambivalence [p. 427 f.] which is dominant in the majority of our intimate relations with other people. The hostile feelings are as much an indication of an emotional tie as the affectionate ones, in the same way as defiance signifies dependence as much as obedience does, though with a 'minus' instead of a 'plus' sign before it. We can be in no doubt that the hostile feelings towards the doctor deserve to be called a 'transference', since the situation in the treatment quite certainly offers no adequate grounds for their origin; this necessary view of the negative transference assures us, therefore, that we have not gone wrong in our judgement of the positive or affectionate one.

Where the transference arises, what difficulties it raises for us, how we overcome them and what advantages we eventually derive from it—these are questions to be dealt with in detail in a technical guide to analysis, and I shall only touch on them lightly to-day. It is out of the question for us to yield to the patient's demands deriving from the transference; it would be absurd for us to reject them in an unfriendly, still more in an indignant, manner. We overcome the transference by pointing out to the patient that his feelings do not arise from the present situation and do not apply to the person of the doctor, but that they are repeating something that happened to him earlier.[1] In this way we oblige him to transform his repetition into a memory. By that means the transference, which, whether affectionate or hostile, seemed in every case to constitute the greatest threat to the treatment, becomes its best tool, by whose help the most secret compartments of mental life can be opened.

But I should like to say a few words to you to relieve you of your surprise at the emergence of this unexpected phenomenon. We must not forget that the patient's illness, which we have undertaken to analyse, is not something which has been rounded off and become rigid but that it is still growing and developing like a living organism. The beginning of the treatment does not put an end to this development; when, however, the treatment has obtained mastery over the patient, what happens is that the whole of his illness's new production is concentrated upon a single point—his relation to the doctor. Thus the transference may be compared to the cambium layer in a tree between the wood and the bark, from which the new formation of tissue and the increase in the girth of the trunk derive. When the transference has risen to this significance, work upon the patient's memories retreats far into the background. Thereafter it is not incorrect to say that we are no longer concerned with the patient's earlier illness but with a newly created and transformed neurosis which has taken the former's place. We have followed this new edition of the old disorder from its start, we have observed its origin and growth, and we are especially well able to find our way about in it since, as its object, we are situated at its very centre. All the patient's symptoms have abandoned their original meaning and have taken on a new sense which lies in a relation to the transference; or only such symptoms have persisted as are capable of undergoing such a transformation. But the mastering of this new, artificial neurosis coincides with getting rid of the illness which was originally brought to the treatment—with the accomplishment of our therapeutic task. A person who has become normal and free from the operation of repressed instinctual impulses in his rela-

[1] [Cf. for what follows here 'Remembering, Repeating and Working-Through' (1914g).]

tion to the doctor will remain so in his own life after the doctor has once more withdrawn from it.[1]

The transference possesses this extraordinary, and for the treatment, positively central, importance in hysteria, anxiety hysteria and obsessional neurosis, which are for that reason rightly classed together as 'transference neuroses'. No one who has taken in a full impression of the fact of transference from his analytic work will any longer doubt the nature of the suppressed impulses that obtain expression in the symptoms of these neuroses, and will call for no more powerful evidence of their libidinal character. It may be said that our conviction of the significance of symptoms as substitutive satisfactions of the libido only received its final confirmation after the enlistment of the transference.

There is every reason now for us to improve our earlier dynamic account of the therapeutic process and to bring it into harmony with our new realization. If the patient is to fight his way through the normal conflict with the resistances which we have uncovered for him in the analysis [p. 438], he is in need of a powerful stimulus which will influence the decision in the sense which we desire, leading to recovery. Otherwise it might happen that he would choose in favour of repeating the earlier outcome and would allow what had been brought up into consciousness to slip back again into repression. At this point what turns the scale in his struggle is not his intellectual insight—which is neither strong enough nor free enough for such an achievement—but simply and solely his relation to the doctor. In so far as his transference bears a 'plus' sign, it clothes the doctor with authority and is transformed into belief in his communications and explanations. In the absence of such a transference, or if it is a negative one, the patient would never even give a hearing to the doctor and his arguments. In this his belief is repeating the story of its own development; it is a derivative of love and, to start with, needed no arguments. Only later did he allow them enough room to submit them to examination, provided they were brought forward by someone he loved. Without such supports arguments carried no weight, and in

[1] [It may be remarked that Freud very much qualified this assertion in his late technical paper on 'Analysis Terminable and Interminable' (1937c). Cf. the Editor's Note to this.]

most people's lives they never do. Thus in general a man is only accessible from the intellectual side too, in so far as he is capable of a libidinal cathexis of objects; and we have good reason to recognize and to dread in the amount of his narcissism a barrier against the possibility of being influenced by even the best analytic technique.

A capacity for directing libidinal object-cathexes on to people must of course be attributed to every normal person. The tendency to transference of the neurotics I have spoken of is only an extraordinary increase of this universal characteristic. It would indeed be very strange if a human trait so widespread and so important had never been noticed or appreciated. And in fact it *has* been. Bernheim, with an unerring eye, based his theory of hypnotic phenomena on the thesis that everyone is in some way 'suggestible'. His suggestibility was nothing other than the tendency to transference, somewhat too narrowly conceived, so that it did not include negative transference. But Bernheim was never able to say what suggestion actually was and how it came about. For him it was a fundamental fact on whose origin he could throw no light. He did not know that his '*suggestibilité*' depended on sexuality, on the activity of the libido. And it must dawn on us that in our technique we have abandoned hypnosis only to rediscover suggestion in the shape of transference.

But here I will pause, and let you have a word; for I see an objection boiling up in you so fiercely that it would make you incapable of listening if it were not put into words: 'Ah! so you've admitted it at last! You work with the help of suggestion, just like the hypnotists! That is what we've thought for a long time. But, if so, why the roundabout road by way of memories of the past, discovering the unconscious, interpreting and translating back distortions—this immense expenditure of labour, time and money—when the one effective thing is after all only suggestion? Why do you not make direct suggestions against the symptoms, as the others do—the honest hypnotists? Moreover, if you try to excuse yourself for your long détour on the ground that you have made a number of important psychological discoveries which are hidden by direct suggestion—what about the certainty of these discoveries now? Are not they a result of suggestion too, of unintentional suggestion? Is it not possible that you are forcing on the patient what you want and what seems to you correct, in this field as well?'

What you are throwing up at me in this is uncommonly interesting and must be answered. But I cannot do so to-day: we have not the time. Till our next meeting, then. I will answer you, you will see. But to-day I must finish what I have begun. I promised to make you understand by the help of the fact of transference why our therapeutic efforts have no success with the narcissistic neuroses.

I can do so in a few words, and you will see how simply the riddle can be solved and how well everything fits together. Observation shows that sufferers from narcissistic neuroses have no capacity for transference or only insufficient residues of it. They reject the doctor, not with hostility but with indifference. For that reason they cannot be influenced by him either; what he says leaves them cold, makes no impression on them; consequently the mechanism of cure which we carry through with other people—the revival of the pathogenic conflict and the overcoming of the resistance due to repression—cannot be operated with them. They remain as they are. Often they have already undertaken attempts at recovery on their own account which have led to pathological results [p. 422]. We cannot alter this in any way.

On the basis of our clinical impressions we maintained that these patients' object-cathexes must have been given up and that their object-libido must have been transformed into ego-libido [p. 420]. Through this characteristic we distinguished them from the first group of neurotics (sufferers from hysteria, anxiety-hysteria and obsessional neurosis). This suspicion is now confirmed by their behaviour in our attempts at therapy. They manifest no transference and for that reason are inaccessible to our efforts and cannot be cured by us.

ANALYTIC THERAPY[1]

LADIES AND GENTLEMEN,—You know what we are going to talk about to-day. You asked me why we do not make use of direct suggestion in psycho-analytic therapy, when we admit that our influence rests essentially on transference—that is, on suggestion; and you added a doubt whether, in view of this predominance of suggestion, we are still able to claim that our psychological discoveries are objective. I promised I would give you a detailed reply.

Direct suggestion is suggestion aimed against the manifestation of the symptoms; it is a struggle between your authority and the motives for the illness. In this you do not concern yourself with these motives; you merely request the patient to suppress their manifestation in symptoms. It makes no difference of principle whether you put the patient under hypnosis or not. Once again Bernheim, with his characteristic perspicacity, maintained that suggestion was the essential element in the phenomena of hypnotism, that hypnosis itself was already a result of suggestion, a suggested state;[2] and he preferred to practise suggestion in a waking state, which can achieve the same effects as suggestion under hypnosis.

Which would you rather hear first on this question—what experience tells us or theoretical considerations?

Let us begin with the former. I was a pupil of Bernheim's, whom I visited at Nancy in 1889 and whose book on suggestion

[1] [This lecture contains Freud's fullest account of the theory of the therapeutic effects of psycho-analysis. His later discussion of the question in his paper on 'Analysis Terminable and Interminable' (1937c) seems in some respects to be at variance with it. Cf. the Editor's Note to that paper. Freud published very little on the details of psychoanalytic technique. See, however, the technical papers in Volume XII of the *Standard Edition*, where a list of his other writings on the subject will be found.]

[2] [Freud subsequently expressed his disagreement with this view of Bernheim's. See footnote at the end of Chapter X of *Group Psychology* (1921c).]

I translated into German.[1] I practised hypnotic treatment for many years, at first by prohibitory suggestion and later in combination with Breuer's method of questioning the patient.[2] I can therefore speak of the results of hypnotic or suggestive therapy on the basis of a wide experience. If, in the words of the old medical aphorism, an ideal therapy should be rapid, reliable and not disagreeable for the patient ['*cito, tuto, jucunde*'], Bernheim's method fulfilled at least two of these requirements. It could be carried through much quicker—or, rather, infinitely quicker—than analytic treatment and it caused the patient neither trouble nor unpleasantness. For the doctor it became, in the long run, *monotonous*: in each case, in the same way, with the same ceremonial, forbidding the most variegated symptoms to exist, without being able to learn anything of their sense and meaning. It was hackwork and not a scientific activity, and it recalled magic, incantations and hocus-pocus. That could not weigh, however, against the patient's interest. But the third quality was lacking: the procedure was not reliable in any respect. It could be used with one patient but not with another; it achieved a great deal with one and very little with another, and one never knew why. Worse than the capriciousness of the procedure was the lack of permanence in its successes. If, after a short time, one had news of the patient once more, the old ailment was back again or its place had been taken by a new one. One might hypnotize him again. But in the background there was the warning given by experienced workers against robbing the patient of his self-reliance by frequently repeated hypnosis and so making him an addict to this kind of therapy as though it were a narcotic. Admittedly sometimes things went entirely as one would wish: after a few efforts, success was complete and permanent.[3] But the conditions determining such a favourable outcome remained unknown. On one occasion a severe condition in a woman, which I had entirely got rid of by

---

[1] [In fact Freud translated two of Bernheim's books: *De la suggestion et de ses applications à la thérapeutique* (1886, translated 1888–9) and *Hypnotisme, suggestion et psychothérapie* (1891, translated 1892).]

[2] [See p. 292 above.]

[3] [An instance of this kind was reported by Freud in an early paper, 'A Case of Successful Treatment by Hypnotism' (1892–3).]

a short hypnotic treatment, returned unchanged after the patient had, through no action on my part, got annoyed with me; after a reconciliation, I removed the trouble again and far more thoroughly; yet it returned once more after she had fallen foul of me a second time. On another occasion a woman patient, whom I had repeatedly helped out of neurotic states by hypnosis, suddenly, during the treatment of a specially obstinate situation, threw her arms round my neck.[1] After this one could scarcely avoid, whether one wanted to or not, investigating the question of the nature and origin of one's authority in suggestive treatment.

So much for experiences. They show us that in renouncing direct suggestion we are not giving up anything of irreplaceable value. Now let us add a few reflections to this. The practice of hypnotic therapy makes very small demands on either the patient or the doctor. It agrees most beautifully with the estimate in which neuroses are still held by the majority of doctors. The doctor says to the neurotic patient: 'There's nothing wrong with you, it's only a question of nerves; so I can blow away your trouble in two or three minutes with just a few words.' But our views on the laws of energy are offended by the notion of its being possible to move a great weight by a tiny application of force, attacking it directly, without the outside help of any appropriate appliances. In so far as the conditions are comparable, experience shows that this feat is not successfully accomplished in the case of the neuroses either. But I am aware that this argument is not unimpeachable. There is such a thing as a 'trigger-action'.

In the light of the knowledge we have gained from psychoanalysis we can describe the difference between hypnotic and psycho-analytic suggestion as follows. Hypnotic treatment seeks to cover up and gloss over something in mental life; analytic treatment seeks to expose and get rid of something.[2] The former acts like a cosmetic, the latter like surgery. The former makes use of suggestion in order to forbid the symptoms; it strengthens

[1] [Freud described this episode again at the end of Chapter II of his *Autobiographical Study* (1925d), (Norton, 1963).]
[2] [This distinction is developed at some length in an early paper of Freud's 'On Psychotherapy' (1905a).]

the repressions, but, apart from that, leaves all the processes that have led to the formation of the symptoms unaltered. Analytic treatment makes its impact further back towards the roots, where the conflicts are which gave rise to the symptoms, and uses suggestion in order to alter the outcome of those conflicts. Hypnotic treatment leaves the patient inert and unchanged, and for that reason, too, equally unable to resist any fresh occasion for falling ill. An analytic treatment demands from both doctor and patient the accomplishment of serious work, which is employed in lifting internal resistances. Through the overcoming of these resistances the patient's mental life is permanently changed, is raised to a high level of development and remains protected against fresh possibilities of falling ill.[1] This work of overcoming resistances is the essential function of analytic treatment; the patient has to accomplish it and the doctor makes this possible for him with the help of suggestion operating in an *educative* sense. For that reason psychoanalytic treatment has justly been described as a kind of *after-education*.[2]

I hope I have now made it clear to you in what way our method of employing suggestion therapeutically differs from the only method possible in hypnotic treatment. You will understand too, from the fact that suggestion can be traced back to transference, the capriciousness which struck us in hypnotic therapy, while analytic treatment remains calculable within its limits. In using hypnosis we are dependent on the state of the patient's capacity for transference without being able to influence it itself. The transference of a person who is to be hypnotized may be negative or, as most frequently, ambivalent, or he may have protected himself against his transference by adopting special attitudes; of that we learn nothing. In psychoanalysis we act upon the transference itself, resolve what opposes it, adjust the instrument with which we wish to make our impact. Thus it becomes possible for us to derive an entirely fresh advantage from the power of suggestion; we get it into our hands. The patient does not suggest to himself whatever he

---

[1] [Cf. footnote, p. 445 above.]

[2] [See the paper 'On Psychotherapy' (1905c), where, incidentally, the German word *'Nacherziehung'* ('after-education') is wrongly translated 're-education'.]

pleases: we guide his suggestion so far as he is in any way accessible to its influence.

But you will now tell me that, no matter whether we call the motive force of our analysis transference or suggestion, there is a risk that the influencing of our patient may make the objective certainty of our findings doubtful. What is advantageous to our therapy is damaging to our researches. This is the objection that is most often raised against psycho-analysis, and it must be admitted that, though it is groundless, it cannot be rejected as unreasonable. If it were justified, psycho-analysis would be nothing more than a particularly well-disguised and particularly effective form of suggestive treatment and we should have to attach little weight to all that it tells us about what influences our lives, the dynamics of the mind or the unconscious. That is what our opponents believe; and in especial they think that we have 'talked' the patients into everything relating to the importance of sexual experiences—or even into those experiences themselves—after such notions have grown up in our own depraved imagination. These accusations are contradicted more easily by an appeal to experience than by the help of theory. Anyone who has himself carried out psycho-analyses will have been able to convince himself on countless occasions that it is impossible to make suggestions to a patient in that way. The doctor has no difficulty, of course, in making him a supporter of some particular theory and in thus making him share some possible error of his own. In this respect the patient is behaving like anyone else—like a pupil—but this only affects his intelligence, not his illness. After all, his conflicts will only be successfully solved and his resistances overcome if the anticipatory ideas he is given tally with what is real in him. Whatever in the doctor's conjectures is inaccurate drops out in the course of the analysis;[1] it has to be withdrawn and replaced by something more correct. We endeavour by a careful technique to avoid the occurrence of premature successes due to suggestion; but no harm is done even if they do occur, for we are not satisfied by a first success. We do not regard an analysis as at an end until all the obscurities of the case are cleared up, the gaps in the

[1] [Freud gives a small example of this in the 'Wolf Man' case history (1918b).]

patient's memory filled in, the precipitating causes of the repressions discovered. We look upon successes that set in too soon as obstacles rather than as a help to the work of analysis; and we put an end to such successes by constantly resolving the transference on which they are based. It is this last characteristic which is the fundamental distinction between analytic and purely suggestive therapy, and which frees the results of analysis from the suspicion of being successes due to suggestion. In every other kind of suggestive treatment the transference is carefully preserved and left untouched; in analysis it is itself subjected to treatment and is dissected in all the shapes in which it appears. At the end of an analytic treatment the transference must itself be cleared away; and if success is then obtained or continues, it rests, not on suggestion, but on the achievement by its means of an overcoming of internal resistances, on the internal change that has been brought about in the patient.

The acceptance of suggestions on individual points is no doubt discouraged by the fact that during the treatment we are struggling unceasingly against resistances which are able to transform themselves into negative (hostile) transferences. Nor must we fail to point out that a large number of the individual findings of analysis, which might otherwise be suspected of being products of suggestion, are confirmed from another and irreproachable source. Our guarantors in this case are the sufferers from dementia praecox and paranoia, who are of course far above any suspicion of being influenced by suggestion. The translations of symbols and the phantasies, which these patients produce for us and which in them have forced their way through into consciousness, coincide faithfully with the results of our investigations into the unconscious of transference neurotics and thus confirm the objective correctness of our interpretations, on which doubt is so often thrown. You will not, I think, be going astray if you trust analysis on these points.

I will now complete my picture of the mechanism of cure by clothing it in the formulas of the libido theory. A neurotic is incapable of enjoyment and of efficiency—the former because his libido is not directed on to any real object and the latter because he is obliged to employ a great deal of his available energy on keeping his libido under repression and on warding off its assaults. He would become healthy if the conflict between his ego and his libido came to an end and if his ego had his libido again at its disposal. The therapeutic task consists, therefore, in freeing the libido from its present attachments, which are withdrawn from the ego, and in making it once more serviceable to the ego. Where, then, is the neurotic's libido situated? It is easily found: it is attached to the symptoms, which yield it the only substitutive satisfaction possible at the time. We must therefore make ourselves masters of the symptoms and resolve them—which is precisely the same thing that the patient requires of us. In order to resolve the symptoms, we must go back as far as their origin, we must renew the conflict from which they arose, and, with the help of motive forces which were not at the patient's disposal in the past, we must guide it to a different outcome. This revision of the process of repression can be accomplished only in part in connection with the memory traces of the processes which led to repression. The decisive part of the work is achieved by creating in the patient's relation to the doctor—in the 'transference'—new editions of the old conflicts; in these the patient would like to behave in the same way as he did in the past, while we, by summoning up every available mental force [in the patient], compel him to come to a fresh decision. Thus the transference becomes the battlefield on which all the mutually struggling forces should meet one another.

All the libido, as well as everything opposing it, is made to converge solely on the relation with the doctor. In this process the symptoms are inevitably divested of libido. In place of the patient's true illness there appears the artificially constructed transference illness, in place of the various unreal objects of his libido there appears a single, and once more imaginary, object in the person of the doctor. But, by the help of the doctor's suggestion, the new struggle around this object is lifted to the highest psychical level: it takes place as a normal mental conflict. Since a fresh repression is avoided, the alienation between ego and libido is brought to an end and the subject's mental unity is restored. When the libido is released once more from its temporary object in the person of the doctor, it cannot return to its earlier objects, but is at the disposal of the ego. The forces against which we have been struggling during our work of therapy are, on the one hand, the ego's antipathy to certain trends of the libido—an antipathy expressed in a tendency to repression—and, on the other hand, the tenacity or adhesiveness of the libido [p. 348], which dislikes leaving objects that it has once cathected.

Thus our therapeutic work falls into two phases. In the first, all the libido is forced from the symptoms into the transference and concentrated there; in the second, the struggle is waged around this new object and the libido is liberated from it. The change which is decisive for a favourable outcome is the elimination of repression in this renewed conflict, so that the libido cannot withdraw once more from the ego by flight into the unconscious. This is made possible by the alteration of the ego which is accomplished under the influence of the doctor's suggestion. By means of the work of interpretation, which transforms what is unconscious into what is conscious, the ego is enlarged at the cost of this unconscious; by means of instruction, it is made conciliatory towards the libido and inclined to grant it some satisfaction, and its repugnance to the claims of the libido is diminished by the possibility of disposing of a portion of it by sublimation. The more closely events in the treatment coincide with this ideal description, the greater will be the success of the psycho-analytic therapy. It finds its limits in the lack of mobility of the libido, which may refuse to leave its objects, and the rigidity of narcissism, which will not allow transference on to objects to increase beyond certain bounds. Further light may perhaps be thrown on the dynamics of the process of cure if I say that we get hold of the whole of the libido which has been withdrawn from the dominance of the ego by attracting a portion of it on to ourselves by means of the transference.

It will not be out of place to give a warning that we can draw no direct conclusion from the distribution of the libido during and resulting from the treatment as to how it was distributed during the illness. Suppose we succeeded in bringing a case to a favourable conclusion by setting up and then resolving a strong father-transference to the doctor. It would not be correct to conclude that the patient had suffered previously from a similar unconscious attachment of his libido to his father. His father-transference was merely the battlefield on which we gained control of his libido; the patient's libido was directed to it from other positions. A battlefield need not necessarily coincide with one of the enemy's key fortresses. The defence of a hostile capital need not take place just in front of its gates. Not until after the transference has once more been resolved can we reconstruct in our thoughts the distribution of libido which had prevailed during the illness.

From the standpoint of the libido theory, too, we may say a last word on dreams. A neurotic's dreams help us, like his parapraxes and his free associations to them, to discover the sense of his symptoms and to reveal the way in which his libido is allocated. They show us, in the form of a wish-fulfilment, what wishful impulses have been subjected to repression and to what objects the libido withdrawn from the ego has become attached. For this reason the interpretation of dreams plays a large part in a psycho-analytic treatment, and in some cases it is over long periods the most important instrument of our work. We already know [p. 218] that the state of sleep in itself leads to a certain relaxation of the repressions. A repressed impulse, owing to this reduction in the pressure weighing down upon it, becomes able to express itself far more clearly in a dream than it can be allowed to be expressed by a symptom during the day. The study of dreams therefore becomes the most convenient means of access to a knowledge of the repressed unconscious, of which the libido withdrawn from the ego forms a part.

But the dreams of neurotics do not differ in any important respect from those of normal people; it is possible, indeed, that they cannot be distinguished from them at all. It would be absurd to give an account of the dreams of neurotics which could not also apply to the dreams of normal people. We must therefore say that the difference between neurosis and health holds only during the day; it is not prolonged into dream-life. We are obliged to carry over to healthy people a number of hypotheses which arise in connection with neurotics as a result of the link between the latter's dreams and their symptoms. We cannot deny that healthy people as well possess in their mental life what alone makes possible the formation both of dreams and of symptoms, and we must conclude that they too have carried out repressions, that they expend a certain amount of energy in order to maintain them, that their unconscious system conceals repressed impulses which are still cathected with energy, and that *a portion of their libido is withdrawn from their ego's disposal.* Thus a healthy person, too, is virtually a neurotic; but dreams appear to be the only symptoms which he is capable of forming. It is true that if one subjects his waking life to a closer examination one discovers something that contradicts this appearance— namely that this ostensibly healthy life is interspersed with a great number of trivial and in practice unimportant symptoms.

The distinction between nervous health and neurosis is thus reduced to a practical question and is decided by the outcome —by whether the subject is left with a sufficient amount of capacity for enjoyment and of efficiency. It probably goes back to the relative sizes of the quota of energy that remains free and of that which is bound by repression, and is of a quantitative not of a qualitative nature. I need not tell you that this discovery is the theoretical justification for our conviction that neuroses are in principle curable in spite of their being based on constitutional disposition.

The identity of the dreams of healthy and neurotic people enables us to infer thus much in regard to defining the characteristics of health. But in regard to dreams themselves we can make a further inference: we must not detach them from their connection with neurotic symptoms, we must not suppose that their essential nature is exhausted by the formula that describes them as a translation of thoughts into an archaic form of expression [p. 199], but we must suppose that they exhibit to us allocations of the libido and object-cathexes that are really present.[1]

We shall soon have reached the end. You are perhaps disappointed that on the topic of the psycho-analytic method of therapy I have only spoken to you about theory and not about the conditions which determine whether a treatment is to be undertaken or about the results it produces. I shall discuss

[1] [Some interesting remarks on the dreams of *psychotic* patients will be found in Section B of 'Some Neurotic Mechanisms' (1922b).]

neither: the former because it is not my intention to give you practical instructions on how to carry out a psycho-analysis, and the latter because several reasons deter me from it. At the beginning of our talks [this year, p. 256], I emphasized the fact that under favourable conditions we achieve successes which are second to none of the finest in the field of internal medicine; and I can now add something further—namely that they could not have been achieved by any other procedure. If I were to say more than this I should be suspected of trying to drown the loudly raised voices of depreciation by self-advertisement. The threat has repeatedly been made against psycho-analysts by our medical 'colleagues'—even at public congresses—that a collection of the failures and damaging results of analysis would be published which would open the suffering public's eyes to the worthlessness of this method of treatment. But, apart from the malicious, denunciatory character of such a measure, it would not even be calculated to make it possible to form a correct judgement of the therapeutic effectiveness of analysis. Analytic therapy, as you know, is in its youth; it has taken a long time to establish its technique, and that could only be done in the course of working and under the influence of increasing experience. In consequence of the difficulties in giving instruction, the doctor who is a beginner in psycho-analysis is thrown back to a greater extent than other specialists on his own capacity for further development, and the results of his first years will never make it possible to judge the efficacy of analytic therapy.

Many attempts at treatment miscarried during the early period of analysis because they were undertaken in cases which were altogether unsuited to the procedure and which we should exclude to-day on the basis of our present view of the indications for treatment. But these indications, too, could only be arrived at by experiment. In those days we did not know a priori that paranoia and dementia praecox in strongly marked forms are inaccessible, and we had a right to make trial of the method on all kinds of disorders. But most of the failures of those early years were due not to the doctor's fault or an unsuitable choice of patients but to unfavourable external conditions. Here we have only dealt with internal resistances, those of the patient, which are inevitable and can be overcome. The external resistances which arise from the patient's circumstances, from his environment, are of small theoretical interest but of the greatest practical importance. Psycho-analytic treatment may be compared with a surgical operation and may similarly claim to be carried out under arrangements that will be the most favourable for its success. You know the precautionary measures adopted by a surgeon: a suitable room, good lighting, assistants, exclusion of the patient's relatives, and so on. Ask yourselves now how many of these operations would turn out successfully if they had to take place in the presence of all the members of the patient's family, who would stick their noses into the field of the operation and exclaim aloud at every incision. In psycho-analytic treatments the intervention of relatives is a positive danger and a danger one does not know how to meet. One is armed against the patient's internal resistances, which one knows are inevitable, but how can one ward off these external resistances? No kind of explanations make any impression on the patient's relatives; they cannot be induced to keep at a distance from the whole business, and one cannot make common cause with them because of the risk of losing the confidence of the patient, who—quite rightly, moreover— expects the person in whom he has put his trust to take his side. No one who has any experience of the rifts which so often divide a family will, if he is an analyst, be surprised to find that the patient's closest relatives sometimes betray less interest in his recovering than in his remaining as he is. When, as so often, the neurosis is related to conflicts between members of a family, the healthy party will not hesitate long in choosing between his own interest and the sick party's recovery. It is not to be wondered at, indeed, if a husband looks with disfavour on a treatment in which, as he may rightly suspect, the whole cata- logue of his sins will be brought to light. Nor do we wonder at it; but we cannot in that case blame ourselves if our efforts remain unsuccessful and the treatment is broken off pre- maturely because the husband's resistance is added to that of his sick wife. We had in fact undertaken something which in the prevailing circumstances was unrealizable.

Instead of reporting a number of cases, I will tell you the story of a single one, in which, from considerations of medical discretion, I was condemned to play a long-suffering part. I undertook the analytic treatment—it was many years ago—of a girl who had for some time been unable, owing to anxiety, to go out in the street or to stay at home by herself. The patient slowly brought out an admission that her imagination had been seized by chance observations of the affectionate relations between her mother and a well-to-do friend of the family. But she was so clumsy—or so subtle—that she gave her mother a hint of what was being talked about in the analytic sessions. She brought this about by changing her behaviour towards her mother, by insisting on being protected by no one but her mother from her anxiety at being alone and by barring the door to her in her anxiety if she tried to leave the house. Her mother had herself been very neurotic in the past, but had been cured years before in a hydropathic establishment. Or rather, she had there made the acquaintance of the man with whom she was able to enter into a relation that was in every way satisfying to her. The girl's passionate demands took her aback, and she suddenly understood the meaning of her daughter's anxiety: the girl had made herself ill in order to keep her mother prisoner and to rob her of the freedom of movement that her relations with her lover required. The mother quickly made up her mind and brought the obnoxious treatment to an end. The girl was taken to a sanatorium for nervous diseases and was demonstrated for many years as 'a poor victim of psycho-analysis'. All this time, too, I was pursued by the calumny of responsibility for the unhappy end of the treatment. I kept silence, for I thought I was bound by the duty of medical discretion. Long afterwards I learnt from one of my colleagues, who visited the sanatorium and had seen the agoraphobic girl there, that the *liaison* between her mother and the well-to-do friend of the family was common knowledge in the city and that it was probably connived at by the husband and father. Thus it was to this 'secret' that the treatment had been sacrificed.

In the years before the war, when arrivals from many foreign countries made me independent of the favour or disfavour of my own city, I followed a rule of not taking on a patient for treatment unless he was *sui juris*, not dependent on anyone else in the essential relations of his life. This is not possible, however, for every psycho-analyst. Perhaps you may conclude from my warning against relatives that patients designed for psycho-analysis should be removed from their families and that this kind of treatment should accordingly be restricted to inmates of hospitals for nervous diseases. I could not, however, follow you in that. It is much more advantageous for patients (in so far as they are not in a phase of severe exhaustion) to remain during the treatment in the conditions in which they have to struggle with the tasks that face them. But the patients' relatives ought not to cancel out this advantage by their conduct and should not offer any hostile opposition to the doctor's efforts. But how do you propose to influence in that direction factors like these which are inaccessible to us? And you will guess, of course, how much the prospects of a treatment are determined by the patient's social *milieu* and the cultural level of his family.

This presents a gloomy prospect for the effectiveness of psycho-analysis as a therapy—does it not?—even though we are able to explain the great majority of our failures by attributing them to interfering external factors. Friends of analysis have advised us to meet the threatened publication of our failures with statistics of our successes drawn up by ourselves. I did not agree to this. I pointed out that statistics are worthless if the items assembled in them are too heterogeneous; and the cases of neurotic illness which we had taken into treatment were in fact incomparable in a great variety of respects. Moreover, the period of time that could be covered was too short to make it possible to judge the durability of the cures.[1] And it was altogether impossible to report on many of the cases: they concerned people who had kept both their illness and its treatment secret, and their recovery had equally to be kept secret. But the strongest reason for holding back lay in the realization that in matters of therapy people behave highly irrationally, so that one has no prospect of accomplishing anything with them by rational means. A therapeutic novelty is either received with delirious enthusiasm—as, for instance, when Koch introduced his first tuberculin against tuberculosis to the public[2]— or it is treated with abysmal distrust—like Jenner's vaccination, which was in fact a blessing and which even to-day has its irreconcilable opponents. There was obviously a prejudice

---

[1] [Freud recurrs to this question in the *New Introductory Lectures*, p. 152, where the therapeutic value of psychoanalysis is again discussed.]

[2] [In 1890. Its promise was not fulfilled.]

against psycho-analysis. If one had cured a severe case, one might hear people say: 'That proves nothing. He would have recovered on his own account by this time.' And when a woman patient, who had already passed through four cycles of depression and mania, came to be treated by me during an interval after an attack of melancholia and three weeks later started on a phase of mania, all the members of her family—and a high medical authority, too, who was called in for consultation— were convinced that the fresh attack could only be the result of my attempted analysis. Nothing can be done against prejudices. You can see it again to-day in the prejudices which each group of nations at war has developed against the other. The most sensible thing to do is to wait, and to leave such prejudices to the eroding effects of time. One day the same people begin to think about the same things in quite a different way from before; why they did not think so earlier remains a dark mystery.

It is possible that the prejudice against analytic treatment is already diminishing. The constant spread of analytic teachings, the increasing number of doctors practising analysis in a number of countries seems to vouch for this. When I was a young doctor, I found myself in a similar storm of indignation on the doctors' part against treatment by hypnotic suggestion, which is now held up in contrast to analysis by people of 'moderate' views.[1] Hypnotism, however, has not fulfilled its original promise as a therapeutic agent. We psycho-analysts may claim to be its legitimate heirs and we do not forget how much encouragement and theoretical clarification we owe to it. The damaging results attributed to psycho-analysis are restricted essentially to passing manifestations of increased conflict if an analysis is clumsily carried out or if it is broken off in the middle. You have heard an account of what we do with our patients and can form your own judgement as to whether our efforts are calculated to lead to any lasting damage. Abuse of analysis is possible in various directions; in particular, the transference is a dangerous instrument in the hands of an unconscientious doctor. But no medical

---

[1] [Some striking evidence of the medical opposition to hypnotism will be found in an early review by Freud of a book on the subject by the well-known Swiss psychiatrist, August Forel (Freud, 1889a).]

instrument or procedure is guaranteed against abuse; if a knife does not cut, it cannot be used for healing either.

I have finished, Ladies and Gentlemen. It is more than a conventional form of words if I admit that I myself am profoundly aware of the many defects in the lectures I have given you. I regret above all that I have so often promised to return later to a topic I have lightly touched on and have then found no opportunity of redeeming my promise. I undertook to give you an account of a subject which is still incomplete and in process of development, and my condensed summary has itself turned out to be an incomplete one. At some points I have set out the material on which to draw a conclusion and have then myself not drawn it. But I could not pretend to make you into experts; I have only tried to stimulate and enlighten you.

Appendixes

BIBLIOGRAPHY
AND AUTHOR INDEX

[Titles of books and periodicals are in italics; titles of papers are in inverted commas. Abbreviations are in accordance with the *World List of Scientific Periodicals* (London, 1952). Further abbreviations used in this volume will be found in the List at the end of this bibliography. Numerals in thick type refer to volumes; ordinary numerals refer to pages. The figures in round brackets at the end of each entry indicate the page or pages of this volume on which the work in question is mentioned.* In the case of the Freud entries, the letters attached to the dates of publication are in accordance with the corresponding entries in the complete bibliography of Freud's writings to be included in the last volume of the *Standard Edition*.

For non-technical authors, and for technical authors where no specific work is mentioned, see the General Index.]

ABEL, K. (1884) *Über den Gegensinn der Urworte*, Leipzig. (179–80, 229–30)

ABRAHAM, K. (1908) 'Die psychosexuellen Differenzen der Hysterie und der Dementia praecox', *Zbl. Nervenheilk. Psychiat.*, N.F. **19**, 521. (415)
[*Trans.:* 'The Psycho-Sexual Differences Between Hysteria and Dementia Praecox', *Selected Papers on Psycho-Analysis*, London, 1927, Chap. II.]

(1916) 'Untersuchungen über die früheste prägenitale Entwicklungsstufe der Libido', *Int. Z. (ärztl.) Psychoanal.*, **4**, 71. (327)
[*Trans.:* 'The First Pregenital Stage of the Libido', *Selected Papers on Psycho-Analysis*, London, 1927, Chap. XII.]

(1922) 'Die Spinne als Traumsymbol', *Int. Z. Psychoan.*, **8**, 470. (488)
[*Trans.:* 'The Spider as a Dream Symbol', *Selected Papers on Psycho-Analysis*, London, 1927, Chap. XIX.]

(1924) *Versuch einer Entwicklungsgeschichte der Libido*, Leipzig, Vienna, Zurich. (563, 564)
[*Trans.:* 'A Short Study of the Development of the Libido', *Selected Papers on Psycho-Analysis*, London, 1927, Chap. XXVI.]

ADLER, A. (1910) 'Der psychische Hermaphroditismus im Leben und in der Neurose', *Fortschr. Med.*, **28**, 486. (237)

(1912) *Über den nervösen Charakter*, Wiesbaden. (381)
[*Trans.:* *The Neurotic Constitution*, New York 1916; London, 1918.]

AICHHORN, A. (1925) *Verwahrloste Jugend*, Vienna. (610, 614)
[*Trans.:* *Wayward Youth*, New York, 1935; London, 1936; revised reprint, London, 1951.]

ALEXANDER, F. (1925) 'Über Traumpaare und Traumreihen', *Int. Z. Psychoan.*, **11**, 80. (491)
[*Trans.:* 'Dreams in Paris and Series', *Int. J. Psycho-Anal.*, **6**, 446.]

ANDREAS-SALOMÉ, L. (1916) ' "Anal" und "Sexual" ', *Imago*, **4**, 249. (315), (565)

* For references to pages 467 through 646, see *The Complete Introductory Lectures on Psychoanalysis*.

ARISTOTLE, *De somniis* and *De divinatione per somnum.* (88)
  [*Trans.*: in *On the Soul*, Loeb Classical Library (trans. W. S. Hett),
  London and New York, 1935.]
ARTEMIDORUS OF DALDIS, *Oneirocritica.* (86, 236)
  [*Trans.* (Abridged): *The Interpretation of Dreams* (trans. R. Wood),
  London, 1644.]
BERNHEIM, H. (1886) *De la suggestion et de ses applications à la théra-
  peutique*, Paris. (448–9)
  (1892) *Hypnotisme, suggestion et psychothérapie: études nouvelles*, Paris.
  (449)
BETLHEIM, S. and HARTMANN, H. (1924) 'Über Fehlreaktionen des
  Gedächtnisses bei Korsakoffschen Psychose', *Arch. Psychiat. Nervenkr.*,
  72, 278. (486–7)
BINET, A. (1888) *Études de psychologie expérimentale: le fétichisme dans
  l'amour*, Paris. (348)
BINZ, C. (1878) *Über den Traum*, Bonn. (86)
BLOCH, I. (1902–3) *Beiträge zur Ätiologie der Psychopathia sexualis* (2 vols.),
  Dresden. (307)
BÖLSCHE, W. (1911–13) *Das Liebesleben in der Natur* (2 vols.), Jena. (354)
BREUER, J., and FREUD, S. (1893) *See* FREUD, S. (1893a)
  (1895) *See* FREUD, S. (1895d)
BRILL, A. A. (1912) *Psychoanalysis: Its Theories and Practical Application*,
  Philadelphia and London. (2nd ed., 1914; 3rd ed., 1922.) (31, 52–3,
  55)
BRUNSWICK, R. MACK (1928) 'Die Analyse eines Eifersuchtswahnes', *Int.
  Z. Psychoan.*, 14, 458. (594)
  [*English Text*: 'The Analysis of a Case of Paranoia', *J. nerv. ment.
  Dis.*, 70 (1929), 177.]
BURLINGHAM, D. (1932) 'Kinderanalyse und Mutter', *Psychoan. Päd.*, 6,
  269. (520)
  [*English Text*: 'Child Analysis and the Mother', *Psychoanal. Quart.*, 4
  (1935), 69.]
DARWIN, C. (1872) *The Expression of the Emotions in Man and Animals*,
  London. (2nd ed., 1899.) (396, 399)
  (1958) *The Autobiography of Charles Darwin*, London. (76)
DEUTSCH, H. (1926) 'Okkulte Vorgänge während der Psychoanalyse', *Imago*,
  12, 418. (518)
  (1932) 'Über die weibliche Homosexualität', *Int. Z. Psychoan.*, 18, 219.
  (595)
  [*Trans.*: 'Homosexuality in Women', *Int. J. Psycho-Anal*, 14 (1933),
  34.]
DEVEREUX, G. (1953) *Psychoanalysis and the Occult*, New York. (467)
DU PREL, C. (1885) *Die Philosophie der Mystik*, Leipzig. (133)
EISLER, M. J. (1919) 'Beiträge zur Traumdeutung', *Int. Z. (ärztl.) Psy-
  choanal.*, 5, 295.
  [*Trans.*: in *The Psychoanalytic Reader* (ed. R. Fliess), New York,
  1948, 378.]
EISLER, R. (1910) *Weltenmantel und Himmelszelt* (2 vols.), Munich. (488)
FECHNER, G. T. (1860) *Elemente der Psychophysik*, Leipzig. (2nd ed., 1889.)
  (90)
FEDERN, P. (1914) 'Über zwei typische Traumsensationen', *Jb. psychoan.*,
  6, 89. (155)

FERENCZI, S. (1913) 'Entwicklungsstufen des Wirklichkeitssinnes', *Int. Z.* *(ärztl.) Psychoanal.*, 1, 124. (351)
    [*Trans.:* 'Stages in the Development of the Sense of Reality', *First Contributions to Psycho-Analysis*, London, 1952, Chap. VIII.]

    (1921) 'Die Symbolik der Brücke', *Int. Z. Psychoan*, 7, 211. (488)
    [*Trans.:* 'The Symbolism of the Bridge', *Further Contributions to the Theory and Technique of Psycho-Analysis*, London, 1926, Chap. LXI.]

    (1922) 'Die Brückensymbolik und die Don Juan-Legende', *Int. Z. Psychoan.*, 8, 77. (488)
    [*Trans.:* 'Bridge Symbolism and the Don Juan Legend', *Further Contributions to the Theory and Technique of Psycho-Analysis*, London, 1926, Chap. LXII.]

    (1925) 'Zur Psychoanalyse von Sexualgewohnheiten', *Int. Z. Psychoan.*, 11, 6, (551)
    [*Trans.:* 'Psycho-Analysis of Sexual Habits', *Further Contributions to the Theory and Technique of Psycho-Analysis*, London, 1926, Chap. XXXII.]

FLIESS, W. (1906) *Der Ablauf des Lebens*, Vienna. (320)

FREUD, S. (1877a) 'Über den Ursprung der hinteren Nervenwurzeln im Rückenmarke von Ammocoetes (Petromyzon Planeri)', *S.B. Akad. Wiss. Wien* (Math.-Naturwiss. Kl.) , III Abt., 75, 15. (340)

    (1878a) 'Über Spinalganglien und Rückenmark des Petromyzon', *S.B. Akad. Wiss. Wien* (Math.-Naturwiss. Kl.) , III Abt., 78, 81. (340)

    (1885d) 'Zur Kenntnis der Olivenzwischenschicht', *Neurol. Zbl.*, 4, Nr. 12, 268. (393)

    (1886b) With DARKSCHEWITSCH, L., 'Über die Beziehung des Strickkörpers zum Hinterstrang und Hinterstrangskern nebst Bemerkungen über zwei Felder der Oblongata', *Neurol. Zbl.*, 5, Nr. 6, 121. (393)

    (1886c) 'Über den Ursprung des Nervus acusticus', *Mschr. Ohrenheilk.*, Neue Folge 20, Nr. 8, 245, and 9, 277. (393)

    (1888–9) Translation with Introduction and Notes of H. Bernheim's *De la suggestion et de ses applications à la thérapeutique*, Paris, 1886, under the title *Die Suggestion und ihre Heilwirkung*, Vienna. (448–9)
    [*Trans.:* Introduction to Bernheim's *Die Suggestion und ihre Heilwirkung, C.P.*, 5, 11; *Standard Ed.*, 71.]

    (1889a) Review of Forel's *Der Hypnotismus, Wien. med. Wschr.*, 39, Nr. 28, 1097, and Nr. 47, 1892. (462)
    [*Trans.: Standard Ed.*, 1, 89.]

    (1892a) Translation of H. Bernheim's *Hypnotisme, suggestion et psychothérapie: études nouvelles*, Paris, 1891, under the title *Neue Studien über Hypnotismus, Suggestion und Psychotherapie*, Vienna. (449)

    (1892–3) 'Ein Fall von hypnotischer Heilung nebst Bemerkungen über die Entstehung hysterischer Symptome durch den "Gegenwillen" ', *G.S.*, 1, 258; *G.W.*, 1, 3. (72, 141, 499)
    [*Trans.:* 'A Case of Successful Treatment by Hypnotism', *C.P.*, 5, 33; *Standard Ed.*, 1, 115.]

    (1893a) With BREUER, J., 'Über den psychischen Mechanismus hysterischer Phänomene: Vorläufige Mitteilung', *G.S.*, 1, 7; *G.W.*, 1, 81. (257, 275)
    [*Trans.:* 'On the Psychical Mechanism of Hysterical Phenomena: Preliminary Communication', *C.P.*, 1, 24; *Standard Ed.*, 2, 3.]

    (1893f) 'Charcot', *G.S.*, 1, 243; *G.W.*, 1, 21. (145)
    [*Trans.:* 'Charcot', *C.P.*, 1, 9; *Standard Ed.*, 3, 9.]

FREUD, S. (1893*h*) 'Vortrag Über den psychischen Mechanismus hysterischer Phänomene' [shorthand report revised by lecturer], *Wien. med. Pr.*, **34**, Nr. 4, 121, and 5, 165. (555)

    [*Trans.*: Lecture 'On the Psychical Mechanism of Hysterical Phenomena', *Int. J. Psycho-Anal.*, **37**, 8; *Standard Ed.*, **3**, 27.]

(1894*a*) 'Die Abwehr-Neuropsychosen', *G.S.*, **1**, 290; *G.W.*, **1**, 59. (215, 336, 357, 480, 540, 557–8)

    [*Trans.*: 'The Neuro-Psychoses of Defence', *C.P.*, **1**, 59; *Standard Ed.*, **3**, 43.]

(1895*b* [1894]) 'Über die Berechtigung, von der Neurasthenie einen bestimmten Symptomenkomplex als "Angstneurose" abzutrennen', *G.S.*, **1**, 306; *G.W.*, **1**, 315. (386, 392, 398, 400)

    [*Trans.*: 'On the Grounds for Detaching a Particular Syndrome from Neurasthenia under the Description "Anxiety Neurosis" ', *C.P.*, **1**, 76; *Standard Ed.*, **3**, 87.]

(1895*c* [1894]) 'Obsessions et phobies' [in French], *G.S.*, **1**, 334; *G.W.*, **1**, 345. (400)

    [*Trans.*: 'Obsessions and Phobias', *C.P.*, **1**, 128; *Standard Ed.*, **3**, 71.]

(1895*d*) With BREUER, J., *Studien über Hysterie*, Vienna. *G.S.*, **1**, 3; *G.W.*, **1**, 77 (omitting Breuer's contributions) . (141, 257, 269, 274, 275, 279–80, 286, 292, 293–4, 296, 396, 431, 449, 504, 538, 584–5)

    [*Trans.*: *Studies on Hysteria*, London, 1956; *Standard Ed.*, **2**. Including Breuer's contributions.]

(1895*f*) 'Zur Kritik der "Angstneurose" ', *G.S.*, **1**, 343; *G.W.*, **1**, 357. (245, 347, 386, 392)

    [*Trans.*: 'A Reply to Criticisms of my Paper on Anxiety Neurosis', *C.P.*, **1**, 107; *Standard Ed.*, **3**, 121.]

(1896*b*) 'Weitere Bemerkungen über die Abwehr-Neuropsychosen', *G.S.*, **1**, 363; *G.W.*, **1**, 379. (268, 554, 584)

    [*Trans.*: 'Further Remarks on the Neuro-Psychoses of Defence', *C.P.*, **1**, 155; *Standard Ed.*, **3**, 159.]

(1896*c*) 'Zur Ätiologie der Hysterie', *G.S.*, **1**, 404; *G.W.*, **1**, 425. (6, 584)

    [*Trans.*: 'The Aetiology of Hysteria', *C.P.*, **1**, 183; *Standard Ed.*, **3**, 189.]

(1897*b*) *Inhaltsangaben der wissenschaftlichen Arbeiten des Privatdozenten Dr. Sigm. Freud (1877–1897)*, Vienna. *G.W.*, **1**, 463. (141, 340 393)

    [*Trans.*: *Abstracts of the Scientific Writings of Dr. Sigm. Freud (1877– 1897)* , *Standard Ed.*, **3**, 225.]

(1898*a*) 'Die Sexualität in der Ätiologie der Neurosen', *G.S.*, **1**, 439; *G.W.*, **1**, 491. (386, 391)

    [*Trans.*: 'Sexuality in the Aetiology of the Neuroses', *C.P.*, **1**, 220; *Standard Ed.*, **3**, 261.]

(1899*a*) 'Über Deckerinnerungen', *G.S.*, **1**, 465; *G.W.*, **1**, 531. (201)

    [*Trans.*: 'Screen Memories', *C.P.*, **5**, 47; *Standard Ed.*, **3**, 301.]

(1900*a*) *Die Traumdeutung*, Vienna. *G.S.*, **2–3**; *G.W.*, **2–3**. (75, 83–239 passim, 272, 287, 315, 329, 335, 342, 397, 428, 429, 467, 472, 474, 478, 480, 487, 490, 552, 553, 565, 603, 625)

    [*Trans.*: *The Interpretation of Dreams*, London and New York, 1955; *Standard Ed.*, **4–5**.]

(1901*a*) *Über den Traum*, Wiesbaden. *G.S.*, **3**, 189; *G.W.*, **2–3**, 643. (122)

    [*Trans.*: *On Dreams*, London and New York, 1951; *Standard Ed.*, **5**, 633.]

(1901*b*) *Zur Psychopathologie des Alltagslebens*, Berlin. 1904. *G.S.*, **4**, 3;

G.W., **4**, (4, 25–79 passim, 107, 111, 201, 202, 504)
   [*Trans.: The Psychopathology of Everyday Life, Standard Ed.*, **6**.]

(1904*a*) 'Die Freud'sche psychoanalytische Methode', *G.S.*, **6**, 3; *G.W.*, **5**, 3. (287)
   [*Trans.:* 'Freud's Psycho-Analytic Procedure', *C.P.*, **1**, 264; *Standard Ed.*, **7**, 249.]

(1905*a*) 'Über Psychotherapie', *G.S.*, **6**, 11; *G.W.*, **5**, 13. (6, 450, 451)
   [*Trans.:* 'On Psychotherapy', *C.P.*, **1**, 249; *Standard Ed.*, **7**, 257.]

(1905*c*) *Der witz und seine Beziehung zum Unbewussten*, Vienna. *G.S.*, **9**, 5; *G.W.*, **6**. (39, 118, 122, 172, 174–5, 197, 235, 236, 497, 504, 553, 562)
   [*Trans.: Jokes and their Relation to the Unconscious*, London, 1960; *Standard Ed.*, **8**.]

(1905*d*) *Drei Abhandlungen zur Sexualtheorie*, Vienna. *G.S.*, **5**, 3; *G.W.*, **5**, 29. (200, 303, 310, 323, 348, 373, 407, 415, 562, 565, 578, 579, 585)
   [*Trans.: Three Essays on the Theory of Sexuality*, London, 1962; *Standard Ed.*, **7**, 125.]

(1905*e* [1901]) 'Bruchstück einer Hysterie-Analyse', *G.S.*, **8**, 3; *G. W.*, **5**; 163. (156, 185, 222, 384–5, 431)
   [*Trans.:* 'Fragment of an Analysis of a Case of Hysteria', *C.P.*, **3**, 13; *Standard Ed.*, **7**, 3.]

(1906*a*) 'Meine Ansichten über die Rolle der Sexualität in der Ätiologie der Neurosen', *G.S.*, **5**, 123; *G.W.*, **5**, 149. (246, 386, 585)
   [*Trans.:* 'My Views on the Part played by Sexuality in the Aetiology of the Neuroses', *C.P.*, **1**, 272; *Standard Ed.*, **7**, 271.]

(1907*b*) 'Zwangshandlungen und Religionsübung', *G.S.*, **10**, 210; *G.W.*, **7**, 129, (263, 309, 632)
   [*Trans.:* 'Obsessive Actions and Religious Practices', *C.P.*, **2**, 25; *Standard Ed.*, **9**, 116.]

(1907*c*) 'Zur sexuellen Aufklärung der Kinder', *G.S.*, **5**, 134; *G.W.*, **7**, 19. (610)
   [*Trans.:* 'The Sexual Enlightenment of Children', *C.P.*, **2**, 36; *Standard Ed.*, **9**, 131.]

(1908*a*) 'Hysterische Phantasien und ihre Beziehung zur Bisexualität', *G.S.*, **5**, 246; *G.W.*, **7**, 191. (99, 371)
   [*Trans.:* 'Hysterical Phantasies and their Relation to Bisexuality', *C.P.*, **2**, 51; *Standard Ed.*, **9**, 157.]

(1908*b*) 'Charakter und Analerotik', *G.S.*, **5**, 261; *G.W.*, **7**, 203. (315, 555, 566)
   [*Trans.:* 'Character and Anal Erotism', *C.P.*, **2**, 45; *Standard Ed.*, **9**, 169.]

(1908*c*) 'Über infantile Sexualtheorien', *G.S.*, **5**, 168; *G.W.*, **7**, 171. (317, 564)
   [*Trans.:* 'On the Sexual Theories of Children', *C.P.*, **2**, 59; *Standard Ed.*, **9**, 207.]

(1908*d*) 'Die "kulturelle" Sexualmoral und die moderne Nervosität', *G.S.*, **5**, 143; *G.W.*, **7**, 143. (310)
   [*Trans.:* '"Civilized" Sexual Morality and Modern Nervous Illness', *C.P.*, **2**, 76; *Standard Ed.*, **9**, 179.]

(1908*e* [1907]) 'Der Dichter und das Phantasieren', *G.S.* **10**, 229; *G.W.*, **7**, 213. (99, 371, 377)
   [*Trans.:* 'Creative Writers and Day-Dreaming', *C.P.*, **4**, 173; *Standard Ed.*, **9**, 143.]

(1909a) 'Allgemeines über den hysterischen Anfall', *G.S.*, 5, 255; *G.W.*, 7, 235. (332, 384, 396)
Trans.: 'Some General Remarks on Hysterical Attacks', *C.P.*, 2, 100; *Standard Ed.*, 9, 229.]

(1909b) 'Analyse der Phobie eines fünfjährigen Knaben', *G.S.*, 8, 129; *G.W.*, 7, 243. (176, 310, 317, 364, 400, 610)
[*Trans.*: 'Analysis of a Phobia in a Five-Year-Old Boy', *C.P.*, 3, 149; *Standard Ed.*, 10, 3.]

(1909d) 'Bemerkungen über einen Fall von Zwangsneurose', *G.S.*, 8, 269; *G.W.*, 7, 381. (85, 261, 266, 301, 337)
[*Trans.*: 'Notes upon a Case of Obsessional Neurosis', *C.P.*, 3, 293; *Standard Ed.*, 10, 155.]

(1910a [1909]) *Über Psychoanalyse*, Vienna. *G.S.*, 4, 349; *G.W.*, 8, 3, (6, 83, 294, 377)
[*Trans.*: 'Five Lectures on Psycho-Analysis', *Amer. F. Psychol.*, 21 (1910), 181; *Standard Ed.*, 11, 3.]

(1910d) 'Die zukünftigen Chancen der psychoanalytischen Therapie', *G.S.*, 6, 25; *G.W.*, 8, 104. (164, 291)
[*Trans.*: 'The Future Prospects of Psycho-Analytic Therapy', *C.P.*, 2, 285; *Standard Ed.*, 11, 141.]

(1910e) '"Über den Gegensinn der Urworte"', *G.S.*, 10, 221; *G.W.*, 8, 214. (179)
[*Trans.*: '"The Antithetical Meaning of Primal Words"', *C.P.*, 4, 184; *Standard Ed.*, 11, 155.]

(1910f) Letter to Dr. Friedrich S. Krauss on *Anthropophyteia*, *G.S.*, 11, 242; *G.W.*, 8, 224. (162) [*Trans.*: *Standard Ed.*, 11, 233.]

(1910h) 'Über einen besoderen Typus der Objektwahl beim Manne', *G.S.*, 5, 186; *G.W.*, 8, 66. (330)
[*Trans.*: 'A Special Type of Choice of Object made by Men', *C.P.*, 4, 192; *Standard Ed.*, 11, 165.]

(1910i) 'Die psychogene Sehstörung in psychoanalytischer Auffassung', *G.S.*, 5, 310; *G.W.*, 8, 94. (308)
[*Trans.*: 'The Psycho-Analytic View of Psychogenic Disturbance of Vision', *C.P.*, 2, 105; *Standard Ed.*, 11, 211.]

(1910k) 'Über "wilde" Psychoanalyse',*G.S.*, 6, 37; *G.W.*, 8, 118. (391)
[*Trans.*: '"Wild" Psycho-Analysis', *C.P.*, 2, 297; *Standard Ed.*, 11, 221.]

(1911b) 'Formulierungen über die zwei Prinzipien des psychischen Geschehens', *G.S.*, 5, 409; *G.W.*, 8, 230. (190, 355, 357, 377, 553)
[*Trans.*: 'Formulations on the Two Principles of Mental Functioning', *C.P.*, 4, 13; *Standard Ed.*, 12, 215.]

(1911c) 'Psychoanalytische Bemerkungen über einen autobiographisch beschriebenen Fall von Paranoia (Dementia Paranoides)', *G.S.*, 8, 355; *G.W.*, 8, 240. (166, 422, 424, 563)
[*Trans.*: 'Psycho-Analytic Notes on an Autobiographical Account of a Case of Paranoia (Dementia Paranoides)', *C.P.*, 3, 387; *Standard Ed.*, 12, 3.]

(1911e) 'Die Handhabung der Traumdeutung in der Psychoanalyse', *G.S.*, 6, 45; *G.W.*, 8, 350. (184, 478)
[*Trans.*: 'The Handling of Dream-Interpretation in Psycho-Analysis', *C.P.*, 2, 305; *Standard Ed.*, 12, 91.]

(1912b) 'Zur Dynamik der Übertragung', *G.S.*, 6, 53; *G.W.*, 8, 364. (149, 287, 292, 374, 431)

[*Trans.*: 'The Dynamics of Transference', *C.P.*, **2**, 312; *Standard Ed.*, **12**, 99.]

(1912*c*) 'Über neurotische Erkrankungstypen', *G.S.*, **5**, 400, *G.W.*, **8**, 322. (350)

[*Trans.*: 'Types of Onset of Neurosis', *C.P.*, **2**, 113; *Standard Ed.*, **12**, 229.]

(1912*f*) 'Zur Onanie-Diskussion', *G.S.*, **3**, 324; *G.W.*, **8**, 332. (317, 591, 619)

[*Trans.*: Contributions to a Discussion on Masturbation', *Standard Ed.*, **12**, 243.]

(1912–13) *Totem und Tabu*, Vienna. 1913. *G.S.*, **10**, 3; *G.W.*, **9**. (254, 267, 332, 335, 355, 629, 630, 641)

[*Trans.*: *Totem and Taboo*, London, 1950; New York, 1952; *Standard Ed.*, **13**, 1.]

(1913*a*) 'Ein Traum als Beweismittel', *G.S.*, **3**, 267; *G.W.*, **10**, 12. (182, 222, 227)

[*Trans.*: 'An Evidential Dream', *C.P.*, **2**, 133; *Standard Ed.*, **12**, 269.]

(1913*b*) Introduction to .Pfister's *Die psychanalytische Methode*, *G.S.*, **11**, 224; *G.W.*, **10**, 448. (610)

[*Trans.*: *Standard Ed.*, **12**, 329.]

(1913*c*) 'Weitere Ratschläge zur Technik der Psychoanalyse: I. Zur Einleitung der Behandlung', *G.S.*, **6**, 84; *G.W.*, **8**, 454. (287)

[*Trans.*: 'On Beginning the Treatment (Further Recommendations on the Technique of Psycho-Analysis, I)', *C.P.*, **2**, 342; *Standard Ed.*, **12**, 123.]

(1913*h*) 'Erfahrungen und Beispiele aus der analytischen Praxis', *Int. Z. (ärztl.) Psychoanal.*, **1**, 377; partly reprinted *G.S.*, **11**, 301; *G.W.*, **10**, 40. (488)

[*Trans.*: 'Observations and Examples from Analytic Practice', *Standard Ed.*, **13**, 193 (in full). Also partly incorporated in *The Interpretation of Dreams*, *Standard Ed.*, **4**, 232, and **5**, 409f.]

(1913*i*) 'Die Disposition zur Zwangsneurose', *G.S.*, **5**, 277; *G.W.*, **8**, 442. (563)

[*Trans.*: 'The Disposition to Obsessional Neurosis', *C.P.*, **2**, 122; *Standard Ed.*, **12**, 313.]

(1913*j*) 'Das Interesse an der Psychoanalyse', *G.S.*, **4**, 313; *G.W.*, **8**, 390. (377)

[*Trans.*: 'The Claims of Psycho-Analysis to Scientific Interest', *Standard Ed.*, **13**, 165.]

(1914*c*) 'Zur Einführung des Narzissmus', *G.S.*, **6**, 155; *G.W.*, **10**, 138. 390, 414–15, 416, 426, 428, 429, 529, 596)

[*Trans.*: 'On Narcissism: an Introduction', *C.P.*, **4**, 30; *Standard Ed.*, **14**, 69.]

(1914*d*) 'Zur Geschichte der psychoanalytischen Bewegung', *G.S.*, **4**, 411; *G.W.*, **10**, 44. (83, 245, 286, 292, 346, 585, 601, 604–5)

[*Trans.*: 'On the History of the Psycho-Analytic Movement', *C.P.*, **1**, 287; *Standard Ed.*, **14**, 3.]

(1914*g*) 'Weitere Ratschläge zur Technik der Psychoanalyse: II. Erinnern, Wiederholen und Durcharbeiten', *G.S.*, **6**, 109; *G.W.*, **10**, 126. (444)

[*Trans.*: 'Remembering, Repeating and Working-Through (Further Recommendations on the Technique of Psycho-Analysis, II)', *C.P.*, **2**, 366; *Standard Ed.*, **12**, 147.]

(1915*a*) 'Weitere Ratschläge zur Technik der Psychoanalyse: III.

Bemerkungen über die Übertragungsliebe', *G.S.*, **6**, 120; *G.W.*, **10**, 306. (431)
[*Trans.*: 'Observations on Transference-Love (Further Recommendations on the Technique of Psycho-Analysis, III)', *C.P.*, **2**, 377; *Standard Ed.*, **12**, 159.]

(1915c) 'Triebe und Triebschicksale', *G.S.*, **5**, 443; *G.W.*, **10**, 210. (323, 350, 360, 375, 415, 428, 537, 561)
[*Trans.*: 'Instincts and their Vicissitudes', *C.P.*, **4**, 60; *Standard Ed.*, **14**, 111.]

(1915d) 'Die Verdrängung', *G.S.*, **5**, 466; *G.W.*, **10**, 248. (286, 404 (377)
[*Trans.*: 'Repression', *C.P.*, **4**, 84; *Standard Ed.*, **14**, 143.]

(1915e) 'Das Unbewusste', *G.S.*, **5**, 480; *G.W.*, **10**, 264. (22, 286, 297, 360, 374, 409, 410, 422, 528–9, 553)
[*Trans.*: 'The Unconscious', *C.P.*, **4**, 98; *Standard Ed.*, **14**, 161.]

(1915f) 'Mitteilung eines der psychoanalytischen Theorie widersprechenden Falles von Paranoia', *G.S.*, **5**, 288; *G.W.*, **10**, 234. (267, 348, 426)
[*Trans.*: 'A Case of Paranoia Running Counter to the Psycho-Analytic Theory of the Disease', *C.P.*, **2**, 150; *Standard Ed.*, **14**, 263.]

(1916c) 'Eine Beziehung zwischen einem Symbol und einem Symptom', *G.S.*, **5**, 310; *G.W.*, **10**, 394. (157, 268)
[*Trans.*: 'A Connection between a Symbol and a Symptom', *C.P.*, **2**, 162; *Standard Ed.*, **14**, 339.]

(1916–17) *Vorlesungen zur Einführung in die Psychoanalyse*, Vienna. *G.S.*, **7**; *G.W.*, **11**. (467–70, 472, 477, 479, 481, 488, 490, 491, 497, 527, 529, 535, 545, 549, 552, 555, 562, 563, 566, 568, 579, 582, 590, 597, 606, 609, 610, 613, 615)
[*Trans.*: *Introductory Lectures on Psycho-Analysis*, revised ed., London, 1929 (*A General Introduction to Psychoanalysis*, New York, 1935) ; *Standard Ed.*, **15–16**.]

(1917a) 'Eine Schwierigkeit der Psychoanalyse', *G.S.*, **10**, 347; *G.W.*, **12**, 3. (209, 285)
[*Trans*: 'A Difficulty in the Path of Psycho-Analysis', *C.P.*, **4**, 347; *Standard Ed.*, **17**, 137.]

(1917c) 'Über Triebumsetzungen insbesondere der Analerotik', *G.S.*, **5**, 268; *G.W.*, **10**, 402. (315, 565)
[*Trans.*: 'On Transformations of Instinct as Exemplified in Anal Erotism', *C.P.*, **2**, 164; *Standard Ed.*, **17**, 127.]

(1917d [1915]) 'Metapsychologische Ergänzung zur Traumlehre', *G.S.*, **5**, 520; *G.W.*, **10**, 412. (237, 372, 419, 497)
[*Trans.*: 'A Metapsychological Supplement to the Theory of Dreams', *C.P.*, **4**, 137; *Standard Ed.*, **14**, 219.]

(1917e [1915]) 'Trauer und Melancholie', *G.S.*, **5**, 535; *G.W.*, **10**, 428. (276, 427, 428)
[*Trans.*: 'Mourning and Melancholia', *C.P.*, **4**, 152; *Standard Ed.*, **14**, 239.]

(1918a) 'Das Tabu der Virginität', *G.S.*, **5**, 212; *G.W.*, **12**, 161. (267, 597)
[*Trans.*: 'The Taboo of Virginity', *C.P.*, **4**, 217; *Standard Ed.*, **11**, 193.]

(1918b [1914]) 'Aus der Geschichte einer infantilen Neurose', *G.S.*, **8**, 439; *G.W.*, **12**, 29. (7, 185, 363, 371, 452)
[*Trans.*: 'From the History of an Infantile Neurosis', *C.P.*, **3**, 473; *Standard Ed.*, **17**, 3.]

1919a [1918]) 'Wege der psychoanalytischen Therapie', *G.S.*, **6**, 136; *G.W.*, **12**, 183. (5, 290)
[*Trans.*: 'Lines of Advance in Psycho-Analytic Therapy', *C.P.*, **2**, 392; *Standard Ed.*, **17**, 159.]

(1919d) Einleitung zu *Zur Psychoanalyse der Kriegsneurosen*, Vienna. *G.S.*, **11**, 252; *G.W.*, **12**, 321. (274, 382)
[*Trans.*: Introduction to *Psycho-Analysis and the War Neuroses*, London and New York, 1921. *C.P.*, **5**, 83; *Standard Ed.*, **17**, 207.]

(1919h) 'Das "Unheimliche" ', *G.S.*, **10**, 369; *G.W.*, **12**, 229. (216)
[*Trans.*: 'The "Uncanny" ', *C.P.*, **4**, 368; *Standard Ed.*, **17**, 219.]

(1920c) 'Dr. Anton von Freund', *G.S.*, **11**, 280; *G.W.*, **13**, 435. (516)
[*Trans.*: 'Dr. Anton von Freund', *Standard Ed.*, **18**, 267.]

(1920g) *Jenseits des Lustprinzips*, Vienna. *G.S.*, **6**, 191; *G.W.*, **13**, 3. (7, 246, 274, 374, 395, 414, 415, 494, 538, 572)
[*Trans.*: *Beyond the Pleasure Principle*, London, 1961; *Standard Ed.*, **18**, 7.]

(1921c) *Massenpsychologie und Ich-Analyse*, Vienna. *G.S.*, **6**, 261; *G.W.*, **13**, 73. (7, 448, 504, 527, 531-2, 597, 598)
[*Trans.*: *Group Psychology and the Analysis of the Ego*, London and New York, 1959; *Standard Ed.*, **18**, 69.]

(1922a) 'Traum und Telepathie', *G.S.*, **3**, 278; *G.W.*, **13**, 165. (223, 237, 501)
[*Trans.*: 'Dreams and Telepathy', *C.P.*, **4**, 408; *Standard Ed.*, **18**, 197.]

(1922b) 'Über einige neurotische Mechanismen bei Eifersucht, Paranoia und Homosexualität', *G.S.*, **5**, 387; *G.W.*, **13**, 195. (457)
[*Trans.*: 'Some Neurotic Mechanisms in Jealousy, Paranoia and Homosexuality', *C.P.*, **2**, 232; *Standard Ed.*, **18**, 223.]

(1923b) *Das Ich und das Es*, Vienna. *G.S.*, **6**, 353; *G.W.*, **13**, 237. (7, 175, 227, 246, 337, 407, 409, 416, 428, 521, 527, 529, 536, 543, 544, 549, 553, 555, 567, 569, 573, 574)
[*Trans.*: *The Ego and the Id*, London and New York, 1962; *Standard Ed.*, **19**, 3.]

(1923c) 'Bemerkungen zur Theorie und Praxis der Traumdeutung', *G.S.*, **3**, 305; *G.W.*, **13**, 301. (117, 238, 475, 478)
[*Trans.*: 'Remarks on the Theory and Practice of Dream-Interpretation', *C.P.*, **5**, 136; *Standard Ed.*, **19**, 109.]

(1923e) 'Die infantile Genitalorganisation', *G.S.*, **5**, 232; *G.W.*, **13**, 293. 327, 563)
[*Trans.*: 'The Infantile Genital Organization', *C.P.*, **2**, 244; *Standard Ed.*, **19**, 141.]

(1924c) 'Das ökonomische Problem des Masochismus', *G.S.*, **5**, 374; *G.W.*, **13**, 371. (275, 528, 572, 574)
[*Trans.*: 'The Economic Problem of Masochism', *C.P.*, **2**, 255; *Standard Ed.*, **19**, 157.]

(1924d) 'Der Untergang des Ödipuskomplexes,' *G.S.*, **5**, 423; *G.W.*, **13**, 395. (317, 556)
[*Trans.*: 'The Dissolution of the Oedipus Complex', *C.P.*, **2**, 269; *Standard Ed.*, **19**, 173.]

(1925a) 'Notiz über den "Wunderblock" ', *G.S.*, **6**, 415; *G.W.*, **13**, 3. (540)
[*Trans.*: 'A Note upon the "Mystic Writing-Pad" ', *C.P.*, **5**, 175; *Standard Ed.*, **19**, 227.]

(1925d [1924]) *Selbstdarstellung*, Vienna, 1934. *G.S.*, **11**, 119; *G.W.*, **14**, 33. (90, 287, 450, 585)

[*Trans.: An Autobiographical Study*, London, 1935 (*Autobiography*, New York, 1935); *Standard Ed.* **20**, 3.]

(1925*f*)   Preface to August Aichhorn's *Verwahrloste Jugend*, Vienna. *G.S.*, **11**, 267; *G.W.*, **14**, 565. (610, 614)
    [*Trans.:* Preface to Aichhorn's *Wayward Youth*, *C.P.*, **5**, 98; *Standard Ed.*, **19**, 273.]

(1925*h*)   'Die Verneinung', *G.S.*, **11**, 3; *G.W.*, **14**, 11. (553)
    [*Trans.:* 'Negation', *C.P.*, **5**, 181; *Standard Ed.*, **19**, 235.]

(1925*i*)   'Einige Nachträge zum Ganzen der Traumdeutung', *G.S.*, **3**, 172; *G.W.*, **1**, 561. (211, 232, 477, 504)
    [*Trans.:* 'Some Additional Notes upon Dream-Interpretation as a Whole', *C.P.*, **5**, 150; *Standard Ed.*, **19**, 125.]

(1925*j*)   'Einige psychische Folgen des anatomischen Geschlechtsunterschieds', *G.S.*, **11**, 8; *G.W.*, **14**, 19. (246, 317, 333, 529, 576)
    [*Trans.:* 'Some Psychological Consequences of the Anatomical Distinction between the Sexes', *C.P.*, **5**, 186; *Standard Ed.*, **19**, 243.]

(1926*d*)   *Hemmung, Symptom und Angst*, Vienna. *G.S.*, **11**, 23; *G.W.*, **14**, 113. (61, 526, 540, 549–52, 554–5, 558, 622)
    [*Trans.: Inhibitions, Symptoms and Anxiety*, London, 1960 (*The Problem of Anxiety*, New York, 1936; *Standard Ed.*, **20**, 77.]

(1926*e*)   *Die Frage der Laienanalyse*, Vienna. *G.S.*, **11**, 307; *G.W.*, **14**, 209. (6, 17, 296–7, 540)
    [*Trans.: The Question of Lay Analysis*, London, 1947; *Standard Ed.*, **20**, 179.]

(1927*c*)   *Die Zukunft einer Illusion*, Vienna. *G.S.*, **11**, 411; *G.W.*, **14**, 325. (6, 499, 610, 632, 635, 639, 643)
    [*Trans.: The Future of an Illusion*, London, 1962; New York, 1928; *Standard Ed.*, **21**, 3.]

(1927*d*)   'Der Humor', *G.S.*, **11**, 402; *G.W.*, **14**, 383. (374)
    [*Trans.:* 'Humour', *C.P.*, **5**, 215; *Standard Ed.*, **21**, 159.]

(1927*e*)   'Fetischismus', *G.S.*, **11**, 395; *G.W.*, **14**, 311. (349)
    [*Trans.:* 'Fetishism', *C.P.*, **5**, 198; *Standard Ed.*, **21**, 149.]

(1930*a*)   *Das Unbehagen in der Kultur*, Vienna, *G.S.*, **12**, 29; *G.W.*, **14**, 421. (23, 146, 372, 574, 575, 579, 597, 632, 643)
    [*Trans.: Civilization and its Discontents*, London, 1930; New York, 1961; *Standard Ed.*, **21**, 59.]

(1930*b*)   Preface to *Zehn Jahre Berliner Psychoanalytisches Institut*, Vienna. *G.S.*, **12**, 388; *G.W.*, **14**, 572. (616)
    [*Trans.:* In 'Personal Memories', in *Max Eitingon In Memoriam*, Jerusalem, 1951, 47; *Standard Ed.*, **21**, 257.]

(1931*b*)   'Über die weibliche Sexualität', *G.S.*, **12**, 120; *G.W.*, **14**, 517. (333, 370, 576, 585)
    [*Trans.:* 'Female Sexuality', *C.P.*, **5**, 252; *Standard Ed.*, **21**, 223.]

(1931*d*)   'Das Fakultätsgutachten im Prozess Halsmann', *G.S.*, **12**, 412; *G.W.*, **14**, 541. (338)
    [*Trans.:* 'The Expert Opinion in the Halsmann Case', *Standard Ed.*, **21**, 251.]

(1931*e*)   Letter to the Burgomaster of Příbor, *G.S.*, **12**, 414; *G.W.*, **14**, 561. (605)
    [*Trans.: Standard Ed.*, **21**, 259.]

(1932*a*)   'Zur Gewinnung des Feuers', *G.S.*, **12**, 141; *G.W.*, **16**, 3. (566)
    [*Trans.:* 'The Acquisition and Control of Fire', *C.P.*, **5**, 288; *Standard Ed.*, **22**, 185.]

(1933a) *Neue Folge der Vorlesungen zur Einführung in die Psychoanalyse*, Vienna. *G.S.*, 12, 151; *G.W.*, 15, 207. (5, 6, 157, 206, 227, 239, 246, 323, 333, 347, 365, 370, 388, 392, 395, 429, 434, 461)
[*Trans.*: *New Introductory Lectures on Psycho-Analysis*, London and New York, 1933; *Standard Ed.*, 22.]

(1933b [1932]) *Warum Krieg?*, Paris. *G.S.*, 12, 349; *G.W.*, 16, 13. (643)
[*Trans.*: *Why War?*, Paris, 1933; *C.P.*, 5, 273; *Standard Ed.*, 22, 197.]

(1933c) 'Sándor Ferenczi', *G.S.*, 12, 397; *G.W.*, 16, 267. (617)
[*Trans.*: 'Sándor Ferenczi', *Int. J. Psychol.-Anal.*, 14, 297; *Standard Ed.*, 22, 227.]

(1937c) 'Die endliche und die unendliche Analyse', *G.W.*, 16, 59. (431, 445, 448, 554, 610, 620)
[*Trans.*: 'Analysis Terminable and Interminable', *C.P.*, 5, 316; *Standard Ed.*, 23, 211.]

(1937d) 'Konstrunktionen in der Analyse', *G.W.*, 16, 43. (50)
[*Trans.*: 'Constructions in Analysis', *C.P.*, 5, 358; *Standard Ed.*, 23, 257.]

(1939a [1937–39]) *Der Mann Moses und die monotheistische Religion*, *G.W.*, 16, 103. (161, 347, 536, 626, 632)
[*Trans.*: *Moses and Monotheism*, London and New York, 1939; *Standard Ed.*, 23, 3.]

(1940a [1938]) *Abriss der Psychoanalyse*, *G.W.*, 17, 67. (333, 338, 355, 374, 553, 576)
[*Trans.*: *An Outline of Psycho-Analysis*, London and New York, 1949; *Standard Ed.*, 23, 141.]

(1940b [1938]) 'Some Elementary Lessons in Psycho-Analysis' [title in English: German text], *G.W.*, 17, 141. (34, 277)
[*Trans.*: 'Some Elementary Lessons in Psycho-Analysis', *C.P.*, 5, 376; *Standard Ed.*, 23, 281.]

(1940c [1922]) 'Das Medusenhaupt', *G.W.*, 17, 47.
[*Trans.*: 'Medusa's Head', *C.P.*, 5, 105; *Standard Ed.*, 18, 273.]

(1941d [1921]) 'Psychoanalyse und Telepathie', *G.W.*, 17, 27. (495, 504–12, 518)
[*Trans.*: 'Psycho-Analysis and Telepathy', *Standard Ed.*, 18, 177.]

(1950a [1887–1902]) *Aus den Anfängen der Psychoanalyse*, London. Includes 'Entwurf einer Psychologie' (1895). (201, 329–30, 357, 374, 384, 553, 585, 603)
[*Trans*: *The Origins of Psycho-Analysis*, London and New York, 1954. (Partly, including 'A Project for a Scientific Psychology', in *Standard Ed.*, 1.)]

(1955c [1920]) Memorandum on the Electrical Treatment of War Neuroses', *Standard Ed.*, 17, 211. (382)
[*German Text* (unpublished): 'Gutachten über die elektrische Behandlung der Kriegsneurotiker].

(1960a) *Briefe 1873–1939* (ed. E. L. Freud), Berlin. (4–5, 603)
[*Trans.*: *Letters 1873–1939* (ed. E. L. Freud) (trans. T. and J. Stern), New York, 1960; London, 1961.]

GRODDECK, G. (1923) *Das Buch vom Es*, Vienna. (536)

HALL, G.S. (1914) 'A Synthetic Genetic Study of Fear', *Amer. J. Psychol.*, 25, 149. (398, 411)

HARTMANN, H., and BETLHEIM, S. *See* BETLHEIM, S., and HARTMANN, H.

HESNARD, A., and RÉGIS, E. (1914) *See* RÉGIS, E., and HESNARD, A. (1914)

HILDEBRANDT, F. W. (1875) *Der Traum und seine Verwerthung für's Leben*, Leipzig. (92-3)

HITSCHMANN, E. (1913) *Freuds Neurosenlehre*, Vienna (2nd ed.). (9)

HUG-HELLMUTH, H. VON (1915) 'Ein Traum der sich selbst deutet', *Int. Z. (ärztl.) Psychoanal.*, **3**, 33. (136-8)

JANET, PIERRE (1888) 'Les actes inconscients et la mémoire', *Rev. Philosoph.*, **13**, 238. (257)

    (1913) 'Psycho-Analysis. Rapport par M. le Dr. Pierre Janet', *Int. Congr. Med.*, 17, Section XII (Psychiatry) (1), 13. (257)

JODL, F. (1896) *Lehrbuch der Psychologie*, Stuttgart. (87)

JONES, E. (1911) 'The Psychopathology of Everyday Life', *Amer. J. Psychol.*, **22**, 477. (31, 55, 56)

    (1912) *Der Alptraum in seiner Beziehung zu gewissen Formen des mittelalterlichen Aberglaubens* (tr. II. Sachs), Leipzig and Vienna. (514–16) [*English Text:* In *On the Nightmare*, London and New York, 1931.]

    (1916) Review of G. Stanley Hall's 'A Synthetic Genetic Study of Fear', *Int. Z. (ärztl.) Psychoanal.*, **4**, 55. (398)

    (1953) *Sigmund Freud: Life and Work*, Vol. 1, London and New York. (Page references are to the English edition.) (5, 274, 625)

    (1955) *Sigmund Freud: Life and Work*, Vol. 2, London and New York. (Page references are to the English edition.) (5, 349, 625)

    (1957) *Sigmund Freud: Life and Work*. Vol. 3, London and New York. (Page references are to the English edition.) (467, 495, 603)

JUNG, C. G. (1907) *Über die Psychologie der Dementia praecox*, Halle. (52, 269) [*Trans.: The Psychology of Dementia Praecox*, New York, 1909.]

KAPLAN, L. (1914)· *Grundzüge der Psychoanalyse*, Vienna. (9)

LAMPL-DE GROOT, J. (1927) 'Zur Entwicklungsgeschichte des Ödipuskomplexes der Frau', *Int. Z Psychoan.*, **13**, 269. (594–5) [*Trans.:* 'The Evolution of the Oedipus Complex in Women', *Int. J. Psycho-Anal.*, **9**, (1928), 332.]

LEURET, F. (1834) *Fragmens psychologiques sur la folie*, Paris. (257)

LÉVY, L. (1914) 'Die Sexualsymbolik der Bibel und des Talmuds', *Z. Sexualwiss.*, **1**, 274; 318. (162)

LICHTENBERG, G. C. VON (The Elder) (1853) *Witzige und satirische Einfälle*, Vol. 2 of New Enlarged Edition, Göttingen. (38-9)

LINDER, S. (1879) 'Das Saugen an den Fingern, Lippen, etc., bei den Kindern (Ludeln)', *Jb. Kinderheilk*, N.F., **14**, 68. (313–14)

MAEDER, A. (1906) 'Contributions à la psychopathologie de la vie quotidienne', *Archives de psychologie*, **6**, 148. (55)

    (1908) 'Nouvelles contributions à la psychopathologie de la vie quotidienne', *Archives de psychologie*, **7**, 283. (55)

    (1912) 'Über die Funktion des Traumes', *Jb. psychoan. psychopath. Forsch.*, **4**, 692. (236–7)

MAURY, L. F. A. (1878) *Le sommeil et les rêves*, Paris. (1st ed., 1861.) (86–7, 92, 94)

MAYER, C., and MERINGER, R. (1895) *See* MERINGER, R. (1895)

MEIJER, A. F. (1915) *De Behandeling van Zenuwzieken door Psycho-Analyse*, Amsterdam. (9)

MERINGER, R. (1895) with MAYER, C., *Versprechen und Verlesen, eine psychologisch-linguistische Studie*, Vienna. (32–4, 42, 43, 49)

NÄCKE, P. (1899) 'Kritisches zum Kapitel der normalen und pathologischen Sexualität', *Arch. Psychiat.*, **32**, 356. (416)

NORDENSKJÖLD, O., `et al. (1904) *Antarctic. Zwei Jahre in Schnee und Eis am Südpol* (2 vols.), Berlin. (132–3)

[*Trans.*: (abridged) : *Antarctica*, London, 1905.]

PLATO *Republic.* (146)

[*Trans.*: in *Dialogue*, Vol. 2 (tr. B. Jowett), Oxford, 1871.]

PFISTER, O. (1913) *Die psychanalytische Methode*, Leipzig and Berlin. (9, 610)

[*Trans.*: *The Psychoanalytic Method*, New York and London, 1917.]

RANK, O. (1909) *Der Mythus von der Geburt des Helden*, Leipzig and Vienna. (160–1)

[*Trans.*: *The Myth of the Birth of the Hero*, New York, 1914.]

(1910*a*) 'Ein Beispiel von poetischer Verwertung des Versprechens', *Zbl. Psychoan.*, 1, 109. (37–8)

(1910*b*) 'Ein Traum der sich selbst deutet', *Jb. psychoan. psychopath, Forsch.*, 2, 465. (185)

(1912*a*) 'Aktuelle Sexualregungen als Traumanlässe', *Zbl. Psychoan.*, 2, 596. (134)

(1912*b*) *Das Inzest-Motiv in Dichtung und Sage*, Leipzig and Vienna. (208, 337)

(1924) *Das Trauma der Geburt*, Vienna. (551–2)

[*Trans.*: *The Trauma of Birth*, London, 1929.]

RÉGIS, E., and HESNARD, A. (1914) *La psychoanalyse des névroses et des psychoses*, Paris. (9)

REIK, T. (1915–16) 'Die Pubertätsriten der Wilden', *Imago*, 4, 125; 189. (335)

(1920) 'Völkerpsychologische Parallelen zum Traumsymbol des Mantels', *Int. Z. Psychoan.*, 6, 350.

(1942) *From Thirty Years with Freud*, London; New York, 1940. (5, 6)

SACHS, H. (1912) 'Traumdeutung und Menschenkenntnis', *Jb. psychoan. psychopath. Forsch.*, 3, 568. (206)

(1945) *Freud, Master and Friend*, Cambridge (Mass.) and London. (Page reference is to the English edition.) (5)

SCHERNER, K. A. (1861) *Das Leben des Trammes*, Berlin. (95, 152, 153, 159)

SCHROTTER, K. (1912) 'Experimentelle Träume', *Zbl. Psychoan.*, 2, 638. (486)

SCHUBERT, G. H. VON (1814) *Die Symbolik des Traumes*, Bamberg. (163)

SILBERER, H. (1909) 'Bericht über eine Methode, gewisse symbolische Halluzinations-Erscheinungen hervorzurufen und zu beobachten', *Jb. psychoan. psychopath. Forsch.*, 1, 513. (487)

(1912) 'Symbolik des Erwachens und Schwellensymbolik überhaupt', *Jb. psychoan. psychopath. Forsch.*, 3, 621. (487)

(1914) *Probleme der Mystik und ihrer Symbolik*, Vienna. (237, 304)

[*Trans.*: *Problems of Mysticism and its Symbolism*, New York, 1917.]

SPERBER, H. (1912) 'Über den Einfluss sexueller Momente auf Entstehung und Entwicklung der Sprache', *Imago* 1, 405. 167)

STÄRCKE, J. (1916) 'Aus dem Alltagsleben', *Int. Z. (ärztl.) Psychoanal.*, 4, 21; 98. (55)

STEKEL, W. (1911) *Die Sprache des Traumes*, Wiesbaden. (149, 237)

STRÜMPELL, L. (1877) *Die Natur und Entstehung der Träume*, Leipzig. (87, 90)

TOULOUSE, E. (1896) *Émile Zola: enquête médico-psychologique*, Paris. (260)

VIENNA PSYCHOANALYTIC SOCIETY, MINUTES OF, Vol. I, New York, 1962. (397–8)

VOLD, J. MOURLY (1910–12) *Über den Traum* (2 vols.) (*German trans.* by O. Klemm), Leipzig. (87, 92, 155, 238)

WUNDT, W. (1874) *Grundzüge der physiologischen Psychologie*, Leipzig. (87)

LIST OF ABBREVIATIONS

G.S. = Freud, *Gesammelte Schriften* (12 vols.), Vienna, 1924–34
G.W. = Freud, *Gesammelte Werke* (18 vols.), London, from 1940
C.P. = Freud, *Collected Papers* (5 vols.), London, 1924–50
Standard Ed. = Freud, *Standard Edition* (24 vols.), London, from 1953
P.E.L. = Freud, *The Psychopathology of Everyday Life*, Standard Ed., Vol. VI
I. of D. = Freud, *The Interpretation of Dreams*, Standard Ed., Vols. IV and V

INDEX OF PARAPRAXES

The source of each parapraxis is given in brackets where it is other than Freud himself.

INDEX OF DREAMS

The names or descriptions in brackets are the dreamer's followed by the reporter's.

INDEX OF SYMBOLS

For things symbolized see the General Index

GENERAL INDEX

This index includes the names of non-technical authors. It also includes the names of technical authors where no reference is made in the text to specific works. For references to specific technical works, the Bibliography should be consulted.—The compilation of the index was undertaken by Mrs. R. S. Partridge and Miss Angela Richards.

Norton Paperbacks
PSYCHIATRY AND PSYCHOLOGY

Freud, Sigmund. *Inhibitions, Symptoms and Anxiety.*

Freud, Sigmund. *Introductory Lectures on Psychoanalysis.*

Freud, Sigmund. *Jokes and Their Relation to the Unconscious.*

Freud, Sigmund. *Leonardo da Vinci and a Memory of His Childhood.*

Freud, Sigmund. *New Introductory Lectures on Psychoanalysis.*

Freud, Sigmund. *On Dreams.*

Freud, Sigmund. *On the History of the Psycho-Analytic Movement.*

Freud, Sigmund. *An Outline of Psycho-Analysis* (Rev. Ed.).

Freud, Sigmund. *The Psychopathology of Everyday Life.*

Freud, Sigmund. *The Question of Lay Analysis.*

Freud, Sigmund. *Totem and Taboo.*

Frieze, Irene H., Jacquelynne E. Parsons, Paula B. Johnson, Diane N. Ruble and Gail L. Zellmann. *Women and Sex Roles: A Social Psychological Perspective.*

Haley, Jay. *Uncommon Therapy: The Psychiatric Techniques of Milton B. Erickson, M.D.*

Hendin, David. *Death as a Fact of Life.*

Hendin, Herbert. *Suicide in America.*

Horney, Karen (Ed.). *Are You Considering Psychoanalysis?*

Horney, Karen. *Feminine Psychology.*

Horney, Karen. *Neurosis and Human Growth.*

Horney, Karen. *The Neurotic Personality of Our Time.*

Horney, Karen. *New Ways in Psychoanalysis.*

Horney, Karen. *Our Inner Conflicts.*

Horney, Karen. *Self-Analysis.*

Inhelder, Bärbel, and Jean Piaget. *The Early Growth of Logic in the Child.*

James, William. *Talks to Teachers.*

Jones, Ernest. *Hamlet and Oedipus.*

Kagan, Jerome. *The Growth of the Child: Reflections on Human Development.*

Kagan, Jerome, and Robet Coles (Eds.). *Twelve to Sixteen: Early Adolescence.*

Katchadourian, Herant. *Human Sexuality: Sense and Nonsense.*

Kelly, George A. *A Theory of Personality.*

Klein, Melanie, and Joan Riviere. *Love, Hate and Reparation.*

Komarovsky, Mirra. *Dilemmas of Masculinity: A Study of College Youth.*

Kosslyn, Stephen Michael. *Ghosts in the Mind's Machine: How We Create Pictures in our Brains.*

Lacan, Jacques. *Ecrits.*

Lacan, Jacques. *The Four Fundamental Concepts of Psycho-Analysis.*

Lederer, William J. *Creating a Good Relationship.*

Levy, David M. *Maternal Overprotection.*

Lifton, Robert Jay. *Thought Reform and the Psychology of Totalism.*

Light, Donald. *Becoming Psychiatrists: The Professional Transformation of Self.*

Lunde, Donald T. *Murder and Madness.*

Mandler, George. *Mind and Body: Psychology of Emotion and Stress.*

May, Rollo. *Psychology and the Human Dilemma.*

Meehl, Paul E. *Psychodiagnosis: Selected Papers.*

Piaget, Jean. *The Child's Conception of Number.*

Piaget, Jean. *Genetic Epistemology.*

Piaget, Jean. *Play, Dreams and Imitation in Childhood.*

Piaget, Jean, and Bärbel Inhelder. *The Child's Conception of Space.*

Piaget, Jean, and Bärbel Inhelder. *The Origin of the Idea of Chance in Children.*

Piaget, Jean, Bärbel Inhelder, and Alina Szeminska. *The Child's Conception of Geometry.*

Piers, Gerhart, and Milton B. Singer. *Shame and Guilt.*

Piers, Maria W. (Ed.). *Play and Development.*

Premack, David and Ann James Premack. *The Mind of an Ape.*

Rank, Otto. *Truth and Reality.*

Rank, Otto. *Will Therapy.*

Ruesch, Jurgen, and Gregory Bateson. *Communication: The Social Matrix of Psychiatry.*

Schwartz, Barry (Ed.). *Psychology of Learning: Readings in Behavior Theory.*

Schwartz, Barry and Hugh Lacey. *Behaviorism, Science, and Human Nature: An Introduction to Conditioning.*

Sullivan, Harry Stack. *Clinical Studies in Psychiatry.*

Sullivan, Harry Stack. *Conceptions of Modern Psychiatry.*

Sullivan, Harry Stack. *The Interpersonal Theory of Psychiatry.*

Sullivan, Harry Stack. *The Psychiatric Interview.*

Sullivan, Harry Stack. *Schizophrenia as a Human Process.*

van den Berg, J.H. *The Changing Nature of Man.*

Walter, W. Grey. *The Living Brain.*

Watson, John B. *Behaviorism.*

Wheelis, Allen. *The Quest for Identity.*

Williams, Juanita H. *Psychology of Women: Behavior in a Biosocial Context* (2d Ed.).

Williams, Juanita H. (Ed.). *Psychology of Women: Selected Readings.*

Zilboorg, Gregory. *A History of Medical Psychology.*

Selected Liveright Paperbacks

PSYCHIATRY AND PSYCHOLOGY

Jones, Ernest. *On the Nightmare.*

Köhler, Wolfgang. *Dynamics in Psychology.*

Köhler, Wolfgang. *Gestalt Psychology.*

Köhler, Wolfgang. *The Mentality of Apes.*

Köhler, Wolfgang. *The Place of Value in a World of Fact.*

Köhler, Wolfgang. *The Selected Papers of Wolfgang Köhler.*

Luria, Alexander R. *The Nature of Human Conflicts.*

Stekel, Wilhelm. *Impotence in the Male.*

Stekel, Wilhelm. *Sexual Aberrations: The Phenomena of Fetishism in Relation to Sex.*